INTELLIGENCE

INTELLIGENCE

SECOND EDITION

NATHAN BRODY

Department of Psychology
Wesleyan University
Middletown, Connecticut

Academic Press

San Diego New York Boston London Sydney Tokyo Toronto

Find Us on the Web! http://www.apnet.com

This book is printed on acid-free paper. ∞

Academic Press
A Division of Harcourt Brace & Company
525 B Street, Suite 1900, San Diego, California 92101-4495

United Kingdom Edition published by
Academic Press Limited
24–28 Oval Road, London NW1 7DX

Library of Congress Cataloging-in-Publication Data

Brody, Nathan.
    Intelligence / Nathan Brody. -- 2nd ed.
        p.   cm.
    Includes bibliographical references and index.
    ISBN 0-12-134251-4
    1. Intellect.   2. Intelligence tests.   3. Nature and nuture.
    BF431.B6844   1992
    153.9--dc20
                                                      91-30772
                                                         CIP

Printed in the United States of America
    98 99 MM   7 6 5 4 3

CONTENTS

4

MULTIPLE AND COMPLEX CORRELATES OF INTELLIGENCE

5

BEHAVIOR GENETICS OF INTELLIGENCE

6

ENVIRONMENTAL DETERMINANTS OF INTELLIGENCE

7

BIOLOGICAL CORRELATES OF INTELLIGENCE

8

CONTINUITY AND CHANGE
IN INTELLIGENCE

9

CORRELATES OF INTELLIGENCE

10

GROUP DIFFERENCES
IN INTELLIGENCE

11

BEYOND IQ: SOCIAL INTELLIGENCE
AND PERSONALITY

12

EPILOGUE: THE FUTURE
OF INTELLIGENCE

PREFACE

Science, politics, and ideology are linked in the study of intelligence. Beliefs about racial and gender differences in intelligence, the heritability of intelligence, declines in intelligence among the aged, the relationships between intelligence and schooling, and the modifiability of intelligence seem to be influenced by a complex mixture of ideology and science. If this is true, it is not unreasonable to expect someone writing a volume about intelligence to explicate his or her political and ideological position. I will do so but not without a sense of reluctance. I prefer scientific anonymity and its implicit stance of objective neutrality.

My interest in the field of intelligence began some twenty odd years ago. My wife, Erness, was teaching Educational Psychology at Rutgers University, and she read Arthur Jensen's article in which he suggested that racial differences in intelligence might have a genetic basis. She knew that I had become interested in the behavior genetics of personality and she asked me what I thought of the article. I read the article and answered her truthfully that I knew little or nothing about the field of intelligence. This was a curious omission in my knowledge since I was writing a book about personality, and I thought of myself as an individual difference psychologist. I had a course in graduate school devoted to the administration of tests of intelligence. The information about intelligence I received in the course was often wrong and largely irrelevant to an understanding of the nature of intelligence. I was disturbed about my lack of knowledge about intelligence. It seemed to me that this was an important dimension of individual differences about which I should know something. Erness and I decided to learn as much as we could about intelligence. We were motivated by a desire to demonstrate that Jensen was wrong. Our collaboration led to the publication of a book by Academic Press in 1976 *Intelligence: Nature, Determinants, and Consequences.*

If the world were as I would like it to be, what I think I have learned about intelligence would not be true. I think that individual differences in intelligence, as assessed by standardized tests, relate to what individuals learn in schools and to their social mobility. And I think that scores on such tests are related, albeit weakly related, to race and social class background. In addition, I think we do not know how to substantially modify or eliminate individual differences in intelligence or the relationship between individual differences in intelligence and what is learned in schools. As long as this is true, individual differences in intelligence will relate to various important social outcomes. In my utopia, children would be equally capable of learning and everyone would be well educated. Differences in status associated with different occupations would be minimized or eliminated. Individual differences, in whatever would be analogous to intelligence in such a world, would be of little relevance. That world is not the world in which we live. In our world, individual differences in intelligence as assessed by standardized tests are important. I have tried to understand these differences and to write about them in what I hope is an objective and honest way.

I have two beliefs that influence what I have written in this volume. First, the study of "traditional" issues surrounding individual differences in intelligence remains important despite recent efforts to change the field by renewed emphasis on theories and methods derived from cognitive experimental psychology. I try to sketch some of the ways in which the traditional study of individual differences relates to the new experimental approach. Second, I believe that scientific analysis is capable of leading us to an approximation of what is "true." I hope that my critics will discover the errors in what is written in this book and lead us to a better understanding of individual differences in intelligence.

There are eleven chapters in this volume. The first two chapters describe the structure of intellect. Chapter 1 is historical and deals with the works of Binet and Spearman, among others. Chapter 2 deals with contemporary psychometric analyses of the structure of intellect and includes a discussion of Gardner's theory of multiple intelligence. Chapters 3 and 4 deal with the experimental study of intelligence. Chapter 3 is concerned with attempts to relate general intelligence to elementary cognitive processes, and Chapter 4 deals with more complex views of the basis of intelligence and includes a discussion of componential analysis. Chapters 5 and 6 deal with the behavior genetics of individual differences in intelligence. Chapter 5 focuses on genetic influences, and Chapter 6 is concerned with environmental influences. Chapter 7 contains a brief discussion of research on the biological basis of intelligence. Chapter 8 deals with stability and change in intelligence over the life span. The three remaining chapters in the volume may be thought of as a discussion of socially relevant issues related to intelligence. Chapter 9 explicitly considers the relationship between intelligence and socially relevant outcomes, including the relationship between intelligence and education. Chapter 10 deals with race and gender differences in IQ. Chapter 11 considers dimensions other than IQ that are related to social competence.

It is a pleasure for me to acknowledge some of the debts I accrued while writing this book. Bob Sternberg and Tony Vernon sent me prepublication manuscripts of books they are editing. Howard Ehrlichman and John Simmons read an earlier version of Chapter 10 and provided valuable comments. I benefited from discussions with a number of colleagues about various issues; Ian Deary was especially helpful. Santina Scalia has been wonderfully patient and hard working in dealing with my inadequacies as a typist and word processor. I am grateful for the good grace with which she typed and retyped many pages of this manuscript.

And, finally, a special expression of love and gratitude to Erness who first interested me in this field and taught me more things than I will ever know—both about intelligence and many other far more important things. It is to her that I dedicate this book.

1
HISTORICAL BACKGROUND

In the last two decades of the nineteenth century, psychologists in America, England, France, and Germany attempted to measure individual differences in intelligence. In England, Galton (1879, 1883, 1885) developed a laboratory to measure individual differences in sensory functioning. He believed that sensory discrimination ability was positively related to intellectual ability. Binet began his investigations of individual differences in intelligence in France with observations on his daughters (Binet, 1890). In 1896 he and Henri (Binet & Henri, 1896) outlined a theoretical project for the development of a test of intelligence based on the attempt to develop tests of several independent complex functions or faculties whose combined influence was assumed to determine an individual's intellectual level. Binet and Henri were critical of the relatively widespread attempt to measure intelligence by the use of simple laboratory procedures. They believed that intelligence was best measured by tests of such complex functions as imagination, aesthetic sensibility, memory, and comprehension.

The first 20 years of research on intelligence accomplished little. Samples were small, laboratory procedures were casual, and quantitative indices reporting relationships among measures were not used. In 1904, Binet and Simon presented a paper to a German psychological society expressing extreme pessimism about the possibility of developing measures that could be used to assess intelligence in an objective way in a limited period of time (see, Wolf, 1973; for additional information about the early history of attempts to measure intelligence, see Peterson, 1926, and Spearman 1904b). The methods of testing outlined by Binet and Henri were tentatively rejected in America by Sharp (1898–1899), who gave a series of tests to 7 Cornell University graduate students and concluded that the measures were not related. In addition, she thought that they did not lend themselves to understanding fundamental psychological processes of the type studied in Cornell's influential laboratory founded by Titchener.

The attempt to study individual differences in simple psychological processes had also floundered. Cattell & Farand (1890) began a series of studies at Columbia University, culminating in an important paper published in 1901 by Wissler (1901). Wissler was the first to use the coefficient of correlation to actually measure the relationship among a set of measures of simple psychological processes. He tested Columbia University students and found that the average correlation among the measures was close to zero and that these measures were not related to measures of academic performance. The Sharp and Wissler studies were extremely influential in America and did much to turn experimental psychology away from the study of intelligence for several decades.

Although little was accomplished in the first two decades of research on intelligence, the two most important papers in this field were written one year apart in 1904 and 1905. Spearman presented the theory of general intelligence in 1904 and Binet and Simon presented the first test of intelligence that was similar to modern tests (Binet & Simon, 1905a,b,c; Spearman, 1904b). Each of these seminal contributions involved creative ways of thinking about traditional problems.

SPEARMAN'S 1904 PAPER

Spearman's paper reported the results of a set of investigations designed to test Galton's observation that intelligent individuals had keener sensory discriminations than individuals who were low in intelligence. In addition, Galton had suggested that it would be valuable to study the relationship between measures of sensory discrimination ability and ratings of individual difference characteristics (see J. M. Cattell, 1890).

Spearman's investigations were closely modeled on Galton's suggestions. He obtained measures of the ability to discriminate visual, auditory, and tactile stimuli and he related these measures to school performance in examinations in different academic subjects as well as ratings of intellectual capacity for several samples of schoolchildren and one sample of adults. He found that the measures of sensory functioning tended to be positively correlated with measures of intelligence.

After obtaining these results, Spearman began a search of the literature and discovered Wissler's paper reporting contradictory results. Spearman (1930) stated that he would not have obtained his data if he had known of Wissler's negative results. The discrepancy between the results he obtained and those reported earlier led Spearman to undertake a review of earlier studies using laboratory techniques to measure individual differences in mental functioning.

Spearman had four criticisms of the literature he reviewed. First, he noted that, with the exception of Wissler (1901), earlier investigators had not calculated quantitative indices of the relationships among their diverse measures. They relied on subjective impressions. Spearman noted that formulas for the calculation of the coefficient of correlation existed and that this statistical measure could be used to summarize the degree of linear relationship between two sets of measures. Second, no one calculated probable errors—a measure of the statistical reliability of the results. Third, the experiments were poorly controlled and included many different variables that might influence the results. Fourth, there was no correction made for the unreliability of measurement. Spearman (1904a) published a paper presenting techniques for calculating corrected coefficients of correlation. In this article he presented formulas to correct obtained correlations in order to provide an estimate of the true relationship between variables after the elimination of the influence of other variables. These formulas included a correction for attenuation. An obtained correlation between two measures will always be lower than the hypothetical "true" correlation between the measures if the obtained measures contain errors of measurement. The reliability of a measure may be estimated and the obtained correlation may be corrected for unreliability. Spearman indicated that previous investigators had not corrected for attenuation.

Spearman's theory was intimately connected with his data analyses. Spearman asserted that he was interested in the relationship between the common and essential elements existing among his measures of sensory discrimination ability and his several estimates of intelligence. Accordingly, he obtained aggregated scores for his subjects by averaging their scores on discrimination tasks and on the several estimates of intelligence. The correlation between these aggregates corrected for unreliability of measurement was 1.00—the maximum possible value. Spearman reached the conclusion that "the common and essential element in the Intelligences wholly coincides with the common and essential element in the Sensory Functions" (Spearman, 1904b).

Spearman assumed that all conceivable measures of intelligence were related to a common general intellectual function. It was not the case, however, that all measures of intelligence were equally good measures of the common function. Spearman assumed that the correlation between any pair of measures of intelligence was determined by the extent to which they were both measures of the common intellectual function. He assumed that scores on a measure of intelligence could be partitioned into two components—a general, or g, component and a specific, or s, component. The g component is the component that is determined by that which the measure has in common with all other measures of the common intellective function. The s component is specific to each measure. This implies that the correlation between any two measures of intelligence will be determined by the ratio of g to s in each of the measures. The higher the ratio, the higher the correlation. This theory is known as the two-factor theory of intelligence.

These assumptions have a number of empirical consequences. They imply that the matrix of all possible correlations among a set of diverse measures of intelligence should exhibit certain regularities. First, the matrix should exhibit a positive manifold. That is, all of the correlations should be positive. This follows directly from the assumption that all measures of intelligence have a g component. Second, it should be possible to rank order the measures in terms of their g-to-s ratio. Since Spearman assumed that the correlation between any two measures of the common intellective function is determined by the amount of g they share, it follows that the measure with the highest average correlation with all other measures will have the highest ratio of g to s. A rank ordering of the measures may be obtained from the average correlation of each measure with all other measures. The rank-ordered measures may be arrayed in matrix form as in Table 1.1. The rank-ordered matrix should be one in which the correlations decrease as one goes across a row or down a column and there should be no inversions of this order in the matrix. Third, Spearman demonstrated later that all possible sets of four measures obtained from the set of all measures must fulfill the law of tetrad differences (Spearman & Holzinger, 1924). The law may be expressed as follows:

$$r_{12} \times r_{34} = r_{13} \times r_{24}$$

There are at least five respects in which Spearman's paper may be considered an important contribution to our understanding of individual differences in intelligence. First, the paper provides an explicit theoretical rationale for the construction of tests of intelligence. Tests of intelligence should contain measures or subscales that have high g-to-s ratios. This principal has not always been followed. For example, the widely used Wechsler tests of intelligence have subscales whose average correlation with all other scales is relatively low—in modern jargon—whose g loading is low. An additional principle of measurement that may be derived from Spearman's theory is that intelligence is best defined in terms of an aggregate index based on diverse measures of the common intellective function. Spearman called the use of aggregates the "hotchpotch" princi-

TABLE 1.1   A Hypothetical Matrix of Correlations among Five Tests[a]

Tests	1	2	3	4	5
1		.60	.54	.48	.36
2			.45	.40	.30
3				.36	.26
5					.24

[a]The correlations satisfy the law of tetrad differences.

ple. And, as we shall see, Spearman believed that his theory provided a rationale for the methods of measuring intelligence that were developed by Binet and his collaborators. The hotchpotch principle implies that it is possible to obtain an estimate of an individual's g level by using any set of intellectual measures that have g loadings. The aggregated score obtained on an intelligence test with diverse subtests will be in substantial agreement with the aggregated score obtained on a test containing a different set of g-loaded measures. This is referred to as the principle of the indifference of the indicator.

Second, Spearman developed methods for analyzing correlation matrices. Spearman's methods were the foundation of factor analysis—a statistical technique that permits one to analyze the sources of variance of a particular measure by examining the pattern of correlations between the measure and other measures. Pearson (1901a,b), the statistician who discovered the formula for calculating the coefficient of correlation, developed techniques for factor analyzing correlation matrices using different procedures 3 years before Spearman published his paper. Spearman was the first to analyze a correlation matrix of psychological measures and to indicate that the understanding of a particular measure can be obtained by an analysis of relationship between the measure and other measures. Spearman's analyses may be construed as the precursor of the use of construct validation procedures that assess the validity of a measure by an investigation of the nomological network of laws and relations surrounding the measure.

Third, Spearman clearly understood that intelligence is a construct and is a hypothetical entity. He would surely have thought a definition of intelligence as that which the test measures is bizarre. Since g was defined as a common intellective function that is variably estimated by any and all possible measures, including those that have not as yet been invented, it cannot be identified with any particular measure or subset of measures.

Fourth, Spearman's theory contains a strong empirical claim that all measures of intelligence are measures of a single common theoretical entity. Whether this is correct or not is an issue of intense debate in contemporary research. There are contemporary theorists who, with some modifications, would accept Spearman's theory of general intelligence.

Fifth, Spearman assumed that there is a relationship between intelligence and performance in relatively simple sensory discrimination tasks. This aspect of Spearman's paper was generally regarded as wrong if not perverse. Binet reviewed Spearman's paper a year after its publication and wrote: "He regards this conclusion as *profoundly* important. It may possibly be. We ourselves are *profoundly* astonished at the conclusion because of the very defective character both of the sensory experiments of the author and of the manner in which he determined or had others

determine general intelligence . . . (Binet, 1905, p. 624, italics in original).
American psychologists tended to accept Wissler's research as a definitive
demonstration that measures of simple psychological processes based on
laboratory techniques had a zero correlation with intelligence as expressed in academic settings. Spearman had two criticisms of Wissler's
research. The subjects, or reagents as he called them, were Columbia
University students and were therefore likely to be intellectually homogeneous. This "restriction in range of talent" must, of necessity, reduce
the magnitude of the obtained correlations. In addition, the conditions of
measurement were less than ideal. Subjects were tested three at a time
and were given 22 tests in 45 minutes. The experimenter also was required to measure the head length and breadth of the subjects and to
record observations of several of the subject's features.

What is interesting about the virtually unanimous rejection of Spearman's results indicating a relationship between sensory discrimination
procedures and more global aspects of intellectual functioning is that
Spearman was probably correct. Deary (1986) has undertaken a careful
review and reanalysis of all of the data obtained in the nineteenth century
and for the first two decades of the twentieth century dealing with the
relationship between performance in simple laboratory tasks and estimates of intelligence. Spearman obtained correlations of .66 and .56 between aggregated measures of sensory functioning and aggregated measures of intelligence as indicated by academic performance in two
different samples. Spearman had actually calculated the correlations in-
correctly. The actual correlations as recalculated by Fancher (1985) were
.38 and .39. These correlations are comparable to the values obtained by
Spearman's contemporaries. In addition, we shall review contemporary
research that indicates that measures of pitch discrimination that are
conceptually analogous to those used by Spearman are correlated with
intelligence test scores. Thus it would appear that the one aspect of Spearman's paper that was assumed to be wrong or even absurd may be valid. It
should be noted that Spearman withdrew his claims of an identity between discrimination ability and general intelligence in a footnote written to a paper on a similar topic by Burt (1909–1910). He asserted that
discrimination ability and teachers' ratings of intelligence were not identical but might better be understood as manifestation of some more fundamental theoretical cause. This formulation is one that is compatible
with the views of some contemporary psychologists.

BINET AND SIMON'S TEST OF INTELLIGENCE

Binet and Simon's papers represented the culmination of a decade-long
effort to develop a test of intelligence based on the theoretical analysis
presented by Binet and Henri (Binet & Simon, 1905a,b,c, 1916). Unlike

Spearman, whose review of the mental testing movement of the 1890s emphasized the lack of quantitative precision and experimental control that was characteristic of this effort, Binet thought that the work was precise but trivial since it failed to measure the important human characteristics that would define individual differences in intelligence. Binet believed that a successful test of intelligence would have to separately measure several intellectual functions or faculties. And, he and Henri concluded, after several years of work on this problem, that tests did not exist for several of the critical faculties. Therefore, it would be impossible to measure an individual's intellectual function in a restricted period of time.

The immediate impetus to the development of the 1905 scale of intelligence was Binet's interest in mental retardation. The French had instituted universal education and the French ministry of education was concerned with the problem of educating individuals who were classified as morons, idiots, or imbeciles. It was recognized that there was no objective method for diagnosing these conditions or for deciding whether a child was able to benefit from the ordinary instructional program of the public schools. A commission was formed, to which Binet was appointed, that was given the task of developing psychological and physical diagnostic procedures for determining retardation.

Binet wanted to develop a testing procedure that would be easily administered without special laboratory equipment and that would permit the psychologist to distinguish between individuals with normal and abnormal intellectual capacity. In order to accomplish this task he was forced to abandon some of his theoretical commitments. Binet had been frustrated by his inability to measure each of the complex intellectual faculties of intelligence. Binet simply abandoned the attempt to separately measure each faculty and decided to use complex tasks that might be influenced by several of the faculties. He came to the conclusion that any complex task must of necessity involve several complex functions and that important intellectual functions such as judgment were measured by any complex intellectual task. Thus, pure measures of intellectual functions, uncontaminated by the influence of certain omnipresent functions, were not attainable.

In order to develop a measure of intelligence it was necessary for Binet to think of a way of scaling items or intellectual tasks. Binet and Simon relied on the method of age-graded norms for items used by Damaye (1903, as cited in Wolf, 1973). Intellectual tasks could be differentiated by a consideration of the age at which a typical child was able to successfully complete each task. The use of age grading for intellectual tasks permits one to define the mental age of a person by reference to the characteristic age level of the intellectual tasks that an individual can complete. Although Binet had thought about intellectual development in age-related terms for many years, he resisted the tendency to use age-related norms as a basis for the construction of a measure of intelligence because of a belief that intelligence varied qualitatively as well as quantitatively. Binet thought the analogy between the reasoning processes of the child and the retarded person was not completely accurate. He and Simon continued to maintain that these processes were qualitatively distinct in the very papers in which they presented their test of intelligence that relied on the implicit assumption that one could measure the intellectual capacities of retarded individuals by comparing their functioning to children of different ages. Their theoretical assumptions were at variance with their measurement procedures.

The actual test developed by Binet and Simon consisted of 30 items arranged in order of increasing difficulty. On the basis of exploratory research that was not completely described in their papers, the items were assigned an age equivalence. The test could be used to arrive at a quasiobjective determination of the age-equivalent performance of different groups of retarded individuals. The test is described here as quasiobjective because the procedure for scoring performance permitted the examiner to take into account qualitative features of performance on the task. The tests could be administered in a relatively restricted period of time and did not require any special laboratory facilities. The test provided a simple and objective way of classifying different grades of retarded individuals. Several of the items on the test are similar to those used in contemporary tests of intelligence.

Binet published a new version of the test in 1908 (Binet, 1908). The new version was based on additional empirical research and included more specific age-graded groupings of items. The 1908 test was also meant to be applied to normal children in order to develop suitable instructional programs for children at each grade level. A further revision of the scale was presented in 1911 (Binet, 1911). The several versions of the tests were translated into English and used in America and subsequently became the basis for the Stanford–Binet test of intelligence (see Peterson, 1926; Terman & Childs, 1912). Binet never specified a method for developing a single score from his tests. It remained for Stern (1912) to demonstrate that it was possible to calculate an intelligence quotient by dividing a person's mental age by their chronological age. This ratio, multiplied by 100, was called the intelligence quotient or I.Q.

BINET AND SPEARMAN

Spearman provided a theory and Binet provided a test. Their contributions continue to be important and certainly defined the world view of psychologists interested in intelligence for several decades. It would be hard to imagine two individuals whose work coexisted in time and influence who were so intellectually distinct. And, they disagreed about the value of each other's contributions. Spearman believed that Binet should have used laboratory measures of the sort he evaluated in his original research. Nevertheless, he recognized that Binet's tests could provide an adequate measure of intelligence because his hotchpotch principle would apply to the set of items selected by Binet (See Spearman, 1923, 1927, 1930). Spearman felt that the derivation of a single index or score on the basis of performance on the Binet tests was entirely appropriate since the score must be construed as an estimate of *g*. He believed that his theory provided the intellectual foundation for the measurement of intelligence by Binet. Binet (1905) thought Spearman's attempt to relate intelligence to simple laboratory measures was wrong and he did not accept Spearman's theory of general intelligence. Although he was never quite precise in his formulation, he thought of intelligence as consisting of several rather distinct things that were involved in an unspecified way to determine an average level of functioning. In one sense it is clear that Spearman has the better part of this argument. One cannot presume to measure intelligence and to derive a single index unless in some way that hypothetical entity that is measured is one thing. If intelligence is many things then a proper test or measure of intelligence must result in several scores that reflect each of the distinct components of intelligence.

Spearman and Binet also differed with respect to their attitudes toward abstraction and quantification. Binet resisted quantitative treatment. He was impressed with the complexity of the phenomena he studied and believed that numerical analyses could not do justice to the qualitatively distinct phenomena that the investigated. Spearman, by contrast, was obviously at home in the realm of quantitative abstraction. He distrusted the surface appearance of things and assumed that measurements were fraught with error. Thus he used quantitative indices and purified them in order to understand conceptual relationships among variables that were not immediately observable. This willingness to turn away from actual observations is apparent in his decision to aggregate his several discrimination procedures and his several measures of intellectual functioning. This decision was justified by the assumption that there is a commonality among the measures that transcends their obvious distinctions. The presence of positive correlations among the several measures provided only partial support for the decision to create aggregate indices. The correlations were less than perfect and it would have been equally possible to emphasize the distinctiveness of the functions measured by each of the tests as well as their commonality. Binet would probably have been more interested in the former characteristic than the latter. Spearman's decision to aggregate his measures required a mind at home with abstractions—one that is willing to turn away from things as they seem in order to postulate an order among things that can only be imagined.

THOMSON AND SPEARMAN

Spearman's two-factor theory of intelligence was criticized on both conceptual and empirical grounds. Spearman's original presentation of the theory left g as an undefined theoretical entity. In 1916, Thomson presented a theoretical interpretation of g that Spearman did not accept (Thomson, 1916). Thomson suggested that the law of tetrad differences and the evidence in favor of the existence of a general factor in matrices of correlations of diverse tests of intellectual ability could be explained on a theory of the mind that he characterized as anarchic. Thomson assumed that there was a large set of independent bonds or units in the mind. Any test of ability is assumed to sample some subset of these bonds. Different tests will sample different units of the total set. The expected value of the correlation between tests on this model will depend on the operation of the laws of probability. If two tests both sample a relatively large number of bonds, then one would expect simply on the basis of chance that they would sample many bonds in common. If two tests each sample a relatively small number of bonds or units the probability that they will sample any units in common is reduced. The expected value of the correlation between tests is solely a function of the number of bonds they share in common. Thomson indicated that his theory explained the law of tetrad differences without assuming that g was a single theoretical entity. He characterized his theory as an anarchic model of the mind as opposed to Spearman's monarchic theory of mind. Thus, for Thomson, the existence of a single common factor of intelligence was expected by the operation of the laws of chance.

Thomson and Spearman engaged in a heated debate for over 20 years about the respective merits of their interpretations of the nature of g (see references in Dodd, 1928, 1929; Thomson, 1939). Spearman indicated that Thomson's theory did not explain the law of tetrad differences since the theory implied that the correlation between tests would only approximate the law. The actual correlations would vary depending on the laws of chance that specified only probabilistic values of overlap among independently sampled units. By contrast, Spearman argued that his theory specified a deterministic model according to which the correlation between tests of intellectual ability would be determined precisely by the amount of g they shared. Thomson pointed out that this argument was correct but irrelevant since the law of tetrad differences was not precisely supported by existing correlation matrices. Therefore, it was disingenuous to argue that Spearman's theory was superior to Thomson's by virtue of its ability to predict exact values satisfying the law of tetrad differences if the exact values did not in point of fact exist in actual correlation matrices.

Spearman also argued that Thomson's theory implied that all individuals would have equal intellectual ability. Thomson correctly pointed out that his theory could accommodate individual differences in intelligence by postulating that each individual possessed only a subset of the universe of bonds. Thomson assumed that individuals differed in the number of bonds or units of intelligence that they possessed.

With the benefit of hindsight, it appears that Spearman's debate with Thomson was sterile. Both theories were able to account for the existence of a general factor of intelligence. They differed metaphorically. Spearman tended to think of the common factor as a singular entity. He suggested that the factor might be related to the overall energy of the mind. Spearman also developed a theory of intelligence based on cognitive principles. He assumed that tests that had high g-to-s ratios called for the "eduction of relations and correlates" which he defined as follows:

> The eduction of relations . . . when a person has in mind any two or more ideas (using this word to embrace any items of mental content . . .) he has more or less power to bring to mind any relations that essentially hold between them.
>
> It is instanced whenever a person becomes aware, say, that beer tastes something like weak quinine . . . or that the proposition "All A is B" proves the proposition "Some A is B". . .
>
> The eduction of correlates . . . when a person has in mind any idea together with a relation, he has more or less power to bring up into mind the correlative idea.
>
> For example, let anyone hear a musical note and try to imagine the note a fifth higher . . . . [Spearman, 1927, pp. 165–166]

The principle of eduction of correlates and relations provides a simple, if somewhat vague, characterization of g. The theory has never been formally tested but it has been used on occasion as a way of distinguishing among tests that differ in their g-to-s ratio. This use of the principle is rather informal since there is no quantitative method of assigning eduction of correlates and relations values to measures.

Contemporary research and theory have not resolved the theoretical debate between Thomson and Spearman. Contemporary theorists who remain committed to a modified version of Spearman's two-factor theory differ with respect to their interpretations of g. Humphreys (1976, 1985, 1989), for example, has endorsed a theoretical interpretation of the general factor in intelligence that is based on Thomson's theory. He assumed that there are many different facets or determinants of the indefinitely large number of potential measures of intellectual ability. It is possible to define an indefinitely large number of relatively homogeneous tests that differ in only one facet and thus will exhibit correlations of less than 1.00. At the same time the correlation between such independent tests will tend to be positive since they are likely to share facets in common.

Eysenck (1988) stated that Spearman's principle of the eduction of correlates and relations still provides the best definition of g. There is even contemporary research on intelligence that is reminiscent of Spearman's energy theory. Haier, Siegel, Neuchterlein, Hazlett, Wu, Paek, Browning, & Buchsbaum (1988) related individual differences in intelligence to measures of the overall metabolism of the brain. They reported a high negative correlation between a measure of the energy expenditure of the brain and scores on a test of abstract reasoning ability. Individuals who score high on a test of intelligence have brains that exhibit less activity during the test than individuals who score low on the test. These findings may be viewed as providing support for a contemporary version of Spearman's theory of mental energy.

The dispute between Thomson and Spearman may be treated as a metaphorical difference in ways of thinking about the general factor in intelligence. It is also the case that different metaphors may have different theoretical consequences and may lead investigators to suggest different research problems. It is sometimes possible to resolve such issues empirically. Loevinger (1951) argued that it is difficult to test Thomson's theory because it is without specific empirical consequences. By contrast, Willerman & Bailey (1987) argued that observations of individuals who have sex chromosome anomalies or sensory handicaps provide evidence that contradicts Thomson's theory. Females with Turner's syndrome, who lack a portion or all of the second X chromosome, have poor spatial ability and have difficulty in dealing with the Block Design test on the Wechsler test of intelligence. They do not exhibit deficits on the verbal subtests of the Wechsler. It is also the case that individuals with Turner's syndrome exhibit correlations between spatial and verbal measures of intelligence that are not substantially different from the correlations obtained from individuals who do not have Turner's syndrome. The existence of a correlation between different tests implies, on Thomson's theory, that the items must share elements or bonds in common. If an anomaly influences a specific intellectual function, then the elements that are affected ought to influence performance on related tasks. Willerman and Bailey asserted that correlations among different intellectual components that are shown by their differential responsiveness to anomalies to be independent might come about because of correlated qualities of independent neural machinery subserving different intellectual functions.

The Willerman and Bailey argument is not decisive for at least two reasons. Evidence that anomalies may influence one type of intellectual function without affecting a correlated but independent intellectual function contradicts Spearman's theory as well as Thomson's theory. If there is a single common intellectual faculty, then anything that influences performance on one type of task should influence performance on other intellectual tasks. Thomson's theory is a theoretical account of Spearman's two-factor theory. Evidence that contradicts both theories cannot be used to support one theory over the other. In addition, it is not clear that Thomson's theory of bonds is contradicted by the assertion that neural machinery exists that subserves entirely different intellectual functions. One could argue that the common elements that lead to relationships among diverse intellectual functions may be conceived as operating by a sampling principle. Thomson (1939) indicated that the bonds that are sampled may be located in diverse areas of the brain and need not be physically contiguous. It is possible that Loevinger's analysis is correct. Thomson's theory is simply too vague to be tested. It remains on the level of a metaphor.

SPEARMAN AND THURSTONE

Spearman's theory was subjected to a more fundamental criticism on empirical grounds. Matrices of correlations among ability tests did not fit the law of tetrad differences. Spearman was aware of this problem as early as 1906 (Spearman & Kreuger, 1906). Tests of intelligence that appeared to be similar with respect to the kinds of intellectual functions they measured would exhibit correlations that were too high. For example, in a correlation matrix derived from a battery of tests of spatial visualization functioning and verbal tests, the correlations among tests belonging to each class of measures is likely to be higher than those expected on the basis of Spearman's theory. The discrepancy occurs because the correlations between tests belonging to the two separate classes of measures are likely to be lower than the correlations among tests belonging to the same class. It is apparent from this hypothetical example that correlations between tests would be determined not only by a shared general intellectual factor but also by similarity in specific factors that are common to a subset of measures. This contradicts Spearman's assertion that specific factors are uniquely present in each intellectual test. Spearman attempted to trivialize this problem by indicating that tests may be only superficially different. A test of letter cancellation in which a subject is required to cross out all instances of the letter "e" is only superficially different from a test of letter instances of the letter "t". Spearman argued that such superficial similarities between tests would lead to high correlations simply because each test was really a parallel version of the other. This analysis is wrong. Tests that are not superficially equivalent to each other exhibit high correlations that cannot be solely accounted for by their shared relationship to a general intellectual factor. Such evidence constitutes a decisive refutation of Spearman's theory. This implies that relationships among tests of intelligence cannot be accounted for by a single common intellectual ability factor.

While Spearman was aware that his theory had been empirically refuted, he continued to emphasize the importance of the common intellectual factor. He tended to treat the possible existence of specific ability factors as minor perturbations of little general importance. It remained for an American psychologist, Thurstone, to construct a theory of intelligence based on the existence of specialized intellectual abilities. Thurstone (1938) argued that Spearman's theory was flawed on conceptual grounds and provided a misleading foundation for the measurement of individual differences in intelligence. He believed that there were separate intellectual abilities that were unrelated to each other. An adequate representation of a person's intelligence would therefore require the specification of a person's score on each of several ability factors. Thurstone believed that such a representation would provide a more accurate assessment of the strengths and weaknesses of a person and would be diagnostically superior to an evaluation that was based on a single score.

Thurstone developed a statistical procedure called multiple factor analysis that permitted him to analyze correlation matrices to determine the number of independent factors or dimensions that were required to account for the relationships among the tests in the matrix (Thurstone, 1931). For this purpose, Thurstone began with several assumptions about the structure of measures of intelligence. He assumed that there were several independent ability factors. This assumption implies that a person's score on one ability factor is unrelated to the person's score on another factor. The number of ability factors that existed in a set of diverse tests was smaller than the number of tests. Each test was assumed to be a measure of one or more factors. A person's score on a particular test could be represented by an equation representing the sum of the cross-products of the person's score on each of the factors that determine performance on the test and a weighting of each factor based on its importance in determining performance on that particular test. In the case of a test determined by two abilities, the equation may be written as follows: $s = a_1x_1 + a_2x_2$, where s equals the person's score on the test, x_1 and x_2 represent the person's score on the factors that determine performance on the test, and a_1 and a_2 represent the weightings of the factors in terms of their importance in determining performance on the test.

Multiple factor analysis is a technique for discovering the number of independent factors present in the matrix of correlations that must be postulated to account for the obtained correlations. While the statistical procedures involved are complex, the basic concepts underlying the procedure are fairly easy to comprehend. Imagine a matrix of correlations derived from tests of mathematical reasoning ability, spatial reasoning ability, and verbal ability. Imagine that correlations among tests belonging to each of these subsets are relatively high and correlations between pairs of tests belonging to different subsets are relatively low. In such a case, it is intuitively obvious that one would have to postulate three different relatively independent factors or dimensions to account for the pattern of correlations obtained in the matrix. The end result of a factor analysis is the creation of a factor matrix that specifies several independent factors and the relation of each of the tests to the factors. The relationship between a test and a factor is called the loading of a test on a factor and is represented as a hypothetical correlation between the test and the factor. The set of loadings of a test on each of the factors provides an analysis of the extent to which performance on a test is determined by each of the factors. The factor analysis partitions the variance of scores on a test into separate components of variance representing the contributions of each of the factors to performance on the test. The factor analysis also permits one to assign a score to an individual on each of the independent factors that are assumed to be represented in the matrix. A person's score on a factor is determined by his or her performance on tests that load on the factor.

There are a number of different criteria and procedures available for determining the number of factors that must be postulated to account for the matrix of obtained correlations. Thurstone used the principle of simple structure to define factors. The factor analyst seeks to define factors that will maximize the loading of each test on one or more factors and lead to zero loadings of the test on remaining factors. In the limiting case, each test will load on a single factor. If a test does not load on a factor it is assumed that factor does not determine performance on the test.

Thurstone reported the first test of his theory in 1938. He obtained scores on a battery of 56 tests from a sample of 240 volunteers who were students at universities. He factor analyzed the matrix of correlations and obtained 13 factors. Of these, 9 were assigned a psychological label. The labels were spatial, perceptual, numerical, verbal, memory, word fluency, inductive, arithmetical reasoning, and deduction. Thurstone believed that his study had conclusively demonstrated that Spearman's theory was incorrect. He replaced the general factor with several independent factors.

Thurstone's rejection of Spearman's theory was premature. Thurstone (1938) noted that the vast majority of correlations in his matrix were positive and the median correlation among the set of correlations fell within the class interval .25 to .35. The correlations among independent tests of ability tended to be positive or zero. He accounted for the presence of positive correlations by indicating that most tests of intellectual ability in common use were psychologically complex, containing loadings on several factors. This would provide a basis for a relationship among tests since any pair of tests was likely to share a common loading on one or more factors. An alternative interpretation of this finding is that the existence of positive correlations among the tests is attributable to a common intellectual ability factor—Spearman's g. Thurstone's study did not provide an ideal vehicle for distinguishing between his theory and Spearman's theory. Thurstone had made the same error that Spearman had accused Wissler of making 30 years earlier. The use of university students had restricted the range of talent of individuals in general intelligence thereby decreasing the magnitude of the correlation among tests of ability. If the average correlation among tests were larger, it would be more difficult to obtain a factor solution in which independent factors satisfied the requirements of simple structure. As the average correlation among tests increases, tests tend to have higher loadings on all of the independent factors and zero loadings of tests on factors cannot be obtained.

Thurstone's conclusions about the absence of a g in his matrix of correlations were challenged by Eysenck (1939), who reanalyzed his correlation matrix using a method that permitted him to define the general factor in the matrix. He found that g accounted for 30.8 percent of the variance in the matrix. After removing the variance in the matrix attributable to g, Eysenck defined eight specific factors that were similar to those defined by Thurstone. The variance accounted for by these factors ranged from 6.61 to .97% of the variance in the matrix. Thus, on Eysenck's analysis, g accounted for substantially more variance than any of the individual factors. Carroll (1988) calculated the percentage of variance of the general factor and the specific factors in each of the tests in Thurstone's battery using the results of Eysenck's factor analysis. Carroll found that g accounted for approximately half of the variance of scores on these tests and that specific factors accounted for the remaining variance. It should be noted that the relative importance of g and of specific factors in Thurstone's results is influenced by the restriction in range of talent of the subjects used by Thurstone. If Thurstone had used a more representative sample, the importance of g relative to specific factors would be increased. This analysis implies that individual differences in performance on the tests used by Thurstone could be accounted for by a general factor and one or more specific factors of the type postulated by Thurstone.

By 1941 Thurstone realized that his research had not conclusively demonstrated that Spearman's theory was wrong (Thurstone & Thurstone, 1941). In his subsequent factor analytic investigations Thurstone used samples of children who were not restricted in range of talent for general intelligence. He found that he was not able to define a factor solution that postulated the existence of independent factors and that satisfied the requirement of simple structure. Thurstone's solution to his problem was to change his way of defining factors. In his original factor analyses Thurstone had defined factors that were unrelated to each other. These factors are called orthogonal. Thurstone abandoned orthogonal solutions for oblique solutions that permitted factors to be correlated or related to each other. It is possible to illustrate the import of this procedure by a simplified example. Assume that a psychologist administered a battery of tests containing subsets of tests of verbal and spatial ability. Assume further that the average correlation among verbal subtests was .70 and the average correlation among spatial tests was also .70. Assume further that the average correlation between a spatial and a verbal subtest was .40. If one were to factor analyze this matrix of correlations it would be possible to identify two independent factors. It is also apparent that tests that loaded highly on one of the factors would have a positive loading on the second factor and the factor solution would not satisfy the requirements of simple structure. One way of attaining simple structure for such a matrix would be to permit the factors to be related to each other. Such an oblique solution in this case would require the factors to be correlated .4. Simple structure could be obtained at the expense of permitting the factors to be nonindependent.

The use of oblique factor analysis left Thurstone without a convincing refutation of Spearman's two-factor theory. What accounted for the positive correlations among the factors? One could argue that the factors were correlated because of the existence of a general factor. It is possible to demonstrate this by additional statistical manipulation of the correlation matrix. It is possible to perform a second-order factor analysis of the correlation matrix formed by examining the correlations among factors. A general factor might emerge that was identifiable as Spearman's g. R. B. Cattell (1941) indicated that Spearman's theory and Thurstone's theory might be reconciled by postulating the existence of a hierarchical structure of ability. The factor g is a general factor present in all measures of ability. Thurstone's factors are represented at a lower level of abstraction in the hierarchy. Thus the higher-order factor is defined by a wider set of variables (tests) than any of the individual factors that collectively define it. The g factor is assigned a singular position at the apex of the hierarchy and may be thought of as a common factor that is present in all of the tests. The g factor is derivable from the relationships that exist among the more specialized factors postulated by Thurstone.

This historical survey has traced the development of a theory of the hierarchical structure of abilities whose outline was clearly established by 1941. In the next chapter several contemporary theories of the structure of abilities will be considered and we shall compare them to the hierarchical structure of ability developed at the beginning of the fifth decade of this century.

2

THE STRUCTURE OF INTELLECT

THE THEORY OF FLUID
AND CRYSTALLIZED ABILITY

Description

R. B. Cattell (1941, 1963, 1971, 1987; see also Horn, 1985) believed that second-order factor analyses provided evidence for more than one second-order factor. He suggested that Spearman's g could be divided into two separate factors called fluid and crystallized ability. He subsequently argued that there was evidence for the existence of five-second order factors (Horn & Cattell, 1966).

The distinction between fluid and crystallized ability was closely related to a theoretical analysis of two types of intellectual factors called intelligence A and intelligence B developed by Hebb (1942) on the basis of observations of intellectual changes in individuals following brain damage. Intelligence A was basic biological capacity to acquire knowledge. Intelligence B was an ability that was influenced by acculturation. Cattell was also influenced by research conducted by Spearman and his students in the 1930s dealing with attempts to derive measures of intelligence that had high g-to-s ratios. Tests of perceptual analogies and classifications were assumed to be good measures of g. Such tests were relatively independent of tests of scholastic achievement and knowledge that was acquired in school settings.

Cattell's theory was based on the results of factor analytic investigations that started with Thurstone's primary mental ability factors. Second-order factor analysis of oblique factors led to a distinction between two second-order factors labeled g_f and g_c (R. B. Cattell, 1963). Factor g_f

fluid ability, was defined by tests that were assumed to measure the
biological capacity of the individual to acquire knowledge. Factor g_c,
crystallized ability, was defined by tests that were assumed to measure
the influence of schooling and acculturation. The factor with the highest
loading on the second-order g_c factor was verbal ability. Tests of vocabulary measure g_c. Inductive reasoning and spatial reasoning factors tend to
load highly on the second-order g_f factor. Cattell developed culture-fair
tests of intelligence that were designed to present individuals with novel
problems of reasoning using common elements of experience. The tests
were assumed to be good measures of the ability to educe correlates and
relations adumbrated by Spearman. Figure 2.1 presents items from the
Cattell Culture-Fair tests. Such items measure g_f rather than g_c.

Cattell's theoretical interpretation of g_f and g_c has several deductive
implications. Changes in the biological state of the organism influence g_f
more than g_c. Intellectual ability may be influenced by brain damage,
prenatal insults, and nutrition. These events influence g_f more than g_c.
Cattell believed that genetic influences were stronger on g_f than on g_c.
Cattell also argued that there were age-related changes in the functioning
of the brain that lead to an inevitable age-related decline in g_f. By contrast, g_c does not decline with age. Changes in the quality of schooling

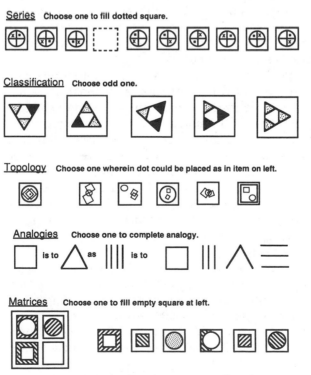

FIGURE 2.1 Items from the Cattell Culture-Fair test (based on R. B. Cattell, 1971).

and other attempts to change intelligence by providing improved intellectual socialization experiences influence g_c more than g_f.

Cattell also developed a causal analysis of the relationship between g_f and g_c. The g_f factor is more likely to influence g_c than g_c is likely to influence g_f. This assertion is related to the fundamental distinction between ability and achievement. To assert that one has an intellectual ability is to assert that one has a capability or potential that may or may not be actualized. An achievement, by contrast, represents the attainment of something for which ability is a necessary condition. Thus it is not possible to acquire knowledge in the absence of the ability to learn. One could have the ability to learn but, for a variety of reasons, one may not acquire knowledge. A person with the ability to learn may have been deprived of the opportunity to learn or, for temperamental or motivational reasons, may choose not to actualize the ability. This implies that ability measures should stand in a causal (but not a unicausal) relation to measures of achievement. At the same time achievements (intellectual attainments) can influence intellectual abilities. One can acquire knowledge and algorithms that change one's ability to acquire new knowledge. This implies that the relationship between abilities and achievements is a complex one that changes over time. While abilities are initially the necessary condition for achievement, achievements can eventually influence abilities. Cattell's causal analysis of the g_f–g_c distinction replicates the ability–achievement distinction in the domain of ability. That is, fluid ability is initially a necessary condition for the development of crystallized ability.

Cattell's second-order factor analyses of Thurstone's primary mental abilities factors provided evidence for additional second-order factors. Cattell was able to identify five different second-order factors. In addition to g_f and g_c, he identified a visualization factor, a memory factor related to retrieval capacity, and a cognitive speed factor (see Horn & Cattell, 1966).

The second-order factors identified by Cattell were not orthogonal. This permitted Cattell to perform a third-order factor analysis of the second-order factors. At the third order, Cattell defined two factors—an educational effectiveness factor and a factor he called historical fluid ability. Factor g_f was the factor with the highest loading on the historical fluid ability factor and g_c was the factor with the highest loading on the educational effectiveness factor.

In recent years much of the research related to Cattell's theory has been conducted by Horn (1985). Horn modified the theory while maintaining the essential commitment to the importance of the g_f–g_c distinction. He believed that five second-order factors were necessary to account for the relationships among first-order ability factors. Table 2.1 presents a representative five-factor solution obtained by Horn for a series of measures used by cognitive psychologists. Horn does not proceed to a third-order analysis.

TABLE 2.1 Second Order Oblique Factors[a,b]

Primary factors	Symbol	g_a	Asd	g_c	g_f	g_v	h^2
Auditory							
Discrimination among sound patterns	DASP	.50	.15	.00	.21	−.04	.68
Maintaining and judging rhythms	MaJR	.35	−.04	−.07	−.09	.29	.32
Temporal tracking of sounds	Tc	.29	−.07	.04	.26	.20	.61
Auditory cognition of relations	ACoR	.23	.08	.17	.24	−.11	.47
Auditory immediate memory	Msa	.22	−.01	−.04	.55	−.18	−.59
Speech perception under distraction/distortion	SPUD	.11	.61	−.02	−.05	−.08	.53
Auditory acuity	Ac	−.01	.39	−.15	.01	.04	.26
Listening verbal comprehension	Va	.11	.30	.43	.08	.03	.66
Visual							
Verbal comprehension	V	−.07	−.16	.50	.16	−.16	.69
Semantic systems	EMS	.02	−.11	.51	−.16	−.01	.50
Semantic relations	CMS	−.03	−.04	.47	.17	−.05	.73
Induction	I	−.07	.01	.28	.26	.13	.59
Figural relations	CFR	.00	−.05	−.04	.57	.09	.61
Visualization	Vz	−.05	−.05	.00	.46	.24	.54
Figural classes	CFC	.01	.02	.10	.19	.40	.28
Speed closure	Cs	−.09	.22	.14	.19	.20	.41
Flexibility of closure	Cf	.02	−.15	−.11	.08	.50	.32
Spatial operation	S	−.05	.02	−.10	.06	.47	.31
Visual memory	Mv	.04	−.16	.16	.00	.16	.18
Factor intercorrelations	g_a	—	.28	.54	.39	.44	
	Asd	.28	—	.00	.28	.34	
	g_c	.54	.00	—	.62	.49	
	g_f	.39	.28	.62	—	.41	
	g_v	.44	.34	.39	.41	—	
Σr		1.91	1.15	1.63	1.70	1.67	

[a]Based on Horn & Stankov (1982).

[b]Abbreviations: g_a, auditory ability; Asd, auditory sensory detection; g_c, crystallized ability; g_f, fluid ability; g_v, visual general ability.

Horn's second-order factors are closely related to Cattell's. Horn used cognitive measures to derive second-order factors rather than Thurstone's primary mental abilities factors (see Horn & Stankov, 1982; Stankov & Horn, 1980). Where Horn differs most fundamentally from Cattell is in his theoretical interpretation of the meaning of the factors. Horn did not interpret g_f as a biological ability factor. He asserted that fluid and crystallized ability are equally heritable although they may be subject to partially independent genetic influences. He assumed that there are separate and distinct physiological and cultural influences on these abilities. Fluid and crystallized ability develop along partially independent pathways and g_f is not causally privileged with respect to its influence on g_c. Horn accepted Cattell's theory of the effects of age on these abilities.

Figure 2.2 presents a summary of Horn's theoretical conception of the organization of abilities. Note that Fig. 2.2 presents both g_f and g_c as broad abilities that are related to the eduction of relations in Spearman's sense. They are influenced to different degrees by other broad ability factors. In this representation, g_f and g_c are assigned privileged status with respect to other second-order ability factors. It is apparent that, through somewhat different conceptual and empirical routes, Horn and Cattell

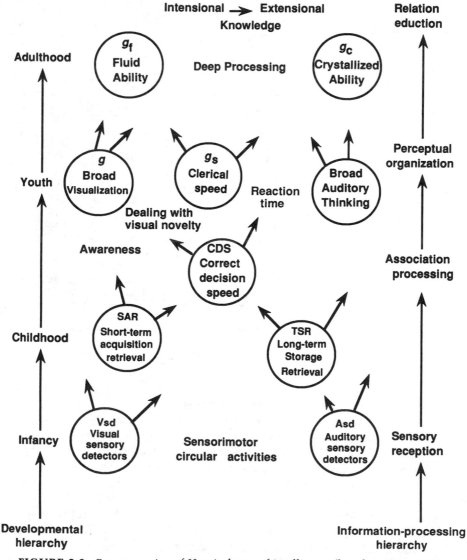

FIGURE 2.2   Representation of Horn's theory of intelligence (based on Horn, 1985).

arrived at structural theories that are quite similar. Cattell proceeds through third-order factor analysis to arrive at two factors that are closely related to fluid and crystallized ability factors derived from second-order factor analysis. The educational effectiveness factor and the historical fluid ability factor may be construed, without excessive distortion, as factors that preserve a privileged hierarchical status for g_f and g_c. Similarly, the theoretical scheme presented in Fig. 2.2 assigns a privileged hierarchical status to g_f and g_c relative to other second-order abilities. Horn assumed that the abilities represented in Fig. 2.2 are hierarchically related. Complex abilities derive from developmentally primitive and simple sensory detection functions and associational abilities. The distance from top to bottom of the hierarchy is inversely proportional to the magnitude of the correlations among the abilities. This implies that the correlation between complex abilities and g_f and g_c will be higher than the correlation between abilities based on developmentally prior and less complex information-processing characteristics and g_f and g_c.

Evaluation

A full evaluation of the theory of crystallized and fluid intelligence requires a consideration of evidence on changes in intelligence with age, research on the behavior genetics of intelligence, and a consideration of the relationship between simple and complex measures of ability. All of these topics are considered in subsequent chapters. In this chapter we shall consider the factor analytic evidence related to the distinction between g_f and g_c.

Both Horn and Cattell propose to replace Spearman's concept of g with a theory that assumes that it is necessary to distinguish between two types of abilities, g_f and g_c. In effect, both theorists propose that Spearman's g is no longer a scientifically useful construct. The evidence in favor of this position would be far less equivocal if g_f and g_c were independent. In point of fact they are not. The correlation between g_f and g_c factors in most studies is close to .5. It is possible to argue that it is necessary to introduce a superordinate g factor in order to explain the relationship between g_f and g_c. We shall consider several different kinds of evidence that suggest that the distinction between g_f and g_c does not constitute decisive evidence against Spearman's theory.

Table 2.2 presents a summary of several third-order factor analyses undertaken by Cattell. For three of the four analyses (those for the three youngest samples) the loading of the g_f factor is higher on the historical fluid ability factor than the loading of the g_c factor on the educational effectiveness factor. The study using adult criminals is the only study that includes the five second-order factors identified by Cattell. Here the pattern of results is somewhat different. The g_c factor is substantially loaded on the educational effectiveness factor and has a near zero loading on the historical fluid ability factor. The remaining second-order factors

TABLE 2.2   Cattell's Summary of His Higher-Order Ability Analyses[a]

A. Children

	$g_f(h)$	Educational effectiveness factor	Possible maturity factor
5- to 6-year-olds (114)			
g_f	.94	−.06	.13
g_c	.41	.38	−.12
Personality			
Factor X	.10	.89	.03
Factor Y	.01	−.01	.93
9- to 12-year-olds (306)			
g_f	.70	−.02	.25
g_c	.57	.48	−.06
Anxiety	−.09	.07	.32
Personality			
Factor 1	−.41	.00	.05
Factor 2	−.02	.62	.04

B. Teenagers and Adults

	$g_f(h)$	Educational effectiveness factor	General personality factor	
			Alpha	Beta
13- to 14-year-olds (277)				
g_f	.69	.00	.02	−.07
g_c	.63	.32	−.04	.07
Anxiety				
U.I. 24	−.01	.79	−.51	−.07
Exvia				
U.I. 32	.18	.23	.01	.00
Corteria				
U.I. 32	.09	.32	−.52	−.07
Personality				
Factor A	.01	−.05	.99	−.03
Factor B	.00	.04	.03	−.74
Factor C	.02	.06	−.69	.08
Adult criminals (477)				
g_f	.53	.02	−.08	−.10
g_c	−.04	.73	.20	.08
g_r	.42	−.21	−.08	−.40
g_s	.60	−.01	.33	.10
g_v	.57	.38	−.13	.18
Person				
U.I.	.00	.11	−.32	−.66
Anxiety				
U.I. 24	−.03	−.41	−.31	.02
Personality				
Factor A	.00	−.01	.45	−.00
Factor D	.34	.00	.11	.21

[a]Based on R. B. Cattell (1971).

24

are all more substantially correlated with the historical fluid ability factor than with the educational effectiveness factor. These analyses indicate that, at the third order, the factor that is more closely related to fluid ability accounts for more variance than the factor associated with crystallized ability.

Humphreys (1967) reanalyzed Cattell's study of 13- to 14-year-old children included in Table 2.2. He derived a two-factor solution for these data. In his solution, all of the Thurstone ability factors and Cattell's culture-fair intelligence tests that are assumed to be measures of fluid ability had loadings ranging from .44 to .64 on the first factor. This factor is broader than the g_f and g_c factors. A second factor was defined by the Cattell culture-fair tests of ability. It had loadings from .20 to .35 on the factor. This factor was not well defined by any of the tests. It weakly resembles a fluid ability factor. Humphreys found that the two factors were correlated .57. In Cattell's solution the correlation between g_f and g_c for these data is .44. Humphrey's analysis indicates that Cattell's data provide substantial support for a single general factor that encompasses both g_f and g_c.

Humphrey's factor solution has much in common with the hierarchical models used by British psychologists such as P. E. Vernon (1961), who first defined a general factor and then proceeded to define two factors called v:ed and k:m. Factor v:ed stands for a verbal–educational factor and k:m stands for a mechanical–spatial ability factor. Vernon, like Humphreys, retained a superordinate g factor in his analyses.

Evidence for the existence of a single general factor is also present in the factor analyses performed by Horn. Table 2.1 presented the results of a factor analysis of auditory and visual tasks reported by Horn & Stankov (1982). The correlations among the five factors obtained in their solution are presented at the bottom of the table. Note that the correlation between the fluid and crystallized ability factors is .62—a value that is higher than the loading of any test in the matrix with any of the five factors derived by Stankov and Horn. The factor with the highest average correlation with the remaining four factors is the fluid ability factor. The correlations between the fluid ability factor and the other factors range from .28 to .62. The auditory comprehension factor, labeled Ac in the table, has the lowest correlation with the fluid ability factor. It is a factor that is not well defined by the existing tests in the matrix. A test of speech perception under distraction loads .61 on the factor. No other test has a loading in excess of .4 on the factor. It is also the case that the five factors extracted by Stankov and Horn are not well defined by the existing tests in the matrix. Only the crystallized and fluid ability factors are defined by two tests that have loadings in excess of .5, and no factor is defined by two tests with loadings in excess of .6. The five-factor solution is not compelling—there is considerable evidence in the matrix for a general factor that is related to all of the other factors in the matrix.

The strongest evidence for the existence of a single general factor in matrices of correlations designed to identify first-order factors and sec-

TABLE 2.3   Loading of Abilities on the g Factor[a]

Factor	Study				Mean
	1	2	3	4	
g_f	1.02	1.01	.95	.94	.98
g_c	.81	.80	.88	.77	.82
g_v	.78	.70	.79	.73	.75
g_s	—	.58	.66	.55	.60
g_r	—	—	.80	.70	.75

[a]Based on Gustafsson (1988).

ond-order g_f and g_c factors comes from studies using confirmatory factor analysis. Gustafsson (1988; see also Gustafsson, 1984) summarized the results of studies using these techniques. Confirmatory factor analyses may be used to test different models of the structure of hierarchical relationships among different tests of ability. In these analyses, the expected structure of relationships based on previous results is specified and then tests are made of the goodness of fit of various models to the obtained relationships. Gustafsson identified five second-order factors in substantial agreement with the theory proposed by Cattell and Horn. Table 2.3 presents the correlations of each of these factors with a third-order general factor. Note that each is substantially related to the general factor and the second-order fluid ability factor is virtually indistinguishable from the third-order general factor. Since g_f and g are essentially the same factor, it is reasonable to remove g_f from the hierarchical order of second-order factors and leave it at the apex of the ability structure. The residual variance in the matrix after the general factor is removed would include a g_c factor that Gustafsson interpreted as being identical to the factor labeled $k:ed$ by Vernon. Gustafsson identified one of the residual second-order factors as being similar to the factor Vernon labels $k:m$. There may be other broad second-order factors identified with memory and auditory ability. Thus Gustafsson's use of confirmatory factor analysis supports a hierarchical structure of ability that combines features of Vernon's theory with the Cattell–Horn theory of several second-order factors. The overall structure of the resultant model is closer to Vernon's model in that g is retained as an essential theoretical construct and fluid ability is assumed to be identical to g. Gustafsson's analyses lead to a decisive refutation of the Cattell–Horn theoretical model.

GUTTMAN'S RADEX THEORY

Guttman's theory is based on a modification of factor analysis. Guttman (1954, 1965, 1970) ordered ability tests in two ways. Tests may be ordered on a dimension of complexity. Such an ordering principle is called a simplex—it permits a rank order. Tests also differ in content. Content differences among tests do not form a simplex. Content relationships among tests form an order that is called a circumplex. Contents may be ordered in a circular way, with contents that are related assigned adjacent positions on the circumference of the circle. The combination of a simplicial ordering principle with a circumplicial ordering system creates what Guttman calls a radex—a radial expansion of complexity. In a radex, each test may be assigned a position in a circular space. Tests that are located near the center of the circle are closer, on the average, to all other points in the space. This forms a simplicial ordering dimension. For any given simplicial ordering, tests with different contents are arrayed circumplicially.

Marshalek, Lohman, & Snow (1983) demonstrated that Guttman's radex theory is compatible with the hierarchical model of intelligence derived from factor analysis. They factor analyzed a battery of tests and were able to specify the g loading of each of the tests. They grouped these tests into three categories—those with high g loadings (between 54 and 60% of the variance), those with intermediate g loadings (between 28 and 46% of the variance), and those with low g loadings (between 4 and 25% of the variance). They used a multidimensional scaling program to determine the distance between tests in their matrix. Figure 2.3 presents the

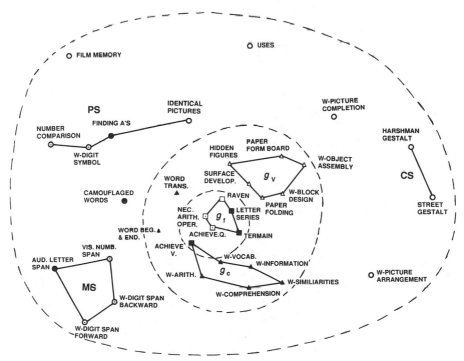

FIGURE 2.3 A radex representation of the structure of ability. Square represent tests with high g loadings, triangles those with intermediate g loadings, and circles represent tests with low g loadings (based on Marshalek, Lohman, & Snow, 1983).

results of their analysis. Note that tests that have high *g* loadings (represented by squares in Fig. 2.3) are located near the center of the radex. Tests with low *g* loadings are located near the periphery of the radex. Tests that were found to have high loadings on fluid ability factors also had high *g* loadings and are located near the center of the radex. Tests with different contents are arrayed at different distances from the center of the radex and are grouped in a circumplicial ordering. It is apparent that the radex representation of the structure of tests of ability is congruent with the hierarchical ordering of tests of intelligence that retains a superordinate *g* factor.

I have argued that there is evidence that supports a hierarchical ability model that retains a superordinate *g* factor. This conclusion would not be acceptable to two additional theorists, Guilford and Gardner. Guilford's theory is based on factor analysis and Gardner's is based on several additional data sources. Both theorists assume that there is no reason to retain *g* in their theories of the structure of intelligence.

GUILFORD'S THEORY

Description

Guilford (1964, 1967, 1985; Guilford & Hoepfner, 1971) based his theory on a three-dimensional taxonomy of intellectual tasks. Intellectual tasks differ with respect to mental operations, contents, and products. He assumed that there were five operations—cognition (knowing), memory, divergent production (generation of alternatives), convergent production (generation of logic-tight conclusions), and evaluation. These operations can be applied to four types of contents—figural, symbolic, semantic, and behavioral. Guilford (1977) subsequently modified the figural category into auditory and visual categories to create five content categories. The end result of the application of a particular operation to a particular content can be expressed in terms of one of six products. These are units, classes, relations, systems, transformations, and implications. This theory implies that there are 150 different types of intellectual tasks. This conclusion is based on the assumption that all possible combinations of these dimensions exist. Guilford asserted that it is possible to develop tests that measure each of these distinct combinations of abilities.

Each of the abilities in Guilford's taxonomy is identified by a three-letter code. And, each ability is assumed to be defined by one or more tests. Consider the following examples. The code CFU refers to the cognition of figural units. It is measured by a test called "Hidden Print." Subjects are presented pictures of digits and letters outlined by dots. There are additional dots on the picture that obscure the digit or letter that is presented. Subjects are required to recognize the digit or letter that is presented. The task involves cognition—the subject is required to gain knowledge about a stimulus. The content of the material represented is figural (visual in Guilford's revised theory). And, the product that results is a unit—a single letter or digit. The code MSC refers to memory for symbolic classes. A test called "Memory for Name and Word Classes" is assumed to measure this ability. The subject is presented a set of names such as IRENE, IRIS, and IRVING. The subject is required to determine in a recognition task whether such words as IRA and IDA belong to the class. The task involves the operation of memory. The stimuli are symbolic and the response involves a determination of class inclusion. A test called "Reflections" is a measure of cognition of behavioral implications (CBI). Subjects are required to pick the best psychological implication of statements of the kind individuals are likely to make in psychotherapy. A subject might be presented with the statement, "I'm just wondering how I'll act; I mean how things will turn out." These statements are accompanied by multiple choice alternatives. The correct answer for the statement is, "She's worried about it." This test deals with knowledge of a behavioral or psychological event. The product is defined as an implication. Evaluation of semantic transformations (EMT) is measured by a test called "Story Titles." Subjects are presented with a brief story and several possible titles for the story. The subject is required to choose the most appropriate title. The test involves an evaluative judgment about semantic (verbal) material and the product of the evaluation is a transformation.

Guilford originally argued that these abilities were unrelated to each other. Instead of a hierarchical model, Guilford postulated a model of 150 independent ability factors. Tests that were similar on two of the three dimensions of his model were not assumed to be correlated with each other more than tests that differed on all of the dimensions of the model. In his original formulation there were no higher-order factors in the model and, clearly, nothing at all that resembled g.

Evaluation

Guilford's theory is based on a large set of factor analyses that he claimed resulted in the identification of many of the factors that were postulated in his theory. These factor analyses used orthogonal rotations that resulted in zero correlations between the factors, thereby providing evidence for the independence of the abilities postulated in the model. In addition, Guilford (1964) explicitly rejected g on the basis of the finding that 17% or 48,140 correlations that he computed among tests of abilities in his investigations fell within the interval of −.10 to +.10. Guilford argued that these findings permit a decisive rejection of g.

It should be noted that Guilford's results do not support his theory. He found that 83% of his correlations among ability measures exceeded .10. If his original theory were correct, correlations among tests of ability would usually be zero except for the case in which pairs of tests belong to one of the 150 abilities defined in the theory. Even with this caveat, it is still difficult to reconcile the assumption of a general ability measure with the finding of a failure to obtain positive correlations among diverse measures of ability. Guilford's findings should be interpreted cautiously for three reasons. First, some of the tests included in his matrices had low reliability. Tests that are unreliable may not correlate highly with themselves and are not expected to correlate highly with other tests. Second, he often used Air Force officer trainees as subjects. These individuals were selected for intelligence. Thus his samples frequently had restrictions in range of talent. Third, some of the abilities in his model may not be related to general intellectual ability. In particular, tests with behavioral contents may or may not be adequate measures of social skills (little evidence of validity exists for such measures), and social intelligence may or may not relate to more traditional cognitive abilities. So, too, tests involving divergent production in which an individual is required to produce several answers to a problem including answers that may only be minimally relevant (e.g., "How many uses can you think of for a brick?") may or may not be good measures of some general cognitive ability. Indeed, Cronbach (1968) argued that such tests are better construed as tests of impulsivity than of intelligence or creativity.

Brody & Brody (1976) examined two matrices of correlations among ability tests obtained by Guilford and his associates. They chose matrices obtained from samples not obviously restricted in range of talent and they excluded correlations among tests of ability with low reliability. Neither of the matrices they examined included tests of divergent thinking or behavioral contents. Tenopyr, Guilford, & Hoepfner (1966) obtained correlations among 50 tests of memory. Brody and Brody excluded seven tests from this matrix that had reliabilities below .6. Only 2% of the 943 correlations among the remaining tests were less than .12, the value required to reject the null hypothesis at the .05 level that the true correlation was .00. This result suggests that the true value of all of the correlations in the matrix was greater than zero. Although Tenopyr *et al.* had obtained a factor solution postulating the existence of 18 separate orthogonal (i.e., unrelated) factors, Brody and Brody found that one of the tests in the battery called the SCAT test that is a good measure of general verbal ability correlated between .16 and .70 with the 42 remaining tests in the battery. The median correlation of the SCAT with the remaining tests was .39. These results suggest that the disattenuated correlation of the SCAT with all of the remaining measures accounts for approximately 25% of the variance in the matrix.

Brody and Brody performed a similar analysis of data obtained by Dunham, Guilford, & Hoepfner (1966), who factor analyzed a battery of tests of ability to learn concepts. After excluding tests of low reliability, Brody and Brody found that less than 1% of the correlations in the matrix had values that were not significantly different from zero. A multiple choice test of vocabulary had correlations ranging between .27 and .60 with all of the remaining tests in the matrix even though Dunham *et al.* reported an orthogonal factor solution with 15 separate factors.

These analyses indicate that Guilford's matrices provide ample evidence for a positive manifold. Guilford's assertion that tests of ability frequently have zero correlations may depend on the use of unreliable tests of abilities of questionable relevance to general intellectual skills with samples that are restricted in range of talent. These analyses also suggest that Guilford's factor solutions may not be compelling. It is hard to imagine how one could obtain results indicating that single tests in a battery have positive correlations with all other tests in the battery and still find evidence for several orthogonal factors in the matrix. This skeptical assertion is buttressed by a closer examination of Guilford's factor analyses.

How is a factor solution justified? There is no single answer to this question. Perhaps the most basic issue involved, as it is for every empirical claim, is replicability. Is it possible to obtain similar solutions when similar batteries of tests are given to different samples? Since factor solutions are derived from correlations among tests, some replicability of correlational relationships is required for the demonstration of factor replicability. Tests should exhibit a comparable pattern of loadings in a new investigation that includes some or all of the same factors. A number of objective indices of factor replicability exist. These involve procedures to compare the loadings of the same tests in different investigations on the same factors. Guilford & Hoepfner (1971) reported that numerical indices of factor replicability failed to provide clear support for their factor solutions. Guilford "solved" the problem of factor replicability by using "targeted" or "Procrustean" rotations. These procedures involve the specification of the expected outcome of the factor analysis. Guilford and his associates attempted to define factors that most closely resemble the factors that are theoretically specified. Guilford did not use confirmatory factor analyses to test the fit between his obtained solutions and the theoretically predicted outcome. Horn & Knapp (1973; 1974; see also Guilford, 1974) examined three of Guilford's studies. They compared the results reported by Guilford and his associates for their factor solutions with results obtained by the use of targeted rotations to randomly generated hypotheses. For each set of data obtained by Guilford, they selected a random factor solution. They then used targeted procedures to define loadings of the variables on the factors. They computed indices of correct placement where a test with a loading of .3 or greater on the specified factor was designated as a hit. If a test did not load on the randomly designated factor with a loading of at least .3 it was designated a miss. The ratio of hits to hits and misses of their randomly selected factors was .83. The comparable ratio for the factor solutions obtained by Guilford was

.84. These data indicate that the evidence obtained from targeted rotations in support of Guilford's theory is not convincing since targeted rotations may be used to provide comparable support for any theory about the factor structure of correlations among tests of ability.

Brody & Brody (1976) examined the loadings of tests on factors in Guilford and Hoepfner's comprehensive report of all of the factor analyses performed prior to 1971. Table 2.4 presents a summary of the frequency distribution of loading they obtained. Table 2.4 indicates that only 7 of the 99 factors identified by Guilford had two or more tests with replicated loadings of .5 or more. Forty-three of the factors had never been replicated. The modal replicated value of the loadings of the test with the second highest loading on the factor fell within the interval of .30 to .39. These analyses indicate that Guilford's factors are not well defined by existing tests.

Guilford (1977, 1981, 1985) modified his theory by replacing a model of 150 unrelated ability factors with a hierarchical ability model. He assumed that factors could be correlated with each other and that factors that shared a common dimension would be more closely related to each other than factors that had no common dimension. The 150 first-order factors would yield 85 second-order factors defined by paired dimensions in the model. The 85 second-order factors would yield 16 third-order factors defined by each of the 16 dimensions of the model. For example, a third-order factor might exist for memory, memory for units would constitute a second-order factor, and memory for semantic units would be one of the 150 first-order actors. Kelderman, Mellenbergh, & Elshout's

TABLE 2.4   Frequency Distribution of Loadings of the Two Tests with the Highest Loading on Each of 99 Factors in the Guilford Model[a,b,c,d]

Loadings	Replicated[d] $f(x)$	Nonreplicated $f(x)$
.70–.79	0	7
.60–.69	1	2
.50–.59	6	36
.40–.49	23	31
.30–.39	26	3
Not replicated	43	—
	99	99

[a]Based on Brody & Brody (1976).

[b]The loading for the factor with the second-highest rating is tabulated.

[c]Singlets are not included.

[d]The replicated value refers to the lowest value obtained in all studies in which the test loaded on the factor. The tabled value represents the lowest loading of the test with the second highest loading on the factor.

(1981) research led Guilford to modify his theory. They used confirmatory factor analysis to compare the relationship between obtained and expected factor structures in seven of Guilford's studies. They found that none of the data sets fit Guilford's orthogonal model. They were able to find a satisfactory fit between obtained and expected results for three of seven studies if they permitted the factors to be correlated. Moreover, the factor correlations were substantial, with the majority of the factor correlations having values in excess of .5. These results indicate that Guilford's theory is frequently not compatible with his obtained data and, where it is compatible, acceptable fits can only be obtained by assuming that the factors are substantially correlated.

Guilford's revised hierarchical theory has not been comprehensively investigated. Since the definition of the first-order factors in the model are suspect, it is difficult to believe that the hierarchical structure that is derived from the first-order factors is valid. Guilford (1981) reported a number of illustrative analyses to provide evidence for the hierarchical version of his theory. He was hampered in this effort by the use of orthogonal rotations in his original studies leading to the definition of factors that were uncorrelated. He arbitrarily defined dimensions based on the amalgamation of scores on tests that were assumed to define factors in his model and then obtained correlations among these aggregate scores. Table 2.5 presents the results of one of these analyses. Table 2.5 presents the loadings of first-order aggregates on two hypothetical factors that share similarity on content and product categories. ST represents symbolic transformations and MT represents semantic transformation. If Guilford's hierarchy were correct, first-order aggregates that share similarity on two of three categories in the model should load more

TABLE 2.5 A Factor Pattern from Rotation of
Two Sets of Transformation Factors[a]

First-order reps	Higher factors[b]	
	ST	MT
CST	.52	.35
MST	.23	.19
DST	.52	.41
NST	.52	.31
EST	.22	.02
CMT	.38	.45
MMT	.48	.48
DMT	.10	.18
NMT	.17	.42
EMT	.09	.15

[a]Angle of rotation was 62°.
[b]Based on Guilford (1981).

substantially on a higher-order factor than those that share similarity on one of three categories. An examination of the data in Table 2.5 provides some support for Guilford's theory, but the support is weak. For example, two of the semantic transformation aggregates have loadings below .2 on the semantic transformation factor (DMT and EMT), and the aggregate with the highest loading on the semantic transformation factor has an equally high loading on the symbolic transformation factor even though it is similar in only one of the three categories. Guilford has not provided comparable data for many other predicted relationships in his model.

Guilford's hierarchical model is incompatible with the hierarchical model based on Gustafsson's confirmatory factor analyses and the congruent model based on the radex theory. Guilford's model does not include a superordinate g factor. It is also the case that the review presented here suggests that Guilford's theory is without empirical support. The factor structure that is postulated appears to be mythical. In the absence of empirical confirmation it cannot be construed as an acceptable alternative to a hierarchical model that retains a superordinate g factor.

GARDNER'S THEORY OF MULTIPLE INTELLIGENCE

Description

Gardner's theory is very different from the theories of the structure of intellect we have considered in this chapter. His theory is not based on the analysis of patterns of correlations among tests of ability. Gardner (1983) assumed that the existence of independent types of intelligence could be established by the use of eight criteria. These are listed as follows:

1. Potential isolation by brain damage. Gardner relied on neuropsychological evidence to argue that there are independent intelligences that are related to different neural structures. Research indicating that localized brain damage influences a particular ability while sparing other abilities provides evidence for the independence and separate identity of the affected ability.
2. The existence of idiot savants, prodigies, and other exceptional individuals. Prodigies are individuals who exhibit precocious intellectual skills. Evidence of precocious intellectual development in the absence of parallel precocity in other intellectual skills argues strongly for the independent development of separate intelligences. Idiot savants are individuals who exhibit an exceptional development of an intellectual ability who are retarded or mediocre in other intellectual skills. The existence of such a pattern of ability argues for the independence of different types of intelligence.
3. An identifiable core operation or set of operations. Gardner believed

that each intelligence is identified by a specific set of operations that is related to a neural mechanism. For example, he indicated that musical intelligence (an independent intelligence according to Gardner) has as one of its core operations the ability to discriminate differences in the pitch of tones. Gardner assumed linguistic intelligence had four core abilities: (1) rhetorical ability, the ability to convince others; (2) mnemonic abilities, the use of language as a way of remembering information; (3) explanatory abilities, the use of language in either written or oral form to teach or explain; and (4) metalinguistic ability, the ability of linguistic analysis to clarify meaning that is exemplified in both the simple question "What did you mean by that?" and in the sophisticated theories of the abstract structure of language developed by linguists.

4. A distinctive developmental history along with a definable set of expert "end-stage" performances. Gardner believed that it is possible to describe the developmental history of each intelligence. In addition, it should be possible to describe the performance of experts. Each intelligence is assumed to have an independent developmental history.

5. An evolutionary history and evolutionary plausibility. Gardner indicated that little is known about the evolutionary history of specific intelligences. He assumed that each specific intelligence has an evolutionary history that is related to some primordial form of expression in other species. For example, social intelligence may be related to primate social organizational abilities.

6. Support from experimental psychological tasks. The methods of the experimental cognitive psychologist may be used to identify the core operations of an intelligence. In addition, these methods may be used to establish the independence of different intelligences. For example, a dual-task paradigm may be used to demonstrate that intellectual tasks that are based on the same intelligence may exhibit more interference than tasks that require separate intelligences.

7. Support from psychometric findings. Psychometric investigations should provide support for the independence of different intelligences. Gardner did not believe that psychometric investigations should be relied on to provide unambiguous support for the independence of different intelligences. He believed that such investigations have not sampled widely among the set of abilities and have relied extensively on tasks that do not relate to the intellectual abilities that individuals exhibit in important social contexts. He also believed that many of the tasks used in psychometric investigations may be solved in different ways. Therefore, they may measure different abilities in different individuals. Despite these caveats, Gardner asserted that psychometric investigations should provide evidence for the independence of different intelligences. Tests of different intelligences should exhibit lower correlations than tests of the same intelligence.

8. Susceptibility to encoding in a symbol system. Gardner assumed that intelligences tend to become encoded in culturally contrived symbol systems. Linguistic intelligence is encoded in a language with formal rules. Musical intelligence may be expressed in a notational language.

Gardner argued that these criteria, when collectively applied, implied that it is possible to distinguish among six different intelligences: linguistic intelligence, musical intelligence, logical–mathematical intelligence, spatial intelligence, bodily–kinesthetic intelligence, and personal intelligence (i.e., the ability to understand one's own emotions and to understand the behavior of other individuals).

Critique

It is difficult to evaluate Gardner's theory because his book does not present specific studies in support of his claims. A fully developed argument in favor of his theory would require the presentation of evidence establishing that each of his intelligences fulfills each of the eight criteria that are assumed to define an intelligence. What I find problematic in his theory is the specific list of intelligences that are defined by the application of his criteria. I shall argue that his list is arbitrary and that his attempt to restructure the theory of intelligence to omit a general factor is no more successful than the attempts of psychometric theorists to dispense with g.

Gardner's criteria may be used to support the independent status of a set of intelligences that is larger than the set postulated by him. Carroll's (1988) psychometric investigations of existing correlational matrices of ability measures provided evidence for the independent status of 30 different intellectual abilities. These investigations do not include three of the six intelligences postulated by Gardner—musical, personal, and bodily–kinesthetic. Gardner indicated that the definition of an intelligence involves a somewhat arbitrary aggregation of abilities that may be partially distinctive. He stated,

> spatial intelligence entails a number of loosely related capacities: the ability to recognize instances of the same element; the ability to transform or to recognize a transformation of one element into another; the capacity to conjure up mental imagery and then to transform that imagery; the capacity to produce a graphic likeness of spatial information; and the like. Conceivably, these operations are independent of one another and could develop and break down separately; and yet, just as rhythm and pitch work together in the area of music, so, too, the forementioned capacities typically occur together in the spatial realm. Indeed, they operate as a family, and use of each operation may well reinforce use of the others. [Gardner, 1983, p. 176]

This quotation indicates that the aggregation of separate components of ability into an intelligence involves an arbitrary decision. Presumably, the aggregation is defined by social conventions that entail the performance of intellectual tasks that are mutually reinforcing, leading to the development of a composite aggregated intelligence. The issue of aggregation is crucial in defining the number of independent intelligences. If the aggregation is to be defined on the basis of socially relevant activities that are mutually reinforcing, there is at least an anecdotal argument to be made that social conventions may involve mutually reinforcing abilities that belong to different intelligences in Gardner's taxonomy. Gardner indicated that physical scientists may use spatial and logical–mathematical intelligences. Other socially defined roles may require an individual to draw on several different intelligences. A choreographer is usually a person who has been a dancer and has a developed bodily–kinesthetic intelligence. Dances are usually choreographed to music. Therefore, the choreographer usually requires a developed musical intelligence. And, dances frequently express emotion and meaning. The choreographer must understand nonverbal expressivity. Finally, dances involve variations on spatial configurations and choreographers must have a highly developed spatial intelligence. Presumably, the practice of choreography mutually reinforces intelligences belonging to each of these four quasiindependent domains. It is as arbitrary to aggregate across the separate abilities that collectively define the spatial domain as it is to suggest the existence of a choreographic intelligence involving the mutually reinforcing family of musical, personal, spatial, and bodily–kinesthetic intelligences.

Research on brain damage and neural structures also indicates that it is possible to define a set of independent intellectual abilities with many more intelligences than are included in Gardner's taxonomy. Prosopognosia provides an excellent example. Prosopognosia is a relatively rare disorder exhibited by individuals with bilateral brain damage in the inferior visual association cortices (Damasio, 1985). The most striking symptom of the disorder is an inability to recognize familiar faces. More generally, the disorder may be described as one of the inability to recognize individual representatives of a visually presented class. Thus, prosopognosics may not be able to distinguish between their car and other cars.

Prosopognosia appears to provide evidence for the definition of an independent intelligence. The condition has a defined neurological basis. Prosopognosics do not, in general, exhibit other intellectual deficits. They have intact linguistic, perceptual, and memory abilities. In fact, some of these patients can discriminate among unfamiliar faces (Benton, 1980). It should be possible to study the development of the ability to recognize and individuate members of a visually presented class of stimuli. The ability also is present at an expert level. Gardner described Jomo Kenyatta's training as a boy in Kenya that enabled him to identify every head of livestock in his family's herd using the cues of color, markings, and size of horns. This example suggests that the intellectual accomplishment related to this ability is socially recognized and valuable. Although I am not aware of any formal research on the issue, it is likely that there are individuals who may be described as idiot savants and prodigies with respect to this ability. John Le Carré created a fictional character of a woman who relies on a prodigious memory for faces to recognize Russian spies. It is also the case that this ability has an evolutionary basis. There is evidence for the presence of cells in the visual cortex of monkeys that respond selectively to faces (Perrett, Mistlin, & Chitty, 1987; Yamane, Kaij, & Kawano, 1988). This brief review of research related to prosopognosia establishes that the separate visual memory for individual members of a class of related objects exists and that this ability constitutes a separate intelligence according to the criteria developed by Gardner. Thus the application of Gardner's criteria does not lead to the set of intelligences that he postulates.

The arguments developed against the specification of particular intelligences defined by Gardner may also be used to undermine his assertion that a model of separate intelligences should be used to replace g. If separate intelligences are defined on the basis of an arbitrary aggregation of quasiindependent abilities, then it is an arbitrary act to refuse to aggregate across several intelligences to define a superordinate general intelligence factor. Certainly the psychometric evidence that I have reviewed in this chapter provides ample evidence for a relationship among those forms of intelligence mentioned by Gardner that are studied by psychometricians—spatial, logical–mathematical, and linguistic. There is also evidence that musical ability is correlated with other measures of intelligence, although the correlation may be weak—approximately .3—and may be present among individuals with IQs below the mean and be less apparent among high-IQ individuals (Shuter-Dyson & Gabriel, 1983).

It is also the case that the neurological evidence for the independence of intelligences cited by Gardner is ambiguous. Gardner indicated that evidence for the neural localization of logical–mathematical intelligence is more ambiguous than the evidence for the localization of other intelligences. He asserted, "Logical–mathematical abilities become fragile not principally from focal brain disease but, rather, as a result of more general deteriorating diseases, such as the dementias, where large portions of the nervous system decompose more or less rapidly" (Gardner, 1983, p. 158). This statement provides an interesting point of contact between Gardner's theory and the hierarchical concept of intelligence derived from psychometric investigations. Abilities that are less dependent on localized neural functioning are more likely to be good measures of g. Since they are involved in more central processing roles they may be highly related to many other abilities. It should be noted that tests that are assumed to be good measures of g in current hierarchical models, such as the Raven's Test of Progressive Matrices, would probably be classified as measures of logical–mathematical intelligence in Gardner's taxonomy. It is also the case that biological evidence establishing the existence of general neural conditions that influence several forms of intelligence exist. For example, Down's syndrome is a condition that influences the development of neural structures. The syndrome leads to the development of low spatial, logical–mathematical, and linguistic intelligences.

Gardner relied on theoretical analyses of mental process that assume that there are independent modules that are responsive to specific stimulus inputs. Psychologists such as Allport (1980) have developed modular theories that postulate specific narrow modular abilities. Gardner's taxonomy is based on the aggregation of specific processing modules to define a more general intelligence. It is also the case that some modular theorists have assumed that there are general processes that are neither modular nor specific to a particular domain. Fodor (1983), a theorist cited by Gardner in support of the notion of independent encapsulated modular processing systems, asserted, ". . . there must be some mechanisms which cross the boundaries that input systems establish. . . . I assume that there must be relatively nondenominational (i.e., domain-*in*specific) psychological systems which operate, inter-alia, to exploit the information that input systems provide" (Fodor, 1983, p. 103, italics in original). Modular theorists whose work is cited by Gardner in support of his theory actually hold theoretical notions that are incompatible with Gardner's taxonomy. Allport's theory supports a taxonomy with many intelligences and Fodor's theory assumes that there are nonmodular general cognitive processes.

Evidence of the independence of intelligences from the study of prodigies and idiot savants is also of questionable relevance in arguing against the existence of a general intellectual factor. Such individuals are rare and the existence of extreme disparities among separate forms of intelligence may in part be attributable to the occasional extreme case that occurs in a normal distribution. Even if two intelligences are substantially correlated in the population, it is still possible that individuals will exhibit dramatic disparities in these intelligences as a result of the normal operation of the laws of chance. The existence of a statistically anomalous disparity may indicate little or nothing about the usual relationship between different intellectual capacities. So, too, the independent functioning of intelligences following brain damage may be of little relevance to understanding the performance of intact individuals. Separate neural structures may operate in a joint and interdependent manner in an individual who is not brain damaged although, following brain damage, the existence of an autonomous psychological function may be apparent. It is also the case that the examples of prodigies and idiot savants cited by Gardner provide less than convincing evidence against the existence of a superordinate general intelligence. This is particularly apparent in the domain of logical–mathematical abilities. Idiot savants

exhibit amazing skills as calculators but their ability to understand complex mathematical reasoning is often quite limited. Mathematical prodigies almost invariably appear to have high IQ. Gardner mentions
Bertrand Russell as an example of an individual with unusual logical–
mathematical ability. Russell was certainly gifted in linguistic intelligence. I doubt very much that he would have scored low on tests of
linguistic and spatial intelligence.

I have argued that a consideration of several sources of evidence used by
Gardner to establish the existence of independent intelligences may be
used to support the existence of a superordinate general intelligence factor. Thus I find his taxonomy to be arbitrary and without empirical foundation. Neither his rejection of a superordinate general factor nor the
specific subset of intelligences that he postulates appears to have a firm
theoretical or empirical basis.

CONCLUSION

This review of contemporary theories of the structure of intellect leads to
several tentative conclusions and leaves many issues unresolved. First, a
positive manifold among measures of various cognitive capacities appears
to exist (I omit from this generalization social intelligence, musical intelligence, and bodily–kinesthetic intelligence). Second, existing knowledge
is best accommodated by the hierarchical structure postulated by Gustafsson in his confirmatory factor analytic studies providing for a superordinate g factor that is best defined by measures of fluid ability, several
second-order factors including crystallized ability, and a number of first-
order factors. These generalizations leave the precise structure of abilities
at the first and second levels of the hierarchy unspecified.

The commitment to a hierarchical structure of ability retaining g at its
apex leaves unresolved many fundamental questions about the general
factor. In this concluding section we shall consider issues that bear on the
validity and generality of the theory of general intelligence. We shall
consider whether the g loading of tests remains invariant in different test
batteries and samples of tests and whether the assumption of a general
intellectual ability is dependent upon a restriction in the types of measures of intelligence that have been investigated.

The Invariance of g

Spearman assumed that every measure of intelligence could be characterized by a g-to-s ratio. This implies that the ratio remains invariant
when the measure is administered to different groups of individuals and
when the measure is part of a different battery of tests. The invariance
over subject samples and test batteries of the g loadings of tests should be

relatively easy to establish. Tests could be assigned a g loading in a particular investigation and the replicability of that number could be ascertained in any other investigation in which the test was included in a battery of different tests given to a different sample of individuals. Relatively little systematic research of this sort exists, although the data required to perform this kind of analysis is clearly abundantly available. This has given rise to somewhat diverse attitudes to the issue of the generality of g loadings. Some authorities write as if g loadings were an invariant property of tests (see Jensen, 1980a); others as if the g loading of a test varies with the composition of the test battery and the sample to which the battery was administered (Ceci, 1990). If it were possible to establish the invariance of g loadings, then it would be possible to examine the relationship between these loadings and the characteristics of tests with high and low loadings on g. This might provide clues to a theory of g.

Thorndike (1987) examined a correlation matrix of 65 tests administered to Air Force cadets. He arbitrarily divided the first 48 tests into 6 groups of 8 variables. He then inserted each of the remaining 17 variables one at a time into each of the 6 artificially created test batteries and obtained the g loading of each of the 17 tests in each of the 6 test batteries. The correlations between g loadings for each of the 15 possible pairs of matrices were obtained. The 15 correlations ranged between .52 and .94. These data suggest that g loadings remain invariant in different test batteries.

Thorndike's results do not provide information about the invariance of g loadings over samples of individuals with different characteristics. All of the correlations were obtained from the same sample. In addition, the test battery he examined included several tests of motor dexterity that had relatively low g loadings and might well be construed as not being tests of intelligence. Table 2.6 presents the 17 tests he used and their respective g loadings in each of the 6 batteries of 8 tests he created. Note that tests 12–16 appear to be tests of motor dexterity. Three of these tests have uniformly low g loadings. Thus the high median correlation among g loadings Thorndike obtained is inflated by the inclusion of tests of dubious relevance to intelligence construed as general cognitive abilities. Such tests have low loadings on g and act as statistical outliers that inflate the correlations among g loadings.

Although Thorndike's investigation is less than convincing, it does provide a model for the kind of research that is needed. Are there other relevant sources of data? Perhaps the most convincing evidence derives from the confirmatory factor analyses reported by Gustafsson (1988). His analyses indicate that the tests that are the best measures of g are those that load on the fluid intelligence factor. This conclusion rests on the study of a particular battery of tests that led to the development of the fluid versus crystallized distinction in the first instance. Other batteries

TABLE 2.6 Factor Loadings of 17 Classification Tests When Inserted
in 6 Different Matrices[a]

Test	Matrix					
	1	2	3	4	5	6
1. Spatial orientation 2	.63	.65	.63	.58	.51	.62
2. Reading comprehension	.62	.47	.54	.53	.52	.68
3. Instrument comprehension	.48	.56	.63	.51	.49	.58
4. Mechanical principles	.43	.61	.59	.47	.33	.57
5. Speed of identification	.52	.48	.48	.51	.59	.53
6. Numerical operations I	.48	.26	.40	.40	.50	.50
7. Numerical operations II	.52	.32	.46	.46	.53	.55
8. Mechanical information	.20	.30	.26	.18	.08	.49
9. General information	.30	.39	.35	.27	.18	.48
10. Judgment	.43	.35	.39	.37	.39	.51
11. Arithmetic reasoning	.61	.48	.56	.53	.51	.62
12. Rotary pursuit	.21	.30	.33	.24	.24	.28
13. Rudder control	.12	.28	.28	.15	.09	.28
14. Finger dexterity	.34	.25	.38	.35	.33	.37
15. Complex coordination	.46	.53	.57	.51	.48	.54
16. Two-hand coordination	.25	.35	.37	.35	.33	.39
17. Discrimination reaction time	.52	.55	.61	.59	.60	.61

[a]Based on Thorndike (1987).

of tests might well yield a somewhat different structure of g loadings. For
example, the subtest on the Wechsler scales with the highest average
correlation with other tests and accordingly with the highest g loading is
the Vocabulary subtest (Mattarrazo, 1972). The Vocabulary subtest is usually construed as a marker for crystallized ability rather than fluid ability.
Thus, tests that are good measures of fluid ability do not invariably have
the highest g loadings in batteries of tests. This counterexample is of
limited value since the Wechsler subtests were not designed to measure a
representative set of cognitive abilities. For this reason, I believe that
Gustafsson's investigations provide weightier evidence with respect to
the invariance of g loadings than research on the Wechsler tests. Clearly,
we need more systematic research on the invariance of g loadings.

The hierarchical structure of ability is derived from correlations among
ability tests. A correlation between tests is derived from an analysis of the
total sample of individuals in a study. If the relationship between measures were different for different subgroups of individuals in the population, then it is possible that different theories of the structure of intelligence might be required to describe these variations. Paradoxically,
individual-difference psychology has often been based on the assumption
that the relationships between measures are invariant across individuals,
thereby creating a restricted conception of the nature of individual differences.

Detterman & Daniel (1989) reported a study that indicates that the g loadings of tests are not invariant for subjects who differ in general intelligence. They used the large standardization samples for the Wechsler tests of intelligence (the WAIS and the WISC). They divided their sample into five groups on the basis of their performance on either the Vocabulary or the Information subtests. They then obtained the average correlations among the remaining subtests for each of these five ability groups. Figure 2.4 presents their data. Note that the average correlations among the tests declines as ability level increases. The effects are substantial. The average correlation among individuals in the lowest ability grouping, with estimated IQs below 78, is approximately twice as large as the average correlation among subtests for individuals in the highest ability level, with estimated IQs in excess of 122. These data indicate that the amount of variance attributable to the general factor in intelligence varies inversely with general intelligence. Detterman & Daniel (1989) indicated that comparable analyses of other test batteries have not been reported. Thus it is not known if the effects they obtained are specific to the Wechsler tests. Given the magnitude of the effect they obtained, it is possible that additional empirical support for this effect would be obtained from analyses of other test batteries. Their research indicates that a general factor is present among the subtests of the Wechsler tests for individuals at all of the ability levels that they examined. The amount of variance attributable to the general factor, however, is not invariant for different ability groups.

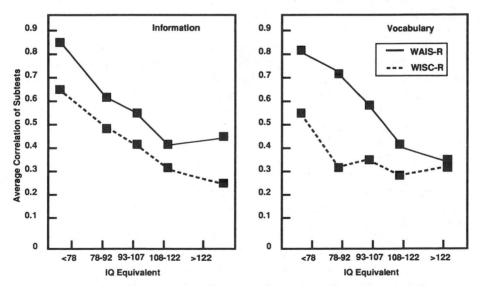

FIGURE 2.4 Correlations among subtests on the Wechsler for individuals differing in performance on the information and vocabulary subtests (based on Detterman & Daniel, 1989).

The Generality of *g* over Tasks

The assumption of a general factor does not provide us with a theory to explain *g* or to account for the ubiquitous relationship among different measures of ability. It is also the case that the evidence in favor of *g* depends substantially on the administration of batteries of tests to individuals. If existing tests, including Guilford's comprehensive attempt to develop measures of different abilities, are limited to a small subset of intellectual skills, then conclusions about a general factor of intelligence may be unwarranted.

Gardner (1983) argued that the support for *g* is substantially based on the examinations of tasks that have limited real-life validity. Ceci (1990) developed a similar argument. He asserted that positive manifolds are found primarily because individuals who are engaged in research on intelligence do not examine performance in real-life contexts. Ceci reported the results of a study by Ceci & Liker (1986) in support of this conclusion. They studied expertise in predicting race-track odds. They selected 30 men who were long-term patrons of harness racing tracks and who were very knowledgeable about racing. They used two measures of skill at predicting the odds chosen by the handicappers paid by the track. They found that the distribution of expertise at predicting odds was bimodal— 14 of the 30 men were able to predict the favorite horses in at least 9 of 10 races and the top 3 favorites in at least 5 of 10 races. The remaining 16 men were not as successful at predicting the odds chosen by the professional handicappers. The two groups did not differ in IQ. Ceci and Liker used another measure of expertise. They presented subjects with a complex body of information about unnamed horses and asked them to set the odds at their winning a race against a single standard horse with defined characteristics. Ceci and Liker used regression techniques to develop a prediction equation for the odds selected for each paired comparison for each of the subjects in their study. They included in their equation a complex interactive variable that was based on a nonadditive combination of variables that they assumed would be related to the reasoning processes used by experts to define odds at the track. They found that their 14 experts were more likely to rely on this complex interactive variable than their 16 nonexperts. A measure of the reliance on this interactive mode of reasoning was correlated with the ability to correctly handicap the 10 original races (Ceci & Liker, 1988). Reliance on this interactive mode of reasoning was also uncorrelated with IQ.

Ceci and Liker concluded that individuals of low IQ are able to reason in a complex way and to solve real-life problems. They asserted that the ubiquitous findings of a positive manifold among tests is dependent on the selection of the limited set of tasks that are used in intelligence tests. In many real-world contexts IQ may be unrelated to the ability to reason in a complex way and to perform as an expert.

Ceci and Liker's conclusions were challenged by Detterman & Spry (1988; see also, Ceci & Liker, 1988). Detterman and Spry argued that Ceci and Liker's measure of expertise was not reliable. Ceci and Liker defined expertise by examining ability to predict odds in 10 races. Their results would have been more convincing if they had demonstrated that individuals who excelled in this ability would have been able to repeat their performance on a second occasion. Ceci and Liker reported that their measure of expertise correlated .56 with the use of complex interactive reasoning in the second task they developed in which individuals had to set odds for hypothetical paired comparisons between horses. This suggests that their measure of expertise was reliable.

Detterman and Spry also criticized Ceci and Liker's sample selection procedures. Their sample of 30 was selected from an original group of 110 patrons of the race track. Detterman and Spry argued that ability to predict odds at the tracks might be correlated with IQ in a representative sample of race-track patrons. Ceci and Liker responded that they were not attempting to establish the relationship between IQ and performance in a representative sample of individuals. Rather, they attempted to see if expertise among a group of knowledgeable individuals was related to IQ. Their strategy was based on the attempt to find individuals who are capable of sophisticated reasoning and skilled performance at an intellectually demanding task who did not have high IQ. They concluded that individuals with low IQ are capable of exhibiting complex patters of reasoning and that high intelligence as measured by IQ tests is not a necessary condition for the attainment of intellectual skills in many real-world contexts. Ceci and Liker asserted that their results were compatible with Gardner's theory of intelligence and contradicted g theory.

My own critique of the import of the Ceci and Liker study rests on issues that are different from those raised by Detterman and Spry. Ceci & Liker's (1986) study identifies a rather limited form of expertise even within the context of harness racing. Expertise in that domain would be reflected by the ability to win money betting on harness races. Ceci and Liker argued that ability to accurately forecast odds is a necessary condition for winning money at the track. Successful betting involves finding horses whose probability of winning is higher than the odds of winning assigned by the track. While this argument is plausible, no evidence is presented by Ceci and Liker that the ability to forecast is associated with the ability to pick horses whose probability of winning is higher than the odds assigned by professional handicappers chosen by the track. This definition of expertise is inherently contradictory. Expertise is defined as ability to predict and emulate the reasoning processes of the handicappers employed by the track to set preliminary odds for the races. The handicappers' odds are highly correlated with the final odds set by the bets of race-track patrons. Since the payoff odds guarantee a profit to the track, the patron who slavishly bet the horses by following the handicappers' odds is guaranteed to lose money. The only way to win money at the track is to bet on the horses using a system to determine odds that is different from the system used by the professional handicappers. Perhaps the non-experts who were inferior at predicting the odds set by the professional handicappers were superior at this task because they reasoned in a different way that might be superior to the professional handicapper in predicting the actual outcome of races.

Ceci and Liker stated that their measure of cognitive complexity was not isomorphic with the complex process of reasoning that were involved in handicapping harness races. They indicated that handicapping actual races in an 8- or 10-horse field involves the formulation of "schemas" that "cast a group of horses into a probabilistic construction of how the race will develop" (Ceci & Liker, 1986, p. 264). Ceci and Liker did not measure the ability to form schemas, nor did they measure the accuracy of the schemas that were developed by their subjects. As a result, there is no evidence that individuals who were expert handicappers in their study did in fact excel at the level of expertise required for successful selection of winning horses in a race.

Ceci and Liker presented an interview with one of their experts with an IQ of 92 who demonstrated an understanding of the complex interactive nature of the relationships among the several variables that are assumed to determine the correct odds of winning a race. They indicated that the majority of their experts and some of their nonexperts were able to articulate the complex reasoning they employed in setting odds. It is possible that individuals might use complex reasoning processes without understanding the processes that they employ. There is a difference between the model developed to explain the performance of an individual and the model that the individual believes he or she is using. It is possible to argue that intelligent behavior is exhibited by the individual who develops a model to explain the behavior of someone who acts intelligently. Acting intelligently without awareness of the basis of the action may or may not be indicative of high intelligence. Consider an example in support of this assertion. In order to explain the behavior of an animal who leaps over a barrier, it is necessary to assume that the animal has coordinated a large number of dynamic variables, including calculations relating to distance, the force of gravity, and the like. The ability to instantaneously coordinate information from diverse stimulus arrays that change as organisms locomote can only be accounted for by a complex model of the sort that has been of concern to Gibsonian students of perception (Gibson, 1979). But this ability, however it is accomplished, is not necessarily indicative of the kind of intelligence that is exemplified in many cognitive tasks used to assess intelligence. Perhaps cognitive tasks used to assess intelligence all involve some ability to articulate and explain the basis for cognitive performance. Although Ceci and Liker interviewed their subjects and found that their experts were more likely to articulate complex patterns of reasoning in their interviews, they did not present these data, nor did they score their interviews for evidence of cognitive complexity of reasoning processes exhibited, nor did they report whether such scores were related to IQ.

This discussion of Ceci and Liker's research deals with lacunae. Let us assume that all of these nagging doubts and questions were satisfactorily answered by a more extensive research project. Suppose that the ability to acquire expertise in reasoning about the outcomes of harness racing was totally unrelated to IQ and that large numbers of individuals could be found who exhibited genuine expertise and had relatively low IQ. Would this support the conclusion that IQ and general intelligence were not related to intellectual performance in many contexts? Perhaps not. Although the pattern of reasoning exemplified by experts in handicapping races is relatively complex, it is possible to argue that its complexity is limited by the relatively small number of variables involved and the relatively encapsulated nature of the activity that is involved. Consider two other "real-world" intellectual activities as comparisons—ability to play chess and ability to function as a physician. On the surface, chess expertise shares much in common with handicapping harness racing. Both activities involve arcane knowledge in a relatively restricted context. Both involve considerations of complex interactive relationships among a limited number of units. In both, the possible outcomes are dependent upon somewhat unpredictable responses. There also appear to be some differences in the activities. The possible set of outcomes in chess readily becomes indefinitely large and there is a large body of formalized knowledge codifying standard responses to standard classes of situations that are likely to be encountered. The expert player of chess must master a large body of formalized knowledge. Expertise at chess also appears to require a good memory and an ability to engage in long and complex chains of reasoning. Is it possible to attain expert status at chess with a low IQ? I don't know the answer to this question. I would find Ceci's arguments far more convincing if he obtained evidence that expertise in chess could be obtained by individuals who are low in IQ.

Expertise as a physician appears to be different from expertise as a handicapper of harness races. Physicians need to be conversant with an extensive body of information. In addition, they need to master technical literature in several scientific disciplines. Admission to medical school is based on successful academic performance that is correlated, as we shall see, with IQ test scores. This leads to a relationship between IQ and the development of expertise in medicine. There are virtually no individuals with medical expertise and low IQ scores. This is a contingent truth that derives from the structure of our educational system. Could individuals with low IQ develop expertise in medicine if we had different standards of admission to medical school? I am inclined to answer this question in the negative. That is, we have extensive evidence indicating that the ability to master complex scientific concepts is related to intelligence.

What do these speculations tell us about the relationship between general intellectual ability and expertise? Real-world tasks may be crudely ordered along such dimensions as the amount of knowledge and the degree of explicit formulation of knowledge that is required for successful performance of the task. General intelligence may be increasingly related to the development of expertise as the size of the knowledge base increases and as the degree of acquisition of formal knowledge required for expertise increases. This leads me to suggest that intensive study of a domain in which (1) the codification of knowledge in formal theories is limited, and (2) the number of variables to be considered is limited may result in the development of expertise for individuals who do not have high general intellectual ability. Such expertise is likely to be domain specific and to apply only to domains of somewhat limited complexity and range of knowledge required. Thus I am tempted to argue that Ceci and Liker's demonstration does not indicate that general intelligence is unrelated to the development of real-world expertise. Ceci and Liker have raised a fundamental question about general intellectual ability. In order to provide convincing evidence in favor of their position they would need to provide somewhat clearer evidence of the relationship between IQ and expertise in harness racing. And, more critically, it would be necessary to obtain information about the relationship between general intelligence and expertise in a variety of situations including those that appear to involve more extensive bodies of information than handicapping harness races. Ceci and Liker's study is too problematic and too limited in scope to support their far-reaching conclusions. We shall return to the issues that they address after reviewing research relating general intelligence to occupational and academic success.

3

g AND BASIC INFORMATION-PROCESSING SKILLS: THE SEARCH FOR THE HOLY GRAIL

Our review of studies of the structure of ability tests supports a hierarchical model of ability with *g* at its apex. Such a taxonomy provides little or no information about the reasoning processes that are measured by various tests. What distinguishes the performance of individuals who are or are not able to solve an intellectual task? Psychometric studies provide little or no insight into the reasons for individual differences in performance on various tests of ability. In the last 15 years many psychologists have developed theories of individual differences in intellectual processes based on experimental research. These theories are reviewed in Chapters 3 and 4 of this volume.

Two broad approaches to laboratory studies of individual differences in ability have emerged. One approach is related to the ideas of Galton and Spearman and is based on the attempt to relate general intelligence to relatively simple information-processing skills (see Carlson & Widaman, 1987). The other approach is based on developments in cognitive psychology and leads to relatively complex models of task performance. The former approach will be considered in this chapter, the latter in Chapter 4.

Psychologists seeking to relate general intelligence to performance in relatively simple tasks tend to share several theoretical assumptions. They assume that individual differences in intellectual ability are influenced by genotypes and other biological events that influence the structure and function of the nervous system. Differences in neural functioning may be indirectly measured by experimental tasks that measure speed or accuracy of processing simple stimuli. Differences in basic parameters of information processing influence the development of the complex intellectual skills and knowledge that are assessed by tests of intelligence. Psychologists in this tradition are usually committed to a "bottom-up" (i.e., the complex derives from the simple) and to a reductionist (i.e., individual differences in intelligence are ultimately rooted in differences in the functioning of the nervous system) model of intelligence. I have somewhat facetiously subtitled this chapter "The Search for the Holy Grail" to capture the commitment shared by many of these psychologists to the development of measures of intelligence that tap fundamental biologically determined processes using tasks that are assumed to be relatively isolated from the cultural experiences of individuals. These psychologists seek to develop laboratory-based measures of intelligence that are relatively "culture free." Such measures may be used to measure ability as opposed to achievement. Measures of intelligence assess an individual's intellectual attainments and, hypothetically, the ability to acquire new information and skills. No measure of intelligence can assess a dormant ability that has not been actualized. The boundary between ability and achievement is fluid. Perhaps measures can be developed that are relatively "uncontaminated" by an individual's achievements. The construct assessed by such measures is akin to Cattell's construct, historical fluid ability. These constructs are archaic; they refer to abilities that are present at birth and even at the moment of conception.

The search for a pure measure of ability using simple information-processing tasks is an intellectually coherent enterprise. If individual differences in general intelligence derive from biologically based differences in the structure of the nervous system that influence the way in which individuals process information, then, in principle, it is possible to develop measures of an archaic biological capacity. Of course, this does not imply that such measures have been discovered. Nor does it imply that the assumptions that are shared by many psychologists working in this tradition are valid. Obtained relationships between measures of general intelligence and performance in simple information-processing tasks may or may not provide independent support for the validity of the assumptions that have motivated this research.

In this chapter I shall review research on reaction time, inspection time, and infant habituation. I shall describe the relationship between performance on these tasks and on tests of intelligence. I shall then consider the somewhat vexed question of the theoretical explanation of the obtained relationships and I shall speculate about the relationship between the results of these studies and the implicit theoretical assumptions held by many psychologists engaged in this research.

REACTION TIME AND INTELLIGENCE

The study of the relationship between intelligence and reaction time to stimuli was initiated by Galton and was periodically investigated during the first three decades of this century (Peak & Boring, 1926). Contemporary research on this topic is largely attributable to Jensen (1982a,b; 1985b; 1987a), who developed an apparatus based on the work of Roth (as cited by Eysenck, 1967) that may be used to obtain measures of several parameters of reaction time. Jensen's apparatus is presented in Fig. 3.1. The subject is instructed to place a finger on the button in the middle of the bottom row of the apparatus. The subject is required to move this finger from the home button to the button below any one of the eight lights that may come on in an unpredictable fashion. In the typical experiment using this apparatus, the subject is instructed to respond as rapidly as possible after the onset of the light. The subject is initially presented with a simple reaction-time task in which only a single light may appear. This is followed by a series of choice reaction-time tasks involving a choice first among two, then four, and then eight lights. The time between the onset of the light and the movement of the finger on the home button is called the reaction time or decision time for the task. The time from the release of the finger from the home button to the button below the appropriate light is called the movement time. Typically, subjects are presented with 15 to 30 trials at each set size of lights (1, 2, 4, and 8). This experimental procedure permits one to obtain several measures of reaction time for each subject. These include the median reaction time for each set size of stimuli, the standard deviation of reaction times at each set size, the median and the standard deviation of movement times at each set size, and the slope and the intercept of the line defining changes

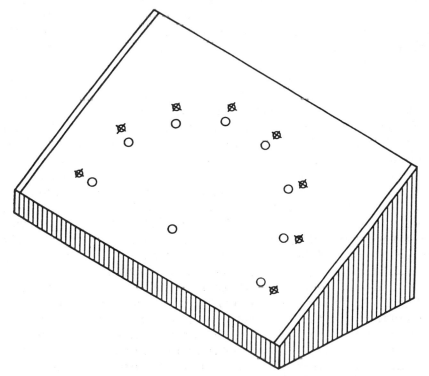

FIGURE 3.1 Jensen's reaction-time apparatus. (Based on Jensen, 1980a.)

in reaction time as a function of set size. Each of these measures may be related to scores on intelligence tests.

Jensen believed that reaction-time measures provide an index of the speed and efficiency with which the nervous system processes elementary information. He found that the slope relating reaction time to set size was positive, providing support for what he called Hick's law (Hick, 1952). Hick found that reaction time was a linear function of the log of set size. Jensen argued that each doubling of the number of alternatives in a choice reaction-time task led to a constant increase in reaction time. He interpreted the linear function relating reaction time to set size as a measure of the ability to process information of increasing complexity. He assumed that intelligence is inversely related to reaction time and to the slope and intercept of the function relating reaction time to set size. Thus intelligence was related to the speed of processing information of increasing complexity.

A substantial body of data has been collected relating intelligence to reaction-time measures obtained using Jensen's apparatus. Jensen (1987a) summarized the results of 31 studies. His conclusions are buttressed by findings obtained by Detterman (1987; see also Barrett, Eysenck, & Lucking, 1986; Carlson & Jensen, 1982) in a study of 860 Air Force enlistees using a related version of the reaction-time task. These data support several generalizations about the relationship between reaction-time measures and scores on various tests of intelligence. Both movement time and reaction time are negatively correlated with intelligence. Jensen (1987a) reports average correlations between median reaction times in the no-choice, two-choice, four-choice, and eight-choice conditions and intelligence of $-.19$, $-.21$, $-.24$, and $-.26$ respectively. The comparable correlations for movement-time measures and intelligence were $-.17$, $-.17$, $-.15$, and $-.14$. These correlations are weighted averages of 15 samples with 1129 subjects. Detterman (1987) reported a correlation of $-.18$ between reaction time and IQ in his sample of 860 Air Force enlistees. These correlations may be corrected for restrictions in range of talent and attenuation. The corrected correlation between the mean of the four reaction times and IQ is $-.309$. Detterman reported a correlation of $-.33$ between mean reaction time and IQ corrected for restrictions in range of talent. Jensen (1987a) reported that the mean correlation in these studies between the slope of the increase in reaction time over set size and IQ was $-.117$. This correlation when corrected for attenuation and restriction in range of talent becomes $-.183$. Detterman obtained a positive correlation of .07 between his slope measure and IQ. Thus, it appears that the slope of reaction-time measures is not consistently related to IQ. Measures of the variability of reaction time are positively correlated with measures of the speed of reaction time. Jensen reported a correlation of .65 between these measures that becomes 1.00 when corrected for attenuation. Since measures of speed and variability of reaction time appear to be redundant, it is not surprising that there is a relationship between the variability of reaction-time measures and general intelligence. Jensen (1987a) reported average correlations ranging between −.21 and −.28 for the relationship between IQ and measures of the variability of reaction time for different set sizes. These correlations, when corrected for restrictions in range of talent and attenuation, ranged between −.33 and −.43. Finally, it is possible to combine several parameters obtained from a reaction-time task into a multiple correlation and obtain multiple r's close to .50 (Jensen & Vernon, 1986; Detterman, 1987).

These date support the generalization that the speed and variability of reaction time is inversely related to IQ. Reaction-time measures considered singly predict approximately 10 to 15% of the variance in IQ. These empirical relationships appear to be well established. The interpretation of these findings remains vexed. The available data contradict several initial assumptions held by Jensen. He assumed that the slope of the function relating set size to reaction time would provide a theoretical index of the rate of processing information based on the functioning of the nervous system and would be related to intelligence. The data indicate that slope measures are not as highly related to IQ as measures of speed and variability of reaction time. He also assumed that choice reaction-time tasks that involve processing of information about the location of a stimulus would be more highly related to IQ than reaction-time measures in which the stimulus appears in a single constant location. The data provide very little evidence in support of this assumption. Although the correlation between the median reaction time in the no-choice condition and IQ is slightly lower than the comparable correlation in the choice reaction-time conditions, the difference is very small (−.19 versus correlations ranging between −.21 and −.26). In addition, the corrected correlation between the variability of reaction-time measures and IQ in the no-choice condition is −.40. The comparable correlations for the choice reaction-time tasks range between −.33 and −.43. These data indicate that there is little or no difference in the magnitude of the relationship between IQ and performance in simple and choice reaction-time tasks.

Frearson & Eysenck (1986) developed a variant of the choice reaction-time task using the Jensen apparatus that may lead to higher correlations between measures of choice reaction time and intelligence than those usually obtained with the Jensen procedure. The procedure used is called the odd-man-out technique and involves the presentation of a stimulus display with three lights. Figure 3.2 presents stimulus displays used by Frearson and Eysenck. The subject is required to choose the stimulus that is located at the greatest distance from the remaining two stimuli that are closest to each other. In their original study using this technique, Frearson and Eysenck obtained a correlation of −.62 between the mean reaction time for odd-man-out presentations and scores on the Raven progres-

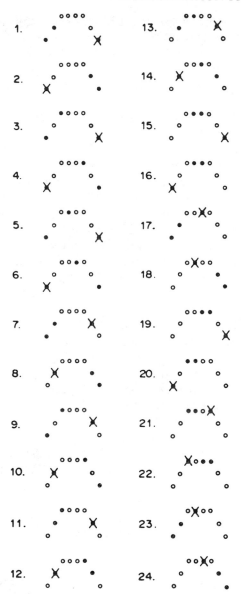

FIGURE 3.2 The 24 patterns used in the odd-man-out paradigm. The target is marked with a cross. (Based on Frearson and Eysenck, 1986.)

sive matrices. They also computed the range of reaction times for each of their odd-man-out presentations and obtained a mean range score. This score correlated with scores on the Raven −.52. The correlations between reaction-time measures obtained in the usual way with the Jensen apparatus and scores on the Raven for this sample of 37 subjects were comparable to those reported by other investigators using the Jensen apparatus. Frearson and Eysenck obtained correlations ranging from −.25 to −.36 between their measures of mean reaction time at each of four set sizes and scores on the Raven. The comparable correlation for measures of the variability of reaction time at each of four set sizes and scores on the Raven varied between −.23 and −.31. These data suggest that the correlations between odd-man-out reaction times and intelligence are substantially higher than correlations between simple and choice reaction times obtained in the usual way with the Jensen apparatus.

Frearson, Barrett, & Eysenck (1988) reported the results of a follow-up investigation using the odd-man-out technique with a sample of 107 subjects. They obtained measures of the mean reaction time for the odd-man-out presentations as well as two measures of the variability of performance on the odd-man-out presentations—the mean of the ranges of response time for each of the stimulus presentations and the mean of the interquartile ranges of response times. In addition, they obtained scores on the Wechsler test of intelligence as well as the Raven test. Table 3.1 presents the correlations between the odd-man-out performance measures and various measures of intelligence as well as correlations between the usual reaction-time measures and the intellectual indices. The correlations presented in Table 3.1 do not provide clear support for the findings obtained by Frearson and Eysenck in their earlier study with a smaller sample. That is, correlations based on the odd-man-out technique are not always substantially larger than correlations between traditional reaction-time measures and intelligence. There is some indication that correlations between measures of reaction time based on the odd-man-out procedure are higher with nonverbal measures of intelligence. And, the correlation between the mean odd-man-out reaction time and performance on the Ravens test (−.48) is higher than the correlation between the Raven test score and the usual reaction-time measures.

The two studies reported by Frearson and Eysenck using the odd-man-

TABLE 3.1   Correlations between Measures of Reaction Time Using Jensen's Apparatus Including Odd-Man-Out Presentations and Measures of Intelligence[a]

	Intelligence			
	VIQ	PIQ	IQ	Raven
Reaction time (RT)				
Mean RT for set size 2	−.22	−.21	−.24	−.17
Mean RT for set size 4	−.17	−.16	−.19	−.13
Variance of RT for set size 2	−.35	−.38	−.39	−.36
Odd-man-out measures				
Mean RT	−.19	−.39	−.30	−.48
Mean range of RT	−.20	−.41	−.30	−.18
Mean interquintile range	−.30	−.33	−.43	−.50

[a]Based on Frearson et al. (1988).

out procedure suggest that this type of choice reaction-time task may be more predictive of performance of measures of intelligence that include a spatial component or that are good measures of fluid or general intelligence than the conventional measures obtained using the Jensen apparatus. The odd-man-out task appears to add to the conventional choice reaction-time task a spatial discrimination component in which the subject is required to compare distances between pairs of stimuli. In the next section of this chapter we shall consider research involving inspection-time tasks that indicates that measures of the ability to discriminate between stimuli that are different may correlate with intelligence more highly than reaction-time measures. From this perspective, the odd-man-out technique may be a hybrid task that combines elements of an inspection-time task involving a discrimination task and a choice reaction-time task. Additional research is needed to establish that odd-man-out reaction-time measures are consistently more predictive of intelligence than other choice reaction-time measures. The preliminary results obtained with the task are promising.

Why is there a relationship between the speed and variability of reaction times and IQ? This question has been answered in two rather different ways. Although Jensen's original theoretical assumptions were not fully supported, he would maintain that the obtained relationship is to be explained by a bottom-up reductive model of intelligence. He believed that the characteristics of the nervous system determine the speed of reaction time and that individuals whose nervous systems function more effectively develop more complex intellectual skills. Thus the reaction-time measures are viewed by him as reflecting culture-free measures of neural functioning. By contrast, many of Jensen's critics argue that reaction-time tasks are not simple, that they provide ample room for the use of strategies, and that the relationship between IQ and reaction time is to be explained by a reversed causal model in which individuals who have good intellectual skills acquire techniques and strategies that enable them to perform in a more optimal manner in a reaction-time task. Let us consider some of the specific issues that have been discussed in the light of the available data.

Longstretch (1984; 1986; see also Jensen & Vernon, 1986) had three criticisms of Jensen's theoretical interpretation of his findings. First, he argued that Jensen's slope measures were confounded with order effects. In Jensen's research, subjects performed the several reaction-time tasks in a fixed order going from simple reaction time to choice reaction time with set sizes of 2, 4, and 8. Reaction-time measures for different set sizes confound set-size and practice effects. It is known that reaction times tend to decrease with practice (Welford, 1980). A short reaction time for a set size of 8 in Jensen's experiments may come about because an individual benefited from practice on the earlier reaction-time tasks. The correlation between the slope of the reaction-time measures and IQ may occur because individuals with high IQ are able to benefit more from practice than individuals with low IQ. Note that this interpretation attempts to provide a theoretical rationale for a relationship between IQ and reaction time that is not reductive. It assumes that general abilities associated with IQ enable individuals to benefit from experience and adapt to novel tasks. In effect, such an explanation reverses the causal analysis explicit in Jensen's theoretical interpretation.

Jensen (1987a) argued that the small number of trials he used in his experiments (typically 15 at each set size) precluded the development of practice effects in his studies. He reported (Jensen, 1987a) that the reaction time for the first three trials is not substantially different from the reaction time for the last three trials for a particular set size. There is, however, evidence of the existence of practice effects in experiments in which the order of presentation of reaction-time tasks is experimentally varied. Widaman & Carlson (1989) found that the slope of the function relating reaction time to set size was lower when they followed Jensen's procedure of using an ascending order than it was when they used a descending order in which the larger set sizes preceded the smaller set sizes. In addition, they found a significant negative correlation between the slope of the reaction-time increase over set size and intelligence when they used the ascending order of presentation used by Jensen ($r = -.26$). The comparable correlation for the reversed order of presentation was positive (.21). These data suggest that the relationship between the slope of the change in reaction time and IQ may be attributable to the rate at which individuals of different IQ are able to benefit from practice effects. (For contradictory results see Larson & Saccuzzo, 1986.) This criticism of Jensen's theoretical analysis does not deal with the findings relating IQ and simple reaction time in Jensen's research. These are typically based on the first 15 reaction-time trials and are unlikely to be attributable to practice effects.

Second, Longstreth argued that visual attention effects might influence reaction-time measures. Subjects who attend to the center of the visual array experience lights from the periphery of the display in regions of the visual field in which optimal visual acuity is unlikely to be present. Widaman and Carlson tested this notion by varying the distance between the lights in various set-size conditions and found little evidence in support of this notion. These attentional effects are not likely to be operating in the simple reaction-time study—the light comes on in a single position in the center of the display—and we have seen that reaction time in the simple reaction-time experimental situation is as highly correlated with intelligence as reaction time in the choice reaction-time experimental situation.

Third, Longstreth argued that response bias effects may be present in the experimental arrangements used by Jensen. The lights occur at different locations and therefore involve different movements to the lights.

Jensen argued that the use of a home button avoids this problem. That is, different amounts of time required to execute the different responses should affect the less important movement-time measures but not the reaction-time measures. Longstreth noted that responses with different movements might require different amounts of preparation. Thus, feedback from the response components of the reaction-time task might influence the reaction-time measure as well as the movement time. There is a second way in which response bias effects might influence reaction-time measures. Individuals might release their finger from the home button before they have determined the direction of the movement response. The decision to move the hand toward the light could be made after the individual has actually responded. Individuals with high intelligence may be more likely to discover the strategy of moving before the information-processing requirements of the task have been completed than individuals of low intelligence. Jensen argued that response bias effects are unlikely to occur in his studies because the response is "ballistic." The term ballistic is used to suggest that the movement response is programmed prior to its execution and cannot be altered once it is in progress. Whatever the possible role of response bias effects described above, it should be noted that they are not present in the simple reaction-time task and thus are unlikely to account for the relationship between reaction-time measures and intelligence since that relationship occurs where they do not exist.

Detterman (1987) asserted that reaction time is not a simple task. Reaction-time measures might be influenced by a variety of exogenous variables including the ability to understand instructions, familiarity with the equipment used, and motivation. While it is plausible to argue that any of these variables may in fact be responsible for the relationship between IQ and reaction time, no evidence exists that any of these variables are responsible for the obtained effects. Some of these variables are unlikely to provide an explanation of the obtained relationships. The equipment should be sufficiently novel for all subjects and the instructions should be unambiguous. Variations in these factors are unlikely to account for the relationship between IQ and reaction time, particularly among individuals who are above average in IQ such as those used by Detterman in his research.

Detterman also argued that reaction-time measures may be influenced by speed–accuracy trade-offs. Speed–accuracy trade-offs usually are evidenced when individuals who respond rapidly are more likely to make incorrect responses than individuals who respond slowly. Such trade-offs occur when individuals adopt different criteria for the execution of a response. Rapid responding can occur at the cost of additional errors in responding. This phenomena cannot explain the relationship between IQ and reaction time since intelligence is negatively correlated with errors in these tasks (Detterman, 1987; Jensen, 1987a). If high-IQ subjects were responding more rapidly at lower levels of accuracy than low-IQ subjects, IQ should be positively rather than negatively correlated with errors.

There is a second more complex way in which speed–accuracy trade-offs may be involved in reaction-time tasks. Brewer & Smith (1984) reported the results of experiments comparing the performance of retarded subjects and college students on choice reaction-time tasks for one to two thousand trials. They studied the trial-by-trial variation in responding following and preceding the occurrence of a wrong response. They noted that subjects tended to decrease their reaction times prior to the occurrence of an error. On the trial following an error, subjects increased their reaction times. These trial-by-trial variations are interpretable by assuming that individuals monitor the trial-by-trial variation in their performance and attempt to adopt criteria of responding that place most of their responses in a narrow "safe" band just above the threshold of response speed that is likely to result in errors. Retarded subjects demonstrated the same phenomena of trial-by-trial variation as the college students, but their adjustments to the occurrence of an error were much less efficient and they tended to overcorrect their response speeds following an error and then exhibit downward drifts that created errors. These phenomena contribute to the obtained increase in the variability of reaction time among the retarded subjects relative to the nonretarded subjects.

To what extent do the phenomena of trial-by-trial variations in adjustments to error explain the relationship between reaction time and intelligence in the studies reviewed by Jensen? There are several reasons to be cautious in accepting the phenomena described by Brewer and Smith as the basis for explaining the IQ–reaction-time relationship. First, Brewer and Smith compared retarded subjects to college students. Larson & Alderton (1990) obtained measures of the increase in reaction time following an error in performing several relatively simple judgment tasks. They found that this measure correlated $-.17$ with general intelligence in a large sample of military recruits. The correlation between a measure of variability of reaction times and intelligence in their sample was $-.36$. The partial correlation between variability of reaction times and intelligence controlling for the degree of post-error slowing was $-.35$. These data indicate that the relationship between variability of reaction times and intelligence is not attributable to differences in a person's ability to moderate changes in reaction times following errors. Second, the phenomena are present in reaction-time experiments in which subjects are given 200 practice trials and 2000 experimental trials. The correlation between the variability of reaction time and intelligence in simple choice tasks is obtained for the first 15 or 30 reaction-time responses following a brief set of practice trials. Third, errors in a simple reaction-time task as opposed to a choice reaction-time task are unlikely to occur. Yet the correlation between variability of reaction time and intelligence does not vary in simple and choice reaction-time tasks. For these reasons, speed–

accuracy trade-offs either of the classic kind or of the type studied by Brewer and Smith are unlikely to provide an adequate explanation of the relationship between reaction-time measures and intelligence.

Attentional mechanisms may mediate the relationship between IQ and reaction time. Speed of responding and variability of responding are highly correlated—indeed they may be perfectly correlated when the obtained correlation is corrected for attenuation. Individuals who are high in intelligence are not consistently faster in responding to a stimulus than individuals who are low in intelligence. The capacity to process stimuli rapidly is not the variable that determines differences in reaction time among individuals who differ in intelligence. High- and low-IQ subjects are likely to exhibit an equal number of rapid responses. Differences in the median reaction time may be an artifact of variations in a subject's ability to maintain a consistent response speed that is close to his or her optimal performance level.

Larson & Alderton (1990) demonstrated that the relationship between variability of reaction times and intelligence was substantially determined by performance on the slowest reaction-time trials. They rank ordered their subjects' reaction times from fastest to slowest and then grouped the rank-ordered trials into 16 groups of 5 trials. They then obtained the mean reaction time for each of the 16 groupings from the fastest to the slowest. This procedure produced 16 reaction time means for each of their subjects. These means were correlated with an index of general intelligence. The magnitude of the correlations increased monotonically from fastest to slowest reaction-time groupings. The correlation between the mean of the fastest band and general intelligence was −.20. The correlation between the mean of the slowest band and general intelligence was −.37. These data indicate that the relationship between reaction-time indices and general intelligence is substantially mediated by performance on trials where subjects are performing at their least optimal level. These data suggest that individuals with high intelligence are able to maintain levels of performance in relatively simple tasks that are close to their optimal level whereas individuals with low intelligence are unable to maintain constantly optimal levels of performance.

It is also possible to explain the relationship between intelligence and the variability of responding in reaction time by the appeal to a neurological or, perhaps, a neuromythological model. Jensen (1980a) assumed that individual differences in intelligence are related to the rate of oscillation of an excitatory function for neurons. Individuals of high intelligence are assumed to have neurons that oscillate more rapidly than individuals with low intelligence. If the onset of a stimulus occurs when the neuron is in an excitatory phase, the reaction-time response will be rapid. If a stimulus is presented during the refractory phase of a neuron, the reaction-time response will be delayed until the neuron enters its excitatory phase. Individuals who differ in intelligence will exhibit equally rapid reaction-time responses for those stimulus presentations that coincide with neuronal excitatory phases. The reaction times of individuals who are low in intelligence will be longer than the reaction times of individuals who are high in intelligence when the stimulus occurs during a refractory phase of neuronal reactivity. This difference in reaction time is attributable to variations in the speed of oscillation of the neuronal excitatory cycle. If oscillations are slow, it will take longer for a neuron to enter the exitatory phase of its cycle when a stimulus is presented during the refractory phase than when oscillations are rapid. And, individuals of high intelligence are assumed to have more rapid oscillatory cycles than individuals of low intelligence.

Jensen's neurophysiological model explains the central feature of the relationship between IQ and reaction time. There is, however, little or no evidence in favor of the model. Evidence of a relationship between intelligence and the oscillatory cycle of systems of neurons does not exist. Such evidence might be obtained by experiments that assess the effects of prior stimulation on evoked potential responses to stimulation. In the absence of any physiological evidence, the model adds nothing more than a physiological metaphor to the assertion that intelligence is positively related to the ability to maintain consistent attention to stimuli. If the physiological model is not supported, the assumption that the relationship between reaction-time measures and IQ is to be understood as providing evidence for a bottom-up reductive explanatory system for intelligence is not justified. Indeed, the causal direction of the relationship remains ambiguous. It is possible that individuals who have high intelligence become skilled at controlling their attention. Consider a fanciful scenario. Individuals who, for whatever reason, excel in academic settings and who develop their intellectual capacities and score high on tests of intelligence may find school a rewarding setting. They become responsive to attentional requirements associated with formal instruction in school settings. The developed attentional skills are manifested in reaction-time tasks. We have no persuasive evidence that favors either of two speculative scenarios—one that assumes that intelligence causes individuals to develop the attentional skills to excel in reaction-time tasks or the other that assumes that basic neurological processes that are related to the performance of individuals in reaction-time tasks cause individuals to develop the abstract intellectual skills that are assessed by tests of intelligence.

To assert that we do not have an appropriate causal explanation of the direction of the relationship between IQ and reaction time does not imply that such an explanation is unattainable. There are three types of research that could, in principle, provide evidence that would support one of these causal analyses. Studies that relate reaction-time performance and intelligence to physiological measures could provide evidence for physiological mediation of the relationship. Behavior genetic analyses of reaction-time measures and other basic psychological processes as well as studies of the genetic and environmental influence on the relationship between the measures (i.e., behavior genetic covariation analyses) could help to clarify the role of genetic influences on the development of the relationship between experimental tasks and individual differences in intelligence. Finally, longitudinal studies could help to elucidate the development of a relationship between intelligence and simple information-processing skills. Although there are few studies of this type that clarify the relationship between reaction time and intelligence, we shall consider related research in this volume.

Given our lack of understanding of the reasons for the relationship between intelligence and reaction time, what, if anything, is the importance of this research? It is surprising to find any relationship between the complex skills and problems found in contemporary measures of intelligence and something as apparently simple as the variability of the time to respond to a light in a simple reaction-time task. At the same time, it should be recognized that the correlation between these variables is not high. Even with adjustments for restrictions in range and attenuation it is unlikely that the true correlation between these variables exceeds .4. Thus reaction-time measures considered singly may account for as much as 16% of the variance in intelligence. This may be too small an amount to assume that reaction-time measures provide insight into the fundamental characteristics that account for individual differences in intelligence.

INSPECTION TIME

It is theoretically possible to measure the speed of apprehension of a stimulus without the use of reaction-time measures. Nettlebeck (1973) and Vickers (1970; Vickers, Nettlebeck, & Willson, 1972) developed an experimental procedure to measure the speed of apprehension of a stimulus. They assumed that judgments about a stimulus occur in a cumulative fashion based on discrete inspections of the stimulus until some criterion level for stimulus judgment is obtained. They attempted to estimate the minimal duration of a single inspection that provides information about a stimulus.

The original inspection-time task involved tachistoscopic presentation of two adjacent vertical lines differing in length in a 1:1.4 ratio followed by a "masking stimulus" that covered both lines and was assumed to prevent additional iconic processing of the stimulus. The duration of presentation of the lines was varied and a psychophysical function was obtained. The task was used to ascertain the minimal exposure time required to attain some predetermined level of accuracy of judgment about which of the two lines was longer. Inspection time was usually defined as the estimated exposure time required to obtain 95% accurate judgments.

Nettlebeck & Lally (1976) reported the first study relating inspection time to IQ and reported a correlation of −.89 between their inspection-time measure and a test of intelligence. Comparably high correlations were reported by Brand & Deary (1982). These extremely high correlations were obtained from small samples that included retarded subjects and normals. The retarded subjects frequently had inspection-time scores that were extreme and these extreme values in small samples tended to inflate the value of the correlations that were reported.

A considerable body of research relating inspection-time measures to intelligence was reviewed by Nettlebeck (1987) and Kranzler & Jensen (1989; see also Brebner & Nettlebeck (1986); Lubin & Fernandez, 1986). The studies differ in many ways. Inspection times have been assessed using visual, auditory, and tactile stimuli. Different procedures to calculate thresholds were used and different stimulus displays were used in different studies. Some psychologists used tachistoscopic displays, others used computer displays. The visual stimuli used varied considerably. In some studies the location of the stimuli on the computer screen varied from trial to trial. The IQ tests used differ and the composition of the samples tested varies by age and IQ range. Kranzler & Jensen (1989) used meta-analysis to summarize all of the available studies dealing with inspection-time measures and intelligence. Kranzler and Jensen's summary of the available literature is based on a total sample of 31 studies and 1120 subjects. Kranzler and Jensen reported that the mean correlation between inspection time and measures of intelligence is .29. The correlation between IQ and inspection time corrected for attenuation and restrictions in range of talent is −.49. The correlation appears to be slightly higher in adult samples ($r = -.54$ versus −.47 for children) and to be higher for performance than for verbal measures of IQ. Kranzler and Jensen also report a meta-analysis that excludes studies that were criticized on methodological grounds by Nettlebeck (1987) in his comprehensive analysis of the inspection-time literature. The corrected correlation between inspection time and IQ is −.54 for this restricted set of studies.

The correlation between inspection-time measures and intelligence may actually be somewhat higher than the value of .54 reported by Kranzler and Jensen as the optimal estimate for the adult population. Raz and Willerman (1985) and their associates (Raz, Willerman, Ingmundson, & Hanlon, 1983) obtained somewhat higher correlations in a series of studies using auditory pitch discrimination measures. These studies were based on an auditory version of the inspection-time paradigm. Auditory stimuli that differ in pitch may be backwardly masked by tones that follow the presentation of the stimuli to be judged. Variations in the interstimulus interval between the offset of the critical stimulus and the onset of the tone can be used to discover the amount of time required to reach some predetermined level of accuracy of judgment. Raz *et al.* (1983) presented subjects with either a low- or a high-pitched tone for 20 ms on each trial. The tones were easily discriminated if they were not masked. Each tone was followed by a masking tone. They varied the interstimulus interval between the offset of the target tone and the onset of the masking tone and determined the briefest interval at which their subjects could accurately judge whether they had been presented with a low or a high tone. Their subjects were college students who had been selected as scoring either high or low on the SAT. They correlated SAT group membership with two threshold values—a threshold score and a logarithmically transformed threshold score. These scores correlated with SAT group membership $-.33$ and $-.53$, respectively. A second experiment was performed as a replication of this study, again using college students selected as high or low scorers on the SAT. In the replication experiment, subjects were administered a Cattell Culture-Fair test of intelligence and thresholds were obtained for stimuli presented for both 20- and 30-ms durations. Four threshold values were obtained—thresholds for interstimulus intervals for stimuli presented at each of two durations and logarithmic transformations of these threshold scores. These scores were correlated with Cattell IQ test scores. The correlations ranged between $-.41$ and $-.73$. Logarithmically transformed threshold scores correlated more highly than the original scores (the correlations were $-.69$ and $-.73$). Performance curves for subjects differing in IQ are presented in Fig. 3.3. An examination of these curves indicates that the largest difference is obtained when the interstimulus interval is low. The results of these two experiments indicate that individuals who score high on an IQ test are able to judge differences in pitch more accurately than individuals who score low on an IQ test when the time available for processing the stimulus is brief.

Raz and Willerman (1985) reported an additional replication of these findings using stimuli that differed both in pitch and in duration. Their high- and low-pitched tones were presented for durations varying between 10 and 20 ms. The subjects were instructed to ignore variations in the duration of presentation of the tone and to judge only the pitch of the tone. The logarithmically transformed threshold values for the interstimulus interval between the offset of the tone and the onset of a masking stimulus and Cattell IQ scores correlated $-.47$, $-.44$, and $-.53$ for three different presentation times.

In the last study in this series, Raz, Willerman, & Yama (1987) introduced a different auditory task. Subjects were presented with two 20-ms presentations of two unmasked tones that were clearly different in pitch. There was an 85-ms interval between the presentations of the first and second tone. The subjects were required to indicate whether the first or the second tone was higher in pitch. The difference in pitch between the tones was reduced and threshold measures were obtained for the minimal

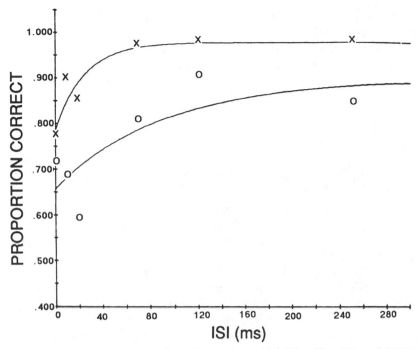

FIGURE 3.3 Performance curves for subjects scoring high (X) and low (O) on the SAT for a pitch discrimination. (Based on Raz *et al.* 1983.)

difference in pitch that subjects could accurately discriminate. The correlations between four different measures of pitch discrimination and Cattell IQ test scores ranged between −.42 and −.52. In a replication experiment using college students selected for extreme scores on the SAT, they obtained correlations of −.50 and −.52 between their measure of pitch discrimination and Cattell IQ scores. Raz *et al.* (1987) do not report data indicating the relationship between their pitch discrimination measure and the auditory inspection-time measures. Since both measures related to IQ, it is reasonable to expect that they are correlated with each other. In addition, both auditory inspection-time measures and pitch discrimination measures require subjects to make a judgment about the pitch of two briefly presented tones. It is also the case that the duration of presentation of the tones is a critical variable in both types of measures. In the case of auditory inspection time, it is the variable that is manipulated, and the threshold that is obtained is a duration threshold. In the case of the procedure used by Raz *et al.* (1987), the use of brief durations (20 or 30 ms) is critical. Pitch discrimination for tones presented for long durations is not related to IQ in relatively high-IQ samples. Deary, Caryl, Egan, & Wight (1989) reported near-zero correlations between pitch discrimination ability and intelligence in a college sample. Although the empirical relationship between pitch discrimination measures for briefly presented tones and auditory and visual inspection-time measures remains to be empirically investigated, it is possible to argue that both kinds of measures may be related to speed of information processing. Deary argued that faster inspection times would enable individuals to make more individual inspections of the characteristics of briefly presented tones thereby increasing the accuracy of the discrimination. He stated, ". . . the argument which pits processing speed against fidelity of stimulus representation may well be a nonargument: the experiments reported here are commensurate with an explanation which states that a fast inspection time is primarily an advantage in information processing speed, and that this results in more faithful representation of briefly presented stimuli" (Deary, 1989).

Willerman and Raz and their associates do not report corrected correlations for any of the correlations they obtained in their studies. They do not report test–retest correlations for their various measures of auditory inspection time and pitch discrimination. In addition, the use of college students with extreme scores on the SAT makes it difficult to apply conventional corrections for restrictions in range of talent. Nevertheless, it is clear that some restriction in range of talent exists in their samples and it is undoubtedly the case that the test–retest correlation of the various experimental measures they use is less than 1.00. Therefore, their obtained correlations are lower than the hypothetical true correlation between their experimental measures and scores on tests of intelligence. If a representative correlation of .5 is corrected for attenuation assuming test–retest correlations of .75 for their experimental measures (the value for test–retest measures of inspection time) and .9 for their measure of intelligence, the corrected correlation is .6, indicating that the experimental measures may account for approximately 36% of the variance in intelligence test scores. Jensen and Kranzler's meta-analysis of all of the inspection-time data suggests that inspection-time measures account for approximately 25% of the variance in scores on intelligence tests. These analyses indicate that inspection-time measures are more predictive of intelligence test scores than reaction-time measures. They also indicate that the relationship between inspection time and intelligence test scores is sufficiently high as to suggest that these experimental measures must be determined by something that is substantially related to the determinants of performance on tests of intelligence. There is no rule or law that indicates when a particular amount of variance accounted for by a measure is to be classified as substantial or trivial. I am comfortable dismissing the relationship between reaction time and intelligence as being too insubstantial to provide important clues to understanding the nature of individual differences in intelligence. I cannot respond in the same way to the data on inspection time. If inspection-time measures account for 25% of the variance in scores on intelligence tests and if the measures used by Willerman and his associates account for 36% of the variance in performance on tests of intelligence, then this relationship is too substantial to dismiss. An understanding of the nature of the relationship should provide clues to an understanding of the nature of individual differences in intelligence.

Several lines of research help to elucidate the meaning of the obtained relationship between inspection time and measure of intelligence. If inspection-time measures are related to a general information-processing capacity they ought to be independent of modality. That is, there should be a relationship between measures of inspection time derived from visual displays and measures of inspection time derived from stimuli presented in other modalities. Deary (1980; 1986; Deary, Head, & Egan, 1989) found that auditory inspection time and visual inspection time were perfectly correlated, but this result was dependent on the performance of retarded subjects. When these subjects were omitted, the correlation was not significantly different from zero. Irwin (1984) also found that auditory inspection time and visual inspection time were unrelated in a sample of 50 schoolchildren. These results may be attributable to methodological problems in the assessment of auditory inspection time. White noise masks were used in these investigations and there is some evidence that they may not have been effective in masking the pure tones. Thus individuals were able to process the tones after the onset of the mask. In addition, the distribution of auditory inspection items was skewed, with some individuals having extremely long inspection times. This was partially attributable to a small subset of subjects who were not able to adequately perform the discrimination task even with relatively long presentation times. Deary et al. (1989) devised an improved auditory inspection-time task using a more effective masking stimulus. They excluded subjects who were unable to make the discrimination accurately when the tones were not masked. They found correlations ranging between .24 and .53 in a sample of 120 undergraduates between their measure of auditory inspection time and three different measures of visual inspection time (see also Nettlebeck, Edwards, & Vreugdenhil, 1986).

Visual inspection time has also been related to tactile inspection-time measures. Edwards (1984, as reported in Nettlebeck, 1987) failed to obtain a relationship between tactile reaction times and visual inspection-time measures. Nettlebeck & Kirby (1983) used a tactile discrimination task in which their subjects were required to report which of two fingers was first stimulated by rapidly vibrating keys. They reported that their subjects complained that their fingers rapidly became numb when performing this task. Nettlebeck (1987) speculated that this problem may have rendered the measures meaningless and this may account for the failure to obtain correlations between tactical and visual inspection times. Deary (1988) speculated that tactile information processing may be less centrally related to higher-order intellectual processes than either visual or auditory information processing.

A number of hypotheses have been advanced to explain the relationship between inspection time and intelligence. It may be the case that individuals with high intelligence understand instructions in these tasks better than individuals who have low intelligence and thus perform better for reasons that have little or nothing to do with their basic information-processing skills. There are two arguments against this hypothesis. Correlations between inspection-time measures and general intelligence test scores have been obtained in children as young as 6. For example, Anderson (1986) reported correlations between visual inspection-time measures and Wechsler intelligence test scores in small samples of children aged 6, 8, and 10. The correlations in these three groups of children were −.38, −.55, and −.33 respectively. If a relationship between inspection time and IQ can be obtained in children as young as 6, it is unlikely that variations among a sample of university students are attributable to a failure to understand instructions. Raz et al. (1987) obtained data in one of their experiments that also provides evidence that contradicts an instructional explanation for the relationship between intelligence and inspection-time measurement. They presented subjects with a loudness discrimination task for tones presented in one of two intervals for 20 ms. The subjects were required to indicate in which of two intervals the tone occurred. They obtained loudness thresholds for three different conditions involving masked and unmasked stimuli. The correlations between their loudness thresholds and Cattell IQ test scores were .16, .17, and −.06, respectively. These correlations should be compared with those obtained between their measures of pitch discrimination and Cattell IQ test scores. The loudness thresholds were obtained from a sample of students with the same characteristics as those used in the experiments on pitch discrimination. In addition, the instructions and the experimental procedures used in both experiments were quite comparable. The obtained correlations are clearly different. Their measure of pitch discrimination threshold for briefly presented tones had a significant negative correlation with IQ and their measure of loudness threshold had a nonsignificant positive correlation with IQ in two of three conditions and a weak negative correlation in the third condition. Raz et al. (1987) indicated that decorticated cats can perform loudness discriminations but are profoundly impaired in their ability to perform pitch discriminations. They interpreted their results as indicating that the characteristics of the information-processing demands associated with simple tasks account for the relationship between IQ and task performance and not the ability to understand instructions. It is also the case that these results provide evidence against the interpretation of the inspection-time–IQ relationship in terms of motivational or attentional variables. It is hard to see why motivational or attentional variables that might explain a relationship between IQ and performance in a pitch discrimination or auditory inspection-time task would not lead to a comparable relationship between loudness discrimination and IQ. The results of the Raz *et al.* (1987) experiment on loudness discrimination need to be replicated. The sample was small ($N = 24$) and reliability data for the three threshold measures were not presented. Quite apart from their substantive relevance, they constitute an important methodological advance. Studies attempting to relate cognitive processing measures to IQ would benefit from the use of control experiments in which subjects are presented with structurally similar tasks using similar instructions and making comparable attentional and motivational demands that measure parameters of information processing that are not assumed to be related to IQ. Such experiments could, in principle, eliminate explanations of relationships that do not focus on information-processing characteristics of the tasks that are assumed to relate to IQ.

Differences in performance between subjects with high and low IQ may be attributable to the capacity of high-IQ subjects to resist boredom. Subjects who are easily bored fail to pay attention and may make frequent errors. Deary (1988; Deary & Caryl, 1990) indicated that this type of reasoning fails to explain the psychophysical regularities obtained in inspection-time research. Subjects who may make frequent errors at one duration of stimulus presentation may well make zero errors at longer durations. If subjects were inattentive, unmotivated, and bored, one would expect to find errors distributed at many different durations of stimulus presentation in inspection-time tasks. Subjects in inspection-time experiments generate regular psychophysical data in which the duration of stimulus presentation appears to be a determining variable of the probability of correct response.

The inspection-time–IQ relationship may be attributable to differential familiarity with inspection-time tasks. Sternberg (1985) proposed that intelligence is best measured in tasks that pose new problems for individuals. If a task is completely novel and the relevance of previously acquired skills and abilities to the task are not apparent, it will not be a good measure of intelligence. If a task may be solved in a habitual way then it may also not engage higher-order intellectual processes and may not serve as a good measure of intelligence. We shall review research related to Sternberg's hypothesis in Chapter 4. If individuals with different IQ test scores were differentially familiar with inspection-time tasks it is possible that this might explain the relationship between IQ and inspection time. Several empirical findings are relevant to an evaluation of this hypothesis. Nettlebeck (1987) indicated that inspection-time measures do exhibit improvement with practice and he reported that studies have found between 17 and 30% improvement as a function of experience with the task. There is no evidence, nor is there reason to believe, that subjects with high IQ scores have had more experience with tasks that are similar to inspection time than individuals with low IQ. The test–retest correlations between initial and terminal performances on inspection-time tasks is high, suggesting that the determinants of performance on the task do not change as a result of practice on the task. Anderson reported that children with experience with video games—an activity that superficially appears to resemble inspection-time tasks—do not have shorter inspection times than individuals who are inexperienced. Raz & Willerman (1985) reported that improvement with practice on their measures of auditory inspection time was not related to IQ. (There was no IQ × trial blocks interaction.) Although subjects do improve with practice on the task, this improvement appears to occur at the same rate for individuals who differ in IQ test score. These findings suggest that the inspection-time–IQ relationship is not attributable to differential familiarity with inspection-time tasks.

The inspection-time–intelligence relationship may be explained by appeal to strategic differences in the approach to the task. Studies of visual inspection time have used light-emitting diodes or computer displays as well as tachistoscopic presentations of stimuli. Many undergraduates performing these tasks report an apparent movement artifact for non-tachistoscopic stimulus displays in which subjects report movements of the lines after the onset of the mask. These cues might be used to solve the problem, and individuals who are able to use these cues might obtain shorter inspection times. In addition, the ability to use such cues might be correlated with IQ. Thus the inspection-time–IQ relationship might be attributable to individual differences in the use of strategies rather than to individual differences in ability to process information. Mac-Kenzie & Bingham (1985) obtained data on the use of strategies in inspection-time tasks. They divided their subjects into two groups—those who reported apparent motion cues and those who did not. They found that the correlation between visual inspection-time measures and IQ in the group of subjects who reported that they did not see apparent motions in the displays was −.72. The comparable correlation in the group who reported seeing apparent motion was −.20. MacKenzie & Cumming (1986) replicated these results and obtained correlations between visual inspection-time measures and IQ of −.66 for 15 university students who reported that they were not able to see apparent motion and a correlation of −.19 for the 22 subjects who reported apparent motion effects. Deary (1988) cited unpublished data obtained by Egan indicating that the correlation between IQ and inspection time is equivalent among individuals who differ with respect to their ability to observe apparent motion effects. The available evidence suggests that the use of a strategy of relying on apparent motion effects does not influence the inspection-time–IQ relationship. In addition, there are several inspection-time tasks where apparent motion effects are attenuated or not present at all. For example, tachistoscopic presentations reduce visual after-effects and such effects are not present in auditory tasks. The relationship between inspection time and intelligence does not appear to conspicuously vary over these different classes of tasks. Where there is reason to believe that the masking stimulus was ineffective in auditory inspection-time tasks using white noise masks, the correlation between inspection time and IQ appears to be low (see Deary, 1988; 1989), and where more effective auditory masks were used the correlation between auditory inspection time and IQ appears to be somewhat higher. And, Raz *et al.* (1987) reported correlations between auditory pitch discrimination and IQ using unmasked stimuli. All of these results do not demonstrate that the inspection-time–IQ relationship is not attributable to the use of strategies that differentiate high- and low-IQ subjects—it is impossible to disprove the mull hypothesis. What can be said is that there is no credible evidence that supports the hypothesis that the relationship between IQ and inspection time is attributable to differences in the use of strategies.

Let us assume that the ability to discriminate between briefly presented simple stimuli is related to the more complex skills tapped in tests of intelligence. Assume further that the relationship is not artifactual and is not attributable to strategies. Would these assumptions establish that heritable characteristics of the nervous system influence information processing and ultimately influence the development of individual differences in intelligence? I think not. The obtained correlation does not establish the direction of influence between its constituents. We have no plausible theory that explains how alleged differences in the functioning of the nervous system might lead to differences in a complex skill such as the ability to define words. Lacking such a theory, we might, perhaps with equal plausibility, speculate about ways in which individual differences in complex reasoning skills might influence the ability to make simple discriminations.

As with research on reaction time, longitudinal research, behavior genetic research, and physiological research might contribute to an understanding of the causal basis of the inspection-time–IQ relationship. What may be concluded is that the relationship is substantial and the basis for the relationship is not clearly understood.

INFANT HABITUATION

Studies of information processing in infancy may contribute to an understanding of the causal direction of the relationship between information-processing abilities and intelligence. Bornstein (1989; Bornstein & Sigman, 1986; see also Fagan, 1984; Fagan & McGrath, 1981; Fagan & Singer, 1983) summarized research indicating that measures of habituation obtained during the first year of life are predictive of IQ scores obtained in early childhood. Infant habituation is defined as a decrement in attention following the repeated presentation of a stimulus. Several different procedures and stimuli have been used in these studies and several different types of measures of habituation have been obtained. Typically, changes in attention are measured by observing the direction of an infant's gaze. Stimuli may be presented for a fixed duration for several trials. Infants usually exhibit a decrease in the time that they attend to stimuli following repeated presentations. The slope of the function defining decline in attention may be obtained. Newer studies tend to use infant-controlled habituation procedures. The duration of the infant's initial attentional response to the stimulus is noted, and the duration of subsequent stimulus presentations is controlled by the duration of the infant's initial responses. The duration is decreased until some predefined criterion of attention is reached—typically 50% of the duration of initial attentional responding. In a number of studies, measures of response recovery are also obtained. If the stimulus is changed, there is usually an increase in attentional responding to the new stimulus. This is called dishabituation or response recovery.

Contemporary theoretical analysis of habituation and dishabituation is usually derived from the work of Sokolov (1958/1963; 1969). Sokolov believed that the presentation of a novel stimulus elicits an orienting response accompanied by a series of psychophysiological changes including visual orientation to the stimulus. Repeated examination of the stimulus is assumed to create a neural model or representation of the stimulus that encodes its properties. Subsequent presentations of the stimulus elicit a comparison process in which the new stimulus is compared to the developed representation of the stimulus. If the stimulus is sufficiently similar to its representation, inhibitory mechanisms lead to the inhibition of the orienting reflex and a decline in attention. If there is a mismatch between the representation of the stimulus and a new stimulus, disinhibitory mechanisms occur, initiating a new orienting reflex and a renewed attention to the stimulus. The rate of habituation is, on this theory, a measure of the rate of development of a representation of external stimuli. Measures of response recovery may be thought of as representing the fidelity of the stimulus representation. Dishabituation can only occur if there has been sufficiently detailed representation of the previous stimulus to permit a mismatch between the representation of the old stimulus and the new stimulus to occur. If the representation of the prior stimulus has failed to encode relevant dimensions of the stimulus, including those features on which the changed stimulus differs from the original stimulus, the probability of a mismatch will decrease. It should be apparent that indices of the rate of habituation and response to novel stimuli are thought to reflect fundamental properties of information processing. These measures are at least metaphorically analogous to the dimensions of information processing assumed to be measured in inspection-time tasks.

Table 3.2 presents Bornstein's summary of studies relating infant habituation measures to measures of intellectual functioning in early childhood (Bornstein, 1989). The studies summarized in Table 3.2 derive from 14 separate experimental reports and include 685 children in all. The correlations reported in the last column of the table are uncorrected correlations. Several generalizations about these data are warranted. The results are remarkably consistent in indicating that infant habituation and recovery measures are consistently related to measures of intelligence and intellectual functioning obtained in early childhood. There is relatively little variability in the reported magnitude of the correlations that have been obtained. With the exception of one study that measures habituation in neonates, all of the correlations are above .30. The habituation measures are all obtained in the first 6 months of life. Thus they occur at a time when the sophisticated skills tapped by intelligence tests in early childhood are not present. Whatever the interpretation of the correlations, it clearly cannot be argued that they occur because children who develop good academic and intellectual skills of the type measured on intelligence tests become skilled in basic information-processing abilities. Intelligence cannot be the cause of the abilities tapped by infant habituation measures unless intelligence is construed as a latent trait that is present prior to its manifestation in performance on tests of intelligence. The available studies summarized in Table 3.2 do not permit one to reach a firm conclusion about the long-term predictability of measures of infant habituation. The studies reporting the correlation between infant habituation and recovery measures and intellectual performance of older children aged 6–8 do report slightly lower correlations than those obtained for the relationship between these infant measures and performance on tests of intelligence administered at ages 2 through 5. Sigman, Cohen, Beckwith, & Parmalee (1986) reported correlations of .36 and .28 between infant measures and IQ obtained at age 8. These are the only studies of children as old as 8 in the set of studies summarized by Bornstein. It is possible that the correlations between infant measures and later IQ will decrease as IQ tests are give at a later age. Or, it is possible that the results reported by Sigman *et al.* (1986) will turn out to be anomalous, and infant measures will be as predictive of later IQ as they are of IQ in early childhood. Additional research is required to reach a firm conclusion on this issue.

Bornstein (1989) summarized data from six studies on the test–retest reliability of measures of habituation. The test–retest correlations decline as the time between test administrations increases. The correlations range between .3 and .7. A reasonable estimate of the long-term stability of habituation measures during the infant years is .4. I calculated the weighted average correlation for all of the data reported by Bornstein and obtained a correlation of .44. If this correlation is corrected for attenuation, assuming a test–retest correlation of .40 for infant habituation measures and a test–retest correlation of .9 for the various intellectual measures, the disattenuated correlation between infant measures and

TABLE 3.2 Summary of Studies Relating Infant Habituation and Recovery to Early Childhood Intelligence[a]

Reference[b]	N	Infancy Measure	Infancy Age (months)	Childhood Measure	Childhood Age (years)	Correlation[c]
Decrement: Habituation and Fixation Time						
Bornstein (1984, 1985a)	20	Amount	4	WPPSI (N = 14)	4	.54
Bornstein (1985b)	18	Index[d]	5	RDLS-R	2	.55
Lewis & Brooks-Gunn (1981)	22	Amount	3	Bayley	2	.61
Miller et al., (1979)	29	Amount	2–4	Language Comprehension	3.3	.39
Rose, Slater, & Perry (1986)	21	Index[g]	1.5–6.5	WPPSI (N = 16)	4.5	.63
				BAS (N = 16)	4.5	.77
Sigman (1983)	96[e]	Fixation time[f]	(Term)	Stanford–Binet	5	.29
Sigman, et al. (1986)	58[e]	Amount	4	Stanford–Binet	5	.44
				WISC-R (N = 56)	8	.28
	96[e]	Fixation time[f]	(Term)	WISC-R (N = 91)	8	.36
Recovery: Novelty Preference, Response to Novelty, and Recognition Memory						
Bornstein (1984)	20	Recognition memory	4	WPPSI (N = 14)	4	.54
Caron, Caron & Glass (1983)	31	Response	5–6	Stanford–Binet	3	.42

74

Study	N	Infant measure	Infant age	Outcome measure	Outcome age	r
Fagan & McGrath (1981)	35	Novelty preference	7	Language scales	3.8	.41
	19	Novelty preference	5	PPVT	4.3	.33
	20	Novelty preference	4–5	Language scales	6.5	.66
	19	Novelty preference	5	Language scales	7.5	.46
Lewis & Brooks-Gunn (1981)	22	Response to novelty	3	Bayley	2	.52
	57	Response to novelty	3	Bayley	2	.40
O'Connor, Cohen & Parmalee (1984)	28[e]	Auditory response to novelty	4	Stanford–Binet	5	.60
Rose & Wallace (1985)	35[e]	Novelty preference	6	Stanford–Binet ($N = 14$)	2.8	.66
				Stanford–Binet ($N = 17$)	3.3	.45
				WISC-R ($N = 19$)	6	.56
Yarrow, Klein, Lomonaco, & Morgan (1975)	39	Novelty preference	6	Stanford–Binet	3.6	.35

[a]Based on Bornstein (1989).
[b]Listed in alphabetical order by author.
[c]All correlations are absolute values and significant at $p < .05$; direction and nature of the correlation depend on the measures.
[d]Latent variable of baseline, slope, and amount.
[e]Sample consists of or includes preterm infants; testing carried out of corrected age.
[f]One trial or first trial.
[g]Mean of total fixation time, duration of first fixation, average fixation duration, and average trial duration.

early childhood intelligence becomes .733, indicating that close to 54% of the variance in childhood IQ is predictable on the basis of measures of infant habituation obtained during the first 6 months of life. The correction reported is conservative. Corrections for restrictions in range of talent were not performed. In any case, this analysis suggests that infant habituation and response recovery measures are remarkably predictive of early childhood intelligence.

What bearing, if any, do these results have on the interpretation of findings relating performance on simple experimental tasks such as inspection time to intelligence? It is difficult to answer this question without knowing more about the relationship between the abilities that are assessed in infant and adult experimental tasks. Inspection-time measures and infant habituation indices may both be construed as measures of the speed and accuracy of processing stimulus information. Whether this represents a superficial and metaphorical analysis or a deep structural relationship is unclear. Research relating performance on an infant version of the pitch discrimination task to intelligence assessed at a later age would be informative. If infant pitch discrimination ability predicted later intelligence, then it would be reasonable to interpret the correlation between adult pitch discrimination ability for briefly presented tones and intelligence as being attributable to the influence of pitch discrimination on intelligence rather than the converse. More precisely, those characteristics of the information-processing system that determine ability in simple tasks could be assumed to be present prior to the development of more complex skills and even, perhaps, to be causally related to the development of the complex skills and knowledge assessed in adult tests of intelligence. Since such research is not available, the exact relationship between the infant research on information-processing ability and intelligence and the adult research on the relationship between intelligence and basic cognitive processing ability remains indeterminate.

Although the prior longitudinal status of the infant measures renders a causal interpretation in which intelligence influences infant habituation nugatory, the alternative causal analysis in which infant habituation is assumed to influence the development of complex intellectual skills may also be unwarranted. The relationship may be mediated by the influence of environmental events that influence the development of infant cognitive processing and childhood intelligence. Two of the studies reported in Bornstein's summary, Sigman (1983) and Sigman et al. (1986), assessed infant habituation at birth. The significant correlations obtained by these investigators cannot readily be interpreted in terms of the influence of postnatal environmental stimulation in infancy and early childhood. It is possible that environmental events that influence development in utero are correlated with postnatal environmental events and that these events influence both infant and early childhood intellectual ability. It is also the case that the correlations reported by these investigators between habituation and intelligence were lower than have reported by other investigators. Perhaps postnatal environmental events contribute to the development of both intelligence and infant habituation and these events are less likely to influence the habituation performance of neonates. Or, it may be the case that the reliability of habituation measures obtained at birth is low. I believe that the causal interpretation of the research on infant intelligence is vexed and the bearing of this research on studies of relationship between IQ and performance on elementary information-processing tasks is indeterminate.

CONCLUSION

In this chapter I have reviewed studies relating scores on tests of intelligence to performance on three kinds of tasks—reaction time, inspection time, and infant habituation and response recovery. The stimuli that are used in these investigations include tones, lines, and lights. None of these investigations used alphanumeric symbols, and thus the role of formal tuition or differential exposure to certain classes of stimuli has been minimized or rendered irrelevant as an explanation of performance on these tasks (see Ceci, 1990). Differential familiarity with flashing lights, line lengths, and tones differing in pitch do not appear to be reasonable interpretations of the obtained correlations between performance on these tasks and intelligence. The stimuli used in the infant habituation tasks are probably equally novel for all infants, but they may be more or less similar to the stimuli that are encountered in the environments of different children. We do not know if performance on the infant tasks is determined by variations in patterns of stimulation encountered in the early postnatal environment. Some of these tasks have nontrivial relationships with performance on intelligence tests and may account for a substantial portion of the variance in intelligence test scores. Given the substantial relationships that have been obtained, it should be the case that a theoretical analysis of the determinants of performance on these tasks should provide insights into the nature of the abilities that are measured by tests of intelligence.

These tasks appear to involve the ability to process information accurately and rapidly. The tasks with the most substantial correlations to intelligence, such as inspection time, pitch discrimination, and infant habituation, all appear to involve the ability to notice differences between stimuli under difficult conditions. The use of backward masking in the standard visual inspection-time tasks forces individuals to detect stimulus differences under conditions where there is limited opportunity to inspect a stimulus. The pitch discrimination task measures ability to distinguish differences between stimuli that are presented too briefly for full examination and extraction of relevant information. The measures of infant performance we have examined are assumed to involve a hypothetical comparison between a representation of a stimulus and a new stimulus. Response recovery requires the ability to distinguish between an old and a new stimulus. Although the infant tasks are not speeded, the infant's limited intellectual repertoire may make the task difficult without the degradation of the stimulus accomplished by the rapid presentations used in the adult tasks.

If the ability to detect differences is the fundamental common element presented in these tasks, it is possible to suggest that Spearman's principles of eduction of correlates and relations are not the optimal definition of the foundation of general intelligence. Before one can note that two different things are related, it is necessary to know that they are different. In the absence of the detection of difference, things which are different will be treated as identical. And, one cannot educe a correlate or relation between two things that are identical. If two things are identical, then the only relation or correlate that may be educed between them is the identity relation.

This discussion leaves unresolved the nature of the discriminatory processes that relate to individual differences in intelligence. It leaves unresolved whether or not the common element that is present in some of the tasks that are related to scores on tests of intelligence is some kind of discriminatory ability. Clearly, discrimination per se is not the fundamental attribute of tasks in which individual differences in performance are correlated with scores on tests of intelligence. Raz et al. (1987) demonstrated that ability to discriminate between tones that differ in loudness does not relate to intelligence. Perhaps the ability to detect variations in the intensity of stimuli does not relate to intelligence. This implies that inspection-time measures for visual stimuli that differ in brightness would not relate to individual differences in intelligence. And, again pursuing the analogy of research on audition, inspection-time indices for stimuli differing in color might be predictive of individual differences in intelligence. It is apparent that there are many different detection experiments that could be done to obtain measures of the ability to discriminate between briefly presented stimuli that differ on some dimension. An examination of the class of discrimination measures that predict individual differences in intelligence, as opposed to the class of measures that do not, might provide insight into the relationship between information-processing skills and intelligence. It is possible to suggest tentative hypotheses to guide this research. Raz et al. (1987) suggested that differences between parallel and serial processing might explain why pitch discrimination correlates with intelligence test scores and loudness discrimination does not. They assumed that pitch discrimination involves parallel information processing and loudness discrimination involves serial processing of information. If this hypothesis is correct, it would be possible to design experiments involving discrimination of simple visual stimuli that tap differences in parallel and serial processing of information. For example, Treisman (1982; Treisman & Gormican, 1988; Treisman & Souther, 1985) indicated that there is a preattentive automatic processing of stimulus features of visual stimuli that appears to involve parallel processing. She finds that the ability to detect stimuli that differ in certain dimensions may not vary as the number of distractors in the set of stimuli increases. Other stimulus features appear to be processed serially since the time to detect a stimulus that differs from others on these features increases as set size increases. It is interesting to note that Treisman suggested that line lengths, the discriminative feature used in the original inspection-times tasks, are discriminable on the basis of preattentive properties that are not related to the number of elements in the set. By contrast such properties of line arrangements as convergence and parallelism are processed serially—the detection time for such properties is an increasing function of the number of distractors presented in the set of stimuli. If the critical feature of discrimination tasks that determines their relationship to intelligence is the presence or absence of serial and parallel processing, then one would expect that the inspection time for judgments of convergence and parallelism of lines, or discrimination thresholds for such lines, would not be predictive of individual differences in intelligence.

There are many other possible hypotheses that could be explored about the class of psychophysical measures that are predictive of intelligence. Consider another possible visual dimension. Livingstone & Hubel (1988) distinguished between two primate visual systems—an evolutionary old magno system that is designed to provide information about moving objects and the overall structure of the visual world, and the parvo system that is important for analysis of the details of visual images. Livingstone and Hubel detail the anatomical and physiological substrates of these systems and relate them to a variety of perceptual phenomena. If it is assumed that variations in the functioning of the parvo system and not variations in the magno system are related to individual differences in intelligence, then Livingstone and Hubel's analysis provides a number of suggestions of the kind of perceptual phenomena that one might examine to obtain possible relationships with intelligence. What should be apparent is that research attempting to delineate the class of psychophysical measures that do or do not predict performance on tests of intelligence should inform us about the nature of individual differences in intelligence.

I have argued that we do not have a firm theoretical understanding of the reasons why performance on some relatively simple experimental tasks is predictive of performance on tests of intelligence. Nor do we understand the way in which the abilities measured by these tasks are causally related to performance on tests of intelligence. Nor do we know if the reductive, bottom-up models favored by some researchers in this area are justified. Such models are, at best, plausible. No more, no less.

4

MULTIPLE AND COMPLEX CORRELATES OF INTELLIGENCE

In this chapter we shall consider several different approaches to the experimental investigation of individual differences in intelligence. The experimental approaches considered in Chapter 3 were examined from the perspective of a monarchical, reductive, bottom-up model of intelligence. In this chapter we shall consider approaches to the experimental study of individual differences in intelligence that relax one or more of the common characteristics of the theoretical perspective used in Chapter 3.

First, we shall consider studies in which performance on several different experimental tasks is related to psychometric indices of intelligence. These studies are designed to measure several elementary components of information processing that collectively define either general intelligence or verbal or spatial ability. Second, we shall consider studies that attempt to define a complex correlate of general intelligence. These studies may be understood as a contemporary version of Spearman's attempt to characterize general intelligence by the ability to educe correlates and relations. Third, we shall consider the componential approach to general intelligence which is distinguished by the effort to study the components of performance on complex tasks.

MULTIPLE COGNITIVE CORRELATES OF INTELLIGENCE

Many different experimental tasks may be used to study the cognitive correlates of intelligence. Several tasks have been studied that are based on well-defined paradigms used in cognitive psychology. E. Hunt (1978) was one of the first researchers to relate individual differences in intelligence to a theoretical parameter derived from the contemporary study of cognitive processes. He used a task studied by Posner, Boies, Eichelman, & Taylor (1969) in which subjects were required to state whether two letters were the same or different. The judgment of similarity may be based on the physical identity of the letters—e.g., the pair "aa." Or the judgment may be based on name identity, as in the pair "Aa." The reaction times for similarity judgments of physically identical letters are shorter than the reaction times for letter pairs with the same name. The difference in reaction times is attributable to the need to access long-term memory for lexical categories in order to judge name identity. Hunt found that the difference between reaction time for name-identity (NI) judgments of similarity and physical identity (PI) judgments of similarity (NI − PI) was inversely related to measures of verbal ability, implying that individuals with high verbal ability are able to access long-term memory codes for lexical material more rapidly than individuals with low verbal ability.

Individual differences in spatial ability have been related to the speed with which an individual is able to rotate a visual image. Shepard & Metzlar (1971) found that the time taken to decide whether the two-dimensional representation of a three-dimensional figure was the same or different from a previously presented target figure was a monotonically increasing function of the angle of rotation of the figure. The slope of the function defining increases in judgment time as a function of the angle of rotation of the target stimulus is a measure of the speed of mental rotation and this measure may be related to spatial ability measures.

Speed of access to memory for arithmetic stimuli may be measured by a task studied by S. Sternberg (1970). Individuals are presented with a set of numerals followed by a single probe digit. The subject judges whether the probe digit was or was not included in the set of stimuli that was previously presented. Decision time is a monotonically increasing function of the number of digits in the initial comparison set, suggesting that individuals engage in serial processing of the stimuli in order to determine whether or not the probe digit is included in the set of stimuli. The slope of the function relating decision times to set sizes may be taken as an index of the speed of scanning memory for digits.

The three tasks described above each provide a slope measure of the speed of processing information. They differ with respect to the kind of information that is processed—lexical, arithmetic, or visual–spatial. The slope measures that are obtained are formally analogous to the slope measure of increase in choice reaction time as a function of set size. Each of these measures is related to a general law in cognitive psychology and variations in a parameter of speed of processing information may be investigated as a correlate of general intelligence or of a specific ability measure. Studies that combine these measures, along with several variants of these procedures, have been undertaken with the aim of surveying the relationship between measures of information processing and intelligence. Such studies are, in principle, capable of clarifying several related issues. Are certain information-processing parameters more predictive of intelligence than others? To what extent are these several measures redundant? Is it possible to combine several measures of information processing into an index that is more predictive of intelligence than any single component? Do measures of information-processing parameters possess discriminant and convergent validity for different abilities? That is, are parameters of spatial processing more predictive of spatial reasoning ability than they are predictive of verbal reasoning, and are parameters of verbal processing of information more predictive of verbal reasoning ability than of spatial reasoning ability? We shall examine these and related questions by considering the results of several studies that have studied one or more of these or related tasks in a single investigation.

P. A. Vernon (1983) obtained reaction-time measures for several cognitive tasks including visual inspection time and simple and choice reaction time using Jensen's apparatus. In addition, subjects were required to judge pairs of words that were either physically identical or not. He used a semantic version of this task in which subjects were required to judge pairs of words that were synonyms or antonyms. A digit recognition task was included that required subjects to indicate whether or not a digit was included in a previously presented list containing from 1 to 7 digits. A dual-task procedure was used in which subjects were given the digit recognition task, interrupted after the presentation of the initial digits by the presentation of a same–different judgment task for words, followed by the presentation of a single digit. The subject indicated whether the digit was or was not present in the previously presented list. Measures of response speed and variability of response times were obtained for each of these tasks and these measures were correlated with performance on tests of intelligence. The multiple correlation between various measures of response times on these tasks and IQ was .46. The subjects in the experiment were college students and therefore had a restricted range of talent for IQ. The multiple correlation, corrected for restriction in range of talent, was .67. Comparable results were obtained for measures of the variability of responding in this sample. The multiple r for the variability measures and IQ was .43, which, when corrected, became .63. These analyses indicate that approximately 40% of the variance of scores on tests of intelligence is predictable from scores on a battery of tests of the speed and consistency of response speed for tasks that have very low error rates. The median latency of responding on these tasks is below 1500 ms, suggesting that they do not involve highly complex reasoning processes. Although the multiple correlations involving the combined results of several measures are higher than the correlations of any individual measure, it is not clear that these values are conspicuously higher than the correlations obtained by Raz & Willerman (1985; Raz, Willerman, & Yama, 1987) for various measures of auditory pitch discrimination and intelligence. Also, the replicability of the multiple correlations remains to be investigated. Vernon, Nador, & Kantor (1985) reported comparable multiple correlations for similar batteries of tests and IQ in different samples. Although the overall magnitude of the multiple *r* is replicable, the exact weights assigned to the several predictor variables that enter into the multiple prediction equation are probably not replicable. These results indicate that it is possible, given several measures of elementary information processing, to predict IQ.

Vernon *et al.* (1985) proposed that the correlation between general intelligence and performance on elementary information-processing tasks is related to the complexity of information processing required for a task. Vernon & Jensen (1984) measured complexity by noting the median latency required to perform each task. They found that group differences in IQ were positively related to median reaction times. Vernon and Jensen reported that the correlation between the mean difference in reaction times between a group of university students and a group of vocational students, whose mean IQ was lower than that of the university students, correlated .97 with the median reaction time on the task. They suggested that median reaction time on these tasks is a measure of the complexity of the information processing required for successful completion of each of these tasks. And, the more complex the cognitive processes involved in performing a task, the more *g* loaded the task. Although the correlation reported has a dramatically high value, the conclusion may not be compelling. The mean differences are not presented in standard deviation units. There is a correlation between the median reaction time for a task and the standard deviation of reaction times on the tasks. It is conventional to compare mean differences in terms of the standard deviations of the scores. If this were done, the correlation would be lower. In addition, tasks that differ in reaction time also differ in a number of dimensions other than complexity. For example, the largest difference in reaction time between university and vocational college students is obtained on a dual processing task that requires individuals to perform a same–different judgment for pairs of words that are interspersed between presentations of a digit recognition task. We shall review evidence suggesting that dual processing tasks are highly correlated with intelligence. Finally, Vernon *et al.* (1985) found a negative correlation of −.95 between mean differences in reaction times on these tasks between two groups of university students who had small differences in IQ (122 versus 117) and median reaction time for the task. In this instance, larger differences between the groups occurred for those tasks that had the shortest reaction time—a result exactly opposite of that reported by Vernon and Jensen for the differences obtained between university students and vocational college students. Obviously, the relationship between differences in the magnitude of mean differences and median reaction times for different tasks for groups differing in IQ is not constant.

Larson & Saccuzzo (1989; see also Larson, Merritt, & Williams, 1988) presented a battery of timed tasks to 343 Navy recruits. They chose tasks that varied in complexity of information-processing requirements and they correlated performance on these tasks with performance on tests of intelligence. They used the following tasks.

1. A simple reaction-time task.
2. A visual inspection-time task.
3. A numbers task in which subjects were given a single target digit to recall followed by a rapid presentation of a sequence of digits. The subjects were required to indicate the digits immediately preceding and following the target digit.
4. A choice reaction-time task called the arrows task in which the position of an arrow cued the appropriate response.
5. A mental counters task in which subjects were required to note the location of a box above or below a line and add +1 for boxes above the line and −1 for boxes below the line. The appropriate score for each trial varied between +3 and −3. A description of this task is presented in Fig. 4.1.

Larson & Saccuzzo (1989) derived three parameters of increasing complexity of information processing from their subjects' performance on these tasks. The first parameter was an encoding parameter defined by a

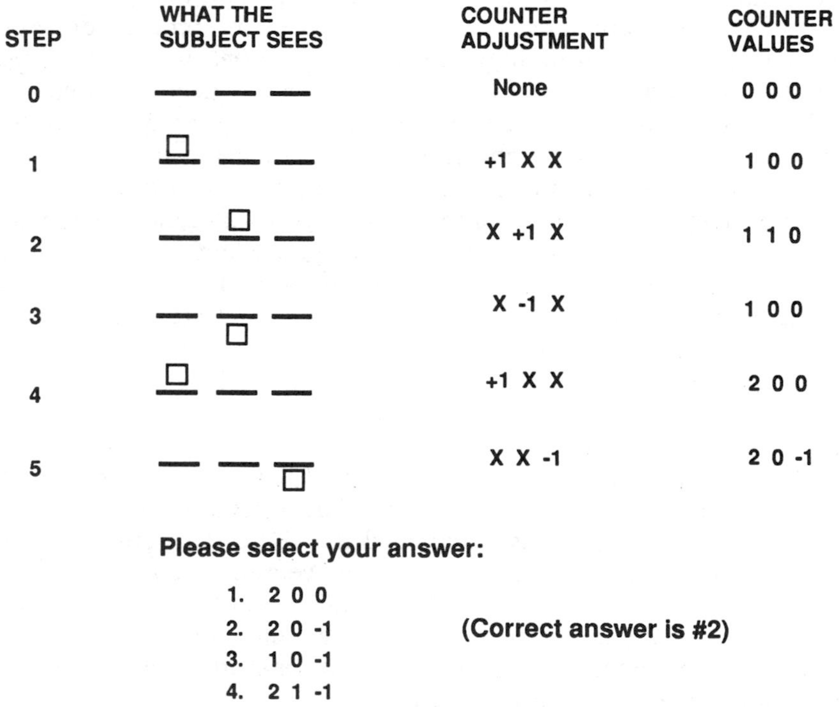

STEP	WHAT THE SUBJECT SEES	COUNTER ADJUSTMENT	COUNTER VALUES
0	— — —	None	0 0 0
1	▢ — —	+1 X X	1 0 0
2	— ▢ —	X +1 X	1 1 0
3	— ▢ —	X -1 X	1 0 0
4	▢ — —	+1 X X	2 0 0
5	— — ▢	X X -1	2 0 -1

Please select your answer:

1. 2 0 0
2. 2 0 -1   (Correct answer is #2)
3. 1 0 -1
4. 2 1 -1

FIGURE 4.1 Sample items from mental counters test. (Based on Larson & Saccuzzo, 1989.)

composite of the inspection-time measure and the standard deviation of simple reaction times. The second level of complexity was encoding plus memory comparison and it was defined by the standard deviation of choice reaction-time performance. This was based on performance on the arrows test that required subjects to respond in a different way to stimuli depending on the position of an arrow that served as a cue. Thus the subject was required to recall the position of the cue while responding to a stimulus. The third level of complexity was called encoding plus memory comparison plus momentary workload. It was defined by performance on the mental counters test. The correlations between these three derived parameters and a composite measure of intelligence were .27, −.29, and .54, respectively. The disattenuated correlations, corrected for unreliability of measurement, were .42, −.45, and .72. The correlations for the first two parameters and a measure of general intelligence are not significantly different. The third parameter, i.e., performance on the counters test, has a significantly larger correlation with IQ than the other parameters.

Larson and Saccuzzo's findings provide only partial support for the hypothesis that complexity of information processing determines the magnitude of the relationship between IQ and information-processing tasks. There was no difference between the first and second parameter. Thus the introduction of a memory component to encoding does not increase the magnitude of the correlation between a simple cognitive task and IQ. This finding is analagous to the results obtained with the Jensen apparatus. The variability of reaction times in a simple reaction-time task is as predictive of IQ as the variability of performance in a choice reaction-time task. The significant increment in predictability associated with their third parameter, performance on the counters test, may be attributable to several possible differences between this task and the other tasks used by Larson and Saccuzzo. Performance on this task is defined by a measure of the number of correct responses rather than by indices based on reaction times. In addition, the counters task requires an individual to perform simple arithmetic calculations. Familiarity with alphanumeric symbols and with the task of performing mental arithmetic may influence performance on this task. It appears less related to a basic ability to encode or respond to simple stimuli than the other tasks and comes closer to being a task where the assertion that performance may be influenced by formal schooling appears to have a *prima facie* validity.

Matthews & Dorn (1989) obtained theoretically defined parametric measures of information processing from performance on a variety of timed tasks and related these measures to performance on the Cattell Culture-Fair test of intelligence. Their subjects were presented with a variety of choice reaction-time tasks and several modifications of these tasks. The choice reaction-time tasks used by Matthews and Dorn included three "control tasks" that required subjects to respond to three different colors, lights, or shapes. They introduced several variations of these three basic tasks in order to derive parameters for more complex information-processing components. The variations included the following tasks.

1. A degraded shape task in which the shapes presented to subjects in the choice reaction-time task were degraded with visual noise.
2. A memory load task in which subjects were presented with seven digits followed by a reaction-time task followed by the request to recall the seven digits that were previously presented.
3. An incompatible response task in which subjects had to respond with different response keys to a previously encountered choice reaction-time task.
4. An alternation task in which subjects had to respond on alternate trials to a shape or a color discrimination task.
5. A rare-event task in which subjects were required to respond to shape stimuli on 90% of the trials and color stimuli on 10% of the trials.
6. A cue control task in which a plus sign signaled the start of a trial followed by the presentation of one of the three choice reaction-time tasks.
7. A category cue task in which different letters cue which of the three choice reaction-time tasks would be presented.

The preceding tasks were used to define several different parameters of information processing. The parameters were as follows.

1. Feature extraction defined as the difference in reaction time for degraded and nondegraded shape control stimuli.
2. Short-term memory: memory load − shape control.
3. Response selection: incompatible response − shape control.
4. Flexibility I: The difference between alternation and the average performance under shape and color control stimuli.
5. Flexibility II: The difference between performance on rare-event trials and the average performance on shape and color control reaction times.
6. Conscious attention. The difference between the category cue and the cue control reaction times.

It should be apparent that each of these derived parameters is assumed to measure performance under conditions in which there is an additional information-processing requirement added to the basic choice reaction-time tasks. A mean reaction time and the standard deviation of reaction times were obtained for each of the measures included. The correlations of these measures with Cattell Culture-Fair IQ tests ranged from −.15 to −.52. The color control choice reaction-time task had the highest correlation with IQ. The more complex versions of the reaction-time tasks did not have higher correlations with IQ than the basic control tasks. Table 4.1 presents the correlations between the mean and standard deviation of control reaction times and IQ as well as the correlations between the means and standard deviation of the several derived parameters and IQ.

Table 4.1 indicates that performance on the choice reaction times without the introduction of additional information-processing demands is more predictive of IQ than the measures of derived parameters. The findings of the Matthews and Dorn study appear to be congruent with the results obtained by Larson and Saccuzzo. Larson and Saccuzzo found that the addition of a dual-task memory component to a reaction-time task did not lead to a significant increment in the prediction of IQ. It is also the case that none of the complexities added to the choice reaction-time tasks presented by Matthews and Dorn involved the use of mental calculations or the use of alphanumeric symbols. Their data support the notion that the increment to predictability of intelligence associated with performance on the counters test is not the result of the added complexity of information processing per se, but rather of the introduction of a mental task that is congruent with activities associated with formal education. Matthews and Dorn tentatively concluded that the relationship between performance on simple information-processing tasks and intelligence is attributable to speed of apprehension ability or encoding ability.

The studies we have considered used multiple measures of performance in a single investigation. E. Hunt (1978; 1987; Hunt, Frost, & Lunneborg, 1973; Hunt, Lunneborg, & Lewis, 1975; Lansman, Donaldson, Hunt, & Yantis, 1982) used a theory of the verbal comprehension process to obtain measures of several correlates of verbal ability. He assumed that these

TABLE 4.1   Correlations between IQ and Means and Standard Deviations of Reaction-Time Measures[a]

	Correlations with	
	Mean	SD
Measures		
Color	−.52	−.35
Shape	−.41	−.32
Cue control	−.42	−.43
Derived Parameters		
Feature extraction	−.26	−.26
Short-term memory	−.15	−.21
Response selection	−.10	.01
Flexibility I	−.15	.10
Flexibility II	−.12	−.19
Conscious attention	−.31	−.12

[a]Based on Matthews & Dorn (1989).

several elementary processes collectively determined individual differences in verbal ability.

Hunt *et al.* (1975) studied individual differences in the ability to identify sublexical units of speech. They presented subjects with phonemes in a dichotic listening task in which different phonemes were presented to each ear. The subjects were required to identify which of the two phonemes was presented first. Performance on this task was contrasted with performance on a similar task in which the stimuli were nonspeech sounds (a buzz, hiss, or tone). Figure 4.2 presents the data obtained by Hunt *et al.* (1975) indicating the number of correct judgments made in

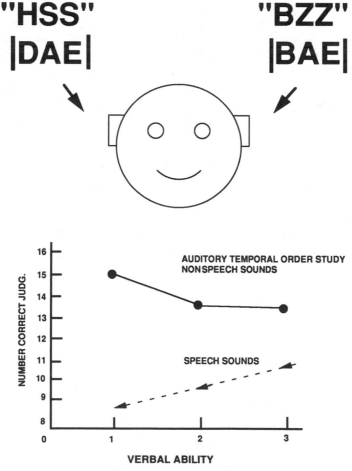

FIGURE 4.2 Verbal ability is related to the ability to perceive sublexical elements. The task was to detect the order of dichotically presented speech or nonspeech sounds. High-verbal people were better at detecting speech sounds than were low-verbal people. There was no difference for nonspeech sounds. (Based on Hunt, 1987.)

this task for the two classes of discrimination problems for individuals who differ in verbal ability. The data clearly indicate that there is little or no relationship between verbal ability and the ability to discriminate the order of presentation of nonspeech sounds. Verbal ability is positively related to the ability to discriminate the order of presentation of phonemes that serve as a sublexical unit of language.

Hunt et al. (1975; see also Hunt et al., 1973) studied the speed of access of written symbols to a language code using the paradigm developed by Posner et al. (1969), who presented subjects with pairs of letters on a computer display that were physically identical (AA) or name identical (Aa) or different (aB). The subjects were required to distinguish between letter pairs that were the same or different and were further instructed to consider the first two pairs as the same. Table 4.2 presents their data relating performance on this task to a classification of subjects as being high or low in verbal ability. Table 4.2 indicates that subjects who are high in verbal ability need less additional time to identify letters with the same name but different physical representations as identical than subjects who are low in verbal ability. These results suggest that verbal ability is related to the speed of access to overlearned verbal codes that are stored in long-term memory.

Goldberg, Schwartz, & Stewart (1977) used an analagous task to study the time required to identify words that were either physically identical (DEAR - DEAR), homophonically identical (DEAR - DEER), or taxonomically identical (DEER - ELK). Their data are presented in Table 4.3, which indicates that high-verbal subjects and low-verbal subjects differ slightly in the time taken to determine the physical identity of words. High-verbal subjects are able to determine the identity of homophonically and taxonomically identical words more rapidly than individuals who score low in verbal ability. These data suggest that subjects who are high in verbal ability are able to access lexical meanings more rapidly than individuals low in verbal ability.

Individuals who differ in verbal ability have also been found to differ in the speed with which they can verify sentences that describe a very simple visual stimulus as true or false. A typical stimulus used in these studies is presented in Fig. 4.3. Hunt, Davidson, & Lansman (1981) obtained measures of performance on a sentence verification task as well as

TABLE 4.2 Mean of Median Reaction Time for Same–Different Identification[a]

	Name identical (NI)	Physical identical (PI)	NI − PI
High verbals	588.1	524.5	63.6
Low verbals	631.7	542.8	88.9

[a]Based on Hunt, Lunneborg & Lewis (1975).

TABLE 4.3   Mean Reaction Times (ms) on Same-Different Identifications for Subjects Differing in Verbal Ability[a]

Matching task	High verbals	Low verbals
Physical	732.8	868.7
Homophone	806.3	1168.7
Taxonomic	907.4	1267.3

[a]Based on Goldberg, Schwartz, & Stewart (1977).

performance on a number of tasks designed to measure speed of access of lexical information in long-term memory. They found that the partial correlation between individual differences in verbal comprehension and performance on the sentence verification task holding constant performance on a semantic matching task was .31. This correlation indicates that verbal ability is related to the speed with which an individual can verify sentences that describe pictures and that this ability is partially independent of the ability involved in determining that words are semantically identical.

We have considered the relationship between performance on several tasks and verbal ability. The tasks may be ordered in terms of the degree to which they approximate complex abilities that are acquired as one gains facility in the comprehension of a language. Clearly, the ability to discriminate between phonemes requires relatively little linguistic sophistication. It may be thought of as a measure of primitive processing capacities that may be related to complex skills. By contrast, the sentence verification task can only be performed by someone who is literate. It is possible to study individual differences in verbal ability using tasks that are dependent on highly developed linguistic skills. Sternberg & Powell (1983) developed a theory of vocabulary acquisition. They assumed that individual differences in vocabulary were not solely attributable to individual differences in exposure to words with different meanings. They assumed that the acquisition of vocabulary was determined by the ability to infer the meaning of words from incompletely specified contexts. All of us are able to define words for which we have never encountered a formal definition. We may be able to do this because we infer the meaning of the word from context. Sternberg and Powell believed that most of the words

PLUS ABOVE STAR

+

FIGURE 4.3   The sentence verification paradigm. The participant is shown a sentence or phrase, followed by a picture. The task is to determine whether or not the sentence accurately describes the picture.

in an individual's vocabulary are acquired in this way. In order to test this theory, they presented high school students with passages containing unusual low-frequency nouns that are almost never encountered in written English. None of the words used were in the working vocabulary of the students. They constructed passages using these words and asked students to provide a definition of the word. They found that a measure of the quality of the definitions provided by the students had correlations of .62, .56, and .65 with IQ, vocabulary, and reading comprehension, respectively. These results explain why individual differences in vocabulary are a good measure of general intelligence. The acquisition of vocabulary is correlated with the ability to determine meanings from imperfectly specified contexts. Thus abstract skills related to fluid ability are probably involved in vocabulary acquisition.

The research we have considered permits one to develop a model of individual differences in verbal ability that assumes that such differences are related to individual differences in partially independent skills. E. Hunt (1987) summarized the theoretical import of research on individual differences in verbal ability as follows.

> What is verbal ability? The theoretical position taken here is that the "dimension" of verbal ability is the result of a somewhat correlated collection of skills. These skills depend upon a variety of more primitive psychological processes, including access to lexical memory, rapid consolidation of information into long-term memory, the possession of knowledge about how to process discourse in general, and the possession of knowledge about the topic of the discourse being comprehended. Some of these primitive processes can be thought of as properties of the brain, closely linked to physiological processes. The efficiency of consolidation of information into long-term memory is an example. Other processes, such as the use of restaurant scripts, are learned, and are highly culture dependent.
>
> If the various verbal skills are distinct, why do psychometric analyses so consistently uncover a single dimension of verbal ability? It could be that all the primitive processes of language comprehension are derived from a single underlying brain process, and that the expression of different processes is correlated across individuals for that purpose. There may be some truth to this, but it is an impossible proposition to prove or disprove. The moderately high correlations between measures of different aspects of language comprehension could also be explained by interactions between them as they are developed. Being able to consolidate information into permanent memory rapidly would aid in the acquisition of lexical knowledge, and increasing one's vocabulary would increase one's ability to develop text and situation models, which could be used to increase lexical knowledge by defining new words in context. Since each subprocess of verbal comprehension encourages the development of the others, it is hardly surprising that, across individuals, the same people are usually good at different verbal comprehension tasks (E. Hunt, 1987).

Keating, List, & Merriman (1985; see also Keating & Bobbitt, 1978) related performance on verbal and spatial information-processing tasks to tests of verbal and spatial psychometric ability. They hoped to demonstrate what is called discriminant and convergent validity for their measures. That is, they assumed that evidence for the theoretical specificity of information-processing parameters would be obtained if various parameters relating to spatial skills would correlate with each other at a higher value than they correlated with parameters relating to the processing of verbal information. In addition, the same pattern of convergent and discriminant validity should be demonstrated for correlations with ability scores. That is, they assumed that parameters of verbal processing of information would correlate with verbal tests at a higher level than they correlated with spatial tests, and parameters of spatial processing should correlate with spatial ability at a higher value than they correlated with verbal ability. They also included data from two different age groups, eighth graders and adults, in order to see if the assumed relationships between elementary processing skills and ability measures were constant across developmental levels.

Among the verbal measures they obtained were differences in name versus physical identity judgments for letters, a delayed version of this task in which the letters were presented sequentially, and a semantic processing measure in which subjects were required to judge whether the second word of a pair of words belonged to the same category as the first word in the pair. They varied the association strength of the first and second word and obtained a measure of the slope of reaction time for words of differing degrees of association. Among the spatial components they investigated was a letter rotation task based on a task developed by Cooper & Shepard (1973) in which letters are presented in normal or reversed orientation and with different degrees of rotation from the upright. Subjects were required to judge whether the letter was presented in reversed or normal orientation. The time required to make these judgments is a monotonically increasing function of the degree of rotation of the stimulus. They obtained a measure of the slope of reaction time to make a judgment of reversed or normal orientation as a function of the degree of rotation of the stimulus. They also included a measure of facial rotation and a measure of letter rotation in which subjects were presented with a cue (an arrow) that indicated the direction of the rotation of the stimulus.

Keating et al. (1985) found little evidence for convergent and discriminant validity for their various parameters of information processing. They reported average correlations of .23 for their three verbal parameters, .37 for their spatial parameters, and .08 for the average correlation between verbal and spatial parameters for eighth graders. The comparable correlations for adults were −.13, .17, and .12. These data indicate that there was little evidence for convergent and discriminant validity in the relationship among these different measures.

The correlations between spatial and verbal ability measures and spatial and verbal parameters derived from information-processing tasks also provided relatively little evidence of discriminant and convergent validity. Table 4.4 presents the correlations between the various measures of information processing and spatial and verbal ability for eighth graders and adults. The data indicate that the correlations are relatively low and inconsistent. For adults, the best predictor of verbal ability is performance on a spatial rotation task. Spatial ability is predicted by performance on rotation tasks, but also by performance on a semantic processing measure. For eighth graders, verbal ability is best predicted by performance on the semantic processing task, but it is also predicted by performance on two of the rotation tasks. Spatial ability is not related to any of these measures.

Keating *et al.* (1985) (see also Keating & Bobbitt, 1978) contended that their results provide little or no support for the attempt to derive cognitive correlates of intellectual skills. They argued that the imposition of more stringent validity criteria and the search for convergent and divergent validity correlations explain the generally negative outcome of their study in comparison to other studies that are reported in the literature. Their conclusion may be premature for two reasons. First, their use of measures of the slope of reaction time to various stimuli, while theoretically justified, may not provide an optimal approach to the discovery of the cognitive correlates of ability. Recall that measures of the variability of choice reaction times to stimuli tend to be more predictive of general intelligence than the slope of reaction times for choice reaction times for different set sizes of stimuli. In short, Keating *et al.* (1985) may

TABLE 4.4 Intercorrelations of Processing Parameters and Ability Measures, Eighth Graders and Adults[a,b]

	Facial rotation (FR)	Standard letter rotation (SLR)	Oriented letter rotation (OLR)	Letter matching (LM)	Delayed letter matching (DLM)	Semantic processing (SP)	Verbal ability (VA)	Spatial ability (SA)
FR	—	.52***	.15	.22	−.04	−.06	−.22	.12
SLR	.18	—	.42**	.11	.18	.12	−.24	−.06
OLR	.02	.30*	—	.03	.16	.02	−.07	−.09
LM	.11	−.17	−.12	—	.26*	.23	−.14	.03
DLM	−.13	.08	.03	−.20	—	.21	.13	.03
SP	.26*	.68***	.20	−.08	−.12	—	−.39**	−.07
VA	−.32*	.02	−.11	−.09	.01	−.08	—	.26*
SA	−.16	−.43**	−.23	.17	−.22	−.38**	.41**	—

[a]Based on Keating, List & Merriman (1985).
[b]Adults' data are below the diagonal; eighth graders', above.
*p < .05.
**p < .01.
***p < .001.

not have used the best measures of elementary cognitive processes in their study.

Second, the difficulty may in part be attributable to the search for convergent and divergent validity correlations in the first place. That is, the relationship between elementary parameters of information processing and intelligence may not be content specific. The parameters may relate to more fundamental processes that correlate with general intelligence rather than the difference between verbal and spatial ability. Keating *et al.* assumed that the search for the cognitive correlates of general intelligence as opposed to spatial and verbal ability is theoretically uninformative. They asserted, ". . . a high correlation of total RT with Raven's matrices' scores demonstrates that they share common variance, but the psychological source is not illuminated by the correlation" (Keating *et al.*, 1985, p. 151). This notion is based on the theoretical assumption that the cognitive correlates of psychometric ability measures exist at the level of specific abilities. If there are cognitive correlates of general intelligence it is entirely possible that experimental tasks that measure reaction times to spatial or verbal stimuli would not demonstrate the pattern of correlations with verbal and spatial ability measures that are required to provide evidence for discriminant and convergent validity demonstrations. The research reviewed in Chapter 3 was undertaken under the assumption that there are cognitive correlates of general intelligence and that these should generalize to measures of verbal and spatial ability in so far as those measures relate to *g*. Thus the data obtained by Keating *et al.* may indicate more about inadequacies of their theoretical assumptions than it does about the general value of research for cognitive correlates of general intelligence.

McGue & Bouchard (1989) related performance on several information-processing tasks to a battery of measures of mental abilities that permitted them to derive separate verbal, spatial, perceptual speed and accuracy, and visual memory factors. They used three experimental tasks—the Posner measure of reaction time for name and physical identity judgments of letters, the Sternberg measure of the time taken to identify a probe digit as belonging to a previously presented set of digits, and the Shephard–Metzler measure of the time to judge visually rotated spatial images as being the same or different from a comparison figure. For each of their experimental measures they derived slope and intercept measures. Table 4.5 presents the correlations they obtained between performance on their experimental tasks and performance on the psychometric tests. Table 4.5 indicates that there is some evidence for discriminant and convergent validity in these data. Parameters derived from the Posner measure of lexical processing of information relate more highly to scores on the verbal tests and the verbal factor than they do to scores on other factors. Similarly, performance on the Shepard–Metzler spatial rotation

TABLE 4.5 **Correlations between Ability Clusters and Information-Processing Measures**[a,b]

Information-processing measure	VR		SP		PSA		VM	
	$\bar{X}$[c]	F[c]	$\bar{X}$	F	$\bar{X}$	F	$\bar{X}$	F
Posner identity								
NI + PI	−.39*	−.49*	−.21*	.10	−.31*	−.36*	−.17*	−.17*
NI − PI	−.13*	−.27*	.07	.13	.00	.06	−.06	−.07
Sternberg probe								
+ Intercept	−.21*	−.23*	−.16*	−.11	−.19*	−.20*	−.07	−.10
− Intercept	−.24*	−.27*	−.16*	−.10	−.21	−.24	−.11	−.13
+ Slope	−.16*	−.22*	−.04	−.01	−.03	−.04	−.03	−.04
Slope	−.13*	−.15*	−.05	−.02	−.10	−.09	.01	−.03
Shepard-Metzlar rotation								
Intercept	−.19*	−.20*	−.29*	−.34*	−.30*	−.17*	−.12*	−.10
Slope	.04	.13	−.13	−.19	−.22	−.19	−.05	−.06

[a]Based on McGue & Bouchard (1989).
[b]VR, verbal reasoning; SP, spatial ability; PSA, perceptual speed and accuracy; VM, visual memory.
[c]$\bar{X}$ = mean score on the subtests that define each factor; F = factor score.
*$p < .05$.

task is more highly related to performance on the spatial psychometric tests than to performance on the other psychometric composites. In addition, these data indicate that the predictability of specific parameters of information processing is not completely content specific. Note that measures that are good predictors of performance on one of the psychometric composites tend to be predictive of performance on the other psychometric composites. For example, the NI + PI scores from the Posner measure is significantly correlated with mean performance on each of the other three psychometric composites. And, the intercept measure of speed of rotation derived from the Shepard–Metzler task is significantly related to verbal ability as well as to the spatial ability and perceptual speed and accuracy composites. These data provide evidence for the pervasive nature of the general ability factor. Specific parameters of information processing that are assumed, on theoretical grounds, to be measures of a content-specific processing parameter are predictive of psychometric performance in other content areas. The data presented in Table 4.5 also indicate that intercept measures are almost invariably more predictive of performance on psychometric indices than slope measures. Note that the best predictor of performance on the psychometric tasks is the NI + PI parameter derived from the Posner task. The parameter that has the clearest theoretical definition, NI − PI, is invariably less predictive of performance on psychometric tests. Thus it is not speed of access to lexical processes that provides an optimal measure of either verbal or general intelligence, but the average speed of judgments involving both

TABLE 4.6   Genetic Model Analysis for Information-Processing Measures[a]

Measure	Monozygotic apart (r)	Dyzygotic apart (r)	h^2
Posner identity			
NI + PI	.46	−.11	.43
NI − PI	.05	.20	.10
Sternberg probe			
+Intercept	.55	.06	.53
−Intercept	.57	.28	.57
+Slope	.06	−.12	—
−Slope	.19	−.07	.17
Shepard-Metzlar rotation			
Intercept	.40	.46	.39
Slope	.42	.19	.39

[a]Based on McGue & Bouchard (1989).

physical and name identities. So, too, the intercept measures derived from the Shepard–Metzler and Sternberg tasks are more predictive of specific and general intelligence than the slope measures that are assumed to measure theoretically defined parameters of speed of rotation and speed of serial processing of digits. These data help to explain the disappointing results obtained by Keating & Bobbitt (1978). Slope measures in reaction-time studies as well as those derived from other information-processing tasks are simply less predictive of psychometric intelligence than intercept measures or measures of the average speed of processing information.

The McGue and Bouchard data were derived from a sample of separated monozygotic and dyzygotic twins. We shall examine twin studies of the heritability of intelligence in Chapter 5. For our purposes here, it should be noted that McGue and Bouchard were able to derive measures of the heritability of the several measures included in Table 4.5. Table 4.6 presents the results of this analysis. These data indicate that heritability estimates for these data are higher for intercept than for slope measures on both the Posner and the Sternberg tasks. The heritability estimates for slope and intercept measures do not differ on the Shepard–Metzlar task. These data provide a possible theoretical explanation of the difference in predictability of slope and intercept measures. Parameters of information tasks that exhibit high heritability are likely to be predictive of psychometric indices of intelligence. These data should be accepted cautiously. They are based on the results of a single investigation, and the sample of dyzygotic twins reared apart is small. Nevertheless they are provocative and they suggest that speed of information processing may be a heritable characteristic of individuals that is related to performance on psychometric tests of ability.

THE COMPLEX CORRELATES OF INTELLIGENCE

What makes a task a good measure of intelligence? Spearman assumed that the eduction of correlates and relations was the defining property of good measures of intelligence. We shall consider two contemporary experimentally based characterizations of such tasks.

Dual-Task Paradigms

Stankov (1983; 1987; 1988) argued that attentional processes are highly related to intelligence and that tasks that use a dual-task paradigm in which individuals are required to work on two different problems at the same time tend to increase the g loading of performance on the task relative to performance of the task in isolation. Roberts, Beh, & Stankov (1988) studied performance in a dual-task paradigm that was designed as an analog of Jensen's reaction-time experiment. They studied performance in a card sorting task in which subjects were required to sort decks of playing cards by color, suite, or number range and suite. These categories constituted sorts into 2, 4, or 8 different categories. The task was assumed to pose information-processing requirements that were analagous to those used by Jensen in his choice reaction-time experiments. Card sorting without information processing was also measured in a task in which subjects were required to sort the cards into two piles alternately without regard to the content of the card. This task is analagous to a simple reaction-time task. A competing task was also introduced in which subjects had to indicate the semantic category of words that were presented orally. Measures of performance on these tasks were correlated with scores on the Raven test.

Table 4.7 presents the correlation between measures of the time taken to sort cards under competing and noncompeting task conditions and performance on the Raven. The data presented in Table 4.7 indicate that performance on the card sorting task is correlated with scores on tests of

TABLE 4.7   Correlations between Card Sorting Performance and Ravens Test Scores[a]

Card sorting task	Single (S)	Competing (C)	C − S
Alternative piles	.03	−.07	−.23
Color (2 categories)	−.21	−.65	−.54
Suite (4 categories)	−.49	−.71	−.62
Number (8 categories)	−.30	−.59	−.75
Sum of reaction times	−.47	−.76	

[a]Based on Roberts, Beh, & Stankov (1988).

intelligence. The correlations appear to be significantly higher than those usually obtained with the Jensen apparatus. Since the sample size was small ($N = 48$) it is difficult to tell whether or not the time taken to sort cards into various categories is more highly correlated with intelligence than choice reaction time to lights. What is perhaps of greater interest in these data is the effect of the introduction of a competing task. The correlations between card sorting times and performance on the Raven test exhibit large increases for card sorting performance under dual-task conditions. The correlation of .76 for the sum of card sorting time and intelligence indicates a very substantial relationship between a relatively simple performance task and intelligence. In addition, the increments in card sorting times under dual-task conditions are also substantially related to performance on the Raven. Intelligence is inversely related to the increment in performance times associated with performing a simple task under dual-task conditions.

The results obtained by Roberts *et al.* should be replicated and the boundary conditions of the phenomena they studied need to be established. Matthews and Dorn found that the dual-task paradigm they used did not add to the predictability for intelligence of a reaction-time task. What may be critical is the use of a dual-task paradigm that involves relatively complex processing skills. The subjects in the Roberts *et al.* study were required to classify words. This task involves higher-order cognitive processes and apparently changed the character of the card sorting task sufficiently to increase its correlation with intelligence. Matthews and Dorn required their subjects to memorize a set of digits and perform a choice reaction-time task while recalling the digits in order to respond to a question about the digits after completing the reaction-time response. In contrast to the results reported by Roberts *et al.*, they found that the dual-task condition was less predictive of intelligence than the reaction-time measure obtained under single-task conditions. The difference in the outcome of these studies may be attributable to the additional cognitive processing demands associated with the dual task used by Roberts *et al.* In their task the subject had to encode semantic information and classify it. By contrast, the dual task used by Matthews and Dorn required the subject to memorize a set of digits but not to process or transform those digits in any way. This suggests that dual tasks in which the secondary or interfering task involves a transformation or categorization of stimulus information will add to the predictability for intelligence of the primary task. Simply performing a primary task while holding untransformed information in memory does not add to the predictability for intelligence of primary tasks.

The results obtained by Roberts *et al.* may also be related to the results obtained by Larson and Saccuzzo with the mental counters task. This task, which is very predictive of intelligence test scores, also measures attention. The subject is required to memorize the results of previous arithmetic calculations while encoding rapidly presented new information that must be transformed from a visual to a numerical code, and then the arithmetic results of the calculation must be added to the previous arithmetic results. Thus the results of previous calculations must be retained while encoding and transforming new inputs. This task would appear to have dual-task components.

A number of issues remain unresolved in this brief review of studies using dual-task paradigms. What is needed is a more precise specification of the properties of primary and secondary tasks that will increase the predictability of primary tasks for intelligence. The data reviewed here suggest that the secondary task must require some transformation of information and must make demands on the attentional resources of an individual. This hypothesis leaves undefined the characteristics of the primary task that is used to predict intelligence in a dual-task paradigm. It is not known if a primary task that involves relatively little transformation of stimulus information would exhibit increased predictability for IQ in a dual-task paradigm. The primary task used by Roberts et al. was analagous to a choice reaction-time task with some initial processing of stimulus information. Would a simple reaction-time task exhibit increased predictability of intelligence if it were paired with the oral classification task for words used by Roberts et al.? This and related questions remain to be investigated.

Sternberg's Theory of Nonentrenchment

R. J. Sternberg (1981; 1982; 1985; Sternberg & Gastel, 1989a,b; Tetewsky & Sternberg, 1986; see also, Raaheim, 1974) proposed that intelligence is best assessed by tasks that cannot be solved in a habitual manner. The hallmark of intelligence is the ability to solve novel intellectual problems. Sternberg indicated that much of the experimental study of the correlates of intelligence used tasks that he describes as entrenched— that is, that measure the ability to solve problems using algorithms that are well practiced. And, he suggested that more substantial correlations between experimental tasks and general intelligence could be obtained by the use of tasks that are relatively novel or nonentrenched.

Sternberg & Gastel (1989a) varied the degree of nonentrenchment of intellectual tasks by presenting undergraduates with a statement verification task in which the subjects were presented with a counterfactual or a familiar presupposition that was relevant or irrelevant to a series of statements that subjects were required to state were true or false. Table 4.8 presents a representative sample of the statements that the subjects were required to verify. They assumed that the verification of statements preceded by counterfactual presuppositions was a more nonentrenched task than the verification of statements preceded by familiar presuppositions and, consequently, they assumed that performance on the former tasks

TABLE 4.8   **Representative Verification Statements**[a]

	Keyed response	
	Familiar presupposition	Counterfactual presupposition
1. Familiar presupposition: Trees need water. Counterfactual presupposition: Trees eat people.		
a. Librarians eat maple trees.	False	False
b. Cherry picking requires great bravery.	False	True
c. Trees are carnivorous.	False	True
d. Trees have branches.	True	True
e. Trees are harmless.	True	False
f. Lumberjacks chop down trees.	True	True
2. Familiar presupposition: Cats are furry. Counterfactual presupposition: Cats are strongly magnetized.		
a. Cats "stick" to refrigerators.	False	True
b. Cats attract paperclips.	False	True
c. Cats have sharp claws.	True	True
d. Cats eat iron filings.	False	False
e. Cats like eating fish.	True	True
f. Catnip is metallic.	False	False
g. Suspended cats tend to face east–west.	False	False
3. Familiar presupposition: Kites fly in the air. Counterfactual presupposition: Kites run on gasoline.		
a. Kites emit exhaust.		
b. Kites need fuel.	False	True
c. Kites have tails.	False	True
d. Kites need wind.	True	True
e. Kites have four wheels.	True	False
f. Kites are faster than airplanes.	False	False
g. Kites can explode when they crash.	False	False
h. Kites are sold in stores.	False	True
	True	True

[a]Based on Sternberg & Gastel (1989a).

would be more predictive of general intelligence than performance on the latter task. They also obtained scores on three measures of fluid ability including the Cattell Culture-Fair test. Table 4.9 presents the correlations between the decision time required to verify different classes of statements and performance on the psychometric tests.

An examination of the correlations reported in Table 4.9 indicates that there is little or no difference in the magnitude of the correlation between ability measures and decision times for novel and non-novel items. And, on the most general measure of fluid ability—the Cattell Culture-Fair test—the correlations are identical. Sternberg and Gastel also obtained a difference score by subtracting the time required to verify statements

TABLE 4.9   Correlations between Decision Times for
Different Kinds of Statements and Fluid Ability Measures[a]

| | Ability measures | | |
	Letter sets	CTMM syllogisms	Cattell Culture-fair
Non-novel	−.46	−.66	−.32
Novel	−.52	−.68	−.32

[a]Based on Sternberg & Gastel (1989a).

with familiar presuppositions from the time required to verify statements
with nonfamiliar presuppositions. These difference scores tended to be
positive, reflecting the added difficulty of verifying statements when exposed to unfamiliar presuppositions. They found that the correlations
between these difference scores and the three psychometric measures—
Letter Sets, Syllogisms, and the Cattell test—were −.34, −.38, and −.15,
respectively. The negative correlations indicate that the incremental time
required to solve novel items is inversely related to performance on tests
of fluid ability. Sternberg and Gastel attributed the difference in correlations between the Cattell test and the other two tests to differences in the
degree to which these three measures shared content with the statement
verification task. The correlation with the Cattell test, which was least
similar in content to the statement verification task, is more likely to be
attributable to an overlap in process than the correlations between the
statement verification task and the other two measures of fluid ability.
    Sternberg and Gastel's data provide relatively little support for the hy-
pothesis that intelligence is best measured by nonentrenched intellectual
tasks. Their data actually provide two different tests of this hypothesis.
First, if nonentrenched measures are more predictive of general intellectual ability than entrenched measures, then the novel tasks should be
more predictive of fluid intelligence than the non-novel verification
tasks. The data presented in Table 4.9 indicate that the correlations between fluid ability and performance on these two types of statement
verification tasks are virtually identical. Second, the difference scores
between performance on these two types of tasks should provide an index
of the ability to respond to nonentrenched tasks and should be predictive
of performance on tests of general intelligence. Sternberg and Gastel do
report that these correlations are negative, as would be expected on their
hypothesis. It should be noted, however, that the correlation between the
difference scores and the Cattell test was not significantly different from
zero. This correlation provides the best test of the hypothesis since the
correlation is least contaminated with content similarity. This correlation should provide the best measure of the extent to which the ability to
deal with novelty is predictive of a nondomain-specific general intellec-

tual ability. (For additional analyses and critique of this research see Humphreys, 1990; Larson, 1990; R. J. Sternberg, 1990.)

Sternberg & Gastel (1989b) obtained measures of performance in a variety of inductive reasoning tasks that varied in entrenchment. They used three types of induction problems—analogies, classifications, and series completions. The problems were either uncued or precued by a relevant or irrelevant statement or cue that preceded the problem. The precue was either familiar or novel. The novel precued items were all counterfactual. Sternberg and Gastel obtained correlations between performance on these tasks and performance on several measures of fluid ability that permitted them to obtain a fluid ability factor. The data obtained from the various induction tasks could be used to derive several measures of a subject's ability to cope with nonentrenched tasks. Difference scores between precued and uncued performance should provide one such measure on the assumption that subjects who were college students would be more familiar with solving induction problems that were uncued. Similarly, induction problems that are cued with novel, counterfactual statements are less entrenched than induction problems that are precued with familiar factual statements, and the difference between these measures should provide an index of the ability to cope with nonentrenched problems. Sternberg and Gastel do not report the correlations between these measures and performance on their psychometric measures of fluid ability. They do report correlations between performance on psychometric tests and performance on cued and uncued induction problems. The relevant correlations are presented in Table 4.10. An examination of the correlations presented in Table 4.10 indicates that the correlations between performance on cued induction tasks and fluid ability are higher than the correlations between performance on uncued induction tasks and fluid ability. The differences between the correlations are clearly not significant, and the difference in predictability of fluid intelligence between relatively nonentrenched tasks and relatively entrenched tasks is trivial. And, Sternberg and Gastel do not provide additional more refined tests of their hypotheses based on the novelty data and on several possible dif-

TABLE 4.10   Correlations between Response Times (RTs) and Error Rates (ERs) with Fluid Ability Measures[a]

	Uncued		Cued	
	RT	ER	RT	ER
DAT verbal reasoning	−.19	−.45	−.23	−.57
Cattell abstract reasoning	−.32	−.02	−.41	−.08
Insight problems	−.20	−.36	−.26	−.39
Reasoning factor	−.31	−.36	−.39	−.45

[a]Based on Sternberg & Gastel (1989b).

ference scores or other measures that could be derived from their data on inductive reasoning.

This brief review of the data presented by Sternberg and Gastel in support of the assertion that nonentrenched measures are better predictors of general intelligence than entrenched measures indicates that their studies do not provide clear support for their theory. Measures of performance on nonentrenched tasks are predictive of performance on tests of general intelligence. They are not conspicuously more predictive than measures of performance on relatively nonentrenched tasks.

COMPONENTIAL ANALYSIS

Componential analysis as a method for studying individual differences in intelligence was first presented in a relatively complete form by Sternberg in 1977 (see also R. J. Sternberg, 1980). Sternberg began by studying performance on analogy tasks that were similar to those used in tests of fluid ability. Performance on these tasks was assumed to be highly related to performance on tests of intelligence since they were assumed to belong to the domain of tests of intelligence. Componential analysis begins with a relatively complete theory of the task. The theory specifies the components or elements of successful task performance and provides rules for the way in which these elementary components combine to determine task performance. In performing a componential analysis of a task, it is necessary to provide estimates of parametric values for each of the elementary processes or components that are theoretically assumed to determine performance on the task. Research in the cognitive correlates tradition usually is based on some model of the cognitive processes that determines performance on the task, but no attempt is made to test the full model in a single investigation. A simple task is selected that is assumed to measure, in isolation, one component of performance on some measure of intellectual ability. By contrast, componential analysis frequently involves a test of a complete theory of performance on a task in a single investigation.

Componential analysis may be thought of as the basis for a process-oriented theory of intelligence. Assume that a componential analysis of some intellectual task has been successfully tested. The theory of the task may specify certain components that are assumed to be general. For example, R. J. Sternberg (1977) assumed that the encoding of the terms in an analogy problem was a general component that was necessary to solve the problem. Encoding of stimulus meanings is clearly an intellectual skill that is required to solve many intellectual problems. In principle, it should be possible to obtain a measure of encoding skill from the componential analysis of performance on an analogies problem that will relate to encoding performance on other intellectual tasks. To the extent that it is possible to specify a sufficiently general set of cognitive components, it ought to be possible to explain performance on different intellectual tasks by developing componential analyses of task performance. Estimates of component abilities should generalize to new tasks. Thus it should be possible to predict a person's performance on a new task from a compilation of component scores derived from other tasks. Components may be construed as the elements of intelligence. It should be obvious that this research program bears more than a superficial similarity to Thurstone's theory of multiple intelligences. Thurstone assumed that it is possible to decompose task performance into the several different independent factors that were assumed to be involved in a particular intellectual task. And, knowledge of a person's score on a particular factor could be used to predict his or her performance on any task. Where componential analysis differs most fundamentally from Thurstone's approach is in the use of a specific theory of task performance and in the use of experimental procedures to test that theory. Thurstone assumed that the factors that determined performance on a task could be determined by a factor analysis of the matrix of correlations among ability tests. By contrast, componential analysis is based on an explicit and testable theory of task performance.

In order to explain componential analysis I shall present in some detail a study by Sternberg & Gardner (1983, Experiment 3) that represents one of the more developed applications of this approach to the study of intelligence. Sternberg and Gardner presented 18 Yale undergraduates with three different kinds of induction problems—analogies, series completions, and classification problems. Each of these problems was further subdivided into three different contents—verbal problems, schematic pictures, and geometric forms. Table 4.11 presents examples of the three classes of verbal induction problems used in this experiment. An example of a geometric classification problem that is structurally analagous to a verbal classification problem is presented in Fig. 4.4. These problems are relatively easy for Yale undergraduates and error rates are low. Performance on these tasks is measured in terms of the time taken to solve these problems.

Sternberg and Gardner developed an explicit theory of task performance for each of the three classes of induction problems that they investigated. They assumed that the time taken to solve an analogy problem was the sum of the time taken to execute each of several components used in the solution. The components are the following: (1) encoding, a component that involves the time taken to classify or encode the first two terms of the analogy, (2) inference, the act of inferring the relationship between the first two terms of the analogy; and (3) application, which is the application of the relationship between the A and the B term to the C term and a hypothetical ideal completion term that is assumed to be an extrapolation of the A–B relationship to the C term. The subject must then encode each of the two D terms provided that complete the analogy, and compare

TABLE 4.11 Examples of Verbal Induction Problems[a,b]

Analogies
    Mouth:Taste::Eye: (a) Help, (b) See
    Shell:Nut::Peel: (a) Orange, (b) House
    Tree:Forest::Soldier: (a) General, (b) Army

Series completions
    Second:Minute:Hour:
        Decade: (a) Time, (b) Century
    Rarely:Sometimes:Often:
        Many: (a) Frequently, (b) Most
    Baby Carriage:Tricycle:Bicycle:
        Measles: (a) Illness, (b) Acne

Classifications
    (a) Dictionary, Encyclopedia   (b) Lemonade, Rum
                            Gasoline
    (a) Furnace, Stove   (b) Refrigerator, Air Conditioner
                            Oven
    (a) Germany, France   (b) Vietnam, Korea
                            Italy

[a]Based on Sternberg & Gardner (1983).
[b]In the analogies, subjects had to choose the answer option that was related to the third analogy term in the same way that the second term was related to the first. The correct answer options are b, a, b. In the series completions, subjects had to formulate a rule that carried over from the first term to the second and the second to the third and then use this rule to carry over from the fourth term to one of the two answer options. The correct answer options are b, b, b. In the classifications, subjects had to chose as the correct answer option the pair of words with which the word at the bottom fits best. The correct answer options are b, a, a. The format of the items that the subjects actually saw (in terms of physical placement of terms on the card) was the same as that for the schematic picture and geometric items.

each of the possible D answers to the ideal. If one is identical to the ideal solution a response could be executed. If it is not, the subject is required to justify one answer as being closer to the ideal than the other. For verbal and geometric analogies the subject is assumed to perform these components in serial order. Each component is assumed to be executed in real time. The time taken to solve a particular item is the sum of the time required to execute each of the component processes.

Sternberg and Gardner were able to develop measures of the speed of executing components that entered into problem solutions. Several procedures may be used to develop parametric estimates of components in componential analysis. In the Sternberg and Gardner experiment the method of precueing was used in which various elements of the problem are cued, leaving a reduced task to be solved. For example, the first two terms of an analogy problem may be presented and the subject may be given a sufficient period of time to encode the terms and infer the relation between them before the second two terms of the analogy are presented. In addition, independent subjects rated several elements of the task with respect to difficulty. The degree of the relationship between the terms to

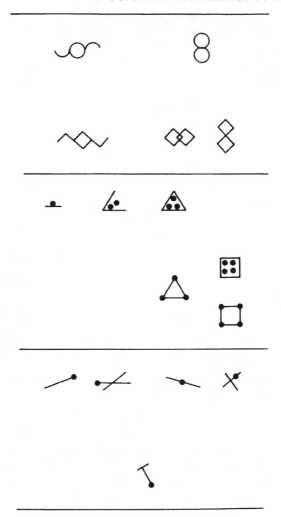

FIGURE 4.4   Geometric induction problems. (Based on Sternberg & Gardner, 1983.)

be encoded in an analogy was rated as well as the distance between a particular solution and the ideal solution. These ratings provide a basis for ordering the problems in terms of the difficulty or time required to execute the particular component.

The model of the task could be tested by comparing the expected time to execute all of the components and the obtained times for each item averaged over individuals. The multiple correlation between expected and obtained solution times for the nine classes of problems investigated ranged from .70 to .97, indicating that the models developed for these tasks were predictive. It was also the case that the models were not perfectly predictive and that there is significant residual variance.

Sternberg and Gardner suggested that models of serial execution of component processes for these tasks may be an oversimplification. In any case there is good evidence that the specific models developed to explain performance on these tasks are valid approximations of the factors that determine performance.

Sternberg and Gardner also demonstrated that performance on these tasks was predictive of performance on psychometric tests. They derived a reasoning factor from a battery of psychometric tests that may be construed as a measure of general intelligence or, perhaps equivalently, of fluid ability. Performance on the nine classes of induction problems correlated with the intelligence factor scores between $-.47$ and $-.72$. The negative correlations indicate that the time to solve these problems is inversely related to intelligence. It is interesting to note that performance on these tasks was not related to a psychometric factor that was defined as a measure of perceptual speed. Thus, rapid performance of component processes in induction tasks is not a measure of speed *per se* but is more optimally construed as the time required to execute complex cognitive processes. Are individual component scores predictive of intelligence? There are individual component scores for each of several components obtained for each of the nine classes of problems investigated by Sternberg and Gardner. The correlations of these component scores with general intelligence are not presented by Sternberg and Gardner. What is presented are the correlations for various collapsed component scores and intelligence. Table 4.12 presents these data. The correlations reported vary considerably. The correlations collapsed over contents provide information about the separate component scores obtained by summing over the different contents in each of the three tasks. An examination of the relationship between component scores for a particular induction problem and intelligence indicates that the most consistent relationships are obtained between the components of reasoning and comparison and intelligence. The reasoning component score is a combined parameter representing the time required to execute the inference of the relationship between elements in the problem and the mapping of that relationship to other terms and extrapolating the relationship to an ideal. Comparison involves a comparison between the ideal and the offered solutions to the induction problem. These data do indicate that at least some components do relate to performance on tests of intelligence. These correlations are based on component scores that are averaged over different tasks. They beg the question of whether individual component scores would relate to intelligence.

Perhaps the most critical test for the componential analysis presented by Sternberg and Gardner concerns the extent to which the component processes that are identified in the different kinds of tasks are related to each other. An analysis of the correlations of component scores across tasks is required in order to ascertain whether the theoretical identity of

TABLE 4.12   Correlation of Component Scores with Factor Scores[a]

Component score	Factor score	
	Reasoning	Perceptual speed
Collapsed over tasks and contents		
Encoding	−.37[b]	−.07
Reasoning	−.79***	.08
Comparison	−.75***	.07
Justifcation	−.48*	−.05
Collapsed over tasks		
Schematic picture		
Encoding	.46	−.03
Reasoning	−.70***	.11
Comparison	−.64**	−.19
Verbal		
Encoding	−.02	−.06
Reasoning	−.61**	.00
Comparison	−.66**	.24
Justification	−.29	−.04
Geometric		
Encoding	−.25	−.11
Reasoning	−.67**	.21
Comparison	−.65**	−.12
Justification	−.37	−.06
Collapsed over contents		
Analogies		
Encoding	.01	−.35
Reasoning	−.70**	.17
Comparison	−.61*	−.12
Justification	−.58*	.07
Series completions		
Encoding	−.51*	.20
Reasoning	−.50*	.01
Comparison	−.66**	.18
Justification	−.19	−.10
Classifications		
Encoding	−.16	−.10
Reasoning	−.64**	.02
Comparison	−.67**	.04
Justification	—	—

[a]Based on Sternberg & Gardner (1983).
[b]Negative correlations indicated faster times are associated with high paper-and-pencil test scores.
*p < .05, two-tailed; **p < .01, two-tailed; ***p < .001, two-tailed.

components extends beyond the fact that some have the same name. Components with the same name that are presumed to measure the same processes should correlate more highly with each other than components with different names. The full correlation matrix was not presented. Sternberg and Gardner reported that the average correlation across tasks for parameters with the same name collapsed over contents was .32. This correlation should be compared with the comparable correlation for components with different names, which was .24. The correlation of .32 is disappointing. The correlation is obviously subject to restrictions in range of talent attributable to the use of undergraduates from a highly selective college. It should be noted that a correction for restriction in range of talent should also be applied to the average correlation for components with different names and this would have the effect of increasing that correlation. The evidence for the identification of separate components that determine performance on these tasks is determined not only by the average correlation of components with the same name but also by the difference between those correlations and correlations of components with different names, and that difference is small.

Alderton, Goldman, & Pellegrino (1985) performed a componential analysis of errors rather than latency on two verbal inductive reasoning problems—analogies and classifications. They presented subjects with subsets of analogies and classification problems in which part of the information necessary to solve the problem was presented. For example, they presented subjects with the first two terms of the analogy. The subjects were asked to infer the correct solution of the problems presented on the basis of partially presented information. The subjects were required to infer the rule governing the relationship between the terms of the problem that were presented or to state the answer that they assumed would be correct. The subject's verbal reports were used to obtain measures of several different components assumed to be involved in correct solution of these problems. These included the following components: accuracy of production, measured by the probability of generating the correct completion term; inference accuracy, the probability of correctly inferring the rule defining the relationship among the elements; recognition, the probability of generating a correct answer for items on which an incorrect completion had been provided; and distraction, the probability of generating an incorrect answer for an item for which a correct completion had been provided. The probability of correct solution of an item was assumed to be determined by the combined relationship among these components.

Alderton *et al.* (1985) found that these component scores could be used to predict performance on the two induction problems. Component scores accounted for 88 and 91.5% of the variance in the probabilities of solving different analogies and classification items, respectively. Component scores are not only predictive of item difficulties, but they may be used to predict variations in performance for each subject in the experiment. Three models of performance were tested on an individual basis: model 1, that assumed that performance was determined solely by the ability to infer the appropriate relationship or completion term plus a guessing factor; model 2, which adds to the equation a recognition factor;

TABLE 4.13 Proportion of Subjects' Best Fit by Each Model
of Forced-Choice Accuracy[a]

Problem	Model 1	Model 2	Model 3
Analogy problems			
All subjects ($N = 80$)	.08	.80	.13
Upper quartile ($N = 20$)	.00	.95	.05
Lower quartile ($N = 20$)	.25	.50	.25
Classification problems			
All subjects ($N = 80$)	.16	.18	.67
Upper quartile ($N = 20$)	.10	.40	.50
Lower quartile ($N = 20$)	.15	.05	.80

[a]Based on Alderton, Goldman, & Pellegrino (1985).

and model 3, which adds to model 2 a distraction factor. Table 4.13 presents the proportion of subjects whose performance was optimally fit with each of the three models of solution. An examination of the data presented in Table 4.13 indicates that the best-fitting model was different for each of the induction problems. Model 3, which includes a distraction parameter, was the optimal predictor for the largest proportion of subjects for classification problems. The distraction parameter was of less importance in analogy problems and was not needed to predict performance for a majority of subjects. The difference in the role of distraction may be explained by a consideration of the role of the initial two terms in an analogy problem as opposed to the role of initial terms in classification problems. The initial term in an analogy problem may constrain the set of acceptable alternative correct answers more rigorously than the initial terms constrain classification problems. Thus subjects who correctly infer the relationship between the initial terms of an analogy problem are rarely distracted by a consideration of alternative incorrect answers to the problem. If initial items in a classification problem are less likely to constrain the acceptable answer to the question, it is possible that a subject who has inferred the correct answer to the problem may be distracted by alternative incorrect solutions to the problem. Table 4.13 also indicates that the best-fitting model varies as a function of ability level. The distraction component is less likely to be important for subjects in the upper quartile of verbal ability than for subjects in the lower quartile of verbal ability.

The multitrait–multimethod matrix for these data indicating the average correlations between the same and different components within problem type and across problem type is presented in Table 4.14. The data indicate that all of the components are positively related to each other. Components from different problems with different names have an average correlation of .42. Two values are presented for the average correlation across tasks for components with the same names, .57 and .51. The former value excludes the application component on the grounds that it

TABLE 4.14 Intercorrelations of Process–Outcome Measures for Analogy and Classification Problems[a]

Process–outcome measure	Mean r
Within analogy, different label[b]	.45
Within classification, different label	.37
Analogy with classification, different label	.42
Analogy with classification, same label[c]	.57 (.51)
Analogy production with classification production	.66
Analogy independence with classification inference	.53
Analogy recognition with classification recognition	.53
Analogy application with classification application	.32

[a]Based on Alderton, Goldman & Pellegrino (1985).
[b]Excludes Distraction.
[c]Correlation in parenthesis includes application.

plays a different role in each of the two tasks. The average correlations including the distraction parameter are not presented. The correlation across tasks for distraction was close to zero. If all of the components assumed to determine performance on these two tasks were included in the average correlation for components with the same name, it is apparent that this correlation would be virtually identical with the average correlation across tasks for components with different names. If the average correlation is computed for the three components that are assumed to operate in a comparable way for both classes of problems, then the correlation for components with the same name is larger than the correlation between components with different names.

The Sternberg and Gardner study and the Alderton *et al.* studies provide a basis for a general discussion of the contributions of componential analysis to an understanding of individual differences in intelligence. Componential analysis represents a genuine advance over traditional psychometric methods of understanding intelligence. The method provides insights into the processes involved in the solution of an intellectual task. These insights are obtained in several different ways. Explicit models of the components involved in the solution of a problem are developed and theories of the way in which these components combine to determine performance on a task are tested. In Sternberg's early research it was not always possible to empirically distinguish between models of the solution of analogies. For example, one can assume that an analogy solution is self-terminating or exhaustive. In the former case, all of the possible correct alternatives are not evaluated with respect to an ideal solution. The evaluation process is terminated when an acceptable solution is found. In the latter case, each of the possible solutions to an analogy is evaluated. Theories of the way in which individuals solve various problems that differ in other respects have been tested. For example, component processes may be executed in a serial fixed order or there may be backtracking and a return to an evaluation of other relationships. Successful attempts have been made to distinguish between different theories of the process of solution of a problem, and the method of componential analysis can be used to distinguish among theoretical models with respect to the extent to which they provide an optimal fit to obtained data. Thus the method permits testing of the adequacy of different process theories.

The ability to test different theoretical models can be extended to the individual subject. Note that Alderton *et al.* indicated that there was a relationship between a person's general verbal ability and the best-fitting model of performance on a task. Perhaps the most dramatic evidence for the ability of componential analysis to distinguish between different processes of solution for different subjects is found in a componential analysis of deductive reasoning reported by Sternberg & Weil (1980). They tested different componential analyses of performance in a deductive reasoning task. They presented deductive reasoning problems to subjects that differed on several dimensions. A typical problem they used was as follows: "John is taller than Bill; Bill is taller than Pete. Who is tallest? John, Bill, Pete." The problems differed on such dimensions as whether the first, second, or question term was marked or unmarked. A marked term is the negative form of a dimension (e.g., shorter, slower). They also differed with respect to whether the premises were stated in the affirmative or negative form and whether the correct answer to the question was found in the initial or second premise. Different models of the solution process for these tasks were tested. Spatial models assume that the solution to problems of this type involves the representation of the problem to be solved as a spatial array. Linguistic models assume that the information in the premises is coded in terms of deep structural representations of the meanings of the assertions. R. J. Sternberg (1980) believed that most subjects use a mixed model that relies on both verbal and spatial representations of the information that is presented. These models make somewhat different predictions about the difficulty of the different deductive problems studied by Sternberg and Weil. That is, some problems are easier to array in a spatial form than others and other problems may be easier to represent linguistically.

Sternberg and Weil obtained solution latencies for solving a series of deductive problems and then attempted to predict these latencies using different models of the process of solution for each individual subject. They found that their subjects differed with respect to the model that provided the optimal solution for their latency data. Thus they were able to classify their subjects with respect to whether a linguistic, spatial, or mixed model provided the best fit for each subject's latencies. Sternberg and Weil also administered psychometric measures of verbal and spatial ability to their subjects. The correlations between the overall score on the reasoning problems and scores on verbal and spatial ability measures for

TABLE 4.15 Correlations between Solution Latencies and Verbal and Spatial Ability for Subjects with Different Models of Solution[a]

	Ability	
Model group	Verbal	Spatial
Mixed (N = 82)	−.47	−.27
Linguistic (N = 15)	−.76	−.29
Spatial (N = 15)	−.08	−.60

[a]Based on Sternberg & Weil (1980).

subjects who differed with respect to the model that fit their latency data is presented in Table 4.15. An examination of these indicates that there are dramatic differences in the pattern of correlation with spatial and verbal ability scores for different groups of subjects. If subjects appeared to use a spatial strategy, then their performance on the deductive reasoning problems was predicted by scores on the spatial ability measure but not by scores on the verbal ability measure. The opposite pattern of correlations was obtained for subjects who apparently relied on a verbal strategy to solve these problems. These data indicate that different individuals may solve the same problem in different ways and these differences in methods of solution will lead to different patterns of correlations with abilities. These data also contain the basis for the development of intervention strategies. If a problem may be solved in different ways it would be advisable to suggest to an individual that he or she select a method of problem solution that will use those abilities on which he or she excels. Thus the optimal strategy for solution of a problem may not be invariant over individuals. The Sternberg and Weil study extends the range of individual-difference research from a consideration of variations in the abilities that are assumed to determine performance on a task to a consideration of individual differences in the abilities that are engaged by the same task.

The methods used to evaluate components have been both varied and rigorous. Statistical tests for the presence of each component have been used to indicate that the component is significantly related to performance on the task. The ability of the component to add to the predictability of a multiple correlation has been considered. That is, does knowledge of a score on a component permit one to predict performance over and above that obtained from knowledge of the other components in the prediction equation? The components have been collectively evaluated against the ideal of accounting for all of the variance in the task. That is, is there a difference between the predictability of performance from component scores and actual performance? The deviations between actual and predicted scores provide measures of the extent to which the components provide an exhaustive account of performance. Componential analyses have failed this test but they have come close to providing exhaustive accounts of the predictable variance. Componential analysis has also led to an integration of cognitive psychology and research on individual differences in intelligence. The models that are used to provide an analysis of tasks are generally drawn from cognitive experimental psychology. In addition, experimental variations in item format and problem type can be introduced as a test of the model. Thus experimentally induced variations are used to estimate components. This provides for an unusually intimate integration of experimental psychology and individual-difference psychology.

Componential analysis provides a general approach to the study of individual differences. As we have seen it may be applied to different kinds of problems and it may be used to analyze latency data as well as error data. Despite the impressive achievements of the method there are, I think, several limitations to this approach as a general model of understanding individual differences in intelligence. Although the method is presented as a basis for understanding individual differences in the processes of thought as opposed to the traditional psychometric emphasis on the products of thought, on closer examination the method leaves unanalyzed many of the processes that are fundamental to the solution of a problem. Consider some of the components that we have considered that are involved in the solution of inductive reasoning problems. Sternberg and Gardner reported that the reasoning component based on the time taken to infer the relationship between terms in a problem and to extrapolate that relationship is predictive of performance on psychometric ability measures. Note that the reasoning parameter is a combined parameter that is itself derivative of theoretically independent components in the model. More critically, no theory or explication of the processes that determine individual differences in the speed of execution of these problems is provided. What accounts for these differences? Similarly, Alderton et al. (1985) found that individuals differ in the ability to infer the correct solution of a problem from partial representations of the problem and that this ability is predictive of performance on psychometric tests. What is left unexplained in this analysis is the basis for these individual differences. The componential analyses we have considered do not provide a fine-grained analysis of the processes involved in solution of a problem. Typically, three or four components are found to account for most of the variance in predicting intelligence. On reflection, these components are self-evidently built into the structure of the problems that are being investigated. It is obvious that it is necessary to encode the terms of an analogy problem in order to solve it and to infer the relationship between the terms. While considerable experimental and theoretical ingenuity is required to develop measures of the independent components that are involved in a solution and to test various models of the way in which these components combine, the end result of the analysis leads to the discovery of components whose relevance to task solution is readily apparent. And, the components function as unanalyzed theoretical terms, leaving mysterious the nature of the processes that account for individual differences in the ability to execute various components that are required for a solution to a problem.

Componential analyses fail a second critical test. There is little evidence that the components that have been identified are generalizable beyond the specific tasks that have been used to identify the components. Evidence for the intertask generality of components is quite limited. Recall that Sternberg and Gardner obtained average correlations of .32 and .24 for the components with the same name and with different names obtained from three different induction problems. These data suggest that components with the same name do not refer to the same process in different tasks. This result is particularly disappointing since the tasks that are used to study the generality of components in the Sternberg and Gardner investigation have a number of methodological similarities. They are based on reaction-time measures obtained during the same experimental sessions and they are obtained by aggregating performance on the same three problem contents. Interactions between the ability to execute particular components such as reasoning and comparison for different classes of stimuli that may involve different knowledge bases or differential ability to work with different contents are not present in these studies. If component scores do not exhibit intertask generality in these quite similar contexts it appears highly unlikely that they will exhibit intertask generality for tasks that are substantially different. For example, encoding, a component defined by the speed with which the subject is able to encode terms in the induction problems, appears to be involved in other tasks. It is necessary to encode the stimulus in a choice reaction-time task. Is the speed required to encode the position of a light related to the speed required to encode the terms in an analogy problem? Or, to refer to a related componential analysis of induction problems using error rates rather than response speeds, is the accuracy of inference from the initial terms in an analogy problem related to the speed of execution of the inference of the relationship between the terms? Recall Alderton et al. also found relatively little evidence that components with the same name derived from different tasks were more highly related to each other than components with different names. Indeed, in their study, there was probably no difference between these average correlations and, even with the exclusion of two of their components that may have had differential relevance to their tasks, the differences between the average correlations were not large.

The data on the intertask generality of components provides more than the hint of the existence of a positive manifold when components are generalized across tasks. If heterotask correlations are all positive then it is possible to inquire about the basis for the generality of componential reasoning. This line of inquiry leads almost inexorably to the unpalatable introduction of the construct that componential analysis was designed to banish—Spearman's g. If individuals who excel in the execution of a component in a particular task are found to excel in the execution of all other components in different tasks, then it is possible to argue that componential analysis has not discovered the components that collectively define individual differences in g. Rather, componential analysis has rediscovered g by fractionating performance on a task into separate components. We are then left to explain why individuals who excel in a component are likely to excel in all other components in different tasks. And, the explanatory burden has simply been displaced from the need to explain why different tasks form a positive manifold to the need to explain why different components of task performance form a positive manifold. This certainly is not the result desired by individuals who are engaged in componential analysis.

Two counterarguments may be advanced against this criticism. It is possible to argue that each component in a componential analysis may be shown to independently predict psychometric intelligence. Thus the components must be partially independent of each other. The difficulty with this argument is that it holds within a task but not across tasks. For example, it has been demonstrated that components that are derived from a given task each independently predict performance outcome and may each independently predict a measure of intelligence. But the small differences in average correlations between components with the same and different names obtained from different tasks imply that increments to predictability across tasks from different components are not likely to be attainable. If one were to predict performance on a new task from an aggregate measure of components on a different task that excluded one of the components it is not likely to be the case that the excluded component will add to the prediction of performance in the new task. If components clearly generalized across tasks and components with the same name always accounted for unique variance in different tasks, then the exclusion of a single component score from a task would always leave the residual aggregate score as a deficient predictor of performance on a task in which the excluded component is assumed to be involved. Little or no evidence exists that componential analysis can meet this test and the available evidence suggests that componential analysis will fail this test.

What does this imply about the virtues of componential analysis as a general model for studying individual differences in intelligence? I think that it implies that the method as presently constituted cannot be used to construct a general model of the determinants of individual differences in intelligence. The method appears more useful as a technique to study the components that determine performance in a particular intellectual task. Components, from this perspective, may be contrasted with g as theoretical constructs by reference to their range of application. As a construct, g provides little or no information about the processes that determine performance on any particular task. Its range of application is self-evidently extensive. It informs us about individual differences in performance, on the average, in virtually everything at the cost of providing us with virtually no information about the performance of an individual on any particular task. Componential analysis, by contrast, may be construed as providing extensive information about the performance of an individual on a particular task (subject to the caveat mentioned above that components are themselves theoretically unanalyzed terms) while at the same time providing little or no information about the details of performance on any other task. One approach tells us too much about too little and the other too little about too much.

R. J. Sternberg (1985) assumed that components differ in their intertask generality. Among the components that are assumed to be general are encoding and metacomponents. We have already indicated that there is evidence that suggests that measures of encoding do not invariably exhibit intertask generality. Metacomponents are assumed to function as executive processes that control the execution of specific performance components. Metacomponents are involved in the allocation of time to different performance components, monitor progress on a task, respond to feedback, and generally control the execution of performance components. Sternberg argues that metacomponents are the most general of all components and are highly related to performance on tests of intelligence. He writes,

> . . . individual differences in general intelligence are attributable to individual differences in the effectiveness with which general components are used. Since these components are common to all of the tasks in a given task universe, factor analysis will tend to lump all of these general sources of individual-difference variance into a single general factor. As it happens, the metacomponents have a much higher proportion of general components among them than do any of the other kinds of components, presumably because the executive routines needed to plan, monitor, and possibly replan performance are highly overlapping across widely differing tasks. Thus, individual differences in meta-componential functioning are largely responsible for the persistent appearance of a general factor. [R. J. Sternberg, 1985].

If metacomponents are the basis of individual differences in general intelligence, then evidence indicating that performance components have limited intertask generality leaves open the question of the generality of components. Generality may not have been found because we have looked for it in the wrong place. Sternberg and his associates have reported some research in which they have related measures of metacomponents to intelligence. We shall review these studies in order to see if they provide evidence for the claims of generality of metacomponents advanced by Sternberg.

R. J. Sternberg (1981) gave subjects a number of analogies problems to solve that had from one to three terms of the analogy missing. Analogies with more than one term omitted were assumed to be nonentrenched. He presented these problems in either blocked or mixed form. In the blocked condition all of the problems had a common format with the same type of analogy problem. That is, the number of terms missing in the analogy was constant for that block of trials. In the mixed condition the format of the problems varied from trial to trial. Sternberg used this task to obtain measures of two different metacomponents he called global and local planning. He assumed that more global planning was involved in the solution of analogies under mixed-block conditions. If the format of a problem varied from trial to trial, the subject must spend time planning the method of solution of the problem that is appropriate for each analogy problem. In the blocked condition global planning is minimized since the subject needs to spend time planning the method of solution only once during the trial block. Local planning parameters were measured in terms of a model of the difficulty of the problems related to the changes introduced by omitting various terms from the analogy. Measures of global and local planning contributed to the prediction of the measure of latency of problem solution. Global planning scores were positively related to solution times and local planning was negatively related to solution time. The positive relationship implies that subjects who spent more time in global planning were able to solve the analogies problems more rapidly. In this instance, the global planning parameter refers to the amount of additional time taken to solve the problems in the mixed rather than the blocked condition. Sternberg correlated metacomponent scores with scores on psychometric tests. He used the Raven test and two tests of ability to solve the letter series problems. The ability to solve analogies in this study was not significantly related to the Raven test. It should be noted that this constitutes additional evidence against the assertion that nonentrenched tasks provide good measures of general intelligence. Since the Raven is generally recognized as a good measure of g, these data suggest that the use of nonentrenched or unfamiliar formats in analogy problems does not necessarily increase the relationship between solution times and general intelligence. Both of the metacomponent measures were related to performance on the letter series tests. The correlations between global planning and local planning measures and performance on the letter series tests were .43 and $-.33$, respectively. The correlation between the local planning measure and performance on the letter series test was not quite statistically significant (the sample size was small, $N = 20$). The positive correlation between the global component measure and performance on the psychometric index was statistically significant. The positive sign of the correlation implies that more time spent in global planning is associated with superior performance on the psychometric test. The conclusion that the global planning metacomponent is substantially related to general intelligence is somewhat vitiated by the failure to report data that incorporates scores on the Raven matrix in the overall index of general intelligence. Presumably, the inclusion of this measure into the index of psychometric ability would decrease the reported correlation between global planning and psychometric ability, perhaps to a nonsignificant level.

Wagner and Sternberg (as cited in R. J. Sternberg, 1985) obtained measures of metacomponential strategies used in solving verbal comprehension problems. In one of their studies subjects were told that they would be asked questions that dealt with the gist of the passage, the main idea of the passage, the details of the passage, or the analysis and application of ideas in the passage. The subjects allocated less time to reading the passages in the first two conditions. A time allocation parameter defined as the difference between the time allocated to reading under the first two conditions and the last two conditions was predictive of overall accuracy in answering questions about the passages. The semipartial correlation, removing the influence of overall ability, was .30.

In a second experiment, subjects read passages from the Graduate Record Examination under three conditions—a control condition, a condition in which subjects were provided with information about the difficulty level of questions about the passages, and a condition in which critical passages were highlighted. A number of different strategy measures were obtained based on the time allocated to various problems and protocols obtained from the subjects about their performance. They found that subjects who reported that they changed their strategy of solving the problems that were presented scored significantly higher on the reading comprehension task than subjects who did not report changing strategies. In addition, the former subjects had slightly higher verbal reasoning test scores. Subjects who read passages in terms of the order of difficulty of the passage did better on the reading comprehension than subjects who did not read passages in order of difficulty. These two groups of subjects did not differ in verbal reasoning ability. Subjects also differed with respect to their tendency to use the specific difficulty information provided to them. Those subjects who used this information tended to allocate different amounts of time to questions depending upon the specific information provided to them about the difficulty of the question. Subjects who used this strategy had lower verbal comprehension scores than subjects who did not. There were no differences between these two groups of subjects in the psychometric test of verbal reasoning ability. Wagner and Sternberg identified three different strategies of reading the highlighted passages. Some subjects read the highlighted passages exclusively. There was no difference in task performance between those subjects who reported using this strategy and those who did not. The subjects who used this strategy scored higher on the test of verbal reasoning ability than the subjects who did not use this strategy. A second related strategy involved reading the highlighted passages more carefully than the passages that were not highlighted. Performance on the task and on the verbal ability measure was comparable for subjects who reported using this strategy and subjects who did not. Another group of subjects reported searching for the answers to the questions in the highlighted portions. Subjects who used this strategy did not do better on this task than subjects who did not use the strategy, and these two groups of subjects did not differ in their scores on the verbal reasoning ability.

The Wagner and Sternberg studies indicate that the metacomponential strategies that were identified were for the most part unrelated to verbal reasoning ability. More generally, the relationships between metacomponents and general intelligence reported in these studies are weak. And, little evidence is presented that indicates that metacomponents are related to each other. For example, is there a metacomponent of efficient time allocation for all classes of problems? The metacomponents that have been studied appear to be relevant to performance of a particular task. No evidence is presented in these or in related studies that metacomponents exhibit wider intertask generality than performance components. Indeed, metacomponents that have been identified appear to be specific to a particular task. Whether one spends more time reading passages that are assumed to be difficult is, by definition, a task-specific metacomponent. Other metacomponents such as the time allocated to global planning may be general, but no evidence is presented that indicates that this metacomponent is correlated with a metacomponent with the same name and definition derived from a totally different type of task. In addition, the evidence presented by Sternberg indicates that this metacomponent is only weakly related to general intelligence. In summary, little or no evidence is presented in support of the assertion that metacomponents have greater intertask generality than performance components, and no evidence is presented that metacomponents are likely to be more substantially related to general intelligence than performance components. Thus the critique presented here of componential analysis as being of limited value in understanding individual differences in intelligence by virtue of the failure to demonstrate intertask generality of component scores is not vitiated by a consideration of research on metacognitive components.

Carpenter, Just, & Schell (1990) reported the results of a simulation analysis of performance on the Raven test that is similar in its goals to a componential analysis of performance on an intellectual task. They asked a group of college students who were taking the Raven test to verbally describe their thought processes and hypotheses as they attempted to solve the problems. In addition, they recorded eye movement patterns permitting them to obtain measures of the elements of the stimuli that individuals looked at as they attempted to solve the problems. They analyzed these protocols in order to develop a model of the reasoning processes of individuals who attempted to solve the Raven test. They then constructed two computer programs that were designed to simulate the performance of their median college student and the best-performing college students in their sample. If the computer programs accurately simulate the performance of college students taking the Raven test, they may be construed as a model of task performance. In addition, a comparison of the programs designed to simulate the performance of individuals with different abilities to solve the Raven may be construed as a theory of individual differences in performance on the task. Since the Raven is assumed to be a good measure of general intelligence, a theory of individual differences in Raven performance may be assumed to be a general theory of individual differences in intelligence.

The computer simulation of Raven performance may be illustrated by a description of the methods used to solve a representative problem that is described in Fig. 4.5. The description of the stimuli (encoding) is accomplished by a symbolic description of the stimuli in the matrix. Thus the process of perceptual encoding is not addressed in the simulation model. This is justified by the assumption that individual differences in encoding ability are not a source of variance among college students in performance on the Raven test. The program encodes stimulus attributes and transfers them to working memory. The program also compares adjacent figures in an attempt to infer the rules governing variations among the stimulus elements of the problem. Among the rules that can be generated by the program are a rule of constant in a row for a particular attribute and quantitative pairwise progression of values of an attribute. Rules that are inferred to describe variations of a figure are tested against variations in the figures in a second row of the problem. The computer simulation is designed to mimic evidence that human subjects solve the Raven by the incremental development of hypotheses and by repeated reiterative testing of these hypotheses. The verbal protocols and eye movement data provided evidence for the emergence of single hypotheses about the rules governing variations in the figures. The rules that are generated are applied to the missing entry and used to choose the correct solution to the problem.

The simulation of the performance of superior subjects on the Raven differs from the program designed to simulate performance of the typical subject on the Raven in several respects. The model is able to infer more rules and more complex rules. For example, the more sophisticated simulation is able to solve problems involving a null argument with a distribution-of-two-values rule in a row (see Fig. 4.5). Problems involving this rule were not solved by the subjects whose performance was at the median of college students but were solved by the best-performing subjects. In addition, the more advanced simulation program incorporated a goal monitor that specifies the order of operation of various procedures and defines rules for modifying the order of execution of a particular operation.

The simulation programs designed by Carpenter *et al.* (1990) reproduce

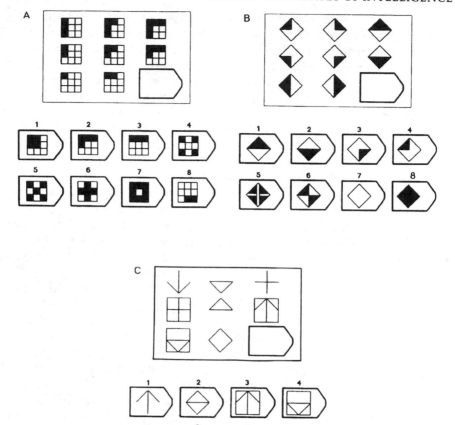

FIGURE 4.5 Problems illustrating rules of the Raven test. (A) The quantitative pairwise progression rule. The number of black squares in the top of each row increases by one from the first to the second column and from the second to the third column. The number of black squares along the left remains constant within a row but changes between rows from three to two to one. The correct answer is 3. (B) The figure addition rule. The figural element in the first column is superimposed on the figural element in the second column to compose the figural element in the third column. The position of the darkened element remains constant in a row but changes between rows from top to bottom to both. The correct answer is 8. (C) The distribution-of-two-values rule. Each figural element, such as the horizontal line, the vertical line, the V, and so on, occurs twice in a row, and the third value is null. The correct answer is 5. (Based on Carpenter, Just, Schell, 1990.)

several features of the performance on the subjects whose behavior they were designed to simulate. The regular program solves the same number of problems as the median subject in their sample and the advanced program solves the same number of problems as the best subjects in the sample. The error patterns of the subjects and the programs were similar. For example, subjects close to the median in performance had error rates ranging from 17 to 70% on easy and hard problems, respectively. The simulation program had comparable error rates of 0 and 90%. Also, the specific rules that were induced by the subjects as indicated by their verbal protocols were similar to those that were induced by the programs.

The comparison of the performance of the simulation programs and the performance of the actual subjects leaves little doubt that the simulation programs captured some of the main features of the processes used by subjects to solve the Raven. While there are differences in details of the performance of real subjects and the computer programs, the overall performance is sufficiently similar to support the assumption that the computer programs have successfully simulated the incremental discovery of separate rules based on pairwise comparisons among figures in the matrix. Does this relatively successful simulation provide insights into the nature of general intelligence? In order to answer this question it is necessary to describe the nature of individual differences in performance on the Raven as construed in the simulation models developed by Carpenter *et al.* (1990). These models provide insights into individual differences in performance as well as insights into what is assumed to be general in all higher-order cognitive processes. Individual differences are present in at least two different dimensions of problem solving. Superior performance on the Raven is associated with the ability to discover abstract representations of the figures that are only loosely tied to the perceptual inputs of the stimuli. Note that the distribution-of-two rule that distinguished typical and optimal performance of both subjects and their simulations may be characterized as an abstract representation of the relationship among perceptual elements. In addition, the simulation of the optimal-performing subjects involved the addition of goal management instructions that specified the order of application of various routines and the modification of procedures depending on the attainment of various subgoals. This element of the program is analogous to the emphasis on metacognitive components in Sternberg's componential analysis of intelligence. In addition to individual differences, these simulations contain a theory of what is general in cognitive performance. Carpenter *et al.* close their paper with this description of what is common to the process of Raven solution:

> Thus what one intelligence test measures, according to the current theory, is the common ability to decompose problems into manageable segments and iterate through them, the differential ability to manage the hierarchy of goals and subgoals generated by this problem decomposition, and the differential ability to form higher level abstractions. [Carpenter, Just, & Shell, 1990, p. 429]

It is certainly possible to develop a plausible argument that many complex cognitive tasks involve similar elements. Indeed, Carpenter *et al.* demonstrated that performance on a problem that is frequently analyzed by cognitive psychologists, the Tower of Hanoi problem, is subject to a similar analysis and is correlated with performance on the Raven. Therefore, a *prima facie* argument can be made that the processes involved in the simulation of performance on the Raven are related to performance on other complex cognitive tasks. At the same time a strong argument can be developed that these simulations do not provide the basis for the development of a complete theory of general intelligence. There are two specific arguments that can be developed to support this conclusion.

First, the claim of a relationship between the simulation of performance on the Raven and performance on other complex cognitive tasks is an argument by analogy. The simulation programs that are provided for the Raven cannot be used to solve other intellectual problems. In order to sustain the argument that these programs provide a model of individual differences in general intelligence, it would be necessary to design a program that is capable of solving a class of problems. And it would be necessary to demonstrate that differences in the parameters that define individual differences in the ability to solve problems would be constant across problems. It should be realized that this argument is another version of the discussion of the intertask generality of components. To what extent is a component with the same name used to explain performance in different tasks a measure of the same characteristic?

Second, there is convincing evidence that the stimulation theory of performance on the Ravens test is incomplete as a model of general intelligence. The theory omits perceptual encoding as a source of variations in individual differences in intelligence. There is a considerable body of evidence that suggests that encoding in both simple and complex tasks is a source of variation in some intellectual tasks. In addition, there are tasks that are at least moderately predictive of performance on the Raven that do not appear on the surface to involve any of the parameters that are assumed to be critical for Raven performance in the simulations developed by Carpenter *et al.* Consider, for example, performance on the relatively simple cognitive tasks reviewed in Chapter 3. How is performance on a visual inspection-time task or pitch discrimination for briefly presented tones related to the simulation parameters in these models of Raven performance? Abstraction ability, hierarchical goal processing, and the ability to decompose problems into manageable segments do not appear to be plausible explanations of performance on such tasks. Yet these tasks are predictive of scores on tests like the Raven. This analysis suggests that what is common to different measures of intelligence may include something other than that which is assumed to explain individual differences in the Raven.

CONCLUSION

The experimental investigation of individual differences has been actively pursued for the last 15 years. Earlier attempts to study intelligence in laboratory contexts became relatively moribund after the development of psychometric tests in 1905. For the brief period of its active revival, re-markable progress has been made. Methods for the determination of indi-vidual differences in cognitive processes on a given task and the analysis of individual models of task solution have been developed. Several corre-lates of general intelligence have been identified. Some of these tasks, such as pitch discrimination and reaction-time measures obtained under dual-task processing conditions, may even have substantial predictive relationships to intelligence. While it is not yet possible to specify with precision the theoretical properties of the class of information-processing tasks that are predictive of general intelligence, it is possible to tenta-tively suggest some general properties of tasks that may serve to provide suggestions about a more precise theory. Measures of the speed and ac-curacy of encoding stimulus information and the ability to maintain near-optimal attentional performance as well as the ability to attend to a simple task under conditions of distraction may all provide at least meta-phorical clues for a more precise theory. It is also possible to indicate that complexity of information processing per se is not a good basis for defin-ing experimental tasks that relate to general intelligence. Theoretically defined parameters involving additional information-processing require-ments are usually not more predictive of performance on tests of intel-ligence than simple measures of speed of processing stimuli.

The research we have considered in Chapters 3 and 4 of this volume was designed either to provide the experimental foundation of Spearman's g construct or to overthrow g either by discovering separate cognitive components or by discovering theoretically defined parameters that would exhibit convergent and discriminant validity for separate ability dimensions. The effort to dislodge g has been less than successful. Com-ponents are positively correlated and do not, in general, exhibit sufficient generality to provide a basis for understanding individual differences in intelligence. Theoretically defined parameters of tasks that are presumed to correlate with specific abilities do not exhibit strong evidence of dis-criminant and convergent validity. The effort to dislodge g by use of the experimental method of investigating intelligence has not as yet been conspicuously more successful than the attempt to dislodge g by psycho-metric methods. And, if anything, evidence that general intelligence is substantially related to ability to process information in relatively simple tasks that appear on surface examination to require minimal formal tui-tion strengthens the need for a theoretical construct of general intel-ligence that is not restricted with respect to specific content. A general ability related to fundamental capacities to encode and attend to stimuli is sufficiently different from a model of content-specific skills to provide a theoretical foundation for a construct that predicts individual dif-ferences in performance on virtually all intellectual tasks.

5

BEHAVIOR GENETICS OF
INTELLIGENCE

INTRODUCTION

Why do people differ in intelligence? The answer to this question is obvious. Individuals have different environments and different genotypes. Behavior genetics provides methods for studying genetic and environmental influences on a trait. The term behavior genetics is clearly a misnomer. This area of investigation is concerned with both environmental and genetic influences. Indeed, behavior geneticists believe that one cannot understand the influence of the environment on a trait without studying the ways in which genotypes may influence the trait.

To what extent are individual differences in intelligence attributable to variability among genotypes? The answer to the question is indeterminate because intelligence cannot, in principle, be assigned an index of heritability. Heritability estimates are not properties of a trait. They are properties of a trait in a given population. Heritability indices may be different in different populations. The extent to which a trait may be heritable in a given population depends upon the variability of genotypes in a population. In addition, the characteristics of the environment encountered by a population of individuals will influence the way in which genes may influence the phenotypic measure of a trait. If we were to provide all members of a population with an environment that is uniform with respect to its influence on intelligence, then estimates of genetic influences would increase. The assertion that estimates of heritability are not properties of traits but are properties of the trait in a particular population is not merely a linguistic refinement; we shall consider research that indicates that the heritability of intelligence test scores may be subject to secular influences (i.e., that it may be changing for individuals born in different time periods), that it may vary with age, and that the heritability of intelligence may be different for different populations of individuals. In addition, there is dramatic evidence that a genetic influence on intelligence may be drastically altered by variations in the

126

environment. The disease phenylketonuria is caused by an inability to metabolize phenylalanine, which interferes with the appropriate development of the nervous system. Untreated individuals with phenylketonuria usually have IQ scores below 50 (Paine, 1957). The disease is an autosomal recessive disorder. Somewhere between .5 and 1% of the population are carriers of the recessive gene. Heritability of phenylketonuria follows classic Mendelian laws and occurs in one of four offspring of parents who are both carriers for the disease. Phenylketonuria can be detected at birth and a treatment program involving the use of phenylalanine-restricted diets usually removes the risk of retardation. Note that the treatment does not alter the genetic characteristics of individuals who have the disease but does alter the influence of the genotype on the phenotype. This example indicates that genotypic influences are not necessarily immutable. The influence of a genotype on a phenotype is subject to environmental intervention.

Behavior genetic analyses may be understood as attempts to partition variance. Variations in a phenotypic characteristic such as a score on a test of intelligence may be attributable to several independent sources of variance. Genetic and environmental sources of variance may each be partitioned into additional sources of variance. Environmental variance may be partitioned into two components, within- and between-family variance. Between-family variance refers to variations in a phenotype attributable to differences in environmental influences associated with being reared in different families. It is the source of variance that is generally considered when we think of environmental influences on intelligence. Within-family environmental influences are environmental influences attributable to different experiences of individuals reared in the same family. These influences encompass both events that occur within the context of the family, such as differential treatment of siblings being reared together, and events that are not associated with experiences within a family, such as the effects of friendships that are not shared by individuals reared in the same family. Genetic variance may be partitioned into additive genetic variance and nonadditive genetic variance. Additive genetic variance derives from the additive influence of each of the genes that influences a phenotype. Nonadditive genetic influences may be attributable to dominance caused by differential influence of one of two genes in the heterozygous case, and epistasis, which is an interactive influence of genes at different locations. Nonadditive genetic variance may decrease the resemblance between parent and offspring.

In addition to these four sources of variance that may influence the phenotype for intelligence, there are two other sources of variance that involve combinations of genetic and environmental influences. Genetic–environmental covariance is a source of variance attributable to the correlation of genes and environments. It is possible that individuals who are likely to have genes that are favorable for the development of high intelligence may also create family environments that are favorable to the development of intelligence. The combined influence of these correlated genetic and environmental effects may contribute to variability in the phenotype for intelligence. Genetic X environmental interaction refers to nonadditive combinations of genetic and environmental influences. Such effects would be present if the influence of genes would vary in different environments. In the most dramatic case it is possible that the influence of one or more genes would lead to high intelligence in one environment and low intelligence in a different environment.

Behavior genetic studies lead to the partitioning of variance in IQ scores and are able to assign numerical values for each of the independent sources of variance that are described above. In this chapter we shall consider research on twins and family and adoption studies in an attempt to outline their bearing on genetic and environmental influences on intelligence. In addition, we shall consider models that combine these sources of data. We shall also consider studies of genetic and environmental influences on development and change in intelligence.

TWIN STUDIES

Monozygotic twins (MZ) are genetically identical. They derive from the splitting of a single fertilized egg. Dizygotic twins (DZ) derive from the fertilization of two different eggs and are no more similar to each other than siblings. If a phenotypic measure of a trait is influenced by genotypes, MZ twin pairs should be more similar to each other than DZ twin pairs. Differences between pairs of DZ twins are attributable to variations in their environment and their genotypes. Differences between pairs of MZ twins are solely attributable to environmental variations. Therefore, a comparison of differences between MZ and DZ twin pairs should provide an index of genetic influence on a trait.

Each source of data that may be used to estimate genetic and environmental influences on a trait is liable to provide distorted estimates for a variety of different reasons. The twin method assumes that the within-pair similarity of environmental influences for MZ and DZ pairs is identical. It is possible that MZ pairs are treated more alike than DZ pairs by virtue of their greater physical similarity and that these environmental differences cause them to be more alike in intelligence. Thus evidence indicating that MZ twins are more alike in IQ than DZ twin pairs does not necessarily provide evidence for genetic influences.

There are several lines of evidence that suggest that an environmental interpretation of differences between MZ and DZ pairs is not tenable. Although MZ twins may experience a more similar environment than DZ twins, this similarity may itself be the result of genetic influences on the environment. For example, if MZ twins are more likely than DZ twins to have the same friends this may be attributable to genetic influences on interests and temperament that influence friendship patterns. More critically, the assertion that MZ twins experience more similar environments than DZ twins does not provide compelling evidence for an environmental interpretation of MZ–DZ differences on a trait unless one can demonstrate that the environmental differences that distinguish MZ and DZ pairs are related to the trait. Vandenberg & Wilson (1979) found that variations in within-pair similarity of treatment of MZ and DZ twins did not correlate with scores on tests of intelligence. There are two other critical sources of data that may be used to investigate the equal-environment assumption. MZ twin pairs who are reared in different families undoubtedly experience environments that are more varied than MZ twins who are reared in the same family. Comparisons between these two groups of twins should provide evidence about the importance of variations in the environment experienced by MZ twin pairs in determining their similarity in intelligence. We shall consider these studies. Another test of the environmental interpretation of MZ–DZ differences for intelligence may be obtained by comparing same-sex and opposite-sex DZ twin pairs. Opposite-sex DZ twin pairs clearly experience larger within-pair environmental variability than same-sex DZ twin pairs. Although I am not aware of any specific empirical research on the topic, it appears obvious that differences between same-sex MZ and DZ twin pairs in within-pair environmental variability are smaller than differences between same-sex and opposite-sex DZ twin pairs. If this assertion is correct, an environmental interpretation of differences between MZ and DZ twin pairs in intelligence implies that the difference between same-sex and opposite-sex DZ pairs for intelligence should be larger than the difference between MZ and same-sex DZ twin pairs. Opposite-sex and same-sex DZ twin pairs appear to be equally similar in intelligence. For example, Mehrota & Maxwell (1950) obtained a correlation of .63 for 182 opposite-sex 11-year-old twins in Scotland—a value comparable to that usually reported for same-sex DZ twins. Herrman & Hogben (1933) obtained slightly larger correlations on the Otis test for opposite-sex twin pairs than for same-sex DZ twin pairs. The failure to find evidence for differences in IQ similarity among same- and opposite-sex DZ twins suggests that variations in the environment experienced by pairs of twins reared in the same home are not the cause of differences between MZ and DZ twin pairs in similarity for IQ. Indeed, it is hard to imagine environmental hypotheses to account for differences in MZ and DZ twin pairs in intelligence that would not predict relatively large differences between same-sex and opposite-sex DZ twin pairs. Equivalence in similarity of intelligence test scores for these two classes of DZ twin pairs appears to render environmental explanations of MZ–DZ differences in intelligence nugatory.

Estimates of different sources of variance in intelligence using twin data are subject to empirical and conceptual difficulties. On a simple additive genetic model, DZ twin pairs may be assumed to have a genetic correlation of .5. This implies, on a purely genetic hypothesis, that the value of the DZ correlation for intelligence should be one-half the value of the MZ correlation and the difference between the correlations multiplied by two should provide an estimate of the heritability of intelligence. There are three difficulties with this simple procedure for estimating heritability. The genetic correlation between same-sex DZ twin pairs may be larger than .5. Assortative mating refers to the tendency of individuals who are genetically alike to mate. Spouses exhibit a phenotypic correlation in IQ of approximately .33. The genotypic correlation among spouses for IQ is a complex theoretical parameter that can only be indirectly estimated and not directly measured. The presence of a genotypic correlation among biological parents for intelligence will inflate the genetic correlation between DZ pairs since they are receiving genes from parents that are similar. Assortative mating will inflate DZ correlations and lead to lower heritability estimates. Dominance and other nonadditive genetic influences will tend to decrease the similarity of DZ twin pairs for purely genetic reasons. These influences do not decrease MZ correlations since MZ twins are genetically identical. In order to use twin data to arrive at estimates for different sources of genetic and environmental variance it is necessary to develop estimates of assortative mating and nonadditive sources of genetic variance. Estimates of genetic and environmental influences on intelligence using twin data may be distorted by special environmental experiences peculiar to twins. Twins may influence each other in ways that siblings who are not twins do not and thus twins may be more alike for environmental reasons that are not shared by other individuals in the population.

In addition to the conceptual difficulties involved in deriving estimates from twin data, there are also possible empirical difficulties in ascertaining the actual values of twin correlations. The determination of zygosity is no longer a serious problem with modern techniques of blood typing. And, if there are errors of determination of zygosity in a study, differences between MZ and DZ twin pairs would be underestimated, thereby decreasing estimates of heritability. A potentially more serious source of bias is volunteer bias. Twin studies require the cooperation of both members of a twin pair. If twins who are dissimilar are more likely to be discordant for the tendency to volunteer to participate, then the surviving members of any twin study are likely to be a biased sample of twin pairs who are more similar to each other than twins in the population. If MZ twins are more alike in personality characteristics that are correlated with the tendency to volunteer and participate in psychological studies than DZ twins, then the population of DZ twins who participate in a study of intelligence are likely to be a more biased sample of their population than MZ twins are of their population. Biases in obtained values of DZ correlations are likely to lead to lower estimates of the heritability of IQ.

Bouchard & McGue (1981) summarized the available literature on kinship correlations for intelligence. They reported a weighted average correlation of .86 based on 34 correlations encompassing 4672 pairings for MZ twins reared together. The comparable correlation for same-sex DZ twins was .60 based on 41 correlations and 5546 pairings. The correlation of .86 may be compared to the test–retest reliability of .87 for the tests of intelligence used in these investigations. The correlation in intelligence for MZ twins reared together is close to the upper bound set by the test–retest reliability of IQ tests. On the simplest genetic model, ignoring assortative mating, these data imply that 52% of the variance on IQ tests is attributable to genetic influences. Considerations of the influence of assortative mating would increase the estimates for the heritability of intelligence.

Loehlin, Willerman, & Horn (1988) reviewed recent twin studies of intelligence published after Bouchard and McGue's review. They noted that several recent studies reported larger MZ–DZ differences. Tambs, Sundet, & Magnus (1984) reported correlations of .88 and .47 for MZ and DZ twin pairs. Wilson (1983, 1986) obtained correlations of .88 and .54 for 15-year-old MZ and DZ twin pairs. Segal (1985) found correlations of .85 for MZ twins and .46 for DZ twins. Nathan & Guttman (1984) obtained correlations of .80 and .34 for their twin pairs. Stevenson, Graham, Fredman, & McLoughlin (1987) reported the only recent data that is compatible with the weighted estimates contained in the Bouchard and McGue report. They obtained correlations of .84 for MZ twin pairs and .61 for DZ twin pairs on the Wechsler. The newer twin studies suggest heritabilities that are somewhat higher than those based on the studies reviewed by Bouchard and McGue. These data are compatible with heritability estimates for additive genetic variance that are close to .7. It is not known if these data represent random perturbations in the obtained values of correlations, systematic changes attributable to differences in methodology, or true secular changes in the heritability of intelligence.

In addition to studies of MZ and DZ twins reared together, there are studies of MZ and DZ twins reared apart. The correlation between MZ twins reared apart provides a direct estimate of the heritability of intelligence. For several reasons, the direct estimate of the heritability of intelligence based on correlations of IQ scores of MZ twins reared apart should be dealt with cautiously. There is only a small number of such studies—data are available from only six studies and the results of one of these studies is generally discounted as being either fraudulent or, at best, untrustworthy. The samples are small and there are less than 200 MZ pairs available, and some of these data are based on older IQ tests that may not have been appropriately normed. In addition, only one study, whose results are not currently available, is based on a systematic sample. The remaining studies obtained samples that may be unrepresentative of the exceedingly small group of separated MZ twins. Finally, many of the MZ twin pairs that are included in the available data were not separated from birth. Many were reared in similar circumstances in families that were similar with respect to socioeconomic background and even in collateral branches of the same family. Thus, the correlation between separated MZ twin pairs cannot be accepted at face value as a direct estimate of the heritability of IQ.

There are six studies of separated twins that provide information about their similarity of IQ. One study, Cyril Burt's, is currently considered to report data that is not trustworthy (see Hearnshaw, 1979; Kamin, 1974; see also Joynson, 1989, for a somewhat contradictory point of view). It shall not be considered here.

Bouchard & McGue (1981) reported a weighted average correlation of .72 for three classical studies of MZ twins reared apart. The correlation is based on three studies and involves 65 twin pairs. These data have been subject to intense scrutiny and dispute. The data are based on three classic studies, Newman, Freeman, & Holzinger (1937), Juel-Nielsen (1965), and Shields (1962). Farber (1981), Kamin (1974), and Taylor (1980) argued that these data cannot be accepted at face value as demonstrating the importance of genetic influences on IQ. They presented four general criticisms of these data. First, they argued that the samples are not systematically ascertained and consist of volunteers who may not be representative of the population. There is one modern study of twins reared apart that is based on a systematic sample, Pedersen, McLearn, Plomin, & Friberg (1985), but results for MZ twins reared apart have not been reported for this study. In addition, Newman, Freeman, & Holzinger (1937) may have introduced an additional source of bias in their study by excluding any twin pairs who described themselves as dissimilar in order to reduce the probability of obtaining DZ pairs that they intended to exclude. Thus they may have unwittingly failed to study MZ twin pairs who were dissimilar in IQ. Their results were comparable to those obtained in other studies in which this procedure was not followed. The possibility that the MZ twins that are included in these studies may for unknown reasons be a specially selected sample whose resemblance in IQ might not be representative cannot be excluded. There is, however, with the possible exception of the Newman et al. study, no reason to believe that biases have been introduced in the sample selection procedure that would result in an increase in the correlation for the MZ twins.

Second, Kamin argued that the results of the Juel-Nielsen and Newman et al. studies are attributable to age confounds. There is a relationship between the age of the twin pairs and their average IQ. Kamin attempted to demonstrate that this age confound, probably attributable to inadequate age standardization for the tests used, accounts for the IQ correlation between them. It is known that there are cohort and age effects for IQ and that cross-sectional data is likely to indicate a negative correlation between IQ and age. The correlations averaged by Bouchard and McGue are age corrected and therefore should be interpreted as being free of age confounds. Kamin objected to the standard methods of correcting for age confounds, arguing that the appropriate age correction should be done separately for male and female twin pairs and even for different subsets of subjects at different points of the age cycle. Kamin created pseudopairings of twins who were adjacent in age. He demonstrated that the correlations for pseudopairs were comparable to those for actual twin pairs. Kamin's approach is dependent on creating separate groupings for male and female pairs and on creating additional arbitrary divisions. The resultant correlations are based on exceedingly small samples and have large standard errors. In addition, there is no reason to assume that age corrections that are required for IQ should be different for male and female subjects. If Kamin had applied his pseudopairing procedure consistently to the entire sample for each of the studies he examined, in all probability the effects of the age correction he used would have been comparable to the standard partial correlation method of age correcting. In addition, Shield's (1962) data are not subject to this criticism.

Third, Kamin and Farber criticized the IQ tests used in these investigations. Juel-Nielsen used a Wechsler test that may not have been adequately standardized for his Danish sample. The Stanford–Binet used by Newman et al. may also have been inadequately standardized. The nonverbal Dominoes test used by Shields required extensive verbal instructions and the outcome of the test may have been biased since Shields administered the test to most of his MZ twin pairs. Bouchard (1982) noted that in each of these three classic studies an additional IQ test was available. Juel-Nielsen reported data for the Raven, Newman et al. administered the Otis quick-scoring test, and Shields had data for a vocabulary test. In each case the intraclass correlations for the MZ twins were comparable for these alternative IQ measures to those obtained from the measures that were criticized by Kamin and Farber. Bouchard concluded that criticism of the outcomes of the separated MZ twin studies based on the adequacy of the tests of intelligence used were not "constructively replicated" for the alternative tests used in these studies.

Fourth, the most fundamental criticism of these data is that the results are attributable to environmental similarity in the rearing conditions of these separated twin pairs. Taylor argued that the similarity between MZ twins reared apart was dependent on environmental similarity. He investigated the effects of age of separation, whether the twins had been reunited, whether they had been reared in related or unrelated families, and the similarity of the social environment in which they were reared. Bouchard (1982, 1983) reexamined the separated twin studies using Taylor's analyses and classifications as a basis for classifying the separated twin pairs. He then used these classifications to compute correlations for a second measure of intelligence obtained by two of the original investigators, Juel-Nielsen and Newman *et al.* This analysis tests the replicability of Taylor's analysis for different measures of intelligence. Taylor's original analysis and Bouchard's constructive replication of this analysis are reported in Table 5.1. An examination of the data in Table 5.1 indicates that Taylor's analyses do not generalize to different measures of intelligence presented to the same twin pairs. Taylor found that age of separation was not related to the degree of similarity; Bouchard found that age of separated was related to twin similarity. Early-separated twins were less similar than late-separated twin pairs. Taylor reported that MZ twins who had been reunited were more similar than the twin pairs who had not been reunited. Bouchard found that this effect does replicate, but the differences in the magnitude of the intraclass correlations are smaller than those obtained by Taylor. Taylor found that the MZ twins reared by relatives were more similar than those reared by nonrelatives. Bouchard found that the results were reversed for the alternative measures. Perhaps the most critical of Taylor's analyses is that based on his classification of twins with respect to the similarity of rearing environment. An examination of the data in Table 5.1 indicates that, on Taylor's analysis, MZ twins reared in similar environments are more alike than those reared in relatively dissimilar environments. Bouchard found that the differences on the alternative measure for Taylor's classification do not replicate—the twins reared in dissimilar environments are slightly and nonsignificantly more alike on the alternative measures than the twins assigned to the

TABLE 5.1   Taylor's Analysis of Variables Influencing MZA Correlations and Bouchard's Constructive Replication[a]

Variable	Taylor's correlation[b]	Bouchard's correlation[c]
Reunion classification		
Reunited	.85	.82
Not reunited	.57	.68
Age of separation		
Late (>6 months)	.70	.79
Early (<6 months)	.67	.42
Rearing classification		
Related	.77	.66
Not related	.61	.77
Environment classification		
Related	.86	.67
Not related	.52	.70

[a]Based on Bouchard (1983).

[b]Taylor's correlations are weighted averages for three studies as recalculated by Bouchard using intraclass *r*.

[c]Bouchard's correlations are weighted averages for two studies using Taylor's post hoc classifications replicated for a second test score for the same subjects.

relatively similar group. Bouchard's reanalysis indicates that Taylor's analysis cannot be used to explain the similarity of MZ twins reared apart by reference to environmental similarity of their rearing conditions.

The results of the classic twin studies are buttressed by the results of a contemporary study, the Minnesota study of twins reared apart. Bouchard, Lykken, McGue, Segal, & Tellegen (1990) reported correlations for three different measures of general intelligence—the WAIS, a combination of the Raven and the Mill–Hill vocabulary test, and the first principal component of a battery of tests for over 40 separated MZ twin pairs. The correlations for these three measures were .69, .78, and .78, respectively. The correlation for a composite index based on the mean of the three measures was .75. Indices of socioeconomic background and retrospective accounts of the intellectual orientation of the family environment were obtained. The correlations between the family background variables of the MZ twins reared apart were obtained and the correlations between family background variables and performance on IQ tests were also obtained. Using these correlations it is possible to calculate the contribution of the similarity of family background variables to the correlation of IQ scores for the MZ twins reared apart. Table 5.2 presents these data. An examination of the data in Table 5.2 indicates that the twins were reared in somewhat correlated environments. It is also the case that the environmental variables were for the most part only negligi-

TABLE 5.2 Placement Coefficients for Environmental Variables, Correlations between IQ and the Environmental Variables, and Estimates of the Contribution of Placement to Twin Similarity in WAIS IQ[a]

Placement variable	MZA similarity (R_{ff})	Correlation between IQ and placement variable (r_{ft})	Contribution of placement to the MZA correlation $(R_{ff} \times r^2_{ft})$
SES indicators			
Father's education	0.134	0.100	0.001
Mother's education	0.412	−0.001	0.000
Father's SES	0.267	0.174	0.008
Physical facilities			
Material possessions	0.402	0.279**	0.032
Scientific/technical	0.151	−0.090	0.001
Cultural	−0.085	−0.279**	−0.007
Mechanical	0.303	0.077	0.002
Relevant FES scales			
Achievement	0.11	−0.103	0.001
Intellectual orientation	0.27	0.106	0.003

[a]Based on Bouchard, Lykken, McGue, Segal, & Tellegen (1990).
**r_{ft} significantly different from zero at $p < 0.01$.

bly correlated with performance on tests of intelligence. And, the last column of Table 5.2 indicates that similarity of rearing environment as assessed in this study accounts for a vanishingly small degree of the similarity of IQ performance in these separated twin pairs. These data indicate that MZ twins reared apart are more similar to each other in IQ than DZ twins reared together. And, these data are compatible with estimates of heritability for intelligence that are close to .7.

McGue & Bouchard (1989) also reported data for separated twins on several special ability measures. Table 5.3 presents intraclass correlations for their sample of 47 MZ twin pairs, 2 MZ triplets, and 25 DZ twin pairs who were reared apart for four groupings of tests of special abilities as well as an estimate of heritability based on an analysis of these data. An examination of the data presented in Table 5.3 indicates that the correlations for MZ twins reared apart range from .29 to .71 on these measures. Note that these correlations, with the exception of the correlation for the spatial ability factor score, are somewhat lower than the general intelligence value of .75 for what is essentially the same sample. It is also the case that the DZ twins who are reared apart exhibit correlations that are not invariably smaller than the MZ apart correlations. The DZ apart correlations are comparable to those obtained in studies of DZ twins reared together. The somewhat high DZ correlations should be accepted cautiously in view of the relatively small sample on which they are based. They are, however, comparable to correlations for DZ twins reared apart reported by Pedersen *et al.* (1985) for a sample of 34 pairs of DZ twins reared apart. They also reported that the differences within twin pairs on intelligence correlated .05 with a measure of the difference in the socioeconomic status of the environment in which members of the twin pair were reared. Thus differences in the favorableness of the environment of these separated DZ twins do not appear to predict the IQ differences within the twin pairs.

The data on separated twins provide additional support for the assumption that the MZ–DZ difference in similarity for measures of intelligence is attributable to differences in shared genetic characteristics. The available literature on separated twins is not extensive and the twins have certainly not been reared in independent environments. There is little

TABLE 5.3 Intraclass Correlations for Special Ability Factors for Twins Reared Apart[a]

Factor	MZA	DZA	h^2
Verbal reasoning	.57	.51	.57
Spatial ability	.71	.40	.71
Perceptual speed and accuracy	.53	.56	.53
Visual memory	.43	.07	—

[a]Based on McGue & Bouchard (1989).

persuasive evidence that the similarity of their environments can account for their similarity in intelligence. Separated MZ twins encounter environments that are more varied than MZ and DZ twin pairs reared together. Yet they appear to be somewhat more alike in IQ than DZ twins reared in the same family. It is difficult to explain these findings without invoking a genetic hypothesis. The correlation for MZ twins reared apart is a direct estimate of the heritability of IQ. Thus these data suggest heritabilities for IQ that are close to .7.

FAMILY STUDIES

Bouchard & McGue (1981) summarized the literature reporting correlations between IQ scores of members of the same family who were reared together. They reported average weighted correlations of .42 for the correlation between a parent's IQ and the IQ of his or her child. The comparable correlation for siblings was .47. These data, considered in isolation, provide little or no evidence about genetic and environmental influences on intelligence. Members of the same family are genetically similar and share similar environments. Their similarity in IQ may be attributable to either of these circumstances. Studies of adopted families provide a way of separating genetic and environmental influences.

There are three contemporary studies that provide information about the relationship between IQ scores of adopted children and their biological and adopted parents. Teasdale & Owen (1984) obtained data on Danish fathers whose biological sons were adopted. They obtained scores on an intelligence test administered for military induction for biological fathers, their adopted sons, and the adopted stepfathers of these children. The correlation between biological fathers and their sons was .20. The corresponding correlation between the intelligence test scores of adopted fathers and their sons was .02. These data suggest that adopted adult children are more likely to resemble their biological parent than their adoptive parent in intelligence. The sample was small and information about possible restrictions in range of talent for either biological or adopted fathers was not presented.

The two remaining studies in this category that we shall discuss are the Texas Adoption Study (Horn, Loehlin, & Willerman, 1979) and the Colorado Adoption Project (Plomin & DeFries, 1985b). Both studies are longitudinal and have large samples that permit several different kinds of comparisons. The Texas Adoption Study is an investigation of a sample of 364 unwed mothers whose children were given up for adoption at an early age. The mothers were given an IQ test, and IQ test data exist for their offspring and the adoptive parents of these children. The mean IQ of the adoptive mothers was 112.4 with a standard deviation of 7.68 and the mean IQ of the adoptive fathers was 115.2 with a standard deviation of

7.52. The mean IQ of the biological mothers was 108.7 with a standard deviation of 8.67. The biological mothers in this sample were quite comparable in mean and variability of IQ scores to the adoptive parents. Both groups exhibit some restriction in range of talent that should decrease the magnitude of obtained correlations between parents and children. Correlations between characteristics of adopted children and their biological parents are frequently explained by reference to the existence of selective placement. Adoption agencies may try to match the background and characteristics of birth parents and adoptive parents. There was selective placement in the Texas Adoption Study. The correlation between the IQ of the biological mother and the IQ of the adopting mother was .14. The comparable correlation between the IQ of the biological mother and the IQ of the adopting father was .11.

Correlations between parents and children in the Texas Adoption Study were reported by Loehlin, Horn, & Willerman (1989). These correlations were obtained when the children were between 3 and 14 years old and again 10 years later. They include correlations between adoptive parents and their natural children as well as correlations between biological mothers and the natural children of the adoptive parents. Table 5.4 presents these data. Several aspects of the data reported in Table 5.4 are noteworthy. At the initial assessment, the correlations between the IQ of the adoptive parents and that of their adopted children were not conspicuously different from the correlations of the adoptive parents with their biological children. The correlations between the IQ of the biological mothers of the adopted children and the children they gave up for adoption were slightly higher than the correlations between the adoptive parents' IQ and these same adopted children. These data provide evidence for the influence of the family environment and genes on IQ. The correlation between the adopting parents' IQ and the IQ of their adopted child suggests that the family environment did influence the development of the IQ of the children who were adopted, and the correlation between the IQ of biological mothers and the IQ of their adopted children provides evidence for a genetic influence on IQ. Each of these correlations exceeds the correlation for selective placement. This implies that the correlations between adopted children's IQ and the IQs of their biological mothers and their adoptive parents cannot be attributed to selective placement.

The second assessment, 10 years later, when the adopted children were adolescents or young adults, provides a different picture of genetic and environmental influences on IQ. The correlation between the IQ of the adopting parents and the IQ of the adopted child is now close to zero and is lower than the correlation between the IQ of the biological mother and her adopted child. The correlation between the IQ of the biological mother and her adopted child has increased slightly and is now clearly larger than the correlations between the adopting parents IQ and the IQ of the same children. These data suggest that between-family environmental

TABLE 5.4   Correlations among Parents and
Children in the Texas Adoption Study[a,b]

Variables[c]	Time 1[d]		Time 2[e]	
	r	N[f]	r	N
F,A	.19	253	.10	253
M,A	.13	246	.05	246
F,N	.29	92	.32	92
M,N	.04	90	.14	90
B,A	.23	200	.26	200
B,O	.12	115	.06	115
B,N	.03	95	.05	95
S,A	.14	256	.11	256
S,N	.17	93	.17	93
Among, offspring, same time:				
A,A	.11	75	−.09	75
A,N	.20	106	.05	106
N,N	.27	25	.24	25

[a]Based on Loehlin, Horn, & Willerman (1989).

[b]IQ tests: WAIS for F, M; Revised Beta for B; WAIS/
WISC/Binet for A_1, N_1; WAIS-R/WISC-R for A_2, N_2.

[c]Abbreviations: F, adopted father; M, adopted mother; A,
adopted child of F and M; N, natural child of F and M; B,
birth mother of adopted child; O, other adopted child in
family that adopted B's child; S, socioeconomic index of
adoptive family.

[d]Initial test.

[e]Follow-up test.

[f]N's are number of pairings or degrees of freedom within
families, as described in text.

variance has a decreasing influence on IQ as individuals age. There is
clear evidence in these data for a genetic influence on IQ and, if one
compares the correlation between the biological mother's IQ and the IQ
of her adopted child to the correlations between the IQ of the adopting
parents and that of their natural children, it is possible to argue that
virtually all of the similarity in IQ in natural families is attributable to
genetic similarity. The Texas Adoption Study thus provides two somewhat contradictory pictures of the influence of genetic and environmental characteristics on IQ. Evidence for genetic influences appears stronger
for the second assessment and the evidence for between-family influences
appears stronger on the initial assessment. We shall see that several other
studies provide comparable data suggesting that between-family influences decline with age and genetic influences increase with age. Data on
sibling correlations from the Texas Adoption Study which I will review
also support this conclusion.

The Colorado Adoption Study is another large-scale longitudinal study
that includes data on the IQ of biological parents and their children given

up for adoption at an early age. Data are also obtained from natural families who are matched to the adopting families. There is little selective placement and the samples are reasonably representative of the middle class population of their communities. There is some restriction in range of talent for IQ for all of the parent samples. Table 5.5 is based on data presented by Phillips & Fulker (1989) for a behavior genetic analysis of longitudinal study for children in the Colorado Adoption Project whose IQs were assessed at ages 1, 2, 3, 4, and 7. The data exhibit evidence for an increasing genetic influence as a function of age. At age 7, the correlation between the biological mother's IQ and the IQ of her adopted child is higher than the correlation between the IQ of the adoptive mother and her adoptive children. The samples are large and the correlations that are reported are for the same sample of adopted children. Correlations between the IQ of the adoptive father and these children at age 7, though positive, are still lower than those between the biological mother and her adopted children. The correlation between the biological mother's IQ and the IQ of her adopted child is larger than the correlation between mother and child in the matched sample of natural families. Thus the correlation between the IQ of the biological mother and the IQ of her adopted child at age 7 may be spuriously high. Nevertheless, the trend of these data seems clear. Adopted children exhibit an increased tendency to resemble their biological mother as they grow older and a declining tendency to be similar in IQ to their adopted parents as they grow older. The data for age 7 IQs suggest that all of the resemblance in IQ in natural families is attributable to shared genetic characteristics among members of the same family.

The results of the Colorado Adoption Project and the Texas Adoption Study are in substantial agreement. These studies provide the best available data on the relationship between the IQs of parents and children in adopting and natural families. There are several other sources of data that provide additional information about the similarity in IQ of members of

TABLE 5.5   IQ Correlations for Adopted Children at Different Ages in the Colorado Adoption Project[a,b]

Child		Biological mother	Adopted mother	Adopted father
N	Age			
212	1	.12	.07	.06
189	2	.04	.07	.03
177	3	.11	.12	.20
158	4	.18	.21	.16
139	7	.37	−.05	.11

[a]Based on Phillips & Fulker (1989).
[b]Based on data for families without natural children, the subset of data with the most adequate sample size.

the same family. There are two older studies that provide data about the IQ of biological parents and their adopted children. Skodak & Skeels (1949) reported that the correlation between the IQ of biological children who were adopted at an early age and the IQ of their biological mothers increased as the adopted children aged and was .41 at age 13. The correlation between the biological mother's educational level and the IQ of her adopted child was .32. The comparable correlation between the adoptive mother and her adoptive child was .02. Kamin (1974), in his critique of this study, noted that the comparable correlations at age 7 exhibited smaller differences. The correlations between the biological mother's educational level and the IQ of her adopted child at age 7 was .24 and the comparable correlation between the adoptive mother's IQ and that of her adopted child was .20. Kamin attributed the changes in the values of these correlations at age 7 and 13 to changes in the composition of the sample. The changes in the composition of the sample were not large and do not appear to provide an adequate explanation for the change in the value of the correlations (see Brody & Brody, 1976, Chapter 5). A more plausible explanation that is compatible with the results of modern studies would be that of an increased genetic influence on the IQ of older children.

Snygg (1938) obtained data on the IQs of biological mothers whose children were adopted early in life and the IQs of their children reared in foster homes. The children were assessed when they were between 3 and 8 years of age. The correlation between the IQ of the biological mothers and their adopted children did not vary with the age of the child. The correlation for the entire sample was .13. For the subset of 70 children who were assessed between ages 5 and 8, the correlation was .12. Snygg assumed that the obtained correlation was attributable to selective placement although no quantitative data about the magnitude of selective placement were presented. The correlation obtained by Snygg was slightly lower than that obtained in modern studies. It is also the case that his sample was relatively young and there was some restriction in range of talent for IQ among the biological mothers. The biological mothers in his sample were low in IQ (mean IQ = 78) and the IQs of the biological mothers in the Colorado and Texas studies were not low in IQ. Any or all of these variables as well as secular changes in the heritability of IQ may have contributed to the divergence in outcome between the Snygg study and the modern studies we have reviewed. It should also be noted that Snygg's results, when one considers the age of his sample, are not dramatically different from those obtained in other studies.

There are adoption studies that report the correlation between the IQ of adopted children and characteristics of their biological mothers other than IQ. The educational and occupational levels of the biological parents are measured as "surrogates" of IQ. As we shall see these are variables that correlate with IQ and therefore the relationship between these characteristics of biological mothers and the IQs of their adoptive children provide indirect evidence about the heritability of IQ. The best modern study of this type for young adults aged 16 to 22 is the Minnesota Adoption Study (Scarr & Weinberg, 1983). The study uses educational background as a surrogate for IQ for parents of adopted children. The children were placed in adopted homes in the first year of life. The adopting parents tended to have upper middle class social status and the biological mothers tended to have working class backgrounds. Table 5.6 presents the correlations reported by Scarr and Weinberg. An examination of Table 5.6 indicates that the correlation between the educational level of the biological parents and the IQs of their adopted children is higher than the correlation between the educational level of the adopting parents and the IQ of these children. The correlations between the biological parents' educational level and the IQs of their adopted children is comparable to the correlation between the educational level of parents and the IQs of their natural children in the control families. These data are compatible with the assumption that the resemblance in IQ between parents and young adults in natural families is attributable to their genetic similarity.

There are also several older studies providing information about the relationship between parents' social characteristics and the IQs of their adopted children. Lawrence (1931) studied a group of 185 illegitimate children reared in an institution for orphans. The children were reared in foster homes until the start of primary school and they were tested at an average age of 12.5. The correlations between the social class background of their biological fathers and the IQ of the children were .26 for boys and .25 for girls. Nothing was reported about the foster homes in which the children were reared. Schiff & Lewontin (1986) noted that the tests used in this study were poorly standardized and IQ scores were inversely related to age. It is not clear how the possible age confound would influence the correlation with parental occupational status unless parental occupational status was correlated with the age at which the test was given. No evidence of this confound exists and the poor standardization ought to reduce the magnitude of the correlation with parental social status.

Jones & Carr-Saunders (1927) studied the relationship between adopted

TABLE 5.6 Parent–Child Correlations from the Minnesota Adoption Study[a]

Parent–child factors	Correlation
Adoptive mother's educational level–IQ natural child	.17
Adoptive father educational level–IQ natural child	.26
Adoptive mother's educational level–IQ adopted child	.09
Adoptive father's educational level–IQ adopted child	.11
Biological mother's educational level–IQ adopted child	.28
Biological father's educational level–IQ adopted child	.43

[a]Based on Scarr & Weinberg (1983).

TABLE 5.7 Mean IQ of Institutionalized
Children as a Function of Occupational Status
of the Biological Father[a]

Class	N	Mean IQ
1	209	106.6
2	92	105.0
3	163	96.0
4	165	95.7
5	251	93.4

[a]Based on Jones & Carr-Saunders (1927).

children and the social class background of their biological parents. Table 5.7 presents their data on mean IQs for children adopted at different ages whose biological fathers differed with respect to social class background. The data indicate that mean IQ for adoptees increases monotonically as the social class background of the biological father is higher.

Burks (1928) reported that the correlation between the biological father's occupational status and the IQ of his adopted child was .07. Burks also compared the relationship between parental characteristics in an adopted family and children's IQ and the comparable relationship in biological families. She matched both groups on social background characteristics and reported that correlations between social background characteristics of foster parents and their adopted children were lower than comparable correlations obtained in natural families that were matched on a variety of social background characteristics. For example, she reported correlations between foster father and mother's IQ and the IQ of their foster children of .07 and .19, respectively. The comparable correlations in the matched control families were .45 and .46. The results of the Burks study provide contradictory data with respect to the influence of genetic characteristics on the relationship between the IQ of children and parents. The correlation between the occupational status of biological fathers and the IQ of their adopted children suggests that there is little or no relationship between the biological parent and the adopted child. The differences in the correlation between the IQs of adopted and foster children and natural parents suggests that the correlation between parents and children is mediated by genetic characteristics if natural families have been appropriately matched to adoptive families.

Leahy (1935) reported the results of a comparable investigation. She reported a correlation of .18 between the adoptive midparent's IQ score and the IQ of their adopted child and a comparable correlation of .60 in the control natural families. The children were between 5 and 14 at the time of testing and Leahy attempted to match the social class background of the adopting and natural families. Leahy did not report correlations for relationships between the characteristics of biological parents and their adopted children.

The matching of the natural and adoptive families in the Leahy and the Burks studies was criticized by Kamin (1974). He argued that there were a number of differences between the adoptive and natural families in these studies that might account for the differences in correlation between foster parents and natural parents and the IQs of their children. He did not demonstrate that these differences actually account for the differences that are reported, but only that they might plausibly be assumed to account for these differences. He argued that the correlation between foster parents and their biological children would provide a more relevant control group for comparing correlations between foster children and their adoptive parents' characteristics. Burks did not provide data of this sort. Leahy reported a correlation of .36 between the adoptive midparent IQ and the IQ of a small sample of 20 biological children of these parents. This correlation is larger than the comparable correlation of .18 reported for the sample of 177 adopted children. Whether the correlation of .36 or the comparable correlation of .60 in the control families is the ideal comparison number is debatable. In any case both values are higher than the correlation of .18 reported by Leahy.

In all the studies we have reviewed correlations between the IQs of adopted children and the characteristics of the adoptive parents are low. These results may be contrasted with the findings of Freeman, Holzinger, & Mitchell (1928), who reported a correlation of .48 between a composite measure of the characteristics of the foster home and the IQ of foster children for a large sample ($N = 401$) of adopted children. They also reported a correlation of .39 for a subsample of 169 of these children between the IQ of the child and the midparent IQ of the foster parents. These results appear to contradict the findings of both Burks and Leahy as well as the results of contemporary investigations. Bouchard & Segal (1985) argued that the results of the Freeman et al. study should not be accepted at face value. In addition to the fact that the correlations they obtained appear to be deviant, the results they obtained with a second nonverbal measure of intelligence provide less dramatic evidence for the influence of the foster family on the IQ of its adopted children. They obtained a correlation of .24 between their foster home rating score and scores on the International Test. Finally, many of the adoptees were late placements and had been given IQ tests prior to placement. For this subset of adoptees the correlation between the IQ of the child and the rating of the characteristics of the foster home was .34 at the time of placement. For these reasons, the results of the Freeman et al. study do not constitute clear evidence for a strong influence of the characteristics of adoptive parents on the IQs of their adoptive children.

I have reviewed both modern and classical literature reporting correlations between the characteristics of parents and children in adoptive and natural families. The most important modern studies—the Texas, Colorado, and Minnesota studies—all have large samples and indicate, at least for older children and young adults, that adopted children tend to have IQs that are more highly correlated with the characteristics of their biological mothers than with the characteristics of their adoptive parents. The older literature, while somewhat more problematic and possibly reflecting true secular changes in the heritability of IQ, is generally supportive of these results. Burks reported a near-zero correlation between the occupational status of the biological fathers in her study and the IQ of their adopted children. The remaining older studies including Skodak and Skeels as well as the two British orphanage studies (Lawrence, 1931; Jones & Carr-Saunders, 1927) did obtain significant relationships between the characteristics of the biological fathers and the IQs of their adopted children. In addition, the older studies, with the possible exception of the Freeman *et al.* study, report relatively low correlations between the characteristics of adoptive parents and the IQs of their adoptive children. These data, taken together, suggest that the correlation between the IQ of natural parents and the IQ of their natural children is at least partially attributable to genetic similarity between parent and child. These studies also suggest that between-family environmental influences may not be of great importance in determining individual differences in adult IQ.

Correlations between biologically unrelated siblings who are reared in the same family provide additional information about between-family influences and genetic influences in determining relationships between biologically related siblings who are reared together. There are four modern studies that provide data on the IQ correlation of biologically unrelated children who are reared in the same family. Teasdale & Owen (1984) reported a correlation of .02 for a sample of Danish adoptive male siblings reared in the same home on selective service IQ tests. Kent (1985, as cited in Plomin & Daniels, 1987) compared 52 pairs of adoptive siblings reared together with 54 pairs of nonadoptive siblings between 9 and 15 years of age. An IQ index derived from a phone interview correlated .38 in the sample of nonadoptive siblings reared together. The comparable correlation for the biologically unrelated siblings reared in the same home was −.16. Scarr & Weinberg (1983) obtained a correlation of −.03 for their sample of biologically unrelated siblings reared in the same family in the Minnesota study of older adopted children. Similar results were obtained in the Texas Adoption Study. Correlations for biologically unrelated children reared in the same family decreased from the initial study to the follow-up 10 years later. The original correlation between pairs of adopted children reared in the same home was .11 and the correlation between the adopted and natural children reared together was .20. The comparable correlations in IQ for these biologically unrelated children reared together decreased to −.09 and .05, respectively. These correlations should be compared to the correlation of .24 for biologically related siblings

reared in these families. These data consistently indicate that biologically unrelated older children reared in the same family exhibit little or
no relationship in IQ. Thus the new data on siblings are congruent with
studies on the relationship between parents and children in IQ in adopted
families. These data also support the conclusion that relationships
among older children and young adults in natural families are mediated
by genetic resemblance among family members. In addition, these data
support the conclusion that between-family variance is not a major con-
tributor to differences in intelligence among older children and young
adults.

These data and other data we shall consider have been subjected to a
variety of sophisticated behavior genetic modeling procedures. We shall
review some of these attempts to test various quantitative models for
these data. It should be recognized that the results of the models, irrespective of their sophistication, are in part dependent upon the quality of
the data on which they are based. All of the adoption studies reviewed
here contain some restrictions in range of talent. Therefore, conclusions
about the relative importance of additive genetic influences and between-
family environmental influences on the IQ of children are strictly relative
to the environments that are sampled. While the adopted families in
these studies vary considerably in education, occupational status, and IQ,
they do not contain many individuals who are at the extreme lower end of
the distribution of these variables. Adoptive families, particularly those
whose adoption has been vetted by social agencies, tend to be intact
families of good reputation in their communities. The foster families that
participate in these research studies are likely to have middle class backgrounds. The homeless, the unemployed, the addicted, and the underclass
are not well represented in these studies, if they are represented at all.
These studies do not inform us about the effects on the development of
intelligence of being reared in extremely deprived circumstances. Consider the results of one of the more important contemporary adoption studies, the Texas Adoption Study. The study deals with a sample of biological
mothers who are roughly matched in mean and variance of IQ scores to
the sample of adoptive parents of their biological children. The biological
mothers and the adoptive parents are both above the mean in IQ and
exhibit some restriction in range of talent for IQ. The samples are predominantly middle class. In these circumstances, the IQ of the adopted
child will be determined principally by the IQ of the adopted child's
biological mother. The adoptive parents will have a decreasing influence
on the IQ of their adopted child. This study does not tell us about the
effects of being reared in extremely deprived environments. Thus, when
we appropriately conclude on the basis of this and related studies that
there may be little or no between-family environmental influence on IQ
for older adopted children we should realize that this conclusion may be
limited to certain defined segments of the population and may not apply

to more extreme variations in between-family environments that are not inlcuded in these samples.

Schiff, Duyme, Dumaret, & Tomkiewicz (1982; Schiff & Lewontin, 1986) attempted to demonstrate that there were large effects on IQ attributable to the effects of being reared in upper middle class families. They obtained a sample of 32 French children whose biological mothers had low occupational status who were given up for adoption at an early age and who were reared in upper middle class homes. They compared these children to their biological half sibs who had the same mother and a different father who were reared by their biological mothers or in a variety of less advantaged social circumstances. The children were tested at an average age of 10.3 with a French version of the WISC test. The adopted children had a mean IQ of 110.6. Their biological half sibs reared by their natural mothers had a mean IQ of 94.2. These values are roughly comparable to what would be expected for children in natural families of comparable social class background. Schiff *et al.* argued that these data imply that differences in average IQ of different social classes are attributable to between-family environmental differences.

Capron & Duyme (1989) reported the results of another French adoption study designed to study the influence of extreme variations in social class rearing on mean intelligence test scores of adopted children. They used a complete cross-fostering design in which they formed four groups of adopted subjects consisting of children whose biological parents were either low or high in socioeconomic status who were reared in adopted homes that were either high or low in socioeconomic status. The children were tested with the French version of the WISC at age 14. Table 5.8 presents the mean IQ for children in each of the four groups. The data in Table 5.8 indicate that there is an influence of both biological background and family rearing on mean IQ scores. The effects of biological background are larger than the effects of family rearing in this counterbalanced design. Capron and Duyme asserted that these data do not provide definitive evidence of genetic influences on IQ because the comparison of the biological parents in their studies confounds possible genetic effects with prenatal influences. While this is technically correct, it should be noted that there were no differences in birth weight or gesta-

TABLE 5.8 Mean IQ of Adopted Children[a]

Biological parents' socioeconomic status	Foster parent status	
	High	Low
High	119.6	107.5
Low	103.6	92.4

[a]Based on Capron & Duyme (1989).

tional age at birth for children in each of their four groups. It is unlikely that prenatal influences that might influence the development of IQ could account for the differences observed in the absence of evidence of neurological differences at birth or differences in birth weight or gestational age. While there is some evidence of prenatal influences on intellectual development, they are unlikely to be of sufficiently large magnitude to account for large differences in IQ. Because of the small sample size (total $N = 38$), the magnitude of the effects should not be taken as definitive. It is also the case that the influence of genetic variables may increase during adolescence. Most of the studies that indicate little or no between-family environmental influence on IQ deal with older samples. It may be the case that the asymptotic value for genetic influences and the decline of between-family influences that appears to occur in longitudinal studies of the development of intelligence is not attained at age 14. For these reasons, the Capron and Duyme study does not provide a definitive analysis of the influence of biological and environmental influences on the development of intelligence. Nevertheless, the results do suggest that extreme variations in between-family environments do influence the IQ of adopted children.

The Capron and Duyme study was designed to provide answers to two questions: (1) To what extent can upper middle class rearing conditions increase the IQ of children whose biological parents have low occupational and socioeconomic status?, and (2) to what extent can lower class rearing conditions decrease the IQ of children whose biological parents have high socioeconomic status? There are other studies that provide data that help to answer these questions. Bouchard & Segal (1985) calculated the mean IQ for a subsample of the children studied by Freeman *et al.* (1928) whose adopted parents had a biological child. The mean IQ of 36 foster children in this sample was 95.1 and the mean IQ of the biological children reared in the same families was 112.4. Willerman (1979) obtained the mean IQ of adopted children whose biological mothers were at the extremes of the distribution of IQ scores obtained from mothers in the Texas Adoption Study. Table 5.9 presents the results of his analysis.

TABLE 5.9   IQs of Adoptees as a Function of Biological Mother's IQ[a]

Biological mother (beta)	Adoptive midparent (beta)	Adoptee (WISC/Binet)[b]	Adoptees ≥ 120 IQ (%)	Adoptees ≤ 95 IQ (%)
Low IQ				
(N = 27; mean = 89.4)	110.8	102.6	0	15
High IQ				
(N = 34; mean = 121.6)	114.8	118.3	44	0

[a]Based on Willerman (1979).
[b]WISC = Wechsler Intelligence Scale for Children; Binet, Stanford–Binet Intelligence Scale.

The children of biological mothers whose IQs were low (below 95) had mean IQs that were over one standard deviation lower than adopted children whose biological mothers' IQs were above 120. The adopted children of mothers with low IQ had IQs that were higher than they would have been if they were reared with their biological mother. One can obtain a crude estimate of the magnitude of this effect. The expected value of the IQ of the offspring of mothers with an IQ of 89.4 depends on spouse effects and regression effects. Assuming an assortative mating correlation of .33 and a correlation of .5 for the midparent to child IQ, adoptive rearing increased IQ by approximately .4 standard deviation units or 6 points. This number ought not to be taken too seriously given the sample sizes involved, the lack of information about the biological fathers of these children, and the use of different IQ tests for mothers and children.

The Schiff *et al.* study is not unique in providing a biological sibling control as a way of assessing the influence of upper middle class rearing conditions. The separated twins studied by McGue and Bouchard were reared in a wide range of social class conditions. The separated-twin study combines the features of an adoption and a twin study. McGue and Bouchard's sample of separated twins were reared in families with a mean number of years of education of 10.8 and a standard deviation of 3.5. The adoptive families of the separated twins were equally diverse in occupational status. Thus the sample of homes in which the twins were reared does not appear to exhibit a restriction in range of talent with respect to global indices of between-family environmental conditions that are assumed to influence the development of intelligence. Recall that McGue and Bouchard found near-zero correlations between social background indices and several measures of special intellectual ability. If we try to put together all of the adoptive data to compare the influence of variations in biological background and in family rearing conditions on the development of IQ of adopted children we are left with some uncertainty. It is clear that we have too few studies in which children with allegedly superior genetic backgrounds are reared in circumstances that are thought to be inimical for the development of intelligence. Although we have more data on children with genetic backgrounds that are thought to be less advantageous for the development of IQ being reared in circumstances that are thought to be favorable for the development of high IQ, even here we do not have a great deal of data that permit comparisons with the most relevant control groups—the biological or adopted siblings of the adopted children. Recall that the biological mothers in the Texas study and the Colorado study rarely had extremely low socioeconomic status. Studies of transracial adoption do provide some additional relevant data but I will defer a discussion of these studies to Chapter 10 dealing with group differences in IQ. Putting all of the data together we can venture some tentative conclusions. Virtually all of the studies indicate that the biological background of adopted children influences the IQ of children. In adoption situations that have relatively equal restrictions in range of talent for intelligence in both the biological and adoptive families, the biological backgrond of the adopted child appears to be clearly more important in determining the IQ of the older child than the characteristics of the adoptive families. Put another way, it could be asserted that over a relatively wide range of variation in adopting families that are chosen to provide adequate nurturance for the development of adopted children, there is a vanishingly small influence on the intellectual development of adopted children attributable to the variations in between-family environmental differences. At the extremes, differences in family rearing conditions do influence the intellectual development of the adopted child. It should be noted that we have virtually no data on children reared in the extremes of poverty whose families are disorganized and on public assistance. Children in such families are rarely studied in behavior genetic research and thus we have little basis to reach any conclusion about the effects of this type of rearing on children's IQ. It does appear likely from the available data that children whose biological parents had low IQ who are reared in upper middle class homes will have an IQ that is higher than they would have had if they were reared in their own homes. The true magnitude of this effect is difficult to gauge. A 1-standard-deviation difference is probably a reasonable estimate of the outer limit of this effect although it might well be less (see Locurto, 1990, for a thoughtful discussion of the malleability of IQ based on an analysis of adoption studies). So, too, we can guess that children whose biological parents had high IQs, between 1 and 2 standard deviations above the mean, would have lower IQs if they were reared in extremely deprived homes than if they were reared by their biological parents. Here we have even less basis for a quantitative estimate, but a 1-standard-deviation difference would probably provide an upper-bound estimate for the size of this effect.

QUANTITATIVE ESTIMATES

The data reviewed above may be used to develop quantitative estimates of the various sources of variance that contribute to the IQ phenotype. These estimates may give somewhat different results depending on the data that are used to estimate sources of variance as well as the assumptions of the model used to derive estimates. Plomin & Loehlin (1989) contrasted what they called direct and indirect estimates of the heritability of IQ and indicated that the former estimates are usually substantially larger than the latter estimates. Direct heritability estimates are based on a single family relationship such as the correlation between MZ twins reared apart. Indirect estimates are based on the difference between correlations such as the difference between MZ and DZ twins. They rely on the weighted averages of correlations for several different kinship relationships published by Bouchard & McGue (1981) and updated by newer research to reach this conclusion. Let us consider some of their comparisons. The correlation for separated MZ twins provides a direct estimate of the heritability of IQ. A reasonable estimate for this value is .70. The indirect estimate is based on the difference between MZ and DZ twins and suggests heritabilities closer to .52 assuming MZ correlations of .86 and DZ correlations of .60. There is some uncertainty about the magnitude of this discrepancy. Recall that more recent research suggests that the DZ correlation may be lower than .60, suggesting that the heritability estimate based on this value for DZ correlations may be too low.

Parent–offspring correlations provide a second way of comparing direct and indirect estimates of heritability. The correlation between biological parent and adopted child doubled provides a crude index of narrow heritability. An indirect estimate of heritability may be obtained from adoption studies by obtaining the difference between the correlation of adopted children and their adopted parents and the correlation of natural children reared in the same family with their biological parents. Plomin and Loehlin indicated that direct estimates of heritability for the follow-up data in the Texas Adoption Project are .70, and the indirect estimate for heritability from the same study is less than half the value of the direct estimate—.32. Plomin and Loehlin discussed a variety of possible explanations for this apparent discrepancy and concluded that no satisfactory explanation exists. The example indicates that different approaches and different sources of data used to estimate the heritability of IQ are likely to provide discrepant results. We shall examine a small number of contemporary attempts to provide quantitative estimates of several possible sources of influence on IQ.

Before proceeding to a quantitative analysis of the relative importance of genetic and environmental influences on IQ it should be noted that these estimates may vary in different populations. Loehlin et al. (1988) noted that estimates of the heritability of the intelligence appear to have increased since the previous review of this area of research in 1982 by Henderson. Henderson noted that estimates of heritability that he reviewed were conspicuously lower than those that were common in psychology in earlier decades. Some of these changes are attributable to changes in methods of analysis, some to changes in the available data that are used to estimate heritability, and some possibly to secular trends in the actual heritability of intelligence.

Heritability estimates may also be subject to cohort effects. The most appropriate method for studying secular trends in the heritability of intelligence is to study cohort effects using similar methods of analysis. Sundet, Tambs, Magnus, & Berg (1988) reported a twin study of this type using data from 11 cohorts of male Norwegian twins who were tested at

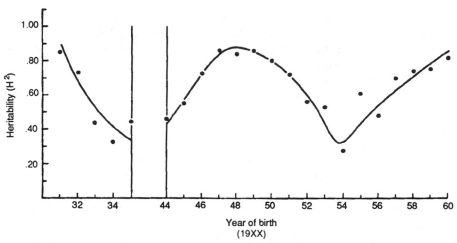

FIGURE 5.1   Cohort influences on heritability of intelligence. (Based on Sundet, Tambs, Magnus, & Berg, 1988.)

the same chronological age when they appeared for armed services examinations. Figure 5.1 presents their data. The secular trends for changes in heritability rise and fall in a complex wave pattern that is not easy to explain by reference to any obvious changes in Norwegian society. It is possible that increased affluence and a more egalitarian educational system resulted in an increased heritability for intelligence for their youngest cohorts. This explanation does not account for the apparent decrease in heritability for the cohorts born immediately after World War II.

DeFries, Johnson, Kuse, McLearn, Polovina, Vandenberg, & Wilson (1979) analyzed sibling and parent–offspring correlations in ability for Caucasian and Japanese children in Hawaii. They found that parent–offspring correlations were generally higher among Caucasians than among Japanese. Sibling correlations for intellectual ability exhibited a reverse pattern. They attributed these effects to changes in the social and economic opportunities available to Japanese-background individuals in Hawaii that resulted in increases in intelligence (Nagoshi & Johnson, 1985). The intergenerational increase in intelligence may have resulted in a decrease in parental–offspring resemblance for Japanese subjects in the study. Changes in correlations among different members of a family will change the outcomes of behavior genetic analyses.

There are other sources of data that suggest that social structural variables may be an important influence on the extent to which intelligence is heritable. Abdel-Rahim, Nagoshi, & Vandenberg (1990) reported the results of a twin study in Egypt. They obtained correlations of .74 for 36 MZ twin pairs and a correlation of .76 for 24 same-sex DZ twin pairs on a measure of general intelligence. The correlations suggest zero heritability for intelligence. Abdel-Rahim et al. indicated that these results might be influenced by a high frequency of arranged marriages in this sample that could contribute to high levels of assortative mating, thereby inflating the DZ genetic resemblance. Whether this is correct or not, it should be noted that this sample was unusual in another respect. The MZ and DZ correlations for height were .96 and .90, respectively. The unusually high DZ correlation for height implies relatively low heritability for a trait that is usually found to be highly heritable. It is also possible that intelligence is not highly heritable in rural Egypt. The role of social privilege may be larger in such a society and between-family environmental influences may play a much larger role in the development of intelligence than they do in Western societies that provide greater access to equal educational opportunities. It may also be the case that heritability varies among different social groups in a society. Fischbein (1980) divided a sample of Danish twins into three groups on the basis of their socioeconomic status. The MZ and DZ correlations for twins in the lowest socioeconomic group on a measure of verbal ability were .66 and .51, respectively. The comparable correlations for twins with the highest socioeconomic status were .76 and .37. Heritability estimates for these data were a monotonically increasing function of the social status of the twin pairs. The sample sizes were small and the data might best be considered as suggestive rather than definitive.

Detterman, Thompson, & Plomin (1990) studied the heritability of intelligence for individuals differing in ability level in a twin study. They found that their twin pairs with high ability had lower heritability of intelligence than their twin pairs with low ability. For example, using a median split of ability level, they found MZ and DZ correlations in intelligence of .57 and .32 for their high-ability twin pairs and comparable correlations of .59 and .09 for their low-ability twin pairs. Note that the low DZ correlations for the low-ability twin pairs leads to an estimate of a heritability of 1.00. The pattern of correlations for the low-ability twins is compatible with the presence of high levels of nonadditive genetic variance.

The results of the Detterman *et al.* study are not in agreement with those of Fischbein based on an analysis of differences in correlations for twins differing in social class background. The differences in outcome may be attributable to differences between an analysis based on social class rather than on differences in intelligence. It is obvious that we know too little about differential heritability of IQ among different groupings of subjects. It is probably premature to speculate about the causes of these differences or even about the findings that require interpretation.

This brief review of studies of differential heritability for intelligence as a function of social background and secular trends should reinforce the caution on the meaning of heritability placed at the beginning of this chapter. The heritability of intelligence is a number assigned to a population, not a trait. Quantitative estimates of heritability should be thought of as results for populations of individuals living in technologically advanced societies. The analyses that we shall consider are derived from studies conducted at different time periods and may confound secular trends and methodologies with sample differences. They may be thought of as a snapshot of what may be a moving target.

Chipuer, Rovine, & Plomin (1990) and Loehlin (1989) used Bouchard and McGue's summary of correlations for IQ similarity to develop behavior genetic models. The modeling procedure is based on a specification of the influences of different environmental and genetic factors on various kinship correlations. Table 5.10 presents the expectations used by Chipuer et al. An examination of Table 5.10 indicates the assumptions that govern the behavior genetic analysis. For example, a nonadditive genetic parameter is assumed to influence the correlation of MZ twins. The value of this parameter for DZ twins is .25. Note also that different parameters are specified for different environmental influences. The influence of the environment of twins is assumed to be equivalent for DZ and MZ twin pairs but the twin environmental parameter is independent of the sibling parameter. The expectations expressed in Table 5.10 are tested against an updated version of Bouchard and McGue's summary of correlations by LISREL procedures. A full model is fitted to these data and provides an adequate fit. This is a model in which each of the separate parameters included in the expectations is assigned a specified optimal value. The model is tested by fixing various parameter values to zero in order to see if this yields a significantly poorer fit to the obtained data, in

TABLE 5.10   Expected Contribution of Genetic and Environmental Factors to Resemblance for 12 Types of Relatives[a,b]

Relationship	Contribution
Monozygotic twins together	$h^2 + d^2 + s^2_T$
Monozygotic twins apart	$h^2 + d^2$
Dizygotic twins together	$.5h^2 + .25d^2 + s^2_T$
Siblings together	$.5h^2 + 25d^2 + s^2_S$
Siblings apart	$.5h^2 + .25d^2$
Parent–offspring together	$.5h^2 + d^2_{PO}$
Parent–offspring apart	$.5h^2$
Parent–adopted offspring	s^2_{PO}
Adopted siblings together	s^2_S
Adopted/natural siblings together	s^2_S
Half siblings together	$.25h^2 + s^2_S$
Cousins together	$.125h^2 + s^2_C$

[a]Based on Chipuer, Rovine, & Plomin (1990).

[b]h^2 are the loadings of the additive genetic factor; d^2 are the loadings of the nonadditive genetic factor; s^2 are the loadings of the shared environment factor for twins (T), siblings (S), parent–offspring (PO), and cousins (C).

effect providing a test of the importance of that particular parameter. It is possible to test various reduced models to see if a simpler model will adequately fit the obtained data. Chipuer *et al.* found that a model that omits a nonadditive genetic parameter led to a significant increase for the Chi Square test of significance, indicating that the fit of the model has declined, implying that it is necessary to include nonadditive genetic influences in order to fit the obtained data. So, too, a simplified model that assumes that the environmental influence is constant for sibs, twins, cousins, and parents and offspring leads to a significant decline in the adequacy with which the model is able to account for the obtained relationships. And, a model that omits the additive genetic parameter is not able to fit the data adequately.

The final parameter estimates derived by Chipuer *et al.* are presented in Table 5.11. Several aspects of these estimates are noteworthy. The heritability of IQ is estimated to be .51. Nineteen percent of the variance in IQ scores is attributable to nonadditive genetic influences. Note that nonadditive genetic influences do not contribute to the relationship between parents and offspring. This will tend to decrease parent–offspring correlations relative to sibling correlations for purely genetic reasons. Nonadditive genetic influences may be masked in analyses that do not consider the influences of assortative mating. Note that assortative mating tends to increase the genetic resemblance of siblings. Chipuer *et al.*'s analysis also indicates that shared environmental parameters vary considerably for different categories of individuals who are reared together.

TABLE 5.11 Parameter Estimates, Standard Errors, and Percentage of Variance Accounted for by Each Parameter, When Assortative Mating Is Included[a]

Parameter	Parameter estimate	Standard error (±)	Variance (%)
Heritability			
h	.569	.024	32
d	.433	.020	19
Environment			
Shared			
Twins	.588	.016	35
Siblings	.471	.016	22
Parent–offspring	.450	.021	20
Cousins	.331	.045	11
Nonshared			
Twins	.374	.004	14
Siblings	.518	.009	27
Parent–offspring	.534	.013	29
Cousins	.616	.031	38

[a]Based on Chipuer, Rovine, & Plomin (1990).

The largest difference is between twins and other categories. This suggests that twins influence each other in ways that are different from the influence of siblings on each other. This analysis also indicates that a substantial portion of the variance in IQ is attributable to within-family environmental differences, i.e., differences experienced by individuals reared in the same family.

Loehlin (1989) also tested various behavior genetic models for a subset of these data. His analysis was addressed to somewhat different issues. He found that it was necessary to assume that direct and indirect estimates of heritability provide different estimates and that separate estimates for these two kinds of estimates improved the fit. He also found that it was necessary to assume that there were genetic influences and between-family influences on IQ in order to obtain an adequate fit for the data and that it was necessary to assume that twins and siblings had different between-family environmental influences. The parametric estimates for additive genetic influence were .41 for direct estimates and .30 for indirect estimates. Nonadditive genetic influence was estimated to account for 17% of the variance in IQ. Thus the heritability of IQ was estimated to vary between .47 and .58. Loehlin indicated that these values are based on correlations that are averaged over different age groups. The heritability of IQ appears to increase with age and thus the values reported for heritability in the two analyses considered here are probably too low for older individuals.

Nonadditive genetic variance may contribute to the phenotype for IQ. This suggests another method of testing for genetic influences on intelligence—the study of inbreeding depression. The study of inbreeding depression is based on a series of genetic assumptions. Offspring of genetically related parents are more likely to be homozygous for various gene loci. It is assumed that harmful or defective traits that survived evolutionary selection are more likely to be recessive and to have their influence masked by dominant traits. Intelligence may be assumed to be influenced by directional dominance effects that are beneficial. If this is correct, offspring of genetically related individuals will be subject to inbreeding depression, i.e., the influence of excessive unmasked recessive genes. A coefficient of inbreeding is a measure of the degree of genetic relatedness of the parents of a child. Incestuous matings of parents and children and of siblings have a high genetic inbreeding correlation of .25. The offspring of first-cousin marriages have a genetic inbreeding correlation of .0625. If intelligence is influenced by genes that exhibit directional dominance, inbreeding depression should occur. The effects of inbreeding depression are difficult to demonstrate. Kamin (1980) and Jensen (1978) reached quite different conclusions about the probity of evidence for the existence of this phenomena. The expected magnitude of the effect is small and in several small sample studies the difference between children expected to exhibit the effect and various control samples is not statistically significant, although it is fair to say that in most of the studies available, the direction of effects distinguishing between the IQ of children whose parents were biologically related and control groups were consistent with an inbreeding depression effect. The difficulty with the interpretation of the results in these studies derives from the search for an appropriate control group. It is usually the case that the biological parents who are genetically related to each other differ from the biological parents who are unrelated to each other. Consider the results of a study reported by Schull & Neel (1965). They obtained IQ scores from a large sample of Japanese children of consanguineous marriages and children of unrelated parents. They found that the mean IQ of the former group was slightly lower than the mean IQ of the latter group. It was also the case that the parents of the former group had lower socioeconomic status than the parents of the latter group. They used multiple regression analyses to adjust for the background differences between their two groups of subjects and statistically adjusted their scores for differences in parental occupational status and educational status. Using these adjusted scores they found a statistically significant inbreeding depression score equivalent to 4.5 IQ points for marriages of first cousins. Neel, Schull, Yamamoto, Uchida, Yanese, & Fujiki, (1970) reported the results of a second study in Japan. They found that the IQ of Japanese children of consanguineous marriages was 2.5 points lower than the IQ of children whose parents were not biologically related. These were adjusted mean differences after statistically controlling for social class differences between the groups. This difference was not statistically significant even though the sample was large (total $N = 1372$). These studies illustrate two of the difficulties that surround research on this topic. The effects are small and difficult to detect, and individuals who choose to marry their relatives may be different from individuals who choose to marry individuals who are genetically unrelated to them. It is always possible to raise questions about the adequacy of the statistical controls for the socioeconomic differences between the two groups.

There are studies reporting inbreeding depression effects where there is little or no socioeconomic difference between the parents of the inbred and outbred children. For example, Agrawal, Sinha, & Jensen (1984; see also Bashi, 1977) obtained a significant inbreeding depression effect on the Raven test for a sample of Muslim children in India. There were no significant differences in socioeconomic status between the inbred and outbred groups. This result may not be conclusive. In addition to differences in socioeconomic status these two groups may differ with respect to attitudes about marriage. In some societies cousin marriage is traditional. The choice of marriage partner may be indicative of one's attitude to tradition and these attitudes may be related to intelligence. Even where there is no difference in the socioeconomic status of inbred and outbred children, the parents of these children may differ in other salient respects. The most convincing control for possible differences between groups used in this research would be intelligence test scores. I am not aware of any studies that equated the intelligence test scores of biologically related and biologically unrelated parents in a study of inbreeding depression. Such a study would provide more convincing evidence of the phenomena than the existing research. At the same time existing studies, though less than perfect, when considered collectively do exhibit a small but relatively consistent effect that is compatible with the phenomenon of inbreeding depression. Perhaps it would be judicious to conclude that the available data are compatible with the existence of inbreeding depression while at the same time failing to conclusively demonstrate that it exists.

DEVELOPMENTAL BEHAVIOR GENETICS

Behavior genetic analyses may also be applied to developmental data. Such analyses address issues of stability and change in IQ. Loehlin *et al.* (1989) analyzed data from the Texas Adoption Study using a behavior genetic analysis of the relationships obtained at the initial testing and at the second testing 10 years later. Their parametric analysis indicated that there are significant genetic and between-family environmental influences for the initial assessment period. The estimates of these paths are .51 and .25, respectively. They tested the significance of a direct path from between-family environmental influences and genetic characteristics to the second assessment. In effect, this tests for the effects of additional environmental and genetic influences on intelligence that have not been expressed at the initial assessment. The path for genetic influences to the phenotypic score for intelligence at the second assessment is .45; the corresponding estimated path value for the effects of the between-family environment is −.11—a value that is not significantly different from zero.

Loehlin and colleagues indicated that this implies that genetic factors continue to influence the development of intelligence. They state,

> A general conclusion from this analysis is that the popular view of genetic effects as fixed at birth and environmental effects as changing has got matters almost backward, at least for the trait of intelligence in this population during these developmental years. Shared family environmental effects occur early in childhood and persist to a degree in the phenotype. But changes in genetic expression continue at least into late adolescence or early adulthood. [Loehlin *et al.*, 1989, p. 1000]

DeFries, Plomin, & LaBuda (1987; see also Phillips & Fulker, 1989) analyzed longitudinal data from the Colorado Adoption Project assessments of children at ages 1, 2, 3, and 4. They also include data obtained by

Wilson (1983) for a longitudinal twin study in which correlations for intelligence were obtained for a sample of MZ and DZ twins at the same ages. Their analysis focused on the relationship between childhood IQ assessments and adult IQ. The relationship between the childhood IQ of an adopted child and the IQ of that child's biological parent is a function of three parameters—the additive genetic variance of the childhood IQ assessment, the additive genetic variance of the adult IQ, and the longitudinal genetic correlation between the two IQ measures. In the absence of selective placement, a correlation between an adopted child's IQ and the IQ of the biological parent can only occur if each of the IQ measures has nonzero heritability and if there is some longitudinal genetic continuity between the genetic influences at both ages. If both childhood IQ and adult IQ are influenced by independent genetic characteristics, the correlation between the biological parent's IQ and the adopted child's IQ will be zero.

The correlations used in the DeFries *et al.* (1987) analysis are presented in Table 5.12. The correlations between biological and adopted parents

TABLE 5.12 Correlations Used for Longitudinal Behavior Genetic Analysis[a,b]

Variable[c]	Phenotypic correlation			
	Year 1	Year 2	Year 3	Year 4
p_M, p_F	.13	.10	.12	.13
p_M, p_O	.07	.20	.16	.21
p_F, p_O	.10	.17	.09	.08
Adoptive families (pooled)				
p_{BM}, p_{BF}	.28	.28	.35	.37
p_{AM}, p_{AF}	.28	.28	.29	.31
p_{BM}, p_{AF}	−.01	−.03	−.03	.07
p_{BM}, p_{AM}	.02	.06	.07	.14
p_{BF}, p_{AF}	−.13	−.08	−.07	.03
p_{BF}, p_{AM}	.04	.11	.10	.19
p_{BM}, p_{AO}	.10	.07	.18	.24
p_{BF}, p_{AO}	.26	.34	.27	.48
p_{AF}, p_{AO}	.09	.08	.15	.11
p_{AM}, p_{AO}	.12	.05	.14	.17
Adult twins				
p_{T1}, p_{T2} (identical)	.86	.86	.86	.86
p_{T1}, p_{T2} (fraternal)	.62	.62	.62	.62
Child twins				
p_{T1}, p_{T2} (identical)	.68	.81	.88	.83
p_{T1}, p_{T2} (fraternal)	.63	.73	.79	.71

[a]Based on DeFries, Plomin, & LaBuda (1987).
[b]Adult and child twin correlations are from Loehlin and Nichols (1976) and Wilson (1983).
[c]M, nonadoptive mother; F, nonadoptive father; O, nonadoptive child; BM, biological mother; BF, biological father; AM, adoptive mother; AF, adoptive father; AO, adopted child; T1, twins; T2, cotwin.

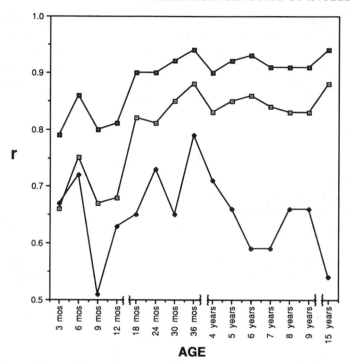

FIGURE 5.2 MZ and DZ correlations at different ages in a longitudinal study. MZ True Score *r*, ■—■; MZ, ◻—◻; DZ, ◆—◆.

and the intelligence scores of the adopted children indicate that IQ scores at age 4 appear to exhibit stronger genetic influences than IQ scores obtained at earlier ages. The twin data exhibit increased divergence between MZ and DZ twins at age 4, and the adoption data indicate an emerging pattern of higher correlations between the IQ of biological parents and the IQ of the adopted child. The quantitative analyses provide a more precise estimate of several parameters. The heritability of IQ is found to increase from age 1 to age 4. The genetic correlation between adult IQ and childhood IQ is estimated to increase from .42 at age 1 to .75 at age 4. These analyses provide insight into the stability of IQ. The phenotypic correlations between childhood IQ at ages 3 and 4 and adult IQ are approximately .4 and .5, respectively. The genetic contribution from childhood IQ to adult phenotypic IQ is estimated to be .18 and .28 for ages 3 and 4, respectively. This implies that approximately half the phenotypic stability from childhood to adult IQ is mediated genetically.

The developmental process investigated in the DeFries *et al.* (1987) analysis is probably continuous for later stages of development. Wilson's longitudinal twin study used in the analysis obtained data for older twins. Figure 5.2 presents the results of this study. Figure 5.2 indicates that MZ correlations approach the test–retest reliability for measures of intelligence. The MZ–DZ discrepancy increases over time. The discrepancy does not appear to have reached an asymptote at age 15. Estimates of the heritability of intelligence based on these data indicate increasing heritability with age and decreasing between-family environmental influence with age. Heritability estimates for these data approach .7 at age 15 (see also Fischbein, 1981). These data suggest that the longitudinal genetic correlation between IQ scores during development and adult IQ is likely to increase as the age of the child increases.

This brief review of the developmental behavior genetics of IQ suggests four conclusions. First, the heritability of IQ increases from infancy to adulthood. Second, between-family environmental influences decline with age—indeed they are hardly detectable over wide ranges of the environment for adult samples. Third, phenotypic continuity in IQ is substantially influenced by genetic continuity. Fourth, genetic influences on IQ not expressed at an earlier age may influence IQ at a later age.

The combination of developmental issues and behavior genetics is also relevant to understanding the influence of an additional source of variance on IQ—genetic–environmental correlation. Genetic–environmental correlations occur when genotypes are correlated with environments. It is reasonable to assume that such correlations exist for intelligence. Parents who are likely to provide their children with genetic characteristics that are favorable for the development of high IQ are likely to provide superior environments for the development of IQ. This potential source of influence is neither genetic nor environmental, it is both. Scarr & McCartney (1983) proposed a developmental theory of genetic–environmental correlation. They distinguished among three kinds of genetic–environmental correlations—passive, reactive, and active. Passive influences simply result from the correlation between the genetic characteristics of the child and the rearing conditions provided by the child's biological parent. Reactive influences result from environmental responses to individuals that are correlated with the child's genotype. Such influences undoubtedly exist for intelligence. For example, a teacher may respond to the intellectual ability of a child and assign that child learning materials that are assumed to be geared to an estimate of the child's intelligence that might contribute to the child's intellectual development. Active influences, sometimes called niche building, refer to a tendency of individuals to select environments that may be compatible with their genotypes. A child with genes that are favorable for the development of high intelligence might chose to engage in intellectual activities that foster the development of intelligence. Scarr and McCartney proposed that the relative importance of these three kinds of genetic–environmental influences changes over time. Passive influences decline and reactive and active influences increase with age.

Although Scarr and McCartney's theory appears plausible, it is difficult to test. Loehlin & DeFries (1987) reported several analyses of the potential role of genetic–environmental correlation for intelligence. A relatively direct test for the presence of this component of variance in IQ test scores can be obtained by comparing the phenotypic variance of IQ scores for adopted children and natural children. Genetic–environmental correlation does not contribute to the variance of adopted children, but it does contribute to the variance of scores of children reared by their biological parents. A comparison of variance differences for phenotypic IQ scores of adopted and natural children, holding constant other relevant influences, should provide a direct estimate of the importance of passive genetic–environmental correlation. Unfortunately, Loehlin and DeFries demonstrated that such estimates are unlikely to be stable for the existing literature due to the standard error of estimates of variance. Small differences in variance estimates for adopted and natural children that could easily occur for the samples that are currently available lead to quite discrepant estimates of genetic–environmental correlation. Loehlin and DeFries recommend the use of path estimates of parent-to-child IQ in adoptive and natural families. There is no genetic–environmental correlation, excluding the influence of selective placement, in adopted families. Loehlin and DeFries estimated the magnitude of genetic–environmental correlational influences on IQ using data from several adoption studies and obtained estimates for different parametric values of heritability and between-family environmental influences. They estimate that this source of variance accounts for 15% of the variance in the phenotype for IQ. If the phenotypic IQ measure is corrected for unreliability, the percentage of variance in true score phenotype for IQ for genetic–environmental correlation increases to 20%. Plomin (1987) indicated that there is some evidence of a decline in the magnitude of the influence of this component for studies with older samples.

There is little formal evidence for the influence of reactive and active genetic–environmental correlations on intelligence. Plomin (1987; see also Plomin & DeFries, 1985b; Plomin, DeFries, & Fulker, 1988) reported one test for reactive genetic–environmental correlational influences on intelligence. In the Colorado Adoption Project, observations of the home environment are made, including the use of a home inventory scale (Caldwell & Bradley, 1978) that is assumed to measure characteristics of the environment that influence the development of intelligence. The correlation between the biological mother's IQ and scores on the home inventory provides a test for the presence of reactive genetic–environmental correlation. Plomin reported correlations between the biological mother's IQ and the home inventory score for the adopted family of that mother's child of − .06, − .02, .12, and .10 for measures of the home inventory taken when the child was 1, 2, 3, and 4 years old, respectively. These data provide some support for Scarr and McCartney's theory. There is evidence of a slight increase in reactive genetic–environmental correlation for IQ as the child becomes older. It should be recognized that this evidence is more in the nature of a demonstration than a definitive attempt to study reactive genetic–environmental correlational influences on the development of intelligence. There are obviously many ways in which the environment may be differentially responsive to individual differences among individuals with different genotypes.

Intelligence may be influenced by genotype × environment interactions as well as the correlation between these components. Interaction effects refer to the nonadditive influences of genes and environments. It is theoretically possible that there are nonadditive combinations of genotypic and environmental influence such that the combined effects of certain combinations of genes and environments are not predictable from knowledge of their general effects. Perhaps individuals with genes that are unusually favorable for the development of IQ experience exceptionally rapid intellectual growth if they are placed in environments that are extremely favorable for the development of IQ. Or, more dramatically, perhaps certain genotypes might predispose individuals to develop high IQ in one environment and low IQ in a different environment. While all of these effects are theoretically plausible, little or no evidence exists for an influence of genotype × environment interaction on IQ phenotypes. One way of testing for the presence of such interactions is to use adoption designs. One can use characteristics of the biological parents as surrogates for genotypic characteristics of the child. Measures of the characteristics of the adoptive home may be used as an index of the environment. The IQ of the adopted child may be studied as an outcome variable in this design to index the presence of potential interactions between genes and the environment. The data presented in Table 5.8 derived from the Capron and Duyme study provide a clear test of genetic–environmental influence on IQ test scores. These data indicate that the characteristics of the biological parent and the characteristics of the adoptive parents each provide an independent and additive influence on the IQ of the adopted child. There is no evidence of the presence of an interaction effect. Plomin & DeFries (1985; Plomin et al., 1988) reported similar tests using data from the Colorado Adoption Project for ages 1, 2, 3, and 4. They performed a number of analyses searching for interactions between the IQ of the biological mothers of the adoptees and characteristics of the adoptive family on the child's IQ. Virtually all of these analyses indicated that there were no significant genotype × environment interactions for the IQ phenotype during early childhood. It is possible that the right environmental measures have not been used in this research. But the most reasonable conclusion, albeit a tentative conclusion, is that genotype × environment interactions are not an important source of influence on the development of IQ.

SPECIAL ABILITIES

It is possible to use behavior genetic methods to analyze specific abilities. Since there is a substantial amount of g variance in most measures of intelligence, it is apparent that a behavior genetic analysis of a specific ability measure should resemble the results of a behavior genetic analysis of general intelligence. It is also the case that the g loadings of specific ability measures vary and that the variance in any measure that is independent of g variance may be determined by genetic and environmental influences that are quite different from those that determine general intelligence or the g component of variance on the measure.

Plomin (1986; 1988) see also Vandenberg & Vogler, 1985) reviewed studies of the behavior genetics of specific abilities. He concluded that heritabilities were higher for verbal and spatial tests than they were for perceptual speed tests. Memory tests had the lowest heritabilities. Contradictory data exist. Plomin cited a study by Partanen, Bruun, & Markkanen (1966) of a large sample of Finnish adult twins. They found comparable heritabilities for tests of verbal ability, spatial ability, perceptual speed, and memory. Similarly, the data reported in Table 5.2 obtained by Bouchard and McGue from separated adult twins in the Minnesota twin study indicate relatively little difference in heritability for a perceptual speed factor and verbal and spatial ability factors. Most of the research reviewed by Plomin that supports the assumption of differential heritability for these factors is based on younger samples. Perhaps differential heritability for different ability factors is less likely to occur among adult samples.

Plomin also indicated that studies of the heritability of general factors may overlook important sources of variance on tests that are grouped as common indices of a specific factor such as spatial ability. The Hawaii Family Study of Cognition (DeFries *et al.*, 1979) provides relevant data. These authors obtained correlations between parent and offspring of different ethnic groups and sibling correlations for specific measures of ability. These data do not permit one to partition the phenotypic variance on any of these measures into genetic and environmental sources of variance. The parent–offspring and sibling correlations that they report provide upper-bound estimates for the influence of additive genetic variance and between-family environmental influences on these measures. The familiality correlations for different spatial ability measures were not equivalent. The parent–offspring and sibling correlations for one of their spatial ability measures, the Elithorn mazes, was .14 or less in different ethnic groups. The comparable correlations for other specific ability measures were higher. Thus additive genetic and or between-family environmental variance must be lower on the Elithorn maze measure than on other measures of spatial ability. It is apparent that it is possible to study the behavior genetics of factors and measures that differ in specificity.

Just as it is possible to define a hierarchical structure of ability measures that contains g at its apex and specific tests or even components of test performance at the lower levels of the hierarchy, it is possible to study the behavior genetics of measures, components, or factors at any level of generality in the hierarchy.

It is possible to perform behavior genetic analyses of the relationship between specific measures. Such analyses indicate whether or not relationships between measures are attributable to genetic or environmental influence. Wilson (1986; see also Segal, 1985) reported greater profile similarity for MZ twin pairs than for DZ twin pairs on the Wechsler tests of intelligence. These data suggest that there are genetic influences on the patterning of scores on intelligence tests. LaBuda, DeFries, & Fulker (1987) analyzed the relationship between subscale scores on the WISC in a sample of twins. Factor analyses of the Wechsler tests usually report a three-factor solution (see Cohen, 1952, 1969; Kaufman, 1975). The factors are defined as Verbal Comprehension, Perceptual Organization, and Freedom from Distractibility. The Vocabulary, Block Design, and Digit Span tests are the best markers for these factors. LaBuda *et al.* analyzed the relationship among these tests. They found that genetic variables tended to determine the underlying factor structure of the tests. Both the between- and the within-family environmental influences were compatible with the assumption that there was a single common factor that influenced scores on all of the factors. The distinctive pattern of scores was primarily determined by genetic influences.

Ho, Baker, & Decker (1988) studied the relationship between measures of the speed of processing information and Wechsler test performance in a sample of 30 MZ and 30 DZ twin pairs. They used tests of rapid naming and the Colorado Speed tests. The rapid naming tests required subjects to name familiar objects, colors, numbers, and letters. The Colorado Speed test presents subjects with a four-letter nonsense syllable and requires individuals to identify which of several letter groups is identical to the target stimulus. Their analyses indicated that the information-processing measures were heritable. They also found that the covariance between these measures and IQ was influenced by genetic characteristics. For their two information-processing measures (rapid automatic naming and the Colorado Speed test) they estimated that the genetic covariance between the measures accounted for 70 and 57% of the variance in the phenotypic correlations between these two measures and IQ. The remaining phenotypic variance was influenced by within-family environmental variance. These analyses imply that the genetic characteristics that determine performance on the tests of speed of information processing are identical to those that determine performance on tests of general intelligence.

Baker, Vernon, & Ho (In press) performed a genetic covariance analysis of the relationship between general intelligence and performance on the battery of information-processing tasks used by Vernon (1983) in his study of the relationship between speed of information processing and intelligence, reviewed in Chapter 4 of this book. They obtained a heritability estimate of .44 for a general measure of speed of information processing. They obtained correlations between a general index of speed of reaction time and verbal and performance IQ of $-.60$ and $-.60$, respectively, for MZ twin pairs. The comparable correlations for DZ twin pairs were $-.36$ and $-.25$. The genetic covariance analysis indicated that virtually all of the correlation between the measures of speed of information processing and intelligence were attributable to correlated genetic influences.

The analyses reported by Ho *et al.* and Baker *et al.* provide a tentative answer to one of the major issues in contemporary discussions of intelligence. Why is there a relationship between performance on information-processing tasks and scores on tests of intelligence? There is evidence that performance on information-processing tasks is heritable. Recall that Bouchard and McGue found that intercept parameters of information processing were heritable. Vernon (1989) reported higher MZ than DZ twin correlations for the battery of tests he used in his studies of the relationship between indices of speed and variability of processing information and IQ (see Chapter 4). Although these data imply that performance on information-processing tasks and performance on tests of intelligence appear to be influenced by genotypes, they do not tell us anything about the covariance or relationship between these measures. The genetic covariance studies, by contrast, suggest that information-processing tasks and IQ may be influenced by the same genes. The remaining phenotypic variance is attributable to within-family environmental factors that tend to individuate twins reared in the same family. It is tempting to extrapolate these findings. Perhaps the information-processing skills tapped by these measures are primitive and are present prior to the emergence of the complex skills assessed by tests of intelligence. These data may be viewed as adding support to the analysis of the relationship between elementary information-processing skills and performance on tests of intelligence advocated by those theorists who are committed to a monarchial, bottom-up, reductive theory of intelligence. At the same time it should be realized that such a conclusion on the basis of these data is extremely premature. These studies leave the causal direction of the influence between information processing and intelligence ambiguous. Strictly speaking, these data are compatible with a model that assumes that genes influence the development of complex intellectual skills and that complex intellectual skills influence the development of information-processing skills. Speed of information processing may be a "slave process" that is not causally related to intelligence but is the consequence of the development of intellectual skills and hence is influenced by the same genes. I am not suggesting that this is correct. A combination of longitudinal research and analyses of the behavior genetics of the covariance between information-processing abilities and intelligence should resolve these questions.

CONCLUSION

In 1974 Kamin wrote a book suggesting that there was little or no evidence that intelligence was a heritable trait. I believe that he was able to maintain this position by a distorted and convoluted approach to the literature. It is inconceivable to me that any responsible scholar could write a book taking this position in 1990. In several respects our understanding of the behavior genetics of intelligence has been significantly enhanced in the last 15 years. We have new data on separated twins, large new data sets on twins reared together, better adoption studies, the emergence of developmental behavior genetics and longitudinal data sets permitting an investigation of developmental changes in genetic and environmental influences on intelligence, and the development of new and sophisticated methods of analysis of behavior genetic data. These developments provide deeper insights into the ways in which genes and the environment influence intelligence. They are, in addition, relevant to an understanding of general issues in the field of intelligence. It is hard for me to imagine how one can write a general thesis on intelligence that omits a discussion of the results of behavior genetic analyses of intelligence. Our ability to address many of the central issues in contemporary discussions of intelligence is enhanced by a knowledge of the results of behavior genetic research.

6

ENVIRONMENTAL
DETERMINANTS OF
INTELLIGENCE

How does the environment influence the development of intelligence? In this chapter we shall consider a variety of research topics designed to provide information about the nature of environmental influences on intelligence. The material to be presented in this chapter is inextricably linked to the concepts presented in Chapter 5. Behavior genetic analyses provide a framework for understanding the role of the environment.

BETWEEN-FAMILY ENVIRONMENTAL EFFECTS

Consider a simple scenario. Children reared in different families are treated differently by their parents. These differences cause children to develop different intellectual skills. There are many studies in the literature that report correlations between parental socialization practices and individual differences in intelligence. These studies may not provide useful information about environmental influences on intelligence. We can illustrate the difficulties involved in studying between-family environmental influences on the development of intelligence by considering research using the Caldwell Home Inventory (Bradley & Caldwell, 1976, 1980; Caldwell & Bradley, 1978).

The Home Inventory is an instrument that is designed to assess the characteristics of a child's home environment. The inventory was designed to assess those characteristics of a child's environment that were assumed to influence the development of intelligence. Table 6.1 presents the items rated by a trained observer that constitute the infant version of the measure. Scores on the Home Inventory are positively correlated with childhood assessments of intelligence. Gottfried (1984) summarized several large-scale longitudinal studies of intellectual development that used this instrument. He calculated an average correlation of .30 between Home Inventory scores obtained at age 1 and childhood IQ scores obtained at ages 1, 2, 3, and between 3.5 and 5. The mean correlation for

TABLE 6.1   Infant Version of the Home Inventory[a]

I. Emotional and verbal responsivity of mother[b]
   1. Mother spontaneously vocalizes to child at least twice during visit (excluding scolding).
   2. Mother responds to child's vocalization with a verbal response
   3. Mother tells child the name of some object during visit or says the name of person or object in a "teaching" style.
   4. Mother's speech is distinct, clear, and audible.
   5. Mother initiates verbal interchanges with observer—asks questions, makes spontaneous comments.
   6. Mother expresses ideas freely and easily and uses statements of appropriate length for conversation (e.g., gives more than brief answers).
   7. Mother permits child occasionally to engage in "messy" types of play.
   8. Mother spontaneously praises child's qualities or behavior twice during visit.
   9. When speaking of or to child, mother's voice conveys positive feeling.
  10. Mother caresses or kisses child at least once during visit.
  11. Mother shows some positive emotional reponses to praise a child offered by visitor.

II. Avoidance of restriction and punishment
  12. Mother does not shout at the child during visit.
  13. Mother does not express overt annoyance with or hostility toward child.
  14. Mother neither slaps nor spanks child during visit.
  15. Mother reports that no more than one instance of physical punishment occurred during the past week.
  16. Mother does not scold or derogate child during visit.
  17. Mother does not interfere with child's actions or restrict child's movements more than three times during visit.
  18. At least 10 books are present and visible.
  19. Family has a pet.

III. Organization of physical and temporal environment
  20. When mother is away, care is provided by one of three regular substitutes.
  21. Someone takes child into grocery store at least once a week.
  22. Child gets out of house at least four times a week.
  23. Child is taken regularly to doctor's office or clinic.
  24. Child has a special place in which to keep toys and "treasures."
  25. Child's play environment appears safe and free of hazards.

IV. Provision of appropriate play materials
  26. Child has some muscle-activity toys or equipment.
  27. Child has push or pull toy.
  28. Child has stroller or walker, kiddie car, scooter, or tricycle.
  29. Mother provides toys or interesting activities for child during interview.
  30. Provides learning equipment appropriate to age-cuddly toy or role-playing toys.
  31. Provides learning equipment appropriate to age mobility, table and chairs, high chair, playpen.
  32. Provides eye–hand coordination toys—items to go in and out of receptacle, fit-together toys, beads.
  33. Provides eye–hand coordination toys that permit combinations—stacking or nesting toys, blocks, or building toys.
  34. Provides toys for literature or music.

V. Maternal involvement with child
  35. Mother tends to keep child within visual range and to look at him often.

(continued)

TABLE 6.1 *(Continued)*

---

    36. Mother "talks" to child while doing her work.
    37. Mother consciously encourages developmental advances.
    38. Mother invests "maturing" toys with value via her attention.
    39. Mother structures child's play periods.
    40. Mother provides toys that challenge child to develop new skills.
VI. Opportunities for variety in daily stimulation
    41. Father[b] provides some caretaking every day.
    42. Mother reads stories at least three times weekly.
    43. Child eats at least one meal per day with mother and father.
    44. Family visits or receives visits from relatives.
    45. Child has three or more books of his or her own.

---

[a]Based on Bradley & Caldwell (1984).

[b]The term "mother" is used to refer to the primary caregiver, regardless of gender. The term "father" is used to a second caregiver, living in the child's home, generally assumed to be of the opposite gender to the primary caregiver.

assessments at the oldest age was .38. Do these data permit us to infer that variations in the environment assessed by means of the Home Inventory are causally related to intellectual development?

The inference from correlation to causation may be difficult. Items on the Home Inventory may be influenced by differences in the genotypes of children. Items 8, 9, and 10 assess the emotional responses of the mother to the child. Genotypes may influence temperament and children with different temperaments may elicit different emotional reactions from mothers. Thus the mother's treatment of the child may be shaped by characteristics of the child. The direction of influence is ambiguous. Items 36 and 42 are designed to measure the provision of intellectual stimulation in the home. Children may, for genetic reasons, be differentially responsive to intellectual activities. Being read to is an activity that may not be equally enjoyable for all children. Children who enjoy being read to may ask questions of caretakers who read to them and reward the caretaker for engaging in this activity. Thus the frequency of occurrence of these activities in the home may, in part, be attributable to the influence of the child on the parent. The mere fact that an instrument is labeled as a measure of the environment and assesses variations in the environment does not necessarily imply that the measure is not influenced by genetic characteristics. It is theoretically possible to study the heritability of items on the Home Inventory. One could, for example, obtain separate Home Inventory observations for MZ and DZ twin pairs and obtain heritability indices for Home Inventory items using these data. I am not aware of research of this type. The assertion that Home Inventory scores may, in part, reflect the influence of genetic characteristics of the child on the home environment presented to the child remains a theoretical possibility rather than a firmly established empirical assertion.

Environmental indices may be influenced by the genetic characteristics of the caregiver. Home Inventory scores may be positively correlated with the intelligence of parents. Parents who differ in intelligence may provide their children with different genotypes for the development of intelligence and these genetic influences may account for the correlation between Home Inventory scores and the intellectual performance of children. Gottfried & Gottfried (1984) obtained IQ scores for mothers and their children as well as Home Inventory scores. They found that the correlation between mother's IQ and the IQ of her child at age 42 months was .22. The multiple correlation between the IQ of the mother and the Home Inventory score and the IQ of the child was .49. The addition of Home Inventory scores to a prediction equation for IQ of a child added significantly to the ability to predict childhood IQ after the influence of mother's IQ was considered. Reversing the order of entry of variables led to different results. The correlation of Home Inventory scores and childhood IQ was .48. The addition of mother's IQ to the prediction equation did not add significantly to the ability to predict a child's IQ. Other studies summarized by Gottfried (1984) used other characteristics of parents in prediction equations combined with Home Inventory scores. These studies usually find that the prediction of childhood IQ is enhanced when scores on the Home Inventory are included in the prediction equation after controlling for parental characteristics such as socioeconomic status and education. These results indicate that the Home Inventory measures characteristics of the home environment that are independent of the intelligence of the parents. And, these results suggest that childhood intellectual performance is influenced by characteristics of the home environment provided to the child that are independent of the genetic characteristics of the parents. Note that these results do not rule out the possibility that genetic characteristics of the child, independent of the genetic characteristics of the parent, influence the nature of the environment provided to the child.

The results of the Gottfried and Gottfried study may be contrasted with the results of a study reported by Longstreth, Davis, Carter, Flint, Owen, Rickert, & Taylor (1981). They used an inventory developed by Wolf (1965) to assess the intellectual stimulation of the home environment of a sample of 12 year olds. They also obtained IQ data for mothers and children in their sample. They found that mother's IQ predicted child's IQ controlling for differences in their measure of the home environment. The partial correlation between mother's IQ (averaged over two measures, the Raven and the Peabody) and the child's IQ was .33. The comparable partial correlation between the home environment index and the child's IQ controlling for mother's IQ was a nonsignificant .18. Longstreth *et al.* found, in contradistinction to Gottfried and Gottfried, that the relationship between the home environment and the IQ of children is substantially mediated by the mother's IQ. This latter finding is compatible with a genetic interpretation of the relationship. The differences in the outcomes of these studies may be attributable to differences in the environmental measures that were used. In my judgment, a more plausible interpretation is to be found in variations in the ages of the samples that were studied. Longstreth *et al.* studied older children. Our discussion of longitudinal behavior genetic studies provides evidence for a declining influence of between-family environmental influences on intelligence as a monotonic function of the age of the child. The children studied by Gottfried and Gottfried had not entered school. The principal intellectual socialization agent of the young child is the parent (or the nursery school for children who spend several hours a day in that setting). For older children, the school tends to displace the parent as the principal intellectual socialization agent of the child. Therefore, it is reasonable to expect a declining influence of the home environment on the intellectual development of the child. That is precisely what is found in developmental behavior genetic analyses and is compatible with the combined results of the Longstreth *et al.* and Gottfried and Gottfried studies.

The correlation between measures of the home environment and childhood IQ may be influenced by the genetic covariance of children and parents in natural families. Children and parents share genes and an environment and their shared genetic resemblance may influence the impact of the environment on the child. This notion may be tested by comparing the correlations between measures of the environment and characteristics of offspring in natural and adopted families. Individuals who are reared in adoptive families do not share genetic characteristics with their adoptive parents. If the correlation between an environmental measure and the characteristic of a child is lower in an adoptive than in a natural family, it is possible to infer that the correlation between the environmental measure and the characteristics of the child is mediated by the genetic similarity between the child and the parent. This analysis provides for the possibility of genetic mediation of environmental influences. Plomin *et al.* (1988) obtained correlations between the Home Inventory scores and childhood IQ at ages 1, 2, 3, and 4 in natural and adopted families in the Colorado Adoption Project. Table 6.2 presents

TABLE 6.2   Home–IQ Correlations for Adoptive
and Nonadoptive Siblings at Different Ages[a]

Age	Nonadoptive correlation	Adoptive correlation
1	.10	.11
2	.38	.09
3	.14	.28
4	.10	.15

[a]Based on Plomin, DeFries, & Fulker (1988).

these data. The data in Table 6.2 provide evidence for possible genetic mediation of the relationship between home environment scores and childhood IQ. At age 2 there is a moderately strong relationship between the Home Inventory score and childhood IQ and this relationship is clearly stronger in natural than in adoptive families. At ages 3 and 4, the relationship between Home Inventory scores and childhood IQ is too weak to find evidence of either genetic or environmental mediation of the relationship. These results suggest that the relationships between Home Inventory scores and childhood IQ may be partially mediated by the influence of the genetic relationship between parents and children. This pattern of genetic mediation of environmental measures is characteristic of a number of other findings in the Colorado Adoption Project, including findings not germane to cognitive development. That is, where correlations exist between measures of the environment and characteristics of children, they are likely to be stronger in the control natural families than in adoptive families (see Plomin, & DeFries, 1985).

It should be apparent that it is difficult to infer causal influences from correlations between measures of the home environment and intellectual development. One way to dissolve the causal ambiguity surrounding these relationships is to treat them as a basis for experimental research that will provide a more definitive test of a causal relationship. A good example of this strategy is found in a study reported by Busse, Ree, Gutride, Alexander, & Powell (1972). They studied the provision of adequate play materials as a factor in intellectual development. They randomly assigned a group of black 4-year-old children to one of two classrooms that differed with respect to the adequacy of play materials that were available for the children. There were no significant improvements associated with a 1-year exposure to the enriched classroom environment. The results of this study lead to a general methodological caveat with respect to studies of the influence of the home environment on intelligence. The observation of a correlation between a measure of the home environment and the IQ of a child does not imply that manipulations of that environmental variable will invariably lead to changes in the intelligence of children.

This discussion of between-family environmental influences on intelligence has been cautious and even skeptical. I have been led to this sense of caution by the results of the recent behavior genetic studies employing older samples. It appears to be the case that reasonably wide ranges of between-family environmental variations encountered by children in western societies have a vanishingly small influence on postadolescent intelligence. It may very well be the case that variations in parenting styles and the adequacy of the home environment have important influences on the early intellectual development of children. These influences may fade and be of diminishing importance for mature intellectual development.

INTERVENTIONS TO INCREASE INTELLIGENCE

Preschool Interventions

Is it possible to increase intelligence by changing the early intellectual environment of the child? Research on this topic was influenced by the development of Project Headstart, which was an attempt to provide an enriched environment for preschool-aged children whose impoverished background was assumed to place them at risk for inadequate intellectual development. It was assumed that the provision of superior early childhood education for these children would increase their intelligence and increase their ability to cope with the educational program of the public schools. Caruso, Taylor, & Detterman (1982; see also Clarke & Clarke, 1976; Zigler & Valentine, 1979) found 65 studies of the impact of Headstart interventions on intellectual development. These studies employed interventions of different durations from short term to up to 2 years in duration. Most used control groups. The children were invariably preschoolers. Perhaps the best summary of the outcomes of these studies was published by a consortium formed for the amalgamation of this body of research (Consortium for Longitudinal Studies, 1983). The Consortium included 14 investigators whose initial samples included 100 or more subjects who were engaged in a longitudinal investigation of the effects of early educational interventions. The samples included in these studies were predominantly black preschoolers with a median IQ of 92 at the time of entry into the program and mothers with a median number of years of education of 10.4. They were predominantly of lower socioeconomic status. The results of these studies as summarized by Royce, Darlington, & Murray (1983) are reasonably consistent. Seven studies used IQ as a dependent variable. They obtained a clear increase in IQ as a result of participation in Headstart. The median IQ benefit at the conclusion of these projects was 7.42 points. Three or four years after the conclusion of these projects the median difference between the experimental and the control group declined to 3.04 points. The last reported assessment includes Wechsler test scores for program participants aged 10 to 17. These assessments occurred 7 to 10 years after the conclusion of the educational intervention. Pooled over a subset of these investigations there were no significant differences between experimental and control groups. Although program children started first grade with an average IQ that was 5.80 points higher than the control group children, these differences were not maintained. Other reviews of early intervention studies based on Headstart reached the same conclusion as the Consortium for Longitudinal Studies. There are no enduring changes in intelligence test scores associated with participation in this program (see Detterman and Sternberg, 1982, and Spitz, 1986, for a discussion of attempts to increase intelligence). The failure of attempts to increase intelligence by early childhood interventions may be attributable to the relatively brief durations of these programs. It is possible that interventions that continued into the first few years of schooling would lead to more enduring changes in performance on intelligence tests. Project Follow Through was designed to extend Headstart interventions in order to obtain more enduring changes. The interventions were based on quite different intervention models. A comprehensive evaluation of the Follow Through Programs compared 22 different intervention models (Bock, Stebbins, & Proper, 1977). Spitz (1986) evaluated the obtained changes on the only test of intelligence used in these studies—the Raven. For 107 comparisons that were available where the children assigned to Follow Through Programs were comparable to their untreated controls, he found 5 significant differences in favor of groups assigned to the intervention, 11 significant differences in favor of groups not provided with the intervention, and 91 comparisons in which there were no significant differences. Variations between different treatment models were smaller than variations within treatment models implemented at more than one setting, suggesting that the theories that governed the intervention model did not determine the effectiveness of the model. These data indicate that interventions extended into the first year or two of elementary school will not lead to enduring changes in intelligence test performance.

The Abecedarian Project provided intensive university-based day-care interventions for a group of children assumed to be at high risk for inadequate intellectual development (see Ramey, Holmberg, Sparling, & Collier, 1977, for a description of the project). The intervention began before the children were 3 months old. The children participated in the program until school entry. Over 90% of the mothers who participated in the program were black, and most were young, without a high school education, and single. Children were randomly assigned to either a treatment or a control group. Ramey, Lee, & Burchinal (1990; Ramey & Haskins, 1981) reported the results of a series of IQ tests administered at 6-month intervals to the children in the experimental and control groups. The largest difference between the experimental and control groups was obtained on the 36-month Stanford–Binet test—14.7 IQ points. On the last test result reported, when the children were 54 months old, the children in the experimental group had IQs that were 8.7 points higher than children in the control group on the McCarthy test. The mean IQ of the children in the experimental group was 101.4. Campbell & Ramey (1990) reported in a paper dealing with performance on Piagetian tests that performance on the WISC IQ test given when these children were 96 months of age indicated that the children in the experimental group had a mean IQ that was .34 standard deviations higher than that of children in the control group. This implies that the children in the experimental group had IQs that were 5 points higher than those of children in the control group, indicating some additional erosion in the effects of the intervention on IQ. These results establish that the Abecedarian intervention led to a significant increase in the IQ of children. It is not at all clear that this effect is of enduring significance. IQ data for older children have not been reported. The magnitude of the effect that was obtained is comparable to that typically reported with the less intensive interventions associated with Headstart programs. Since the change associated with this intervention is no larger than that typically obtained using the less intensive interventions characteristic of Headstart programs, it is possible that the long-term effects of this intervention will be no different than the lasting effects of Headstart.

The Milwaukee Project provided an intensive preschool educational intervention to a group of black children living in a publically assisted housing project whose mothers had IQs below 75. A total of 40 children participated in the project, 20 in the experimental group and 20 in the control group (Heber & Garber, 1972, 1975). Five children left the project leaving a sample of 35 children. Children in the experimental group were exposed to intensive psychological interventions designed to increase intelligence prior to the age of 6 months. The intervention included extensive home visits to train mothers in child care and the provision of intensive day care with extensive intellectual stimulation for several hours a day in an infant-stimulation center. The experimental intervention ended at age 6. In addition to the provision of preschool intellectual stimulation, special efforts were made to place the experimental subjects in public schools whose students scored at or above the norm of academic achievement. The children in the experimental and control groups were repeatedly given IQ tests including the Stanford-Binet and Wechsler tests. Follow-up tests were given at ages 7, 8, 9, 10, and 14.

It was difficult to interpret the results of the Milwaukee Project for many years. The project was funded from 1966 to 1981, but technical details of the project were not available in the scientific literature. Controversy surrounded the project in part because one of the principal investigators was convicted of fraud in connection with the administration of funds in another project (see Sommer & Sommer, 1983). Fortunately, the long awaited complete technical report of the outcome of the project was published in 1988 providing the necessary data for an evaluation of the project's outcome (Garber, 1988). At the conclusion of the project, there were large IQ differences between the control and experimental subjects on the Stanford-Binet. At age 6, the experimental group had a mean IQ of 119 and the control group had a mean IQ of 87. The experimental group's IQ was 2.92 standard deviation units higher than the control group's IQ. However, the IQ differences between the experimental and control group declined over time. The difference in favor of the experimental group was 22 points at age 7, and 10 points at age 14. The mean IQ of the experimental group was 101 at age 14, and the mean IQ of the control group was 91, a difference of .87 standard deviation units.

There are two aspects of these data that are noteworthy. First, the mean IQs of both the experimental and control groups are relatively high for individuals whose mothers had a mean IQ of 67. Jensen (1989) attributed this relatively high IQ to the effects of repeated testing and familiarization with the test contents. In this connection it should be noted that the project participants were tested 13 times with Binet tests and 9 times with various versions of the Wechsler tests. Second, the experimental group had a significantly higher IQ than the control group 8 years after the completion of the project. Note that the effect of the experimental treatment in this project seems to be both more enduring and larger in magnitude than those obtained in the Abercedarian project. Jensen (1989) suggested that the experimental intervention may not have resulted in large scale changes in intelligence despite the evidence of changes in IQ test scores. He argued that the intervention may have included intensive training on items that were similar to those appearing on the IQ tests. This training may have decreased the construct validity of the tests as a measure of g. Jensen's interpretation of these data is supported by the performance of experimental and control children on tests of scholastic achievement. On the Metropolitan Test of Achievement, the experimental group declined from the 49th to the 19th percentile from the first to the fourth grade. The comparable scores for the control group declined from the 32nd to the 9th percentile. In math, the experimental group declined from the 34nd to the 11th percentile from first to fourth grade. The comparable percentiles for the control group were the 18th and 9th for the first and fourth grade, respectively. It is clear that differences between the control group and the experimental group in academic performance were not as large as differences in IQ. These results support Jensen's suggestion that the experimental intervention did not result in large changes in intellectual ability. Normally, differences between two groups in IQ are reflected in differences of comparable magnitude in indices of academic achievement (see chapter 9 of this volume). The discrepancy between the academic achievement of the children in the experimental group and their IQ is compatible with the view that the IQ scores of these children have been artificially inflated. An alternative interpretation of these data is that the academic performance of the children in the experimental group was depressed by environmental influences or the quality of the schools they attend. There is some uncertainty about the outcome of the Milwaukee Project. The experimental effects of the intervention appear to be decreasing. It is possible that further declines in the difference in the IQs of the experimental and control groups would occur if they were tested when they were older. Also, the true magnitude of the changes in intelligence that were obtained as a result of the intervention remains uncertain. The use of additional tests, including tests of fluid ability that were not similar in format to the specific training experiences of children in the experimental group, would provide information about the scope of changes in general intelligence. In any case, changes in scores on an IQ test that are not accompanied by comparable changes in academic performance are of questionable value.

There is no credible evidence that experimental interventions during the preschool years will create enduring changes in performance on tests of intelligence. There are two different interpretations of this generalization. Children in the various experimental groups in these studies increased their intelligence but these gains could not be maintained without totally changing the postexperimental environment to which these children were exposed. Presumably the changes that are required include those associated with the family, the school, and the neighborhood. Alternatively, it is possible to argue that the changes that were obtained in these interventions were superficial and did not represent true changes in intelligence. There are two investigations that may be interpreted as providing evidence for the latter interpretation of the findings. Jacobsen, Berger, Bergman, Milham, & Greeson (1971) provided 20 hours of training in solving two choice discrimination problems to a group of children attending a preschool day-care center for children from poor families. They obtained a 13.3-point increase in Stanford–Binet IQ as a result of this training. The largest gains were obtained by a group of children whose preexperimental IQ was low (mean = 72.8). Children in this low-IQ group gained 20 points on the Stanford–Binet. These results suggest that preschool IQ scores may be volatile and it is possible that children may exhibit rather large gains in performance that may not be meaningful as a result of various experimental interventions. Zigler, Abelson, & Seitz (1973) obtained a 10-point gain on the Peabody Picture Vocabulary test for a group of 4- and 5-year-old children living in poverty when the test was given a second time 1 week later. The comparable gain for middle class children whose initial score on this test was 35 points higher was 3 points. These investigators also found that children from impoverished backgrounds benefited more than middle class children when a second test was administered by the same examiner rather than a different examiner. These results suggest that some of the deficit in IQ exhibited by children from impoverished backgrounds in preschool IQ test performance may be attributable to test familiarity and other motivational factors. Gains of the order of magnitude of those obtained using more intensive interventions can be obtained in the IQ scores of preschool age children from impoverished backgrounds with relatively minor interventions of brief duration. It is unlikely that the latter interventions resulted in enduring changes in intellectual functioning. And, by implication, it is unlikely that changes resulting from more enduring interventions were meaningful.

Although evidence for true changes in intelligence as a result of preschool interventions is equivocal, there is evidence that children exposed to these programs did change in meaningful ways. Royce et al. (1983)

reported results for seven studies participating in the Consortium for Longitudinal Studies of special education placements and grade retentions for program participants. Either of these decisions by school authorities may be taken as an index of inadequate educational progress by a student. Of the Headstart program participants in these studies, 29.5% had either been retained in grade or assigned to a special education class by the end of the seventh grade. The comparable percentage for control subjects was 44.6. This was a highly significant difference for this total sample of over 800 children. This difference in reaction of the schools to these children was obtained in each of the eight studies for which data were available, although the difference was not statistically significant in most of the studies. Although experimental and control children in Headstart programs were treated differently by the schools there was relatively little difference between these groups of children in objective indices of academic performance. There was some evidence that experimental children were slightly better in math achievement in some grades but not in reading skills as assessed by objective tests. By the end of sixth grade, there were no differences between control and experimental subjects in academic achievement as assessed by tests. One way of interpreting these results is to suggest that Headstart programs never resulted in true intellectual changes in children. They may have changed motivation, familiarity with test materials, and school-related social behaviors. These changes may have been apparent to elementary school teachers who responded to these children. Children exposed to Headstart may have behaved in ways that school authorities found more acceptable than children in the control groups in these investigations. These changes, however, were not accompanied by enduring changes in cognitive functioning either as assessed by intelligence tests or by the ability to acquire the skills that constitute the standard curriculum of the public schools.

Interventions with Older Samples

Is it possible to increase intelligence after students enter school? There have been several attempts to change performance on tests of intelligence following various interventions. Perhaps the most extended intervention of this kind is contained in an experiment conducted by the Rumanian psychologist Kvashchev. The results of this study were reported by Stankov (1986). Kvashchev randomly assigned classes of students in their first year of high school to an experimental or a control group. The experimental group was provided with 3 to 4 hours per week of training in creative problem solving for 3 years. The exercises usually involved presenting students with difficult problems followed by various suggestions about the barriers to problem solution. Stankov reports the results of pretest and posttest comparisons on a battery of 28 different tests of intelligence. He estimated that the experimental group began the experiment 2.62 points lower than the control group on a composite IQ index with a standard deviation of 15. At the end of the experiment the experimental subjects were 3.04 points higher than the control group and, on a final retesting 1 year after the conclusion of the experiment, the experimental subjects were estimated to have an IQ that was 5.66 points higher than that of the control group. The initial difference between the groups may reflect sampling error and thus the differences that were obtained at the initial testing were not substantially larger than the differences that were present in students whose classes were assigned at random to participate in the experiment or to the control group. This is probably an overly conservative interpretation of the results. Alternatively, it is reasonable to assert that 1 year after the conclusion of the study there was a gain of slightly less than 8 points for subjects in the experimental group. The gains were larger on tests in the battery that were considered to be markers for fluid intelligence than on tests that were assumed to be measures of crystallized intelligence. The effects that were obtained were present for 17 of 28 tests used on the final assessment. It is unlikely that they represent specific acquaintance with the test material. These effects are best interpretable as the development of an increase in fluid ability as a result of intensive instruction in creative thinking skills. There are some unresolved questions about Kvashchev's results. In addition to the obvious question of the duration of the effects that were obtained, his results leave unresolved the educational significance of the intervention. If one were to provide a subject with the answers to a test of intelligence, changes in that person's score on the test would self-evidently be dismissed as being due to a procedure that compromised the construct validity of the test. Test scores as an outcome of an intervention are of no interest in their own right. They are of interest in the first instance because, as we shall see, they are predictive of educational outcomes. From this perspective, changes in a test score may reflect changes in the construct of which the test is alleged to be a manifestation, changes in the score without changes in the construct as in the case of providing answers to the test, or both. It would be interesting to know if Kvashchev's experimental intervention was accompanied by changes in the academic performance of students, particularly on those aspects of the high school curriculum that deal with problem solving and creative ability to apply insights to new tasks. Did the students in the experimental group improve in their ability to solve novel mathematical problems? Did their ability to analyze literary works improve? In short, were they more sophisticated learners? It is theoretically possible that time devoted to the development of abstract reasoning skills led to a decrease in the acquisition of standard curriculum knowledge. Until we have a fuller assessment of the academic consequences of this type of intervention, it is premature to call for its widespread implementation in the schools. Leaving aside the practical implications of the program, Kvashchev's experiment demonstrates that an intensive program of structured learning presented to high school students will increase fluid intelligence.

The SAT (Scholastic Aptitude Test) is used by many colleges as an aid to admission. The test measures verbal and quantitative aptitudes. While the test is not described as a measure of intelligence, scores on the test are correlated with scores on tests of intelligence. Messick (1980; see also Anastasi, 1981; Messick & Jungeblut, 1981) summarized studies of attempts to increase SAT scores by coaching, including commercial coaching programs. The coaching programs that are available differ with respect to their duration and the extent to which they provide emphasis on test-taking skills as opposed to more general attempts to focus on changes in the cognitive abilities that are assessed by the test. The available studies are flawed in different ways. Several studies did not use random assignment of subjects to experimental conditions. Evidence of differences between experimental and control groups in these studies confound the effects of the experimental intervention with the effects of self-selection. Students who elect to participate in a coaching program to increase their SAT scores may differ from other students in their motivation and in other ways. No comparison group is truly comparable and totally satisfactory as a control group. Studies that have used random assignment of subjects to experimental conditions often used special administrations of the SAT that were not used for admission purposes. Students in the control group may have been less motivated to perform well on these exams. In some of these studies subjects in the untreated control groups exhibited declines in SAT scores, a result that is contrary to the usual outcome. Messick's review of these studies clearly indicates that they are flawed in different ways.

Messick reported that the weighted average increase in SAT scores for 10 studies that used random assignments of individuals to treatment and control groups was 9.1 on the verbal SAT and 13.0 on the quantitative SAT. The comparable differences for studies that did not use randomized assignments of subjects were 38 and 54 points on the verbal and quantitative SAT, respectively. Messick does not report the standard deviations of scores for subjects participating in these studies. SAT scores range from 200 to 800 and standard deviations for unselected samples are usually close to 100. Thus the average weighted obtained changes as a result of coaching on the SAT are usually less than .5 standard deviation. The effects for studies using random assignment of subjects to conditions are considerably smaller.

Messick noted that the time devoted to interventions varied considerably in these studies from a low of 4.5 hours to a high of 300 hours. The rank-order correlation between the effects of coaching and the duration of the intervention was .60 for 22 studies of the verbal SAT and .80 for 11 studies of the quantitative SAT. The function defining magnitude of benefits associated with coaching on the SAT and the duration of the intervention is logarithmic rather than linear. This implies that the expected increments from coaching decline. Gains are more easily attainable at the beginning of an intervention program than they are after considerable exposure to the intervention.

Studies of the effects of coaching on SAT scores do indicate that it is possible to increase SAT performance. The gains that are attainable are relatively slight. These studies also leave unresolved the nature of the changes that are obtained. Some of the changes that are attained may be attributable to hints about techniques to deal with the multiple-choice format of these tests. These studies have not attempted to measure the effects of the interventions on other measures of intelligence nor have they included follow-up tests. Therefore, these studies do not indicate whether or not the interventions led to enduring changes in general intelligence.

Feuerstein (1979) is an Israeli psychologist with extensive experience testing Israeli immigrants from non-Western countries. His experiences led him to challenge the meaning of standardized intelligence test scores obtained from individuals from culturally different backgrounds. He believed that many low-scoring individuals had higher intelligence and greater learning potential than was revealed by their test scores. He found that many of the immigrants to Israel he tested responded impulsively to test questions, did not reason in a planned manner, and exhibited a variety of cognitive deficits on these tests. Feuerstein was inclined to accept the test scores as a valid index of the intellectual functioning of the individuals he tested. He believed, however, that IQ scores were not adequate indices of the intellectual capability of individuals and he argued that systematic interventions could provide skills that would enable low-scoring individuals to score at a high level on tests. He developed a modification of the standard methods of test administration that changed the role of the examiner from that of an objective reporter of the examinee's responses to that of an active participant who demonstrated correct answers and attempted to change the performance of the examinee in order to assess the response of the examinee to potential attempts to remediate his or her intellectual deficits. On this analysis, a conventional test score is not viewed as an index of intellectual ability but merely as an index of current functioning. By contrast, an intellectual assessment using Feuerstein's "Dynamic Assessment of Learning Potential" is viewed as an assessment of the potential of the individual to respond to interventions designed to improve intellectual functioning (for a critical analysis of the assessment procedures used by Feuerstein see Glutting & McDermott, 1990; In press).

There are studies that purport to demonstrate that intellectual performance may be increased by the techniques advocated by Feuerstein. In one of his studies he dramatically improved the performance of low-scoring individuals on the Raven test after giving them information about the analogical principles used in the tests. The results obtained as a result of training in Feuerstein's work should be interpreted cautiously for two reasons. Many of his demonstrations and findings are based on samples of individuals who are recent immigrants who have limited exposure to Western education. Depressed scores among such individuals may not have the same meaning as low scores obtained by individuals who have had less deviant educational experiences. Also, demonstrations that performance on a particular task may be altered tell us little about the generality of the results that are obtained. The research reported on the effects of the interventions used by Feuerstein in which outcome is assessed by more global indices of intellectual performance are somewhat less encouraging.

Feuerstein, Rand, Hoffman, & Miller (1980) assigned a group of culturally deprived and socially disadvantaged 12- to 15-year-old youth to a regular curriculum or a special intellectual enrichment curriculum that involved 5 hours of training per week for a 2-year period. At the end of the 2-year intervention, there were small differences in raw scores on the Thurstone tests. The experimental group obtained a mean score of 172 versus a control group mean score of 164. Follow-up data were available for military induction examinations 2 years after the completion of the program. The approximate IQ of the experimental subjects was 102 compared to an IQ of 96 for the control group subjects. These IQ scores may be compared to a mean Thurstone IQ score of 80 obtained at the beginning of the intervention. The increase in IQ that was obtained for all subjects participating in the study is probably attributable to acculturation effects. The results obtained as a result of the experimental intervention appear comparable to those obtained by Kvashchev with a group of students who were representative of high school students in his country.

Feuerstein reported the results of another intervention in Israel in which outcomes were assessed using the Thurstone test of intelligence. In this study, pupils attending a residential vocational high school who came from a residential program for culturally deprived disadvantaged pupils were assigned to heterogeneously grouped classes rather than homogeneous classes. The usual practice of the school was to assign these pupils to homogeneously grouped classes. Feuerstein argued that the score of these pupils on the Learning Assessment Potential test indicated that they had more potential than was apparent from their initial level of functioning. Feuerstein administered the Thurstone test to these pupils and a control group of regular students in the vocational school entering the ninth and tenth grades at the start of the intervention and 1 year later, after exposure to a heterogeneously grouped classroom. In addition, scores for military induction tests were available 2 or 3 years after the conclusion of the intervention. Table 6.3 presents these data. An examination of the data presented in Table 6.3 indicates that the low-scoring groups did exhibit increases in IQ test performance on some measures.

TABLE 6.3 Scores on Military Induction Exams for Subjects in the Hodayot Study[a]

Measure	9A (N = 30)		9B[b] (N = 25)		10A (N = 27)		10B[b] (N = 15)		t values*	
	$\bar{X}$	SD	$\bar{X}$	SD	$\bar{X}$	SD	$\bar{X}$	SD	9A versus 9B	10A versus 10B
DAPAR	57.28	10.73	52.41	10.26	57.44	13.61	51.27	18.58	1.64	1.12
KABA	46.43	8.19	44.76	8.17	44.15	10.37	40.27	10.48	0.75	1.06
Hebrew	7.76	0.94	7.35	0.98	7.84	1.07	7.60	1.64	1.58	0.50

[a]Based on Feuerstein (1979).
[b]Groups 9B and 10B were the low-scoring groups whose original Thurstone tests were .86 standard deviations lower than those of the control groups (9A and 10A).
[c]None of the t values were significant.

The effects were small. The weighted mean difference between regular pupils and the special background pupils in the ninth and tenth grade in performance on the Thurstone at the start of the intervention was 0.86 standard deviation units using the standard deviation of the regular pupils. On the military induction general intelligence exam, the groups differed by .40 standard deviation units. These data indicate that the special background pupils gained .46 standard deviation units in intelligence relative to the regular pupils from the start of the intervention to their testing for military induction. These results cannot be attributed to their assignment to heterogeneously grouped classrooms. There was no control group and no way of knowing whether these pupils would have gained in IQ relative to their classmates if they had not been assigned to homogeneously grouped classes. In addition, increases in IQ would be expected with the passage of time for low-scoring individuals as the result of regression toward the mean. Finally, the changes that were obtained were less than one-half a standard deviation.

The Feuerstein program was tested at three sites in the United States. Adolescent students who were assigned to special education classes were provided with interventions for 3 or 4 hours per week designed to increase their intellectual functioning (Haywood & Arbitman-Smith, 1981). Initial assessments indicated that the experimental subjects had a mean increase in IQ from 83 to 90 after 58 hours of intervention. The control group's mean IQ increased from 84 to 87. Thus the experimental group had a mean increase in IQ that was 4 points larger than the increase in the control group.

Blagg (1991) reported the results of a comprehensive analysis of the Feuerstein program. The program was instituted in four secondary schools in Somerset, England. The pupils in these schools had a mean IQ of 92 and had poor math and reading achievement scores. The pupils were trained on Feuerstein's instrumental enrichment program. The training was extensive with a mean duration of 112 hours of training. There were no significant effects of the program on general intelligence or on performance on standardized tests of math or reading skills. The Blagg study conclusively indicates that Feuerstein's programs have little or no influence on the development of intelligence.

Although Feuerstein presented dramatic case histories of increases in IQ associated with his intervention procedures, controlled studies generally indicate that the changes in IQ obtained with his interventions are relatively modest.

This brief review of attempts to increase general intelligence in school-age populations suggests that scores on intelligence tests increase following interventions. The long-term effects of the interventions are unknown but there is some evidence that they persist for as long as 2 years after the intervention. Well-controlled studies usually obtain relatively small changes in IQ as a result of interventions—generally less than .5.

standard deviation. There is no evidence that general intelligence can be substantially changed as a result of experimental interventions.

CHANGES IN INTELLIGENCE ATTRIBUTABLE TO EDUCATION

Intelligence and educational accomplishment are linked and may be subject to bidirectional influences. Intelligence test scores predict performance in academic settings. The knowledge that is acquired in academic settings influences one's ability to solve problems and one's general intelligence. If the knowledge that is acquired in school influences scores on tests of intelligence, it is reasonable to assume that variations in the quantity and quality of education relate to performance on tests of intelligence. How might this assumption be tested? We could assign individuals with the same IQ to different kinds of schooling and then assess their intelligence using a longitudinal design. Changes in intelligence following different educational experiences could be unambiguously attributed to the effects of the educational experiences of individuals. There are no studies that follow this simple randomized design. The assumption that differences in educational experience influence intelligence is supported by a variety of studies that rely on indirect demonstrations of the influence of schooling.

The studies that we shall review are addressed to two different questions: (1) Does the amount of schooling obtained influence one's score on an intelligence test?, and (2) do variations in the quality of schooling one obtains, holding constant amount of schooling, influence scores on an intelligence test?

Evidence that amount of schooling influences scores on an IQ test is based on direct and indirect evidence. There are studies of the effects of schooling in third-world countries where schooling is not routinely provided to individuals (Scribner & Cole, 1981). This literature will not be reviewed here. I am concerned with the narrower issue of the extent to which variation in amount of schooling influences performance on tests of intelligence among children who attend schools in industrialized countries in which school attendance is mandatory and universal. A study by Harnqvist (1968a,b; see also Lorge, 1945, for a related study) illustrates some of the difficulty in interpreting studies of the influence of schooling on intelligence. He studied a sample of 10% of the male population born in Sweden in 1948. He obtained IQ data from tests given at age 13 and again at 18 as part of a military induction examination. Harnqvist studied changes in intelligence associated with the quality and amount of secondary schooling received. Adolescents in Sweden choose educational tracks that are designed to prepare students for higher education or that are terminal. Adjusting for initial differences in IQ, Harnqvist estimated that students who had the most rigorous academic education gained .62 standard deviation units in intelligence relative to pupils who were assigned or chose less academic secondary school education. Harnqvist's conclusions are reasonable, however, they are not compelling. Individuals who chose or were assigned to an academic track might have gained in IQ even if they had been randomly assigned to a less rigorous academic education. Consider two individuals with the same IQ who elect to enter different educational tracks at the secondary school level. The student who chooses the academic track may like to read books more than the individual who chooses a less academic track. Differences in intellectual interests may be related to changes in IQ. Differences in IQ associated with different educational experiences obtained in the Harnqvist study may be attributable to the effects of educational experiences or to characteristics of persons that led them to be assigned to different educational experiences.

The problem of self-selection for different educational experiences cannot be overcome even with a study that controls for genetic differences. Newman et al. (1937) obtained correlations of .79 and .58 between differences in the IQ scores of MZ twins reared apart and ratings of the quality of their educational experiences using two different measures of intelligence. The twin with the higher IQ was more likely to have a better education than the twin with the lower IQ. It is reasonable to interpret this finding as demonstrating an influence on the quality of education on IQ scores. This interpretation is not compelling. Differences in IQ may influence educational experiences. Differences in educational experiences between MZ twins may be caused by differences in IQ rather than the converse.

Cahan & Cohen (1989) used a "between-grade-level" approach to study the influence of schooling on intelligence. They studied the influence of schooling by comparing pupils in the same grade who differed in age with pupils in different grades. The difference in test scores between the youngest and the oldest child in a grade in an elementary school in which children are assigned to grade level by chronological age is attributable to the influence of age rather than amount of schooling. Differences in test scores between the youngest child in a grade and the oldest child in the immediately preceding lower grade are attributable to the influence of amount of schooling. A 1-day difference in ages clearly will have a trivial influence on differences in intelligence associated with grade-level assignment. Cahan and Cohen administered tests of intelligence to all children attending Jerusalem's Hebrew schools in the fourth, fifth, and sixth grades. They excluded all students who were in grades that were inappropriate for their age level. Using a regression procedure they estimated the effects of attending school for 1 year on test performance by noting discontinuities in the regression of age on test scores associated with grade differences. The influence of age on test scores was estimated by comparing individuals differing in age within the same grade. They compared estimated gains in test performance associated with 1 year of age and 1 year of schooling on 12 tests of intelligence. The average gain in test scores associated with 1 year of age was .15 standard deviation units. The comparable change for 1 year of schooling was .275 standard deviation units. The average ratio of the effects of schooling divided by the effects of age was 2:21 for these 12 tests. These results clearly establish an influence of education on intellectual development. Schooling increases performance on tests of intelligence independent of changes in age associated with schooling. These results extend findings associated with the effects of formal schooling in third-world countries (see Scribner & Cole, 1981) to the effects of schooling in a technologically advanced society. In addition, this result is compatible with other research on the influence of delayed or minimal schooling in isolated and deprived communities (see Ceci, 1990, for a review of this literature).

Do variations in the quality of schooling independent of the amount of schooling influence IQ test scores? There are a number of indirect studies of this issue. Jencks (1972) summarized research on this issue and concluded that variations among schools had a vanishingly small effect on variations in cognitive abilities of students. Much of this research deals with what is learned in school as opposed to scores on tests of intelligence. We shall review this literature and the controversies that it has generated in Chapter 9, dealing with the relationship between intelligence and what is learned in schools. One of the studies reported by Jencks deals with the effects of attendance in different high schools on vocabulary test performance—a good measure of general intelligence. Jencks used Project Talent data for this analysis (see Flanagan & Cooley, 1966). Data were obtained from 5000 students attending 91 different high schools in the United States. The students were tested at the ninth and twelfth grades. An average terminal level of performance for each school was obtained. Variations between schools accounted for 10.7% of the variance on academic achievement. An expected twelfth grade achievement score was obtained for each school by using a regression equation that took into account ninth grade performance as well as information about socioeconomic status and aspirations for education. These expected scores were related to twelfth grade obtained scores. Only 14% of the between-school variance in twelfth grade performance was unexplained, implying that only 1.5% of the variance in differences in academic performance among individuals is attributable to the school that one attends. This number is an upper-bound estimate of the influence of secondary school attendance on changes in vocabulary. More effective control for additional entry characteristics at the ninth grade that may influence vocabulary growth could decrease this number. It is also the case that school effects in one subject were not necessarily predictive of school success in a second area. A school that increased vocabulary more than was expected on the basis of the entry characteristics of its students may not have been equally successful in increasing math skills. Jencks's analysis should be seen as being relative to variations in the schools studied. More extreme variations among schools, such as those in urban ghettos or isolated rural communities, might have been associated with larger variations in school effects. Also, these results tell us about variations associated with attendance in different comprehensive high schools in the U.S. in a particular time period. It is possible to imagine variations among secondary schools that are more extreme than those included in the Project Talent sample. Private and parochial schools were not included and schools that are based on various radical approaches to education were not studied. Jencks's analysis indicates that variations in the secondary comprehensive high schools that a student attends in the U.S. are not likely to influence scores on tests of intelligence. The IQ score that a student obtains at the end of secondary education is largely predictable from knowledge of the IQ scores that the student has at the beginning of secondary education as well as other background characteristics of the student.

Firkowska, Ostrowska, Sokolowska, Stein, Susser, & Wald (1978) relied on a naturalistic experiment to study the effects of schooling on IQ. They studied the population of all children born in 1963 living in the city of Warsaw in Poland in 1974. The city had been rebuilt after World War II and families were assigned almost at random to housi..g and consequently to schools. All of the subjects in their study were given the Raven test. They obtained information about the education and occupation of the parents of their subjects as well as information about differences in the schools their subjects attended and the neighborhoods in which they lived. The school characteristics included data about average class size, academic qualifications of the teachers in the school, and the percentage of pupils repeating grades in the school. They also developed indices of the social advantage of the neighborhoods of their subjects. They obtained data on the accessibility of cultural facilities and the demographic characteristics of the neighborhood. Information about background characteristics of pupils was used to predict scores on the Raven. Their results are reported in Table 6.4. The data presented in Table 6.4 indicate that the IQ scores of students were related to the occupational and educational backgrounds of their parents. Knowledge of school characteristics and neighborhood characteristics was trivially related to IQ test scores. These results should be considered cautiously. The appeal of this study is that it is based on a massive social experiment initiated by a Communist country that attempted to allocate individuals of different social backgrounds to different neighborhoods in a random fashion. The validity of the experiment derives from the assumption that allocation to schools and neighborhoods approximated a random assignment of individuals to con-

TABLE 6.4   Multiple Correlation and Proportion of Variance in Raven Scores Accounted for by District, Family, and School Variables in Three Casual Models[a]

Step	Variable entered	Multiple correlation (r)	Variance accounted for (r²)	r² Change
Model 1				
1	District	.126	.01586	.01586
2	School	.147	.02161	.00575
3	Family	.326	.10618	.08485
Model 2				
1	School	.115	.01315	.01315
2	Family	.324	.10482	.09168
3	District	.326	.10618	.00136
Model 3				
1	Family	.320	.10271	.10271
2	District	.324	.10514	.00244
3	School	.326	.10618	.00104

[a]Based on Firkowska, Ostrowsha, Sokolowska, Stein, Susser, & Wald (1978).

ditions. This ideological commitment would no doubt be accompanied by an equally fervent attempt to create relatively equal educational opportunities for individuals attending different schools. If one assumes that an egalitarian society was able to assign individuals at random to schools, then it is equally plausible to assume that these schools would be substantially similar. And, under these conditions, one would not expect variations in education to be substantially associated with intelligence test scores. Whether schools that vary considerably in social composition and educational programs would influence scores on intelligence tests cannot be confidently determined from the results of the Firkowska *et al.* study.

Variations among schools do not appear to be a major influence on IQ. There are, however, other studies of changes in intelligence that indirectly implicate variations in education as being critical factors in producing differences in IQ. Jensen (1977) studied a sample of pupils attending schools in rural Georgia. He used a sibling control study in which he compared younger and older siblings in the same families on scores on the California Test of Mental Maturity. He obtained different results for black and white students in his sample. Among white students, there was relatively little difference in test scores between younger and older siblings. The black students in the sample exhibited a linear decrease in IQ as a function of age differences between siblings. Younger siblings had higher test scores than older siblings in this sample. The regression line predicted a 1.42-point decline in IQ per year of difference in age. The cumulative effects of this decline between age 6 and 16 was approximately a one-standard-deviation difference in IQ. Jensen attributed the declines in his black sample to environmental rather than genetic influences. He indicated that an early study (Jensen, 1974a) using the same methodology in California failed to find evidence of differences in test scores between younger and older siblings in a black sample. He attributed the differences he obtained in Georgia to the effects of a cumulative deficit for individuals with extremely low socioeconomic status. The environmental influences that may contribute to the decline observed by Jensen are not isolated. The effects are not solely attributable to the schools that these students attend. Presumably the white students attended the same schools as the black students and they did not exhibit declines in IQ. Of course the educational experience of attending the same schools may be quite different for white and black students. This may be peculiarly relevant for the students studied by Jensen. The study was published in 1977 and the average age of the students was 12 years. Jensen does not state when the data were collected, but it is quite likely that the oldest students in his sample started school in the mid-1960s. Schools in Georgia were segregated in the 1960s and the early school experiences of the older subjects in Jensen's sample must have occurred in a segregated school setting or shortly after the end of segregated schooling in this region of the United States. Whether these changes in the character of education experienced by these black students account for sibling differences in IQ test scores is not known.

Jensen's results are based on a small and isolated subsample of the U.S. population. There are studies demonstrating secular changes in IQ for many industrialized countries. Flynn (1984) summarized data for the United States that demonstrated secular increases in IQ. Using data from various standardization samples of different versions of the Wechsler and Binet tests, he estimated that IQ increased in the U.S. between 1932 and 1978 13.8 points. He subsequently extended this analysis to 14 industrialized countries (Flynn, 1987). Table 6.5 presents his results. The gains are widespread and substantial. They vary in magnitude for different countries. Flynn calculated a value of 3 points per decade for the United States. Lynn & Hampson (1986b) estimated increases of 1.71 points per decade for Great Britain. They also estimated gains of 7.7 points per decade for Japan through the 1960s followed by a declining rate of gain in IQ. Although some of the studies reviewed by Flynn may be flawed and subject to alternative interpretations, there are studies based on very large relatively representative populations of male subjects who appear for universal selective service examinations in The Netherlands, Belgium, France, and Norway that leave little doubt that secular increases in test scores have occurred.

There is no obvious or simple explanation for the increase in test scores. Evidence of increases in IQ observed in selective service examinations administered to recruits in World War I and World War II were explained by reference to changes in the amount of formal education (see

TABLE 6.5 Recent IQ Gains: Locations Grouped by Test and Ranked by Rate of Gain[a]

Location	Test	Rate[c]	Age (years)	Period	IQ gain (points)	Status[d]
Leipzig	Ravens	1.250	11–16	1968–1978	10–15	3/2
France	Ravens	1.005	18	1949–1974	25.12	3
Belgium	Ravens	0.794	18	1958–1967	7.15	1
Belgium	Shapes	0.716	18	1958–1967	6.45	1
Netherlands	Ravens	0.667	18	1952–1982	20.00	1
Norway	Matrices	0.629	19	1954–1968	8.80	1
West Germany	Horna-Ravens[b]	0.588	12–16	1961–1978	10.00	4
Australia	Jenkins	0.490	10–14	1949–1981	15.67	3
Edmonton	Ravens	0.402	9	1956–1977	8.44	1
Australia	Ravens	0.337	10–16	1950–1976	8.76	4
Norway	Matrices	0.217	19	1968–1980	2.60	1
Great Britain	Ravens	0.189	8–14	1938–1979	7.75	3
Great Britain	Ravens	0.181	20–30	1940–1979	7.07	3
Japan	Wechsler[b]	0.835	6–15	1951–1975	20.03	3/4
Vienna	Wechsler	0.824	6–15	1962–1979	12–16	4

192

Sample	Test	Correlation	Age[c]	Period	IQ points[c]	Rating[d]
West Germany	Wechsler[b]	0.741	7–15	1954–1981	20.00	3/4
Zurich	Wechsler	0.652	9 and 12	1954–1977	10–20	4
Edmonton	CTMM	0.525	9	1956–1977	11.03	1
France	Wechsler	0.380	6–15	1955–1979	9.12	4
United States	Wechsler–Binet[b]	0.300	2–18	1932–1972	12.00	2
United States	Wechsler[b]	0.243	16–75	1954–1978	5.95	3
Solothurn	Wechsler	0.186	8–9	1977–1984	1.30	4
Saskatchewan	Otis[b]	0.628	10	1958–1978	12.55	2/3
Norway	Verbal–math	0.582	19	1954–1968	8.15	1
Belgium	Verbal–math	0.408	18	1958–1967	3.67	1
France	Verbal–math	0.374	18	1949–1974	9.35	
Saskatchewan	Otis[b]	0.348	13	1958–1978	6.95	2/3
New Zealand	Otis	0.242	10–13	1936–1968	7.73	1
Norway	Verbal–math	−0.133	19	1968–1980	−1.60	

[a]Based on Flynn (1987).
[b]The content of these tests was substantially altered.
[c]IQ points per year.
[d]1, verified; 2, probable; 3, tentative; 4, speculative.

Tuddenham, 1948). Increases in IQ are present for post-World War II cohorts that have not had substantial differences in the amount of education that they have received. It is also interesting to note that the changes are apparently larger on tests of fluid ability than they are on tests of crystallized ability. For example, they appear to be larger on the Wechsler performance tests than on the Wechsler verbal tests. Flynn estimated that the median rate of gain per year for culture-reduced tests such as the Raven is .588 IQ points compared to .374 points on verbal tests. He argued that gains are more likely to be manifested on those tests that are assumed to measure decontextualized problem-solving ability than on those tests that come closer to measuring specific knowledge. Flynn argued that increases in scores on intelligence tests may occur even though the quality of education is declining. He argued that declines in performance on the SAT were occurring at the same time that gains were occurring on tests of intelligence. The SAT required advanced academic skills and he assumed that the quality of American secondary school education was declining at the same time that intelligence as assessed by tests of decontextualized problem-solving ability was increasing.

Lynn & Hampson (1986b) and Teasdale & Owen (1989) analyzed changes in IQ for individuals with different IQ scores. Their analyses indicate that gains were larger for low-scoring individuals than for high-scoring individuals. Lynn and Hampson reported that gains in IQ in Britain varied with the age of the sample and the IQ of the sample. The correlation between the increase in IQ on the Raven for different cohorts and the age of the sample was .90 for individuals at the tenth percentile in IQ scores. The comparable correlation for high-IQ individuals at the ninetieth percentile was −.56. Gains in IQ for 14-year-old individuals were 12 points for low-IQ individuals and 6 points for high-IQ individuals. Teasdale & Owen (1989) examined test scores for Danish military examinations for individuals born between 1967 and 1969. They compared these scores to scores obtained for cohorts born between 1939 and 1958. There was a significant increase in IQ for this cohort relative to cohorts born earlier. The magnitude of the increase varied inversely with IQ. The maximum gains occurred at the eleventh percentile and at the ninetieth percentile the curves converged. It is not known if the results obtained by Lynn and Hampson for England and by Teasdale and Owen for Denmark are characteristic of IQ changes in other countries.

We can only speculate about the appropriate explanation for these phenomena. Clearly, changes of this magnitude cannot be attributable to genetic changes. They are not likely to be explained by amount of education. Changes in socioeconomic and occupational status are not likely to provide satisfactory explanations. Teasdale and Owen argued that changes in Danish schools with better provision for remedial education explain the increase in IQ among low-scoring individuals. This hypothesis is not incompatible with results showing that increases are larger for tests of what Flynn calls decontextualized abstract reasoning than for tests of crystallized ability. Recall that Stankov found that Kvashchev's intervention led to larger increases on tests of fluid ability than on tests of crystallized ability. Scribner & Cole (1981) reviewed the effects of formal schooling on cognitive ability and they found that formal schooling led to large increases in tests of fluid ability. Combining these speculations leads to the hypothesis that changes in performance on tests of intelligence are associated with the quality of schooling. It is possible that an increased egalitarian tendency in industrialized societies with improved access to educational opportunities has increased the average intellectual ability of low-scoring IQ cohorts. It should be recognized that this hypothesis is highly speculative. We need better data on changes in IQ in different countries for different groups of individuals. And, it would be extremely valuable to relate obtained changes in sociological and demographic indices as well as to analyses of educational policies and opportunities.

Lynn (1990a) argued that secular changes in intelligence are attributable to nutrition. He indicated that secular changes in intelligence were accompanied by comparable secular changes in height and head circumference. These changes are probably attributable to changes in nutrition. Both height and head circumference have been related to intelligence. And, there is evidence that nutrition is related to intelligence. Lynn argued that educational changes and changes in intellectual stimulation were less plausible explanations for secular changes in intelligence since the changes appear to be larger on nonverbal and fluid measures of intelligence than on verbal and crystallized measures of intelligence. He cited evidence from adoption studies indicating that adoption in superior homes influences verbal abilities more than nonverbal abilities. Therefore, secular changes in intellectual stimulation should be manifested more clearly on verbal measures than on nonverbal measures of ability. Lynn's argument does not provide evidence against the hypothesis that secular changes in intelligence could be attributable to educational changes since there is evidence that educational interventions may change fluid ability more than crystallized ability. Lynn's arguments do not, in my judgment, persuasively rule out an educational interpretation of secular changes in intelligence. He has, however, persuasively argued that nutritional changes may contribute to secular changes in intelligence. In order to provide stronger evidence for his hypothesis it would be necessary to obtain indices of secular changes in nutrition and height and to relate these measures to secular changes in intelligence in different countries. It is interesting to note that Japan is a country that experienced very large secular gains in intelligence for cohorts born before World War II and large gains in intelligence. Whether secular changes in height and nutrition in different countries are correlated with secular changes in intelligence remains to be determined.

Flynn argued that the secular changes in intelligence that he reported indicated that intelligence tests were not good measures of intelligence. Changes of this magnitude in intelligence should be accompanied by changes in academic achievement and in various indices of intellectual accomplishment if tests of intelligence are actually measures of intelligence. Lynn (1990a) argued that Flynn's argument is not based on systematic evidence. It is possible that there are true secular changes in indices of intellectual accomplishment that have not been studied. In this connection he noted that the percentage of the population attending college increased in most countries. We need more systematic data about secular changes in intellectual accomplishment that may or may not be correlated with secular changes in intelligence.

Secular changes in intelligence remain mysterious. Nutrition and educational changes may be responsible. We have no explanation for these changes that is not speculative. And, we do not really know if the changes reflect true changes in the theoretical construct indexed by tests of intelligence. I believe, in common with Lynn, that a reasonably strong case can be made that the index is a good measure of the construct and it is unlikely that large changes in intelligence test scores could occur that are not accompanied by some change in the construct of which the test is a putative index.

WITHIN-FAMILY ENVIRONMENTAL INFLUENCES

Behavior genetic research indicates that intelligence is influenced by the within-family environment (Plomin & Daniels, 1987). In what follows I will present some speculations about this source of variance in intelligence.

We do know that there are conditions under which the intelligence of siblings reared in the same family is not influenced at all by within-family environmental variations. MZ twins reared together correlate in IQ .86. The test–retest reliability of the measures of intelligence used in these studies is estimated to be .87. These data imply that the disattenuated correlation in IQ for MZ twins is close to unity. Thus there can be few or no within-family environmental influences on IQ for this class of siblings. It is also the case that DZ twin pairs are more alike in intelligence than nontwin sibling pairs. What does this tell us about the influence of within-family environmental variation on intelligence? This question may be answered in different ways. We have seen that quantitative behavior genetic analyses imply that twins experience environments that are more similar to each other than do other classes of siblings. An analysis of the ways in which twins differ from other sibling pairs may provide clues to within-family variables that may influence intelligence. Twins spend time together and have more extensive opportunities to interact with each other than do nontwin siblings. The opportunity to interact extensively and to influence each other need not automatically lead to identity on all traits among MZ twin pairs. MZ twins exhibit correlations on measures of personality that are considerably lower than the test–retest correlation of the tests (see Brody, 1988, Chapter 3). Rose & Kaprio (1987) reported that MZ correlations for neuroticism were positively related to the degree of contact of twin pairs. Among female MZ pairs the correlations for neuroticism declined from .71 for adult twins living together to .26 for MZ twins who rarely contacted each other. Rose and Kaprio asserted that these findings imply that social contacts between adult twins influence their personality and their degree of similarity. An alternative interpretation of these findings is possible. Twins who are similar for whatever reason choose to maintain social contact with each other. A longitudinal study is required to distinguish between these alternative interpretations. Comparable data have not been reported for MZ resemblance in intelligence. There is little evidence that MZ correlations in intelligence are lower among adult MZ twins than among younger twin pairs. For example, Tambs et al. (1984) reported MZ correlations of .88 for a sample of adult MZ twins on the WAIS. Adult MZ twin pairs experience less intimate contact than younger MZ twin pairs. The decrease in social contact that tends to accompany adult twin experience does not appear to result in a decrease in resemblance in intelligence. It is possible that the extended social contact experienced by MZ twins during childhood creates similarity in IQ and this similarity then persists through the adult years. This interpretation is contradicted by other data indicating that IQ resemblance for biologically unrelated individuals living in the same family decreases as children living together grow older. Alternatively, it could be argued that the increased social contact characteristic of MZ twins is not of substantial relevance in producing IQ resemblance since variations in social contact that occur after the twins leave home do not decrease IQ resemblance.

There are additional data that suggest that social contact among twin pairs is not a major factor in determining their resemblance in IQ. DZ twin pairs appear to be more alike in IQ than nontwin siblings. Opposite-sex DZ twin pairs are as similar as same-sex DZ twin pairs. I assume that opposite-sex DZ twin pairs have less social contact that same-sex DZ twin pairs. This implies that variations in social contact do not determine the degree of resemblance of twin pairs in intelligence.

Although there is considerable uncertainty about all of this, it does not appear that a strong case can be made for the role of social contact as a factor in producing IQ resemblance among twins. What other factors might differentiate twins from nontwin siblings? Perhaps the most obvious difference between twin and nontwin sibling pairs is that they differ in age. In most studies of resemblance among family members in IQ, twins are usually tested at the same age. Nontwin sibling correlations are influenced by sources of variance that do not influence twin correlations attributable to age variations. Wilson (1983) reported that changes in childhood intelligence were heritable. He found that changes in IQ were more highly correlated among MZ twin pairs than among DZ twins. Spurts and declines in scores on childhood indices of IQ appear to be heritable. It is not clear if these effects are present in older children. The presence of heritable developmental changes in IQ suggests that differences between DZ twin correlations and nontwin sibling correlations in intelligence may be influenced by genetic characteristics. A critical test of this hypothesis could be obtained by varying the age of testing of siblings. Differences in the correlations between nontwin siblings and DZ twins ought to decrease if nontwin siblings are tested at the same age.

Variations in the age of testing of nontwin siblings may introduce "time-of-testing" variance. Social changes characteristic of different times of testing may influence test scores. Controls for time-of-testing effects still leave secular changes in IQ as a potential source of variance that could cause differences in IQ resemblance of nontwin siblings that is not present in twin data. The influence of this variable is not likely to be large. Secular changes are usually reported to be 2 to 3 points per decade. IQ scores are usually determined in terms of the relationship between an individual's score and the score of his or her age cohorts. Appropriate renorming of IQ scores is not done on a yearly basis. Failure to adjust IQ scores annually for cohort effects will produce changes in IQ that could decrease the resemblance of nontwin siblings. In addition, if one uses a measure of intelligence that is not cohort normed, such as the Raven test, secular influences may contribute to IQ differences among nontwin siblings. It should be realized that secular influences are not likely to have dramatic within-family effects on IQ. Secular changes in IQ of 2 to 3 points per decade are not likely to be a major source of variance between siblings who have small differences in their ages.

It is possible to study within-family environmental differences using the same variables used to study between-family environmental differences. In order to do this it is necessary to study variations among individuals reared in the same home. Consider some possible ways in which this might be done. There is a large literature on the relationship between the socioeconomic status of parents and the IQ of their children. The socioeconomic status of a family is not invariant. Siblings who differ in age may have parents whose socioeconomic status differs at different stages of their development. We have examined whether variations in schools that one attends influence intelligence. Siblings in the same family may not attend the same schools. Siblings in the same family may be socialized in different ways. Temperamental differences between children may influence the quantity and quality of parental interaction. The amount of time that a parent spends with a child may vary with changes in family circumstances. A mother may be employed during the preschool years of one of her children and remain at home during the preschool-age years of a second child. It is obvious that virtually any variable that has been studied as a potential source of between-family environmental influence on intelligence can be studied as a within-family environmental influence by studying differences between children reared in the same family.

There are few if any studies that I am aware of that attempt to relate within-family environmental differences to differences in intelligence among siblings reared together. We can only speculate about the viability of this research strategy. An argument can be developed that studies of variations within families based on an examination of the variables that are used to characterize differences between families will not provide information about the characteristics of the within-family environment that influence intelligence. Consider socioeconomic status. White (1982) performed a meta-analysis of studies relating socioeconomic background and IQ. He reported that the correlation between parental socioeconomic status and the IQ of a student is .33. Some portion, perhaps a substantial portion, of that variance is attributable to genetic influences. The between-family influence of socioeconomic status on IQ on White's analysis accounts for 10% of the variance in IQ. Disputes exist, as we have seen, about the extent to which this correlation is mediated genetically, and one can argue whether parental socioeconomic status has any influence on IQ that is independent of a genetic relationship between parent and child for postadolescent individuals. Whatever one's position on this issue, it is clear that variations between siblings in the socioeconomic status of their parents at different stages of their development are likely to be small relative to variations between families. And, if variations in socioeconomic status between families have a vanishingly small influence on IQ, then it is unlikely that the much smaller variations within families will have a large influence on IQ. And, even where families experience drastic changes in their socioeconomic status, there is a carry-over in some of the characteristics associated with their previous status. A well-educated parent whose occupational status changes from upper middle class to lower class is unlikely to adopt all of the mannerisms and social characteristics of his or her newly acquired social status. Literature and life histories are filled with examples of individuals whose social status changes over the course of their lifetime and who continue to maintain the vestiges of attitudes and mannerisms that are appropriate to a previous social status. Think of D. H. Lawrence's autobiographical novel, "Sons and Lovers." Many of the characteristics of Paul (the character who represents D. H. Lawrence) are traced to the influence of his mother, whose attitudes and behaviors reflect the residual effects of a childhood socioeconomic background that is higher than that of her husband, who is a miner.

In order to study within-family environmental influences using those variables that are assumed to contribute to between-family environmental influences on intelligence it would appear to be necessary to identify variables that fulfill two criteria: (1) Variations must exist both between families and within families on the variable; and (2) there must be evidence that between-family variance relates to variations in intelligence. The second criterion is not easily fulfilled. Are there any between-family environmental variables that relate to the intelligence of older individuals that are independent of genetic influences? The answer to this rhetorical questions is not self-evident. The only variable that I can think of is the secular variable studied by Flynn.

It is possible to study within-family environmental influences on intelligence using variables that are not derived from the study of between-family environmental variables. Birth order is the classic example of a within-family environmental variable. It is also the only within-family environmental variable for which an explicit theoretical model exists relating variations in birth order and birth spacing to intelligence. Zajonc & Marcus (1975; Zajonc, 1976) developed the "confluence" model to explain data collected by Belmont & Marolla (1973) from a population of Dutch selective service registrants relating family size and birth order to intelligence. The data they analyzed are presented in Fig. 6.1. These data present scores on the Raven test as a function of the size of one's family and birth order within the family. There are several features of the data in Fig. 6.1 that are noteworthy. Excluding only children, performance on the Raven declines as the family size increases. Performance on the Raven decreases as birth order increases. This latter generalization is violated by data for families within eight and nine members, where the next-to-last sibling has higher performance than the preceding sibling. The function relating birth order to family size is quadratic. The differences between birth orders exhibit smaller declines with the exception of the last sibling. Last siblings exhibit large drops in performance. Only children score close to the level of firstborn children in families of four.

Zajonc and Markus explained these data by making assumptions about the impact of the intellectual atmosphere of family members on the development of intelligence. They assumed that the impact of the family environment on intelligence was a positive function of the average level of intelligence of members of a family. They assumed that a newborn child has zero intelligence. If each of that child's parents has an average intelligence of 100, the average family intellectual environment experienced by that child at birth is 66.67—the average value of the intelligence of each of the members of the family including the child. If the child is born into a family with a single adult caretaker of average intelligence,

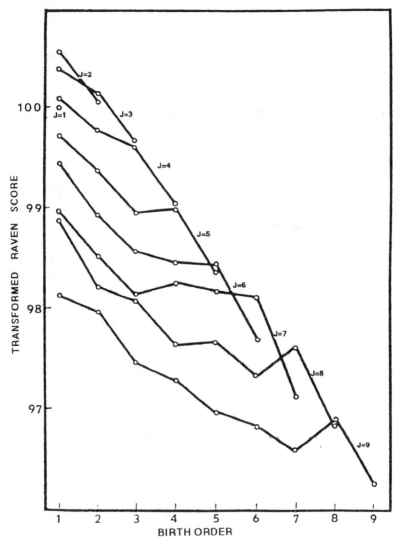

FIGURE 6.1 Birth order, family size, and intelligence. (Based on Zajonc & Markus, 1975.)

the average intellectual level of the family would be 50, leading to the prediction that children reared in families with a single adult caretaker would on average have lower intelligence than children reared in families with two or more adult caretakers. If a second child is born into a family with two adult caretakers with an IQ of 100 and an older sibling who has reached half of an adult level of intelligence of 100, the average value of the intellectual environment affecting that child will be 62.5 (the average of 100, 100, 50, and 0). Note that the second child of a two-parent family tends to have an environment that is assumed to be less favorable for the development of intelligence than the first child in that family. These differences, depending on parametric assumptions, could be reversed if the birth of a second child in a family is delayed. If the second child in the example above is born when the first sibling has attained three-fourths of his or her adult intelligence, the second child's family environment will be more favorable for the development of intelligence than the first child's environment. Therefore, the spacing of children becomes a critical variable in the model. The assumption that the average level of environment influencing a child's intellectual development is a function of the average level of intelligence of all of the members of a family explains several features of the data in Fig. 6.1. Large families tend to have more individuals who have not attained their terminal levels of intelligence and therefore the average level of intelligence of family members tends to be lower in large than in small families. In effect, the parent's mature intellectual development is diluted by the presence of many children. Later-born children tend to experience the diluting effect of the averaging of children with adults at a more intense level than early-born children. There are simply more children present, decreasing the intellectual level of the family with each successive birth in the family. The quadratic function (excluding the last-born child) relating birth order to intelligence is explained by noting that the proportional decline associated with the addition of a new child decreases for each successive child. In addition, younger children in large families are older at the birth of each succeeding sibling and their average intelligence level is therefore higher. The assumption that the impact of the family environment on the child is a function of the average intellectual level of the family does not explain the precipitous decline for the last-born child in each family. Nor does it explain the anomalous position of the only child, who might be expected to have a more favorable environment for the development of intelligence than siblings in any other family configuration. In order to explain these last two characteristics of the data in Fig. 6.1, Zajonc and Marcus assumed that children benefit from the opportunity to teach younger siblings. Only children and last-born children are deprived of this opportunity and hence, uniquely among all other siblings, experience a decline in intelligence attributable to an inability to teach their younger siblings.

Although confluence theory is able to explain, in a general way, several features of the Dutch data, it should be noted that birth-order effects and family-size effects are relatively small. The data presented in Fig. 6.1 are aggregated data presenting means for a very large population. At the individual level, birth order and family size explain a relatively small portion of the variance in test performance. Stein, Susser, Saenger, & Marolla (1975) reported that the correlation between birth order and Raven performance was .10 and between family size and the Raven was .24. This latter correlation may not be attributable to the influence of the environment. Individuals who decide to have different sized families may differ genetically. Family size may be positively or inversely related to social class. The appropriate control for a study of the environmental impact of family size involves studying children whose parents have the same intelligence but differ in family size.

The confluence model was developed to explain the data presented in Fig. 6.1. In several respects these data do not provide an ideal test of the model. The data do not permit one to test hypotheses about single parents and spacing. The data as presented are aggregated over social class. Family size is, as we have noted, a between-family variable. Some attempt should be made to control for differences in parental characteristics before examining the effects of family size. Birth order, by contrast, is a within-family effect and should be tested by within-family data analyses that contrast siblings in the same family. Marjoribanks & Walberg (1975) demonstrated that the curves in Fig. 6.1 were not the same for different social classes. They divided the Dutch selective service data into three social class groups and demonstrated that the functions relating family size and birth order to intelligence differed in each of the groups. For example, in the lowest socioeconomic group there was a slight increase in IQ as family size increased. The confluence model assumes that the environmental influences of these variables should be invariant and therefore should not lead to different results for families with different social backgrounds unless there are differences in birth spacing that are related to social class or differences in the presence of caretakers who are hired or who are members of an extended family. Without additional ad hoc assumptions, the confluence model cannot explain the separate functions for different social classes obtained by Marjoribanks and Walberg for the original data set used to derive the model.

Several investigators obtained data on family size and birth order that they claimed could not be explained by confluence theory. Brackbill & Nichols (1982) obtained Stanford–Binet and Wechsler IQ test scores for a sample of 53,000 children participating in a study of the effects of prenatal and perinatal events on development. They tested five hypotheses derived from confluence theory.

1. Children in father-absent homes will have lower IQs than children reared in homes in which both parents are present. Their data for black and white children on the Binet test administered when the children were age 4 and on the Wechsler test administered when the children were age 7 supported this prediction. The biserial correlations between the dichotomous father-absent or father-present variable and IQ scores ranged from .07 to .12 in their black and white samples for both of these tests. When they controlled for social class differences, the correlations became negative, ranging from −.02 to −.06. These data suggest that father absence has a slight positive influence on IQ when social class differences are controlled.

2. Single surviving twins will have a higher IQ than surviving twin pairs. It is known that twins have lower IQs than singletons. Confluence theory explains this phenomenon by appeal to the decrease of the average family intellectual environment associated with the birth of twins as opposed to singletons. Brackbill and Nichols found that surviving members of twin pairs reared as singletons were not significantly higher in IQ than twins in which both members of the twin pair survived. For the sample of black twins, single surviving members of twin pairs had lower IQ (but not significantly lower) than twins belonging to pairs in which both members of the twin pair survived.

3. Confluence theory predicts that as birth interval increases the effects of family size on ability should decrease. The data obtained by Brackbill and Nichols provided support for this prediction. After controlling for socioeconomic status, both birth order and the interval between births were related to intelligence. Later-born children had higher intelligence and children born with long intervals between births had higher IQ.

4. Only children are expected to score lower in IQ than the firstborn children of small families. Brackbill and Nichols used a regression technique to predict the expected value of an only child's IQ from regressions of birth order and family size on IQ. There were no differences between expected and obtained IQs. Only children did not exhibit the expected decrement in IQ because of inability to teach other children.

5. Children reared in homes with an extended family and additional adults should have higher IQs than children reared in families with two adults. There were no significant differences in intelligence between children reared in homes with more than two adults and children reared in homes with two adults.

Brackbill and Nichols's tests of the confluence of model failed to provide support for the assumptions of the model. They attribute their negative results partially to their ability to control for social class differences. The failure to find significant effects for father absence or for extended families implies that the average level of intellectual stimulation in the home cannot be calculated from averages derived from the composition of the family. Any parametric version of confluence theory implies that the number of adults present in the home influences the intellectual development of the child. If the central assumption of confluence theory is incorrect, how are we to explain those findings that indicate that birth order and birth spacing may influence intelligence? Brackbill and Nichols indicated that obstetrical and epidemiological studies reported that short birth intervals are adversely related to several indices of pregnancy outcome including mortality and birth weight. Therefore, the effects of birth spacing may be mediated by prenatal events.

Gailbraith (1982b) studied Mormon students at Brigham Young University and obtained results that were not easily explained by a confluence model. Gailbraith found that average performance on the American College Test used for admissions at Brigham Young University was positively related to family size. He did find evidence that birth order within family size was inversely related to test scores. These differences were not related to birth spacing. Berbaum, Marcus, & Zajonc (1982) argued that the distinctive pattern of results obtained by Gailbraith was attributable to the use of a Mormon sample. Mormons value large families and emphasize the importance of providing attention to each of their children. The effects of these socialization practices may be interpreted in terms of the central explanatory mechanism of the confluence model. It should be noted, however, that the appeal to distinctive socialization practices dissipates the quantitative elegance of the model and suggests that one cannot specify the effects of family composition variables on intellectual development without additional information about family socialization practices.

Zajonc, Markus, & Markus (1979; see also Berbaum & Moreland, 1980; Marcus & Zajonc, 1977; Zajonc, 1983; Zajonc & Bargh, 1980) developed a number of modifications in the model and attempted to explain several large-scale data sets relating family size and birth order to intelligence. Gailbraith (1982a,b; 1983) was able to show that the various mathematical models developed by Zajonc and his collaborators led to unreasonable results and were not necessarily internally consistent (see also Berbaum et al., 1982). One difficulty in assessing the confluence model is that critical tests of the model require one to assess the impact of the family environment on a child at several different times. Family composition may change in any of several ways: New children enter a family, older children may leave home, adult caretakers may change through divorce and separation, and changes in the presence and absence of members of a child's extended family can occur. All of these changes will change the average intellectual level of members of a family and should influence the child's intellectual development according to confluence theory. Large-scale data sets assessing changes in family composition and changes in intelligence in a longitudinal design do not exist. Therefore, critical tests of the confluence model based on the most appropriate data sets have not been done.

This brief review of the confluence model leads to several tentative conclusions. The effects of birth order and family size are small and after controlling for socioeconomic status are not invariably present. The exact relationship between these variables and intelligence may vary in different social groups. Some of these differences are probably attributable to between-family differences that determine decisions about family size and spacing between children. The central assumption of confluence theory about the impact of family environment on the child's intelligence appears to be contradicted by several findings in the literature. All of this suggests that the composition of the family is not an important determinant of the intelligence of a child.

There are many other potential differences in the treatment of children within the same family. Parents may favor one child over another. Sibling interactions may influence development. Each child may occupy a unique position within the family. We know very little about the systematic influence of these variables. Daniels & Plomin (1985) developed an inventory to assess differences in sibling experiences. The relationship between these differences in perception of treatment and differences in intelligence has not, to my knowledge, been studied. In addition to differences in experiences within the context of the family, siblings may differ with respect to extrafamilial influences. Siblings may have different friends and this could influence the development of intelligence. It is also possible that many of the within-family environmental influences on intelligence are virtually idiosyncratic. Intelligence may be influenced by many unpredictable events that occur in a virtually random fashion. Everything from illnesses, to books read, to the influence of charismatic adults such as teachers or religious leaders might change the activities of an individual and influence scores on a test of intelligence. These influences may be idiographic, i.e., they may be important influences in an individual life but not necessarily in the lives of many individuals. It should be apparent that we do not know very much about within-family environmental influences on intelligence other than that they appear to be important.

THE BIOLOGICAL ENVIRONMENT AND INTELLIGENCE

Intelligence may be influenced by biological events. Illnesses, prenatal experiences, the effects of birth and delivery, and nutrition are among the biological events that have been assumed to influence intelligence. One impetus to the study of the influence of the biologic environment came from the hypothesis of "the continuum of reproductive casualty" (Passamanick & Knobloch, 1966). This hypothesis implies that there is a continuum of the effects of prenatal events and the birth process that have enduring neurological consequences. Individuals without obvious neurological disease may in subtle ways be influenced by the consequences of prenatal events and the birth process. Birch & Gussow (1970) argued that the relationship between social class and intelligence might be influenced by the biological environment. They argued that inadequate prenatal care and nutrition might influence the development of intelligence and school failure. It is difficult to study the influence of such events since they are correlated with a number of parental characteristics that may influence intelligence. Parents who are not likely to obtain adequate prenatal care for their children may be genetically different from parents who do obtain adequate prenatal care, and they may be less likely to provide their children with an optimal intellectual environment than parents who obtain adequate prenatal care for their children. This problem may be circumvented by controlling for variables that may be correlated with biological variables that influence intelligence. A good example of this strategy can be found in the Collaborative Perinatal Project, a large-scale study of the influences of the biological status of the child at birth on the development of intelligence (Broman, Nichols, & Kennedy, 1975). Data on the status of a child at birth for 132 variables were obtained for over 50,000 newborn children. The data included information about birth weight as well as birth complications obtained from hospital records. Information about the social background of the family was included. The children were given IQ tests at ages 4 and 7. Broman *et al.* (1975) performed a series of regression analyses predicting age 4 Stanford–Binet IQ test scores for the children in their sample. In one of their analyses they entered mother's education and socioeconomic status prior to a consideration of all other variables including all of the information about the biological status of the child at birth. Table 6.6 presents the results of these regression analyses considered separately for four subsamples based on a division of the total sample by race and gender. These data indicate that information about mother's education and socioeconomic status predicts somewhere between 6 and 18% of the variance in childhood IQ in the four subsamples of the Collaborative Perinatal Project. Additional information about the biological status of the child at birth as well as other aspects of the family medical history may add 3 to 4% more predictive variance to the ability to predict 4-year-olds' IQ scores. Very few of the variables that measured the status of the neonate were predictively related to IQ at 4 years of age. Among the variables that were significantly related to IQ at age 4 in both black and white subsamples were birth weight, birth length, and head circumference. The

TABLE 6.6 Stepwise Regression Analysis in Four Samples Relating Prenatal and Neonatal Variables to IQ at Age 4[a]

Sample	Contribution of mother's education and socioeconomic status (r)	Final contribution considering all other significant variables (r)
White male	.42	.46
White female	.42	.47
Black male	.25	.30
Black female	.28	.34

[a]Based on Broman, Nichols, & Kennedy (1975).

correlations for these three variables in these two samples ranged from .06 to .11. Three other variables characterizing the biological status of the neonate were predictively related to IQ in both black and white samples—evidence of neonatal brain abnormality, neonatal serum bilirubin, and neonatal respiratory distress. The correlation for these three variables and IQ in black and white samples ranged from −.03 to −.09. These data indicate that information about the biological status of the child at birth is only weakly related to his or her 4-year-old IQ. And, after controlling for mother's education and socioeconomic status, all of the information considered collectively does not add appreciably to ability to predict IQ.

The interpretation of the regression analyses reported by Broman *et al.* (1975) is difficult. The contribution of the biological status of the neonate to the development of childhood IQ may be overestimated or underestimated by the regression analyses summarized in Table 6.6. The control for the socioeconomic status of the mother may be interpreted as an over- or an undercontrol for relevant background variables. Mothers who are impoverished may have less adequate access to prenatal care than more privileged mothers. Inadequate prenatal care may increase the probability that the biological status of the neonate will be impaired. A control for the socioeconomic status of the mother thus may control for variables that influence the biological status of the neonate and thus may be considered to be an overcontrol for relevant variables. On the other hand, the control for socioeconomic characteristics of mothers may fail to control for genetic differences that influence the ability of mothers to gain access to prenatal care. It is difficult to know whether the variables entered into the regression equation prior to a consideration of the influence of variables that reflect the biological status of the neonate are appropriate control variables. In any case, the simple uncorrected correlations between biological variables and IQ are very low. Few account for more than 1% of the variance in IQ. It should be noted that in individual instances these variables may have a large impact on the development of a particular child. Children with very low birth weight may be neurologically impaired and the consequences of this impairment may influence their intellectual development (see Drillien, 1964). In a large and representative sample these variables do not account for a substantial portion of the variance in IQ.

Streissguth, Barr, Sampson, Darby, & Martin (1990) studied the effects of prenatal alcohol exposure on the development of intelligence. They used an interview method to assess alcohol use of women in the fifth month of pregnancy in a predominantly middle class sample. After controlling for educational backgrounds of the parents as well as a number of other potential influences on IQ, they found that their measure of fetal alcohol exposure correlated −.11 with a Wechsler test of intelligence administered when the children were 4 years of age. They also studied the effects of smoking and aspirin ingestion during pregnancy on childhood

IQ. Smoking was unrelated to IQ but aspirin ingestion was inversely related to childhood IQ. Their measure of aspirin use correlated with IQ −.12 after adjusting for differences in parental educational level. The decrease in IQ associated with alcohol ingestion does not appear to be attributable to differences in the postnatal environment. The Home Inventory was administered and was found to be unrelated to alcohol ingestion during pregnancy. A division of the sample of mothers into two groups on the basis of alcohol ingestion was associated with a 4.8-point difference in IQ. Data indicating whether the effects of prenatal alcohol exposure decline or persist for measures of intelligence beyond early childhood have not been reported. While the effects of alcohol exposure may be small, they are only one of several possible teratogenic influences on intelligence. The cumulative effects of all of the potential influences of the biological environment on the child may be large.

The Collaborative Perinatal Project focused on the biological status of the neonate. Other studies of the influence of the biological environment on intelligence have considered measures of the biological environment that are not restricted in their impact to the prenatal period and the birth process. There has been considerable controversy about the influence of lead exposure on intelligence (see Lansdown & Yule, 1986; Needleman, Gunnoe, Leviton, Reed, Peresie, Maher, & Barrett, 1979; Smith, 1985). More extensive research with large samples appears to have documented a clear effect of exposure to environmental lead on intelligence. Fulton, Thomson, Hunter, Raab, Laxen, & Hepburn (1987) administered an intelligence test to 501 children 6 to 9 years of age in Edinburgh and obtained blood samples permitting them to measure lead concentrations. Information about the social and academic background of the children's parents was also obtained. Edinburgh was chosen as a site for investigation because of the presence of a large number of houses with lead plumbing. The sample was divided into deciles on the basis of lead concentrations. There was a linear dose–response effect. Adjusting for parental social background and other relevant variables, children in the highest decile of lead concentration in their blood had IQ scores that were .43 standard deviations lower than children in the lowest decline of lead concentration in their blood. Lead concentrations in the blood accounted for less than half of 1% of the variance in IQ. Therefore, they clearly are not a major source of variance in IQ scores. At the same time these data clearly indicate that high levels of exposure to lead do depress IQ test scores.

McMichael, Baghurst, Wigg, Vimpani, Robertson, & Roberts (1988) reported analogous results in a study conducted in Port Pirie, Australia, an industrial town with a lead-smelting plant and high levels of lead pollution. They obtained measures of lead concentration in the blood at birth and at periodic intervals for a sample of 548 children. In addition, they administered the McCarthy test of intelligence to these children at age 4 and they obtained Wechsler maternal IQ scores as well as data on the

Home measure as well as a number of other parental background indices. They found a linear dose–response effect for lead concentration and IQ. Adjusting for background covariates, the optimal regression line suggests that children with the highest lead concentrations in their blood would have an IQ that was approximately 1 standard deviation lower than children with the lowest lead concentrations. The strongest effects for measures of lead concentrations were obtained for measures that integrated observations taken at several different periods in the child's life. This is compatible with the notion that the effects of lead exposure are cumulative and a constant high level of exposure to lead has a more deleterious effect on IQ scores than high-level exposure at one period in a child's life.

The results of the McMichael *et al.* and Fulton *et al.* studies provide clear evidence that exposure to high levels of lead in the environment has an adverse impact on the development of intelligence. Whether the effects persist beyond early childhood is not known, but there is no obvious reason to believe that the effects of lead exposure, if constant, would dissipate. The range of covariates used in both of these studies is large and it is unlikely that the effects of lead concentrations are artifactual.

Variations in nutrition may be an additional environmental influence on IQ. Children who are extremely malnourished tend to have low IQ (see Stein & Kassab, 1970). Studies of malnourished children tell us relatively little about the influence of nutrition on intelligence since clinical malnutrition is invariably accompanied by neglect, poverty, poor schooling, and a host of other variables that might have a negative impact on the development of intelligence. Even studies that have used sibling controls and compared children who are malnourished with their siblings who are relatively better nourished are not critical. Children who receive different amounts of nutrition within the same family may be treated differently by their parents in many ways other than in the amount of food they receive. We shall examine several different attempts to isolate nutritional variables and to study their impact on intelligence.

Stein *et al.* (1975) studied selective service registrants in Holland who had experienced famine prenatally. Approximately one-half of the population of The Netherlands experienced a severe famine during World War II. Stein *et al.* obtained military induction tapes for over 400,000 male 19 year olds who were born during the period of the famine. They compared Raven test scores for individuals who experienced famine conditions at different prenatal and postnatal periods. By noting place of birth they were able to compare individuals born at the same time who did not experience prenatal famine conditions. They found no effects of famine exposure on Raven scores at age 19. There was little doubt that their subjects experienced severe prenatal malnutrition. While pregnant women might have received more food than other individuals in the famine area, there was evidence of depressed birth weights and excess fetal mortality attributed to the famine conditions. It is possible that the parents who were more resourceful were able to obtain more food and that the surviving children were a biased nonrepresentative sample of the potential population of children who would have survived in nonfamine conditions. This hypothesis cannot be tested. What is clear is that the presence of inadequate prenatal nutrition did not have a detectable effect on IQ under conditions in which adequate nutrition was provided postnatally.

Although the Dutch famine study suggests that prenatal nutrition is not a critical influence on intelligence, there are other data that suggest that prenatal nutrition may influence intelligence. Lynn (1990a, in press) reviewed studies of MZ twins that obtained data on birth-weight differences and differences in intelligence. He found seven studies of this kind. In each study the MZ twins who were heavier at birth had higher IQs than their lighter twins. The differences across the studies ranged from 1.9 to 9.0 points in IQ. The birth-weight differences are reasonably attributable to differences in the adequacy of prenatal nutrition. Therefore, these data are compatible with the assumption that variations in prenatal nutrition influence IQ.

Winick, Meyer, & Harris (1975) compared the IQs of three groups of Korean children who were adopted by American parents before age 3. The children were divided into groups on the basis of an estimate of how well nourished they were at the time of adoption. At age 10 the children who were assumed to be malnourished (they were below the third percentile of Korean norms for height) had IQs that were 10 points lower than the children judged to be well nourished. It is possible that the poorly nourished children differed in a number of other respects from the well-nourished children.

Rush, Stein, & Susser (1980) used a experimental design with random assignment of subjects to conditions to study the effects of prenatal dietary supplements on development. They randomly assigned black pregnant women thought to be at high risk for delivering a low birth-weight babies to one of three groups—a group receiving a high-protein liquid supplement, a group receiving a high-calorie liquid supplement, or a control group. Rush, Stein, Susser, & Brody (1980) tested the children resulting from these pregnancies at age 1 on a visual habituation task. They found that the children whose mothers received liquid protein supplements habituated more rapidly and exhibited larger response recovery to a change in the visual stimulation pattern than children whose mothers received a high-calorie dietary supplement or were in the control group. The differences in these habituation indices were approximately one-quarter of a standard deviation. Since the design involved a moderately large sample ($N = 376$ for the habituation measures) and a random assignment of women to conditions we can be reasonably sure that the effects are attributable to the influence of prenatal nutrition. The long-term consequences of the effects of protein supplementation of prenatal diet were not investigated in this study. Research reviewed in Chapter 3 indicates that indices of habituation are correlated with IQ test scores up to age 7. If we assume that the effects of the changes in habituation observed by Rush and colleagues are related to later IQ in the usual manner ($r =$ approximately .5) this would imply that prenatal protein dietary supplementation could have increased IQ by about an eighth of a standard deviation. Since these children were not tested after age 1 this account remains speculative. It is interesting to note that the changes in visual habituation as a result of prenatal protein supplementation in this study were obtained in a sample that was not clinically malnourished.

Schoenthaler, Amos, Eysenck, Peritz, & Yudkin (1991) reported the results of a randomized trial of vitamin and mineral supplements for a sample of 615 California eighth grade students. The students were assigned to one of four groups who received either a placebo or dietary supplements that contained supplementation of 50, 100, or 200% of the USDA dietary guidelines for these nutrients for 13 weeks. All subjects were given Wechsler tests prior to the start of the experiment and at the conclusion of the study. All of the groups exhibited equal gains on retesting on the verbal part of the tests (approximately 2-point gains). Table 6.7 presents the results for changes in nonverbal intelligence on the WISC. An examination of these data indicates that the supplemented groups gained more than the placebo groups. The results indicate that the dose effects were not linear—the 100% supplemented groups exhibited the largest gains and statistical tests indicated that only this group was significantly better than the placebo groups. If we average the results for the three supplemented groups, it appears that the supplemented groups were approximately .29 standard deviations higher in nonverbal intelligence than the placebo group. There was some evidence that the changes in intelligence were associated with changes in academic performance. The 100% supplemented group gained more than the placebo group in performance on the California test of basic skills in such areas as math, reading comprehension, and science.

The results of the Schoenthaler *et al.* study are promising. The duration

TABLE 6.7 Changes in Performance IQ on the WISC for Different Nutritional Supplement Groups[a]

Group	Mean*	SD	N
Placebo	8.9	7.3	100
50% Supplement	10.1	8.9	100
100% Supplement	12.6	7.9	105
200% Supplement	10.4	7.6	105

[a]Based on Schoenthaler, Amos, Eysenck, Peritz, & Yudkin (1991).

*$F = 3.86, p < .01$.

of these effects is unknown. And, the results, although based on a relatively large, well-controlled study, require replication. Other attempts to demonstrate gains in intelligence using dietary supplements with smaller samples and a somewhat different composition of the supplement failed to find significant differences between supplemented and placebo groups (see, Crombie, Todman, McNeill, Florey, Menzies, & Kennedy, 1990; Yudkin, 1988). Nevertheless, these results suggest that some gains in nonverbal intelligence are possible with the use of dietary supplements in relatively well-nourished populations.

Sigman, Neumann, Jansen, & Bwibo (1989) studied a sample of 7- and 8-year-old Kenyan children growing up in a rural area that was subject to frequent droughts and food shortages. The children were given the Raven and a verbal test of intelligence, their nutritional intake was observed for 2 days, and indices of nutritional intake were derived for each child. Sixty-five percent of the boys and 73% of the girls in this sample were estimated to have daily caloric intakes that were below the optimal level. Parental literacy and socioeconomic status were also assessed. Table 6.8 presents correlations between nutritional indices and scores on intelligence tests for male and female subjects controlling for parental socioeconomic status and literacy. The correlations are all positive, indicating that intelligence test performance is positively related to indices of nutritional intake. It is difficult to know if these correlations under- or overestimate the influence of nutrition on intelligence. Assessments of nutritional intake for a 2-day period do not provide an adequate index of the adequacy of nutrition experienced by each child over his or her lifetime. More comprehensive indices of nutritional intake would probably result in higher correlations with scores on intelligence tests. On the other hand, the possibility that adequacy of nutrition provided to children may be correlated with parental characteristics that are independent of socioeconomic status and literacy that influence intelligence cannot be ruled out. The most reasonable interpretation of these data is that malnutrition decreases performance on tests of intelligence. The effects of

TABLE 6.8 Correlation between Cognitive Score and Food Intake with SES Covaried[a]

	Females (N = 60)	Males (N = 73)	All (N = 133)
Kcal	.37*	.12	.18*
Protein	.39*	.15	.21*
Animal protein	.29*	.34*	.31*
Fat	.44*	.27*	.31*
Carbohydrate	.30*	.07	.13
SES (when food intake covaried)	.34*	.37*	.38*

*$p \leq .05$.
[a]Based on Sigman, Neumann, Jansen, & Bwibo (1989).

malnutrition on intelligence may be mediated by an influence on attention that influences school performance. Sigman *et al.* (1989) found that nutritional intake was inversely related to off-task behavior in classroom observations for females but not for males. Female children who were well nourished were more likely to exhibit appropriate classroom attentional behavior than children who were poorly nourished. Alternatively, it is possible that the influence of nutrition on intelligence is not mediated by attentional variables and is dependent upon a direct influence of nutrition on the development of the brain.

The influence of nutrition on intelligence observed by Sigman *et al.* (1989) is probably dependent on the fact that their sample was one in which there was chronic malnutrition. Comparable studies relating nutritional intake to intelligence with controls for parental characteristics have not been reported for well-nourished samples. Although it is possible that malnutrition among individuals in extremely impoverished circumstances in some Western countries may contribute to the negative impact of poverty on intelligence, there is no evidence that nutritional variables are substantially related to intelligence in technologically advanced countries.

There are many other potential influences of the biological environment on IQ. I am not aware of any research demonstrating that any single biological environmental variable is substantially related to IQ. The cumulative influence of all biological environmental events might be substantial.

CONCLUSION

Chapters 5 and 6 have reviewed research on genetic and environmental influences on intelligence. Current lower-bound estimates for heritability of intelligence are above .4 and some authorities believe that, for older samples, the heritability of general intelligence may be close to .7. We have examined many possible environmental influences on intelligence. With the possible exception of secular influences that are not well understood, there is little evidence that any single source of environmental influence is highly correlated with IQ. Variables as diverse as exposure to lead in air and water supplies, quality and quantity of schooling, and birth order may each exert a small but discernible influence on intelligence. It may be difficult to increase scores on intelligence tests because the environmental influences on tests are diverse.

7

BIOLOGICAL CORRELATES
OF INTELLIGENCE

Intelligence is a heritable trait. This implies that there are biological correlates of intelligence. It is relatively easy to discover the biological correlates of intelligence but it is relatively difficult to determine the causal relationship between a biological measure and intelligence. Imagine an experiment in which a measure of brain function is obtained based on positron emission scanning. This technique permits one to measure activity in different regions of the brain. Individual differences in activity level of the brain are correlated with individual differences in intelligence. How is the correlation to be interpreted? Consider some possibilities. The relationship might be best understood in terms of a purely environmental influence on both intelligence and brain functioning. Individual differences in intelligence might depend on the degree of intellectual stimulation received by an individual. Individuals who differ in intelligence might approach problems in different ways and differences in the way in which they approach problems might result in differences in measures of metabolic rates in different regions of the brain. In this example it is assumed that environmental events influence intelligence and that individual differences in intelligence influence the functioning of the brain, creating a correlation between intelligence and measures of brain functioning.

Consider another scenario. Rats who are exposed to an enriched environment develop brains that are structurally different from the brains of rats exposed to "ordinary" laboratory environments. This suggests that environmental events could influence structural properties of the brain. The correlation between a structural property of the brain and intelligence could be interpretable by assuming that environmental events changed the brain and these changes in the brain influenced the development of intelligence.

There are other possibilities. The characteristics of the biological environment might be related to both individual differences in brain characteristics and individual differences in intelligence. For example, individual differences in nutrition might plausibly be assumed to be related to both individual differences in intelligence and brain characteristics. The relationship between intelligence and brain functioning might be mediated by the direct influence of the biological environment. More complex interpretations are possible. The relationship might be influenced by genetic–environmental correlations. Individuals who differ in genotypes for intelligence may differ in their ability to obtain adequate nutrition. Other interpretations are possible. Individual differences in the quality of nutrition provided to a child may be correlated with adequacy of the intellectual stimulation provided to the child by his or her parents. Nutrition may influence the development of the brain and intelligence but the correlation between a measure of brain function and intelligence may be completely adventitious. That is, individual differences in intelligence may be influenced by the quality of the environmental stimulation provided by a child's parents, and the relationship between a measure of brain functioning and intelligence on this analysis would not provide any insight into the biological basis of intelligence.

It is apparent that a relationship between a biological measure and intelligence is difficult to interpret and may occur for many different reasons. Jensen & Sinha (In press) analyzed genetic and environmental relationships between physical characteristics and intelligence. They indicated that an environmental correlation between two phenotypic measures that are each highly heritable can occur. They presented the following example. In a particular population brunettes may be nutritionally favored and blondes nutritionally deprived. This may lead to a correlation between hair color and stature. The correlation could be reversed to zero in one generation by equalizing the nutrition of individuals who differ in hair color.

Jensen and Sinha distinguish between two types of genetic correlations between traits. A between-family genetic correlation between traits can occur when there is no inherent or causal connection between heritable traits but both traits have been subject to common social influences. For example, assume that both intelligence and height are heritable traits. Assume that in a particular society assortative mating exists for both height and intelligence. This will tend to create a correlation between height and intelligence.

Jensen and Sinha distinguish between genetically linked traits that exhibit only between-family correlations and genetically linked traits that exhibit both between- and within-family relationships. For example, a pleiotropic correlation between traits can occur if one or more genes influence both traits. Such an influence will be present in both within- and between-family relationships.

Jensen and Sinha's distinctions about environmental and genetic bases for correlations between traits are useful in describing studies reporting relationships between physical traits and intelligence.

ANATOMICAL AND PHYSICAL CORRELATES OF INTELLIGENCE

Height

Height and weight are correlated, and both height and weight are correlated with intelligence. Since most of the studies have focused on height, I shall deal only with studies relating height to intelligence. Jensen & Sinha (In press) reviewed studies of the relationship between height and intelligence. They analyzed seven modern studies of young adult populations with samples sizes varying from 203 to 7500. The correlations obtained between height and intelligence vary from .12 to .29 with a mean value of .22 and an N-weighted mean value of .23. There is little doubt that height and intelligence are significantly correlated. The correlation between height and intelligence may be decreasing. Teasdale, Sorenson, & Owen (1989) reported a secular decrease in the correlation for large samples of Danish military recruits born between 1939 and 1967. The decline in the correlation is approximately .03 per decade, although there is some indication that this decline is less apparent for the younger cohorts in their study.

Jensen and Sinha interpreted the correlation between height and intelligence as attributable to cross-assortative mating. Both intelligence and height are related to social mobility. If individuals choose mates who are tall and intelligent, the genes associated with both of these traits will be found to covary. They noted that the correlation between height and intelligence is not substantially decreased when indices of socioeconomic status are controlled and therefore they do not believe that the correlation is substantially attributable to environmental variables that influence both stature and intelligence. It should be noted that there is an environmental variable that may plausibly be linked to both intelligence and height—nutrition. Whether the linkage between height and intelligence is mediated environmentally or by cross-assortative mating leading to an adventitious genetic covariance, the correlation between these variables ought to be substantially diminished when it is derived from within-family comparisons. This is exactly what is found. Jensen and Sinha reviewed several studies that compared within- and between-family correlations for height and intelligence and indicated that they uniformly found that between-family correlations for these variables were invariably larger than within-family correlations, which were often close to zero. For example, Jensen (1980b) obtained IQ test scores and heights for 8000 California children in grades 2 through 8. The between-family correlations averaged over grade levels had a mean of .10. The comparable within-family correlation was .03. If the within-family correlation between height and IQ is close to zero, then these traits are not influenced by the same genes and, to the extent that both traits are influenced by environmental influences, they are influences that do not create similarities among children reared in the same family.

Brain Size and Head Circumference

The study of the relationship between indices of brain size and intelligence has its origins in the nineteenth century and was studied by Binet (see Paterson, 1930, for a review of the older literature). Correlations between brain size and intelligence are not usually based on direct measurement of brain size. Noninvasive techniques for the measurement of brain size did not exist until recent years. Typically, head circumference is used as an indirect index of intelligence. Head circumference itself is only imperfectly correlated with brain size. Van Valen reviewed studies correlating head circumference and brain size and concluded that the correlations typically reported ranged from .6 to .7. Van Valen (1974) cited studies that reported correlations as low as .36. Brain size is related to body size and it is necessary to statistically control for this variable in estimating the relationship between intelligence and brain size as indirectly measured by head circumference.

Jensen & Sinha (In press) reviewed this literature relying on a comprehensive review by Van Valen, who obtained a weighted mean correlation of .27 between measures of head size and intelligence and a partial correlation of .19 between these variables with height partialled out. Van Valen's review may be supplemented by two recent large-scale studies. Broman, Nichols, Shaughnessy, & Kennedy (1987) obtained correlations between head circumference and WISC IQ for a sample of 36,000 black and white 7 year olds studied as part of the Collaborative Perinatal Project. They reported correlations of .24 and .18 between these variables for their white and black samples, respectively.

Sausanne (1979) reported a correlation between head circumference and a composite index of intelligence for a representative sample of over 2000 Belgian males eligible for military service. Susanne obtained a correlation of .24 and a partial correlation with height controlled of .19. Jensen and Sinha used Sausanne's data to estimate the correlation between brain size and intelligence. They indicated that there are uncertainties surrounding some of the appropriate corrections to use and that the precise correlation between head circumference and brain size is not known. They estimated, on the basis of reasonable calculations and assumptions, that the correlation between brain size and intelligence is .38. This value is compatible with the results reported by Willerman, Schultz, Rutledge, & Bigler (1989), who used magnetic resonance imaging to obtain direct measures of brain size in a sample of 40 college students who differed in their SAT scores. They reported a correlation between brain size and scores on the Wechsler test of .35. (This was actually an adjusted correlation to take account of the use of groups with extreme scores). The Willerman et al. study needs replication with larger samples. These data, when combined with the findings of studies indicating a correlation between head circumference and IQ, support the inference that there is a correlation between brain size and IQ. It is possible that the correlation between anatomical features of the brain and intelligence may be underestimated in studies relating brain size to intelligence. It is probably the case that correlations between more refined measures of the size of specific regions of the brain and intelligence would be higher than the correlations that have been obtained between imperfect indices of total brain weight and intelligence. With the availability of newer techniques of imaging it ought to be possible to study the relationship between anatomical features of the brain and intelligence.

It is not known whether the correlations between brain size and intelligence is present in within-family correlations. Jensen & Sinha (In press) reported the results of analyses performed by Jensen of the relationship between indices of head size and intelligence in a sample of 82 pairs of MZ twins and 61 pairs of DZ twins. The correlations they obtained are presented in Table 7.1. The differences in between-family correlations for MZ and DZ twins suggest that the correlation between these variables is mediated genetically. The correlation of .28 for the within-family DZ correlation suggests that differences in head size within families are predictive of differences in general intelligence. Jensen and Sinha noted that these results must be interpreted cautiously in view of the relatively small sample size involved. Note that three of the four correlations reported in Table 7.1 are not statistically significant.

Myopia

Myopia, or nearsightedness, is correlated with intelligence. Myopia is a condition in which light rays entering the eye have a focal point before the retina. The focal point of light rays on the retina is a continuous variable. Myopia is a heritable trait which is thought to be relatively

TABLE 7.1   Correlations between Head Size
and Intelligence for MZ and DZ Twins[a]

Source	r
MZ (between family)[b]	.39*
MZ (within family)	.17
DZ (between family)	.15
MZ (within family)	.28

[a]Based on Jensen & Sinha (in press).

[b]Between-family correlations are based on the mean score for twin pairs in each family for each of two dependent variables—IQ and a composite index of head size. Within-famiy correlations are based on difference scores for each twin pair on each of the two dependent variables.

*$p < .01$; for all other r's $p > .05$.

uninfluenced by degree of literacy or use of the eyes for close reading. Jensen and Sinha reported the results of several large-scale studies that indicate that myopia and intelligence correlate between .20 and .25. Karlsson (1976) reported that California high school seniors wearing corrective lenses for myopia had IQs that were 8 points higher than those who were not wearing such lenses. Teasdale, Fuchs, & Goldschmidt (1988) reported that the frequency of myopia was monotonically related to scores on a group IQ test for a large sample of over 15,000 military recruits in Denmark. Myopic individuals had IQs that were 7 points higher than nonmyopic individuals. Rosner & Belkin (1987) reported comparable results for a national sample of over 150,000 Israeli recruits.

There is evidence indicating that the correlation between myopia and intelligence is present within families as well as between families. Benbow (1986) selected adolescents whose ability scores on the SAT were in the top one-half of 1% of over 100,000 students taking the test. She found that over 50% of this group was myopic, which was over twice the frequency of myopia found in the general population. She mailed a questionnaire on myopia to the parents of these adolescents and found that 36% of their siblings were myopic. Although the intellectual ability of the siblings was not assessed, it is reasonable to infer that it was lower than that of the intellectually gifted students studied by Benbow. This conclusion follows from a consideration of the influence of regression effects. Cohn, Cohn, & Jensen (1988) selected a group of 15 years olds with high IQ and measured their degree of myopia. They compared their scores on intelligence tests and myopia to that of their siblings. The adolescents with high IQ had IQs that were 14 points higher on the Ravens test than their siblings. The high-IQ siblings had myopia scores that were .39 standard deviation units higher than those of their siblings. Thus the correlation between myopia and intelligence appears to be present in comparisons of individuals who are reared in the same family, suggesting that the influences that cause individuals reared in the same family to differ in intelligence are correlated with the influences that cause individuals in the same family to differ in myopia. Genetic influences are plausible candidates. It is possible that the genes that influence myopia also influence intelligence.

FUNCTIONAL PROPERTIES OF THE NERVOUS SYSTEM AND INTELLIGENCE

Nerve Conductance Velocity

Vernon & Mori (1989) measured nerve conductance velocities of the median nerve of the arm. They obtained a correlation of .42 from their measure of nerve conductance velocity and a general measure of intelligence on a sample of 85 university students. The nerve conductance velocity measure is a measure of speed of nerve conductance in the peripheral nervous system and involves no obvious cognitive activity. Vernon replicated these results in a second study of 46 university students and obtained a correlation of .40 between the measures of nerve conductance velocity and general intelligence. Vernon (1991) is conducting a twin study to ascertain genetic and environmental influences on the covariance between nerve conductance velocity measures and intelligence. It should be realized that the study of nerve conductance velocity as a possible biological correlate of intelligence is at a very preliminary stage. Reed & Jensen (1991) were unable to replicate Vernon's findings and the results of Vernon's twin study are not available. Therefore, speculations about possible relationships between nerve conductance velocity and intelligence, including a consideration of the reasons for the relationship, are premature.

PET Scans

Another promising area of investigation of the biological correlates of intelligence involves the use of positron emission tomography (PET) measures of brain functioning. This technique, which is based on the ingestion of a radioactive substance, permits one to obtain *in vivo* measures of activity levels of different regions of the brain. Haier *et al.* (1988) obtained PET scan measures of cortical functioning following the completion of a Ravens test for a small sample of subjects $(N = 8)$. The levels of activity recorded in the brain following the completion of the test may be interpreted as an index of activity in brain regions during the performance of the test. The correlations were negative and statistically significant despite the small sample size. There are other preliminary reports of negative correlations between metabolic functioning as assessed by PET scans and performance on tests of intelligence (see Haier, In press; Parks, Lowenstein, & Dondrell, 1988). Research relating PET measures to intelligence is at a very preliminary stage and its is premature to speculate about possible relationships between individual differences in metabolic activity in different regions of the brain and performance on tests of intelligence.

EEG and Intelligence

The attempt to relate EEG measures to intelligence has a long history— studies have been conducted on this topic for five decades (see Vogel & Broverman, 1964, for a review of older literature). Deary & Caryl (In press) presented a comprehensive analysis of the available literature. Conclusions about the relationship between EEG measures and intelligence have ranged from the assumption that there are defined EEG biological markers of general intelligence that are better measures of g than psychometric tests (Eysenck, 1988; Eysenck & Barrett, 1985) to the assertion that there are no relationships between EEG measures and general intelligence (Howe, 1988a, b).

It is difficult to reach clear conclusions about the relationship between EEG indices and intelligence for several reasons. Many investigators working in this area have used small samples. There are few clear replications of findings and therefore promising relationships are often based on a single investigation. Also, many investigators have computed many EEG measures and related them to intelligence, increasing the likelihood of obtaining spurious nonreplicable correlations. Standardized indices of EEG performance are not used. Investigators used various mathematical procedures to derive measures from the EEG. Some used evoked potential indices that attempt to define characteristic responses to stimuli presented to a subject; other investigators have used nonaveraged EEG measures with no attempt to relate the measures to stimulus presentations. Stimulus presentations varied considerably. Stimuli have varied in modality (e.g., visual, auditory) and in intensity. Subjects have been given quite different instructions and tasks to perform while EEG indices were obtained, ranging from passive observation of stimuli to some type of intellectual task. In addition to this plethora of indices and stimuli, technical procedures for the administration of the EEG have varied. The number of electrodes, the location of electrodes, and various procedures for removing "artifacts" in the data differ. Given the plethora of methods and techniques and the general failure to report replications of findings, it is not surprising that different reviewers have reached somewhat different conclusions about the probity of the evidence indicating possible relationships between EEG indices and intelligence.

In addition to the difficulty of summarizing studies that employed different methods, it should be apparent that there is considerable conceptual confusion surrounding the meanings of any EEG–intelligence relationship. The EEG may be construed as a measure of a "hard-wired" biological index of neural functioning. Alternatively, EEG measures may reflect information-processing characteristics of the brain that have developed as a result of experience. Thus a correlation between the EEG and intelligence is casually ambiguous. This is particularly true for EEG measures derived from subjects engaged in some intellectual task. Differences in the way in which subjects process stimuli might be related to differences in EEG parameters. Differences in intelligence could cause individuals to respond to stimuli in different ways and the EEG could act as a neural index of these differences.

It is beyond the scope of this book to review all of the studies relating EEG indices to intelligence (see Deary & Caryl, In press, for a comprehensive review). I have chosen not to do so because of the inherent ambiguity and nonreplicability of the findings in this area of research. They do not appear to me to lead to clear conclusions. I shall review a series of studies reported by Hendrickson and Hendrickson (Blinkhorn & Hendrickson,

1982; Hendrickson, 1982; Hendrickson & Hendrickson, 1980) that reported substantial correlations between IQ and EEG indices.

Hendrickson & Hendrickson (1980) presented a theoretical analysis linking intelligence to EEG parameters. They assumed that intelligence was related to the fidelity of neural transmissions. Errors in transmission of neural impulses at the synapse were assumed to influence evoked potential responses. They assumed that the complexity of the wave form of the evoked potential response was inversely related to errors of transmission and positively related to intelligence. They used a "string" measure which, in effect, superimposes a string over the wave. More complex wave forms with more components and greater deviations from the baseline would result in higher values of the string length measure. They assumed that string length would be positively correlated with IQ.

Blinkhorn & Hendrickson (1982) tested this theory on a sample of 33 undergraduates. Average evoked potential responses were obtained in response to auditory stimuli delivered to subjects who were instructed to relax and keep their eyes closed. They obtained a correlation of .54 between scores on the Raven test and their measure of string length.

Hendrickson (1982) conducted a similar investigation with 219 secondary school students with a mean Wechsler IQ of 108. The correlation between string length of the average evoked potential response to auditory stimuli and IQ was .72. A combined index based on a composite of the string length measure and a measure of the variability of wave forms correlated .83 with intelligence in this large relatively unselected sample. Hendrickson reported that the string length measure correlated .80 in a sample of 16 court stenographers with above-average IQs. Hendrickson reported that string length measures were very high in a sample of retarded subjects, possibly indicating that the determinants of EEG wave forms in very-low-IQ subjects are different from the determinants of evoked potentials in the normal IQ range.

Eysenck & Barrett (1985) reported the results of a factor analysis of the data collected by Hendrickson relating performance on the Wechsler to evoked potentials in secondary school students. They factor analyzed the WAIS and obtained a general factor. They found that the composite variance—string length measure loaded .77 on the general intelligence factor derived from the WAIS and had a loading that was as high as any of the WAIS subtests, suggesting that the EEG measure could be construed as a marker for the general intelligence factor.

The dramatic findings obtained in these studies should be accepted cautiously. There are at present too few replications to assume that these results constitute a firm basis for assuming that the complexity of the evoked potential response constitutes a biological marker for intelligence. In addition, the studies that attempted to replicate these findings have differed both in methodological detail and in relevant findings. Shagass, Roemer, Straumanis, & Josiassen (1981) failed to find a correlation between the Raven test score and the string length measure in a sample of adult psychiatric patients and their normal controls. It should be noted that their experimental procedure differed from that used by Hendrickson in several details. They presented stimuli in different modalities and the interstimulus intervals were different. Whether these or other differences in methodology accounted for the different results is not clear.

Haier, Robinson, Braden, & Williams (1983) obtained average evoked potentials in response to visual stimuli that differed in intensity from a sample of 23 nursing students. They obtained correlations ranging between .23 and .50 between string length and the Raven scores in this sample. Higher correlations were obtained for stimuli at medium-high and high intensities. They also reported that the string length measure was correlated .80 with the difference in amplitude of the N140 and P200 components. This measure correlated between .38 and .69 with Raven test scores, with the highest correlation occurring at the medium-high intensity.

Haier, Robinson, Braden, & Krengel (1984) reported the results of a replication of the study by Haier et al. (1983). They began with a sample of 27 subjects but excluded 12 subjects who were outside the age range previously studied or for whom they suspected measurement errors in the evoked potential indices. The remaining 15 subjects exhibited a pattern of results that were partially similar to those previously reported. They obtained correlations ranging from −.15 to .50 between the N140–P200 measure and scores on the Raven. The highest correlation was obtained for EEG measures derived from stimulus presentations at the medium-high intensity (luminance = 75 ft L).

Stough, Nettlebeck, & Cooper (1990) reported the results of an attempted replication of the relationship between string length measures and IQ using a sample of 20 first-year psychology students. They used auditory stimuli and procedures that were similar to those originally used by Blinkhorn and Hendrickson. They obtained a correlation of .43 between a string length measure based on the first 250 ms of the average evoked potential response to the auditory stimulus and WAIS IQ. This correlation may be corrected for restrictions in range and test reliability, leading to a corrected value of .58. They also reported that the largest value of the correlation was obtained for a measure based on the string length for the period from 100 to 200 ms after stimulus onset. String length for this period correlated with IQ .60 uncorrected and .74 corrected. In contradistinction to the studies reported by Haier et al. (1983) and Robinson, Haier, Braden, & Krengel (1984), Stough et al. (1990) reported a zero correlation between N140–P200 magnitude and IQ. In addition, they reported that their string length measures were unrelated to scores on the Raven, thus failing to replicate the results of the Blickhorn and Hendrickson study. Some of the discrepancies in results reported may be attributable to sample differences or to the instability of correlations based on small samples.

The studies based on the string length measure, although inconsistent with respect to details of outcome, present a promising beginning for a more detailed analysis of the relationship between EEG parameters and intelligence. Given the uncertain status of the attempts to replicate the dramatic findings of Hendrickson and the relatively small number of relevant studies it is, in my judgment, premature to assume that string length indices constitute a biological marker for general intelligence.

String length measures are derived from experimental situations in which subjects are not required to actively engage in any intellectual activity. Schafer (1982; see also Jensen, Schafer, & Crinella, 1981) suggested that differences in EEG indices obtained when subjects were required to process predictable sensory input and unpredictable input would be related to intelligence. He assumed that subjects who were high in intelligence would commit few neurons to processing predictable stimuli and many neurons to processing unpredictable stimuli. In order to test this theory he presented subjects with auditory click stimuli under three conditions: (1) a condition in which stimuli were presented every 2 seconds, (2) a condition in which subjects were presented stimuli at intervals they selected to be random in which they controlled the stimulus presentations, and (3) a condition in which the clicks were presented automatically at intervals that matched those selected by the subjects in the second condition. He obtained indices of the total integrated amplitude of the average evoked potential for each of these conditions and constructed a "Neural Adaptability" index defined as the difference between the integrated amplitude measures for the third minus the second condition divided by the average amplitude of all three measures plus 50, a constant to ensure that all measures were positive. He obtained a correlation of .66 between this index and full-scale IQ for 74 adult subjects.

Zhang, Caryl, & Deary (1989b) explored the relationship between intelligence and average evoked potential responses to stimuli in an inspection-time task. They presented subjects visual inspection-time stimuli under conditions in which they were required to make a visual inspection-time judgment and under conditions in which they were asked to look at the stimuli but were not required to judge which of two stimuli was longer in length. They were particularly interested in an EEG parameter that was related to inspection-time performance—the rise time for the P200 response. They found that P200 rise time was positively correlated with inspection time. Since inspection time is known to be inversely related to intelligence, this relationship may be explained by assuming that intelligence may be positively associated with the speed with which individuals exhibit transitions between different EEG components. The correlation between Zhang al.'s measure of P200 rise time and IQ in a sample of 35 university students with obvious restrictions in range of talent was −.34, indicating that rise times for the P200 component were associated with high IQ. This correlation dropped to .05 for trials in which subjects were not required to judge the stimuli. These data, and the data obtained by Schafer, suggest that there may be relations between EEG parameters obtained from situations in which individuals are required to respond to stimuli and intelligence. Further research using these and related techniques is required to ascertain the magnitude of the relationship between intelligence and EEG indices obtained while individuals are engaged in various tasks.

While the search for EEG measures that relate to intelligence has a long and somewhat unproductive history, the studies reviewed above do indicate that there is at least the promising foundation for additional research. It appears to be reasonably clear that there is a nontrivial relationship between some EEG parameters and intelligence. It is premature to speculate about the theoretical basis for the reasons for the relationship. It is possible that some EEG parameters that are highly heritable may be related to intelligence. And, it is possible that genetic covariance analyses will indicate that the relationship between such hypothetical EEG parameters and intelligence is genetically mediated. But it should be recognized that the studies that would permit us to reach such conclusions do not exist. For the present, it is reasonable to conclude that it is likely that there is a nontrivial relationship between the EEG and intelligence and further research is needed to specify with greater precision the nature of the relationship. We need to have a better empirical understanding of the relationship as well as a theoretical analysis of the reasons for the relationship.

CONCLUSION

The study of the biological correlates of intelligence has a long history in psychology, going back to Galton in the nineteenth century. It may also be said to have a brief recent history in which it is being resurrected. The status of this area of research may be compared to the study of the relationship between psychometrically assessed intelligence and performance in cognitive experimental situations whose recent history is approximately 15 years in duration. The contemporary study of the biological basis of intelligence is still more recent—many of the topics dealt with in this brief chapter constitute contemporary revivals of research issues that have been resurrected in the last 5 years. It is my guess that the next decade will lead to some progress in understanding the biological basis of general intelligence. The development of new methods of studying the brain (e.g., PET scans and NMR) will provide information about individual differences in the structure and function of the brain. Such indices may be related to psychometric measures, providing a potential for better understanding of the biological basis of individual differences in intelligence. The available data, though far from definitive, do indicate that there are relationships between biological indices and intelligence. With the possible exception of the relationship between myopia and intelligence, there is relatively little evidence that suggests that the relationships may be understood in a causal way—although a causal model that attempts to relate individual differences in intelligence to features of the nervous system is plausible given the evidence for a genetic influence on intelligence.

8

CONTINUITY AND CHANGE IN INTELLIGENCE

IS INTELLIGENCE FIXED?

Is intelligence fixed? It is sometimes asserted that the psychometric approach to intelligence assumes that intelligence is a fixed unchanging characteristic of individuals. In their book on intelligence, Kail & Pellegrino (1985) quote Hunt, who wrote about psychometricians as follows: "The very significance of his research and practice lies in the capacity of the tests to predict performance at a later time and to predict other kinds of performance. A faith in intelligence as a basic and fixed dimension of a person is probably the faith on which one can most readily rest such a professional function" (J. M. Hunt, 1961, p. 14). Sternberg (1986) also asserted that psychometricians believe in a doctrine of intelligence as a fixed characteristic of a person. In the initial chapter of a book on intelligence, Sternberg listed "five red herrings"—that is, erroneous beliefs held about intelligence. Sternberg wrote, "Conventional testers of intelligence obviously have something to gain by selling the notion of intelligence as a fixed entity. After all, what good would the tests be if scores were unstable, varying from one time or place to another? . . . But is intelligence really a fixed entity? The bulk of the evidence suggests that it is not. Intelligence can be increased, and there are now a variety of programs designed to do just that" (Sternberg, 1986, p. 9). It is apparent that experts in the field of intelligence believe that psychometrically oriented psychologists, in contradistinction to cognitive psychologists interested in intelligence, are committed to the view that intelligence is a fixed entity of a person. I find these assertions puzzling. Kail and Pellegrino do not cite any psychometricians who hold these views, but quote Hunt who is opposed to a psychometric conception of intelligence. The assertion that psychometricians believe that intelligence is fixed is a canard and is not representative of the views of psychometricians. Perhaps the mistaken notion that psychometricians believe that intelligence is fixed derives from evidence that we shall review that IQ is a relatively stable characteristic of a person. Despite Sternberg's assertions, there is relatively little evidence that general intelligence is easily changed by intervention programs. Perhaps the commitment of many psychometricians to an investigation of the behavior genetics of intelligence led psychologists opposed to this view to wrongly infer that genetic influences have an immutable influence on the phenotype of intelligence.

What do psychometricians believe about the stability and change of IQ? If there is any legitimate claim to a notion of fixed intelligence, it might most plausibly derive from a genetic conception of intelligence. It is possible to define intelligence as the ability to acquire knowledge. Such an ability is, by definition, logically and chronologically prior to the acquisition of the knowledge that is enabled by possession of the ability. Since abilities are always prior to achievements, the postulation of an ability inexorably leads to a consideration of the origins of the ability. The earliest possible origin of an ability is the moment of conception that determines an unchanging genotype. If intelligence is assumed to be theoretically equivalent to genetic ability, then it is possible to assert that intelligence does not change and is a fixed characteristic of a person. But any such theory refers only to a hypothetical entity that is not isomorphic with any index of developed intelligence. Indices of intelligence are the product of interactions between a hypothetical genetic potential and the acquisition of skills and knowledge that influence future ability to acquire knowledge. No test of intelligence may be correctly construed as a measure of primordial genetic potential to learn. It is possible to imagine some physiological index of intelligence that might be derived from an examination of a person's genotype, or from physiological measures of brain functioning obtained neonatally or prenatally, that would index the primordial intellectual capacity of an individual. Such a construct belongs to science fiction rather than to science.

Apart from science-fiction concepts, how does intelligence change? Consider some of the changes we have considered.

1. There are secular increases in intelligence. These changes are not attributable to genetic influences. Indeed, as we shall see in Chapter 9, fertility patterns in the U.S. have, if anything, been dysgenic, that is, compatible with a decrease in the genetic potential for IQ. If the gene pool for intelligence has remained constant or has actually changed to create a lower genetic potential for the development of intelligence, the increases in intelligence that occurred over the last several decades must be attributable to changes in the influence of genotypes on phenotypes leading to an increase in measured intelligence for younger cohorts.

2. Even the most ardent proponent of genetic influences on intelligence believes that there are environmental influences on the phenotype for intelligence. Hence the genetic potential that constitute a rationale for

a belief in intelligence as a fixed entity must have a variable influence on the phenotype dependent upon the nature of the environment that is encountered.

3. The way in which genetic and environmental influences combine to influence intelligence changes over an individual's life. Our review of developmental behavior genetics in Chapter 5 indicated that genetic factors may be more important determiners of adult IQ than of IQ in childhood. This implies that the IQ index is not a measure of the same construct at different points of a person's life. If it were, the determinants of the construct would not change.

4. The content of intelligence tests changes over the life span. Items used to assess intelligence in a 4 year old are not the same as items used to assess intelligence in adults. In this respect, IQ is not like height, which increases but can be assessed by the same instrument at different times in a person's life. The means of assessing intelligence are not constant over the life span and hence the increase in intelligence is indexed by different instruments.

5. It has been argued that there are age-related changes in the biological basis of fluid intelligence over the life span. Therefore, some components of intelligence may be influenced by age-related changes in the biological basis of test performance.

6. While IQ test scores are stable, the test–retest correlation is less than perfect. IQ is only relatively fixed or unchanging. As the time between administrations increases, the test–retest stability of IQ decreases.

7. The intellectual skills that a person develops depend crucially on a person's cultural experiences. For example, the Puluwat, who inhabit the Caroline islands in the South Pacific, are skilled navigators who develop complex mental maps of their islands and integrate this knowledge with meteorological observations to navigate (Gladwin, 1970). One might argue that intelligence would be defined as skill in navigation for the Puluwat and that intelligence in their society would obviously be a different construct than intelligence assessed in our society. It is clear that the knowledge that is acquired in different societies is different. Such examples are often taken as self-evident demonstrations of the cultural relativity of the concept of intelligence. Actually, the example does not resolve a number of critical issues about the cross-cultural validity of the concept of general intelligence. It is possible that there are individual differences in the ability to acquire the navigational skills that are important to the Puluwat. And, further, these individual differences might be related to a cross-culturally valid index of general intelligence and be related to the same construct that determines individual differences in intelligence studied in the U.S. In principle, this is even a testable hypothesis. A cross-fostering study in which children whose parents differ in navigational skills as defined by the Puluwat could be reared by Americans. Con-

versely, children whose American parents differ in intelligence as assessed by standard IQ tests could be reared in Puluwat families and their skills as navigators could be assessed. It is possible that there are additive genetic differences in intelligence that are related to the acquisition of intellectual skills among both the Puluwat and Americans. Consider another design. It is possible to use measures of infant attention to predict early childhood IQ. Such measures assess abilities that may be relatively disembodied from a particular cultural context. Such measures might be predictive of the development of navigational skills among the Puluwat. R. B. Cattell (1971), a psychometrician, used the metaphorically resonant term "investment" to describe the process of differentiation by means of which individuals develop special intellectual skills and abilities from a generalized intellectual capacity. Cattell's investment theory is the antithesis of a view of intelligence as a fixed characteristic of a person.

What is actually known about the stability of IQ? There have been a number of longitudinal studies of IQ in which the same individuals are repeatedly given IQ tests. Contemporary IQ tests are not based on the mental age divided by the chronological age index of IQ. They are based on deviation IQs that compare an individual's performance to that of his or her age cohort. IQ is defined in terms of a distribution in which the mean is usually set at 100, and the standard deviation is equal to 15. Therefore, an IQ of 115 may be understood as implying that an individual has scored 1 standard deviation above the mean of his or her age cohort. The test–retest correlation obtained from longitudinal studies provides information about the relative position of an individual in the distribution of scores for age cohorts. Thus an individual who receives the same IQ score on two different occasions may have changed substantially in ability to answer questions on an IQ test. The similarity of scores on two occasions merely indicates that his or her change is equivalent to the changes experienced by age cohorts used to norm the test.

Table 8.1 presents test–retest correlations for IQ test scores from ages 2 to 15 based on Wilson's longitudinal twin study (Wilson, 1983, 1986). An examination of the data presented in Table 8.1 indicates that the correlations follow a lawlike pattern. The magnitude of the test–retest correlation decreases as the time between test administrations increases. By ages 8 and 9, IQ test scores are highly predictive of scores at age 15. Humphreys (1989) calculated the year-to-year stability for true score values for these data and arrived at a value of .95 or .96. If one assumes that the change in IQ is constant over years, the correlation between any number of years for true score values of IQ may be calculated as .95 or .96 raised to the power of the number of years intervening between tests. The test–retest reliability for a 10-year period would be between .63 and .70. Predicting from one period of time to another involves the use of the

TABLE 8.1   Intercorrelations of Intelligence over Ages 2 to 15 Years [a,b]

Age	2	3	4	5	6	7	8	9	15
2		74	68	63	61	54	58	56	47
3			76	72	73	68	67	65	58
4				80	79	72	72	71	60
5					87	81	79	79	67
6						86	84	84	69
7							87	87	69
8								90	78
9									80
15									

[a]Based on Humphreys' (1989) analysis of data derived from Wilson (1983).
[b]Note that decimal points have been omitted.

standard regression formula in which the predicted IQ score, in z score terms, would be the value of r times the z score value for the first test. Humphreys indicated that a child with an IQ of 140 on initial testing might be expected to have an IQ of 125 ten years later. Of course there will be considerable variability around this predicted score. It is obvious that IQ test scores are only relatively stable.

One way of increasing the test–retest reliability of IQ is to aggregate scores obtained on more than one occasion of testing. Table 8.2 presents data derived from the Berkeley Growth Study, a longitudinal investigation of a white sample with above-average IQ (Jones & Bayley, 1941; Pinneau, 1961). Aggregated scores were obtained for three administrations of IQ tests starting with the first month of life. These aggregates were related to

TABLE 8.2   Correlations between IQs Averaged over Different Ages and the Mean of IQs at 17 and 18 in the Berkeley Growth Sample

Average of months or years	r
Months	
1, 2, 3	.05
4, 5, 6	−.01
7, 8, 9	.20
10, 11, 12	.41
13, 14, 15	.23
18, 21, 24	.55
27, 30, 36	.54
42, 48, 54	.62
Years	
5, 6, 7	.86
8, 9, 10	.89
11, 12, 13	.96
14, 15, 16	.96

an aggregate score based on tests given at ages 17 and 18. Note how the use of aggregate indices permits one to obtain high test–retest correlations. IQ at the end of high school can be predicted by IQ tests given at ages 5, 6, and 7 with a correlation of .86. And, IQ at the preadolescent or early adolescent ages predicts IQ at the end of the high school period with a correlation of .96. Although the test–retest correlations are relatively high, it should be noted that any individual IQ test score is subject to considerable change. Table 8.3 presents data for the Berkeley Growth sample indicating the mean change and the standard deviation of IQ changes for tests administered at different ages and age 17 IQ. Note that the standard deviation of changes decreases as the time between tests decreases. It is obvious that single tests given early in life may be poor indicators of young adult IQ.

Test–retest correlations for intelligence may be interpreted in terms of a model developed by Anderson (1939, 1946; see also Bloom, 1964). The model may be fit to changes in height as well as changes in intelligence. One may think of the height of a person at time 2 as equal to height at time 1 plus gains in height from time 1 to time 2. Since the height attained at time 1 is a component or subset of the total height attained at time 2, a correlation between height at time 1 and height at time 2 is guaranteed. A teenager who is tall will not become short if he or she is retested at a later date. On this model, test–retest correlations would be positive even if growth in height and original attained height were uncorrelated. Anderson analyzed data on changes in intelligence and attempted to demonstrate that gain scores in intelligence were uncorrelated with previously attained intelligence. Positive test–retest correlations for intelligence test performance would occur because previous intellectual

TABLE 8.3 Changes in IQs Given at Different Ages and IQ at Age 17 in the Berkeley Growth Study

Age at testing	Range of changes	Mean change	Standard deviation of change
6 months	2–60	21.6	15.7
1 year	1–75	16.6	14.9
2 years	0–40	14.5	9.5
3 years	0–39	14.1	9.4
4 years	2–34	12.6	8.0
5 years	1–27	10.8	7.0
6 years	0–34	11.1	7.8
7 years	1–27	9.2	7.4
8 years	0–25	8.7	6.3
9 years	0–22	9.6	5.7
10 years	1–26	9.5	6.4
11 years	1–21	7.8	5.4
12 years	0–18	7.1	4.9
14 years	0–18	5.8	4.7

growth is a component of intellectual performance at a later time. Humphreys (1985, 1989; Humpreys & Parsons, 1979) fit test–retest correlations for intelligence to a model that assumed gain scores for true scores in intelligence are uncorrelated with previously attained true score values for intelligence. He found that the model fit the data quite well. Note that models of this type imply that test–retest correlations decline as the time between administrations of the test increases during the period in which individuals are gaining in intellectual capacity.

There are number of problems with a model that assumes intellectual growth is uncorrelated with previous intellectual performance. The analogy between intelligence and height is strained. Height is measured by the same techniques at any period. Also, height is a ratio scale number with a well-defined metric. Intelligence is measured by different items at different ages and growth in intelligence has both a qualitative as well as a quantitative dimension. Individuals reason differently at different developmental periods. Cronbach & Snow (1977) argued that the choice of a metric is critical for determining if gain scores are or are not correlated with previously attained intelligence. They indicated that the correlation between scores and gains could be influenced by the selection of items to assess intelligence. If the gains in items answered correctly on a test were positively correlated with prior IQ scores, the rank orderings of IQ would not be changed. Individuals with high IQ might have to exhibit more rapid gains in ability than individuals with low IQ in order to maintain their initial lead (Pinneau, 1961). Although Humphreys's analyses indicate that a model that assumes that gains are uncorrelated with initial performance is a good fit to data on the stability of IQ, the model should only be considered as an approximation. It is entirely possible that it is an artifact of the way in which intelligence is assessed. The assumption that intelligence may be understood as the ability to acquire knowledge is compatible with the assumption that gains are always positively correlated with prior attainments. Such a model is logical. The available data do not provide support for this model. The model may be wrong or the available data and the measurement problems inherent in a measure that samples items in order to assess intelligence may not permit us to obtain a strong test of the model.

LIFE-SPAN CHANGE

How does intelligence change over the life span? Prior to 1968 it was widely assumed that intelligence declined after the third or fourth decade of life and that the decline accelerated in middle and old age. This belief was based substantially on the results of cross-sectional analyses in which representative samples of the population at different ages were tested. IQ scores, which are age adjusted, mask the magnitude of decline in intelligence as a function of age. Younger adults would have to score at a higher level than older adults in order to obtain the same IQ score. It is obvious that cross-sectional studies of changes in intelligence over the life span are subject to a major methodological flaw. Age is completely confounded with time of birth. Thus, evidence of declines in intelligence may be attributable to the effects of aging or to cohort effects. The discussion of cohort effects in Chapter 6 of this volume clearly demonstrates that intelligence has been increasing. Therefore, cohorts born earlier in the century will have lower intelligence than cohorts born later in the century and this might account for some or all of the cross-sectional declines in intelligence. Schaie & Strother (1968) provided clear evidence that age effects and cohort effects were confounded in cross-sectional analyses of the effects of age on intelligence. They combined a cross-sectional and a longitudinal design. They administered Thurstone tests to a sample of individuals ranging in age from 20 to 70 and retested them 7 years later. The cross-sectional analyses provided clear evidence of declines. The longitudinal data provided relatively little evidence of declines over the 7-year period for each of their cohorts born at different times.

The work of Schaie and Strother suggests that some of the decline in intelligence with age that was reported in cross-sectional studies was attributable to cohort effects. It might be concluded from these data that the decline of intelligence with age is best characterized as a myth. The appropriate interpretation of studies contrasting and combining longitudinal and cross-sectional procedures is controversial. Horn & Donaldson (1976) argued that the use of longitudinal methods to disentangle cohort and aging effects in the study of intelligence is not a panacea (see also Baltes & Schaie, 1976). They noted that longitudinal studies of aging are not able to maintain their samples. Individuals lose contact with researchers. People die or in old age are no longer able to live independently in the community. Therefore, samples of the elderly who persist in longitudinal studies are increasingly nonrepresentative subsamples of the population. While such data may provide evidence of changes in intellectual functioning among a subset of aged individuals who are healthy enough to live independently and whose mental abilities have remained sufficiently intact to permit them to maintain contact with longitudinal researchers, their performance cannot be considered as representative of the population at large.

Over the last two decades, the results of longitudinal and cross-sectional studies have gradually given a clearer picture of adult-related changes in ability.

Schaie continued to study samples of individuals using a combined longitudinal and cross-sectional design. Schaie & Hertzog (1983) administered Thurstone tests to individuals born between 1889 and 1938. These individuals were tested at 7-year intervals on three occasions. They ranged in age from 25 to 81 at time of testing. Table 8.4 presents changes in their longitudinal data over a 14-year period for different cohorts for each of five separate Thurstone tests. An examination of the data in Table 8.4 provides clear evidence for longitudinal changes in intelligence over a 14-year period as a function of the age of the individuals who are tested. Note that the changes are relatively uniform for each of the five tests. There is evidence of small gains in intelligence between ages 25 and 39. Intellectual declines are evident for the period between ages 53 and 67 and average approximately .2 standard deviations for this 14-year period. Declines increase between ages 60 and 74. For this period, the mean decline is .29 standard deviations. The comparable decline is larger for the age period between 67 and 81, where the average decline is .59 standard deviation units. Note the pattern of accelerated declines between the sixth and ninth decades of life. There are some limitations to these data. Schaie and Hertzog indicated that there is some evidence of cohort × age interactions, suggesting that the pattern of age changes in intelligence may not be constant for different cohorts. There are wide individual differences present in these data and therefore declining intelligence with age is not an inexorable result of aging. Aging is an idiosyncratic process and different individuals may exhibit quite different patterns of changes in intelligence over time. Nevertheless, these data do provide evidence for relatively substantial declines in intelligence after age 50. Adding the results for the 28-year period between ages 53 and 81 there is the suggestion of a one-standard-deviation decline in performance. These results may underestimate the magnitude of declines in general intelligence in the population. The sample studied in the Schaie and Hertzog investigation is not representative of the population. The sample is middle class, relatively well educated, and in good health. Individuals in poor health or whose health has deteriorated to the point where they are not able to

TABLE 8.4 Changes in Thurstone Ability Scores for 14-Year Longitudinal Data for Different Age Cohorts[a,b]

Age cohort	Ability test				
	Verbal meaning	Space	Inductive reasoning	Number	Word fluency
25–39	.29	.20	.13	.13	.22
32–46	.18	.15	.04	−.02	.05
39–53	.04	−.01	.06	−.09	−.19
46–60	.08	−.00	−.01	−.13	−.28
53–67	−.17	−.17	−.16	−.19	−.32
60–74	−.33	−.28	−.31	−.22	−.30
67–81	−.63	−.55	−.53	−.53	−.70

[a]Based on Schaie & Hertzog (1983).
[b]Changes are expressed in standard deviation units.

reside in the community may be assumed to exhibit larger declines in intelligence with age.

Schaie (1980; see also 1988) attempted to assess the influence of dropouts and nonrepresentative samples in longitudinal research on the influence of age on intelligence. He obtained 7-year longitudinal data on a sample, and for each age group he studied he obtained an independent sample. The independent sampling of age groups controlled for cohort effects may be assumed to reflect changes in intelligence for samples that are representative of the original samples recruited in the study. Schaie presented his data in terms of a standard of "meaningful" decline defined as the twenty-fifth percentile of performance of 25 year olds. I used these data to estimate the standard deviation of performance for his independent and longitudinal samples on verbal meaning and induction components of the Thurstone battery. These tests were selected for analysis since they may be assumed to function as markers for crystallized and fluid ability factors. Recall that these abilities are assumed to show a different pattern of change and decline over the life span. Fluid ability is assumed to decline more than crystallized ability. Table 8.5 presents these data. An examination of the data in Table 8.5 clearly indicates that the longitudinal data give a different picture of changes in intelligence than independent cohort-controlled samples of individuals. The latter groups exhibit more declines than the former groups. This indicates that the Horn and Donaldson critique of the combined longitudinal cross-sectional design has considerable merit. Longitudinal analyses for verbal meaning, the marker for crystallized ability, exhibit increases from ages 25 to 60. This index of crystallized ability remains above the 25-year-old performance level even at age 81. The independent samples indicate that there is very little age-related change in verbal meaning from ages 25 to 46. After age 46, evidence of decline is present, and 81 year olds are estimated to be one standard deviation lower in verbal meaning than 25 year olds. The data for induction, a marker for fluid ability, exhibit more pronounced declines. Longitudinal samples exhibit slightly lower induction performance from ages 32 to 60. After 60, declines are manifest, reaching a value of .88 standard deviations at age 81. The independent samples again exhibit more decline than the longitudinal samples. The decline appears more or less constant over the adult life span, reaching a level of 1.52 standard deviations lower than the norm for 25 year olds at age 81.

The data indicating age-related declines in IQ almost certainly underestimate the true magnitude of the decline of intellectual functioning with age. The samples of older individuals represented in these studies, even in the data based on independent samples, are almost certainly increasingly nonrepresentative of the population as older samples are studied. The aged who agree to participate in these studies are those who are able to live in the community (nursing home residents are not included in these samples) and who have sufficient community ties and are sufficiently intellectually intact to cooperate with researchers. Since the probability that individuals will possess these characteristics declines with age, the sample of individuals studied is increasingly nonrepresentative. A better index of the normative declines with age in intellectual functioning may be obtained from studies that attempt to sample representative groups of individuals of a given age whether or not they are living in the community or in institutions. Such studies would undoubtedly provide evidence of larger declines in intelligence than the independent samples studied in Schaie's research. Declines in fluid ability over the life span up to age 80 might well average 2 standard deviations. Schaie typically presents his data in such a way that the average declines in performance associated with aging are minimized. His data presentations accomplish this in two ways. Longitudinal data are sometimes presented indicating that the percentage of individuals who decline is relatively small. Of course, his own data indicate that longitudinal presentations deal only with a selected subset of the population. And, he frequently uses an arbitrary reference point to define meaningful declines or statistically significant declines. For example, his presentation of the data in Table 8.5 included an index of meaningful decline based on the twenty-fifth percentile of the performance of 25 year olds. This is clearly an arbitrary number. It appears to me that it is more meaningful to describe the performance of individuals relative to their own estimated baselines at age 25. An individual whose performance on a test of intelligence was 2 standard deviations above the mean at age 25 who has declined to .5 standard deviations below the level of performance of 25 year olds has experienced a large and meaningful decline in his or her intelligence, although such an individual would not be described as exhibiting a meaningful decline by Schaie. If fluid ability declines 2 standard deviations over the adult life span, this implies that only 2% of the population does not exhibit declines in intelligence over the life span. Even on crystallized

TABLE 8.5   Age-Related Changes in Two Indices of Intelligence in Longitudinal and Independent Samples[a]

		Age							
	Index	32	39	46	53	60	67	74	81
Verbal meaning	L[b]	.30[c]	.51	.68	.81	.85	.72	.43	.13
	I[b]	.08	.08	.00	−.20	−.20	−.47	−.80	−1.04
Induction	L	−.20	−.10	−.10	−.17	−.14	−.31	−.61	−.88
	I	−.10	−.32	−.52	−.78	−.91	−1.17	−1.36	−1.52

[a]Based on Schaie (1980).

[b]L, longitudinal design; I, independent sample.

[c]All values are expressed in terms of the mean and standard deviation of the performance of the 25-year-old samples.

ability tests that are assumed to measure past learning rather than the ability to acquire new knowledge, declines may be expected to be close to 1.5 standard deviation units of the adult life span, suggesting on the basis of normal curve statistics that no more than 7% of the population may be expected to avoid intellectual declines over the adult life span.

Additional evidence for declines in intelligence may be found in data reported by Schaie (1990) in which he reported data for a 28-year longitudinal sample. Schaie reported changes in Thurstone ability scores for a sample of 16 individuals studied over the 28-year interval from ages 53 to 81. Table 8.6 presents his data. Note that the sample is small and therefore the values reported should be considered as approximations of what would be obtained in a large-scale longitudinal study. The data reported in Table 8.6 indicate that there is an approximately equal decline in the markers for fluid and crystallized abilities. The composite index, which may be considered as an approximation of a general intellectual index, exhibits a decline over this age period of .88 standard deviations. Note that the standard deviation of decline scores for this sample is .45, indicating that the mean decline was almost 2 standard deviations from the value of zero, suggesting that almost all of the subjects in this sample exhibited some decline in general intelligence. Again, these results underestimate the true magnitude of decline in unselected samples. Individuals who maintain 28-year contact in a longitudinal study are a hyperselected subset of the population of the aged.

Although Schaie's data provide evidence for declines in intelligence over the adult life span, he has argued that these declines are not global and are rarely general. He used his longitudinal samples to ascertain the number of abilities that had exhibited declines in each 7-year longitudinal sample from ages 53 to 81 (Schaie, 1990). A decline was defined as a reduction in a subtest score for a 7-year period that was equal to 1 standard error of the baseline score at the beginning of each 7-year period. Such a decline is a statistically meaningful criterion, suggesting that the changes were not attributable to chance variations in performance. Table 8.7 presents the proportion of individuals in each 7-year longitudinal study who exhibited declines in excess of 1 standard error. It is obvious that relatively few subjects exhibit consistent declines on all abilities.

TABLE 8.6   Declines in Primary Mental Abilities from Ages 53–81[a,b]

	Verbal meaning	Inductive reasoning	Composite[c]
Mean	.875	.819	.875
S.D.	.507	.808	.452

[a]Based on Schaie (1990).
[b]$N = 16$.
[c]Composite is based on five tests: Verbal Meaning, Spatial, Inductive Reasoning, Number, Word Fluency.

TABLE 8.7 Proportions of Individuals Exhibiting Declines in Abilities[a]

Number of abilities	Age			
	53–60	60–67	67–74	74–81
None	41.3	26.7	24.3	15.5
One	35.3	35.1	37.7	37.2
Two	17.0	22.0	21.8	24.8
Three	4.9	10.3	11.8	14.0
Four	1.2	5.0	3.9	6.2
All five	.5	.8	1.1	2.3

[a]Based on Schaie.

Even in the 74- to 81-year-old subgroup, only 2.3% of the subjects exhibit statistically significant declines on each of the five tests in the Thurstone battery. It is also the case that declines are not consistent across time periods. For the small subset of subjects with the 28-year longitudinal data, no subjects exhibited declines in all four time periods on any ability measure or on the composite measure of ability.

Schaie argued on the basis of these data that declines were not global and were not linear over the age range that he studied. Most individuals exhibit constant performance on most abilities over most time periods. Schaie's conclusions are based on the idiosyncrasies of his data-analysis procedures and his selection of a sample to study. It is possible to argue that these conclusions are not justified for several reasons. First, the longitudinal sample is not representative and therefore may not be informative of the pattern of change associated with aging in the general population. Second, the use of a single point estimate based on a criteria of statistical significance is arbitrary. Third, the use of several ability indices is not an optimal or exhaustive representation of the statistical structure of this set of measures. Schaie, Willis, Jay, & Chipuer (1989) found that factor structures for ability tests given to separate age cohorts across the adult life span are relatively congruent. Thus, the statistical relationships among ability tests may be assumed to be relatively invariant for the samples included in these studies. The discussion of the statistical relationships that obtain among these types of measures in Chapter 2 of this book clearly established that these measures would form a positive manifold supporting the existence of a single common factor that accounts for a substantial portion of the variance in the correlation matrix for these tests. The attempt to treat each of these ability tests as if they are statistically independent of each other does not account for the common variance of the tests. A more meaningful analysis of these data would analyze changes in common variance before examining changes in specific components of variance. The linear and nonlinear trends for changes in common and specific components of variance as a function of age could be analyzed. Such an analysis might be more informative than an analysis based on the proportion of individuals who exhibit an arbitrary statistically defined magnitude of decline on each of several nonindependent ability measures.

Declines in fluid ability with age are correlated with changes in performance on a variety of other cognitive tasks. This has led to the development of different theoretical characterizations of the basis for intellectual decline. I shall briefly consider four approaches to this issue.

The declines in intelligence obtained in longitudinal studies of aging may be attributable to changes in the speed of processing information. Hertzog (1989) reported the results of a cross-sectional study of age differences in intelligence as assessed with the Thurstone battery for adults between ages 43 and 89. He obtained a measure of the speed of processing information that was a composite index of the perceptual speed measure from the Thurstone battery and a measure of the time required to mark correct answers when they were supplied to the subjects. Hertzog calculated cross-sectional changes in intelligence for Thurstone ability measures that were not adjusted for speed and that were speed adjusted. His results are presented in Figures 8.1 and 8.2. These data indicate that a substantial portion of the age-related declines obtained in intelligence are associated with age-related changes in a speed-of-processing variable. It is also the case that the effects of partialling out speed measures lead to quite different cross-sectional age-related changes in different measures of intelligence. For induction, a good marker for fluid ability, there is an age-related decline of approximately .4 standard deviations from ages 60 to 80 for speed-adjusted scores. Comparable data for verbal comprehension, a good marker for crystallized ability, indicate that speed-adjusted performance increases until age 70 and exhibits little or no decline between ages 70 and 80. These data imply that adjustments for the speed of responding have a larger effect on fluid ability measures than on crystallized ability. It should be noted that speed-adjusted scores should not be thought of as pure measures of ability adjusted for a methodological artifact. Speed of filling out a form in which correct answers are supplied is, like many other deceptively simple tasks reviewed in Chapters 3 and 4, correlated with more complex intellectual skills. Hertzog reports correlations ranging between .18 and .62 between this measure of speed of reasoning and Thurstone ability scores for four different age cohorts—the median correlation was .34. This implies that corrections for speed remove true score variance for intelligence as well as a possible methodological artifact in assessment.

Salthouse (1982, 1985, 1988) developed a resource theory to explain declines in fluid ability. He administered tasks to young and old adults that were assumed to vary in the number of times the same operation needed to be applied in order to successfully complete the task. He used a visual synthesis and a geometric analogies problem that varied in com-

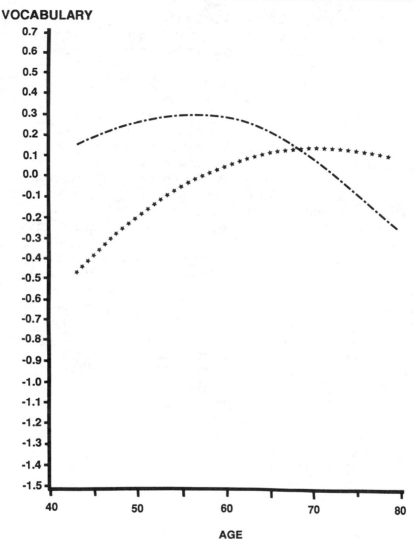

FIGURE 8.1 Speed-adjusted (stars) and unadjusted (lines) cross-sectional changes in crystallized ability. (Based on Hertzog, 1989.)

plexity. The geometric analogies task involved deciding whether the D term of a geometric analogy was correct or not. Variations in the complexity of the analogy were introduced by varying the number of elements included in each of the terms of the analogy. Salthouse assumed that the manipulation of the number of elements in the problem did not influence the strategies used to solve the problem. Such a manipulation is assumed to involve increases in the number of repetitions of the same operation. The slope of the increase in decision time for the analogies is assumed to be a function of the number of resources available to a person to solve this

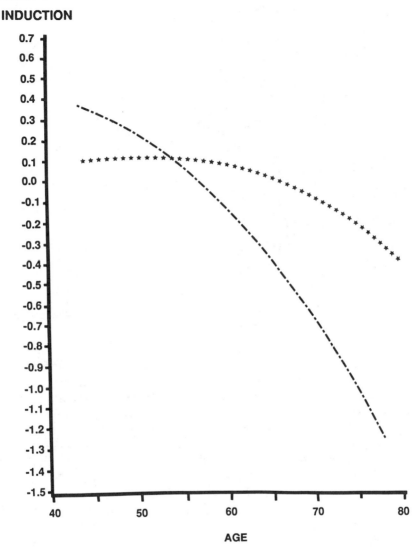

INDUCTION

FIGURE 8.2 Speed-adjusted (stars) and unadjusted (lines) cross-sectional changes in fluid ability. (Based on Hertzog, 1989.)

type of problem. Figure 8.3 indicates that decision times and errors exhibit steeper slopes as a function of complexity among older adults varying between 57 and 67 years of age than among young adults varying in age between 18 and 25. Comparable results were obtained for other tasks in which the slope of performance as a function of the complexity of the task was obtained. As in the geometric analogies task, complexity was conceptualized in terms of the number of recurrent operations of the same type required for solution.

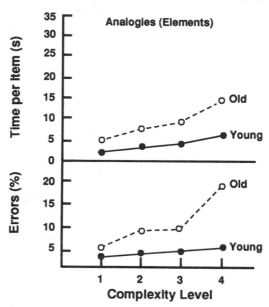

FIGURE 8.3 Performance by young and old adults on a geometric analogies task as a function of complexity level of the task. (Based on Salthouse, 1988.)

Salthouse found that slope measures for different tasks were positively correlated. For example, the slope for the geometric analogies problem and the slope for a visual synthesis problem differing in complexity had a correlation of .47 for older adults in one of his studies (see Salthouse, 1988, Experiment 3). By comparing the magnitude of the slope differences for various tasks, Salthouse derived an estimate of the ratio of processing resources of old adults to young adults. He found that older adults in his studies were estimated to have approximately 60% of the processing resources of young adults. The relationship between age and resource capacity was substantially mediated by the relationship between each of these variables and performance on the Digit Symbol substitution task of the Wechsler test. Control for performance on this task led to a reduction in the common variance of age and performance on the tasks used to measure resource capacities from 28.7% of the common variance to 4.8% of the variance.

Salthouse's studies provide a theoretical foundation and language for an analysis of the relationship between age and fluid intelligence. Aging is accompanied by a loss of the ability to repeatedly perform the same operation rapidly. This inability is indexed in part by speed of performance of the digit symbol tasks and also by more complex reasoning tasks involving the repeated execution of the same type of mental process. The effect is relatively general and appears to provide a basis for understanding declines in fluid ability.

Raz, Moberg, & Millman (1990) obtained data suggesting that age-related declines in fluid ability might be related to basic information-processing capacities. They obtained pitch discrimination thresholds for briefly presented tones. Previous research by Raz *et al.* (1987) reviewed in Chapter 3 of this book indicated that pitch discrimination thresholds for briefly presented tones were correlated with general intelligence in college-age samples. They obtained Cattell Culture-Fair IQ test scores and vocabulary test scores for a sample of 44 adults with a mean age of 40 (S.D. = 20). The correlations among ability measures, age, and their index of pitch discrimination are presented in Table 8.8. An examination of these data indicates that pitch discrimination is related to fluid ability but not to vocabulary. Age is inversely related to the Cattell measure of fluid ability and positively related to vocabulary. Note that age is positively related to pitch discrimination. These data indicate that age is associated with declines in both fluid ability and pitch discrimination for briefly presented tones. These data are compatible with a model that assumes that some of the age-related decline in fluid ability is attributable to a decline in basic information-processing indices that relate to general intelligence in younger age groups. These data should be accepted cautiously. The sample is small and the obtained correlations are somewhat anomalous. Correlations between vocabulary and the Cattell Culture-Fair test are quite low and this somewhat unusual low correlation may contribute to the finding that the pitch discrimination index is related only to fluid and not to crystallized ability.

Declines in fluid ability are thought to be accompanied by changes in the brain. While it is relatively easy to document physiological changes in the nervous system and the brain associated with aging, there is relatively little research that relates changes in physiological functioning that accompany aging to changes in intelligence. It is only recently that noninvasive techniques were developed that permit one to measure anatomy and functioning of the human brain in intact individuals. The use of computerized imaging techniques permits one to measure structure and functioning of the human brain in intact individuals. In principle, changes in brain structure and functioning associated with aging can be measured and these changes can be related to changes in intellectual

TABLE 8.8   Correlations among Age, Pitch Discrimination Index, Cattell Culture-Fair IQ, and Vocabulary[a]

	Pitch	Cattell	Vocabulary
Age	.46	−.77	.24
Pitch		−.52	−.00
Cattell			.09

[a]Based on Raz, Moberg, & Millman (1990).

functioning, providing insights into the biological basis of age-related changes in intelligence. There is relatively little research of this type available. The techniques are expensive and have not been widely used in the study of individual differences in intelligence. Raz, Millman, & Sarpel (1990) performed a study that illustrates the promise of these techniques. They used magnetic resonance imaging to obtain changes in water contents of gray and white cerebral tissue in the medial temporal lobes in a sample of 25 adults ranging in age from 18 to 78. They also administered a vocabulary test as an index of crystallized intelligence to these subjects and the Cattell Culture-Fair test as an index of fluid intelligence. Correlations among age, intelligence indices, and the ratio of gray to white matters pin-lattice relaxation times are presented in Table 8.9. Age is negatively correlated with the gray/white ratio and with Cattell IQ scores. Cattell IQ scores are positively correlated with gray/white ratios. Vocabulary scores have a negative correlation with gray/white ratios. These data should be considered exploratory because of the relatively small sample. Nevertheless, they are interesting. A biological index of aging is negatively correlated with performance on a measure of fluid ability. The same index does not predict scores on tests of crystallized ability. The physiological index does not predict fluid intelligence independently of its association with age. It would be interesting to obtain this index in a sample of older individuals of the same age to see if this provides an independent index of fluid intelligence. There are many potential psychological indices of changes accompanying the aging process. Some of these may be predictive of changes in intelligence among older adults. The Raz, Millman, & Sarpel (1990) study does not indicate whether the physiological index they used was merely a correlate of aging or whether it was an index of changes in fluid intelligence that is independent of age.

It is obvious that changes in fluid ability with age are related to a variety of physiological changes and changes in basic information-processing capacities. In addition to the four approaches briefly discussed above, Horn, Donaldson, & Engstrom (1981) related changes in fluid ability with aging to measures of concentration, encoding organization, incidental memory, eschewing attentional irrelevancies, dividing attention, and working memory. The changes in basic information-processing abilities that occur with age are probably related to physiological changes in

TABLE 8.9   Correlations among Age, Cattell IQ, Vocabulary, and Gray/White Ratio[a]

	Cattell	Vocabulary	Gray/white
Age	−.71	.32	−.57
Cattell		.18	.55
Vocabulary			−.28

[a]Based on Raz, Millman, & Sarpel (1990).

the brain. It is clear that these changes appear to have a differential influence on fluid and crystallized abilities. And declines in the former type of intelligence are larger and appear to be more clearly related to physiological changes and changes in basic information-processing abilities. Differences in the relationship between basic information processes and physiological indices and declines in crystallized and fluid intelligence provide a strong rationale of the theoretical distinction between these two types of intelligence.

What is the practical significance of the decline in intelligence associated with aging? Willis & Schaie (1986) related performance on psychometric indices to tests of ability to perform everyday tasks in a sample of older adults ranging in age from 60 to 88. They administered a battery of psychometric tests and a test of basic skills including the ability to understand labels, read maps and charts, understand a paragraph, understand forms, advertisements, and technical documents, and comprehend news stories. They factor analyzed their ability tests and obtained a four-factor solution that included a fluid ability factor, a crystallized ability factor, a memory span factor, and a perceptual speed factor. Scores on the first two factors were related to performance on the basic skills test. Fluid ability was more highly related to performance on basic skills than crystallized ability ($r = .58$ and $.29$, respectively). These data indicate that the component of intelligence that exhibits the largest decline with age is substantially related to the intellectual ability required to perform activities that are necessary to be a competent adult. Willis and Schaie argued that many of the basic skills they studied were "nonentrenched" and required subjects to solve problems in ways that involved the application of general principles applied to novel tasks. As such, they were better measures of fluid ability than crystallized ability. The distinction between novel tasks and entrenchment may be generally useful in understanding the intellectual competence of older adults. It is possible that aged individuals may be relatively successful in performing intellectual tasks that draw heavily on previously acquired crystallized abilities and knowledge. Studies of scientific productivity have failed to document clear-cut evidence of declines with age (Cole, 1979). Of course this type of evidence deals with the performance of a small number of hyperselected individuals and typically does not include performance of individuals past the normal retirement age of 65. Note that the Willis and Schaie study is concerned with the performance of many adults who are past normal retirement age.

In intellectual declines occur and they are of some significance in ability to perform everyday activities it would be useful to devise programs to increase intelligence among older adults.

Baltes, Kliegl, & Dittmann-Kohli (1988) attempted to change fluid intelligence in a group of healthy volunteers aged 63 to 87. The subjects were randomly assigned to one of three groups. One group took a battery of fluid ability test on two occasions. A second group was given 10 hours of training in ways of solving fluid ability problems. A third group was permitted to take the battery of intelligence tests three times during a 10-hour period without feedback or specific instructional guidance. The battery of tests included two tests generally construed as good markers of a fluid ability factor—the Cattell Culture-Fair intelligence test and the Raven's test. The control group had mean scores that were .45 and .04 standard deviation units higher on the posttest than on the pretest on the Cattell and Raven, respectively. The comparable gains expressed in standard deviation units of the pretest scores for the group given practice tests in the battery without feedback were .82 and .29 standard deviation units. The group given specific training on the test gained .64 and .20 standard deviation units, respectively.

These data permit us to reach several conclusions about the benefits of training in improving fluid ability among older adult subjects. First, the gains associated with training are modest. On general fluid ability tests such as the Cattell and the Raven, specific training was associated with gains of less than one-fifth of a standard deviation unit relative to the gains obtained from a simple retesting. Second, the gains that were obtained as a result of practice without expert guidance were, if anything, slightly larger than those obtained as a result of specific training. Baltes et al. interpreted these findings as indicating that training effects may be largely attributable to helping individuals use skills that are already in their repertoire.

Schaie & Willis (1986) used their longitudinal sample to attempt to remediate changes in intelligence among older adults. Their sample ranged in age from 62 to 95. They divided their sample into those who had exhibited declines in abilities relative to a prior testing 14 years before and those who had not exhibited such declines. The subjects were provided with 5 hours of training designed to assist them in solving either spatial problems or reasoning problems. Subjects were tested on both the ability they were specifically trained on and the ability for which they were not specifically trained. The largest gains as a result of training were exhibited by subjects who had declines in ability and who were tested on the specific ability that they had been trained to perform. For example, subjects who were classified as decliners who were trained in reasoning ability exhibited gains of slightly less than .8 standard deviation units on reasoning on their retest. These gains returned over 40% of these subjects to the level of performance they had exhibited in the test given 14 years earlier. The gains in intelligence exhibited by these subjects were somewhat specific to the abilities on which they were trained. When tested on the generalization ability, the gains for subjects ranged from approximately .2 to .3 standard deviation units.

The results of the Schaie and Willis study tentatively support several conclusions. First, while it is possible to remediate declines in specific abilities associated with aging, the effects of the remediation are smaller on other abilities. This implies that changes in general or fluid intelligence, if any, obtained as a result of the intervention were smaller than changes on specific abilities that were remediated. Second, gains in fluid or general ability as manifested on the generalization task were modest—less than .3 standard deviations in magnitude. Third, there were no controls for changes attributable to the effects of retesting. Note that Baltes *et al.* obtained changes in fluid ability in a comparable sample merely as result of taking tests on two occasions. This suggests that the generalization gains obtained in the Baltes and Willis study may have been attributable solely to the effects of taking the test on two occasions. There is considerable uncertainty about this matter since Baltes and Willis did not include a group who were not given training but were given the test on two occasions. In any case, gains in fluid or general intelligence that were obtained as a result of specific training, when adjusted for an unknown test–retest component, are vanishingly small. Fourth, the results of this remediation may under- or overestimate the general effects of remediation. It is quite possible that longer and more intensive interventions that are directed to a broader range of abilities might lead to larger changes in general intelligence. The long-term effects of the interventions are unknown and it is possible that such interventions may fade over time.

This brief review of two intervention studies suggests that the effects of interventions to increase general intelligence among the aged may be comparable to the effects of interventions designed to increase intelligence in young children. In both instances, the changes that are obtained as a result of the interventions are not large.

CONCLUSION

Baltes & Willis (1979; see also Dixon, Kramer, & Baltes, 1985; Willis & Baltes, 1980) abstracted four conceptions from research on the development of intelligence in adulthood and old age. These are:

1. Multidimensionality, the notion that intelligence is composed of multiple mental abilities, each with potentially distinct structural, functional, and developmental properties.
2. Multidirectionality, signifying that there are multiple distinct change patterns associated with these abilities.
3. Interindividual variability, a conception reflecting the observed differences in the life-course change patterns of individuals.
4. Intraindividual plasticity, which indicates that, in general, throughout the life course individual behavioral patterns are modifiable.

While there is a support for each of these, it is also the case that it would be possible to emphasize the converse principles of unidimensionality, undirectionality, interindividual stability, and intraindividual constancy from an examination of this literature. Consider each of these concepts.

Unidimensionality. Although crystallized and fluid ability exhibit somewhat different changes with age, both decline and it is possible that changes in fluid ability may be more significant. Evidence indicating that fluid ability is isomorphic with *g* and occupies a different hierarchical level than crystallized ability may be relevant to understanding age-related changes in intelligence. That is, it may be correct to say that fluid ability, which is isomorphic with the most general conception of intelligence, exhibits declines and therefore changes in intelligence in adulthood may equally be characterized as unidimensional as well as multidimensional. In a sense this issue mirrors debates about the structure of intellect considered in Chapter 2 of this book.

Unidirectionality. Since analyses of independent samples adjusting for dropout effects (see Table 8.5) indicate that declines occur in both crystallized and fluid ability, it may be just as appropriate to discuss unidirectional change as it is to describe the changes that occur as multidirectional.

Interindividual constancy. Long-term longitudinal data reported in Table 8.6 indicate that virtually all individuals exhibit declines in fluid ability if studied for a sufficiently long period of time. While there is considerable interindividual variability in changes in fluid ability over the life span, it is also correct to state that virtually everyone who survives into the ninth decade of life may be expected to exhibit declines in fluid ability. Therefore, one could say with equal justification that there is interindividual stability in the change in intelligence associated with aging.

Intraindividual constancy. Despite the belief in the plasticity of intelligence, there is, in my judgment, relatively little convincing evidence that existing programs designed to modify general intelligence are able to substantially increase intellectual ability. Intelligence is not particularly malleable. While small changes may occur as a result of interventions, there is relatively little evidence that the changes that occur are of enduring and general significance.

It should be apparent that research on life-span changes in intelligence may be approached from multiple perspectives. Although the concept of fixed intelligence is a caricature of the psychometric tradition, there is a sense in which it is possible to study life-span changes by appeal to a model that emphasizes the importance of the unfolding of a biologically influenced latent ability construct that influences the response to cultural opportunities presented to individuals. Evidence for genetic influences on intelligence, preliminary suggestions from some of the behavior genetic analyses of genetic influences on changes in intelligence, and relationships between biological mothers' IQ and the early intellectual performance of their adopted children suggest that some of the longitudinal stability in IQ is attributable to genotypic influences that influence both early childhood intellectual development and adult intellectual development (see the discussion of longitudinal behavior genetics in Chapter 5). Similarly, the emerging evidence indicating that information-processing indices obtained shortly after birth are related to childhood IQ (see Chapter 3) suggests that some of the continuities in intelligence extend from the first year of life. It is possible that age-related declines in fluid ability may be partially determined by genetic factors that influence physiological changes. Thus, life-span development may be viewed through the lens of inexorable changes in a biologically influenced disposition. While such an approach may have some validity, it should be apparent that it is a gross oversimplification. Genetic predispositions constantly interact with environmental events. Intelligence is clearly determined from the prenatal period on by both the social and the biological environment encountered by individuals. It may be equally wrong to see intelligence over the life span as the inexorable unfolding of a predetermined disposition as it is to see it as a characteristic of persons that is plastic, malleable, variable, multidirectional, and multidimensional. Both perspectives are necessary to understand the changes that occur.

9

CORRELATES OF INTELLIGENCE

From its inception, the study of intelligence has been concerned with the relationship between measures of intelligence and real-world accomplishments. This issue has not been dealt with in the previous chapters in this book. In this chapter we shall consider relationships between intelligence and education, occupational success, criminality, and fertility.

INTELLIGENCE AND EDUCATION

Description

There is a large amount of literature relating scores on tests of intelligence to performance in various academic settings. Lavin (1965) summarized the older literature. Tests of intelligence correlate with measures of academic performance. The correlations that are obtained are usually close to .5. Higher correlations are obtained for elementary school performance. The lower correlations that are obtained for performance in the high school years are probably attributable to some restriction in range of talent. Students usually have some choice of subjects that they study at the high school level and these choices may be related to IQ. The homogeneity of grouping on intelligence may influence the magnitude of the correlation between IQ and mastery of subject matter taught at the high school level.

The correlation between IQ and academic achievement does not invariably decrease as the time between the administration of IQ tests and the administration of measures of academic achievement increases. For example, Butler, Marsh, Sheppard, & Sheppard (1985) obtained reading achievement scores for a large sample of children in the first, second, third, and sixth grades in Sydney, Australia, using a longitudinal design. IQ test scores were obtained in kindergarten. The correlations between IQ and a reading score factor for children in the first, second, third, and sixth grades were .38, .39, .46, and .46, respectively.

Feshbach, Adelman, & Fuller (1977) administered IQ tests to two large samples of kindergarten children and related these scores to reading achievement scores in the first, second, and third grades. They obtained correlations of .32, .40, and .45, respectively. In a second replication sample, the comparable correlations were .42, .48, and .45. Horn & Packard (1985) reported the results of a meta-analysis of studies relating IQ measures administered to children in kindergarten and first grade and reading achievement of children in elementary school. The mean correlation for nine studies relating IQ to reading achievement in the first grade was .52. The comparable correlation for studies relating IQ test scores obtained in kindergarten and first grade to reading achievement in the second and third grades was .54, again indicating little or no change in the predictability of IQ test scores obtained at the beginning of elementary school and indices of academic achievement obtained at different periods of time.

These results may be attributable to two processes. Early achievements may relate to later achievements. Therefore, attainment of reading skills in first grade provides a foundation for subsequent acquisition of new skills. It is also the case that general intelligence may be related to the acquisition of new skills not assessed in previous measures of achievement.

Tests of intelligence are not only related to indices of academic performance; they are also related to measures of the number of years of education that individuals receive. The number of years of education that a person receives is related to a person's occupational status. Occupational status hierarchies, as determined by subjects' rankings, are positively correlated with the years of education that are required to meet entry requirements for a particular occupation. If IQ is related to the number of years of education that a person receives, IQ measures should be related to the occupational status that a person attains. We indicated in Chapter 6 that parental social status is correlated with IQ ($r = .3$), and it is possible that parental social status may influence the amount of education a person receives. Therefore, the relationship between IQ and the amount of education that a person receives, and ultimately the social status that a person attains, may be attributable to the influence of parental social background on IQ and education.

The sociologists Blau & Duncan (1967) were among the first to attempt to study relationships among IQ, parental social status, education, and occupational status. They obtained IQ data on students in school and followed these individuals in order to determine the number of years of education that they obtained. Duncan, Featherman, & Duncan (1972) developed path analytic models for these data using several historical data sets. For example, Benson (1942) obtained IQ scores for a group of elementary school children in the sixth grade in Minneapolis. She found that the correlation between sixth grade IQ test scores obtained in 1923 and the number of years of education that a person obtained was .57. A path model relating these variables is presented in Fig. 9.1. An examination of the model indicates that intelligence is a more important influence on the number of years of education that a person obtains than a person's socioeconomic background. The number of years of education that a person obtains is an important influence on the occupational status of a person's first job. Duncan *et al.* estimated that intelligence by itself accounts for 29% of the variance of educational achievement. Intelligence and socioeconomic background account for 44% of a person's educational attainment. While there are a number of complex issues surrounding the interpretation of these data, including questions of secular change and the estimation of parameters using different data sources, all of the sociological analyses of this type of data for the U.S. are in agreement with certain features of this analysis. Individual differences in intelligence as estimated by scores obtained early in a person's educational career account for more variance in educational attainment than a person's social class background. Social class background, as we have seen, is only weakly related to IQ. Therefore, IQ measures a characteristic of persons that influences their educational experiences that is independent of their social class background. Since the number of years of education that a person obtains influences a person's occupational status, intelligence is related to intergenerational occupational mobility. Individuals with high intelligence are more likely to attain an occupational status that is higher than their parents than individuals who are low in intelligence. It is interesting to note that a system of assigning individuals to educational tracks that would determine the amount of education a person obtains solely on the basis of a person's IQ test score would decrease the class bias in the amount of education that a person receives.

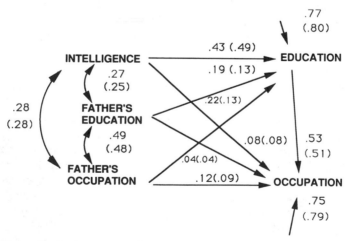

FIGURE 9.1   Abridged version of the final model of ability and achievement with path coefficients for two populations. (Based on Duncan, Featherman, & Duncan, 1972.)

Jencks (1979; see also 1972) presented a comprehensive analysis using several different surveys relating IQ to educational attainment and occupational status. He indicated that there is very little evidence of secular changes in the magnitudes of the correlation between IQ and the number of years of education that a person obtains for data collected from 1920 to 1970. The correlations between these variables are usually in the high 50s, suggesting that IQ accounts for approximately 34% of the variance in educational attainment. Jencks's analyses of the available survey data also indicated that intelligence is related to the amount of income that person obtains independent of the effect of the amount of education that a person obtains. The effects are small. Jencks indicated that the importance of adolescent IQ in determining a person's earnings increases with age. A 1-standard-deviation increase in IQ is associated with a 14% increase in earnings with education and social class background held constant. Also, IQ has been related to earnings for men within the same occupation. Jencks reported that in one sample of individuals from Michigan, a 1-standard-deviation difference in IQ was associated with an 11% increase in earnings for individuals in the same occupation. There is considerable uncertainty surrounding these values since they are based on complicated adjustments for social class background and education. Nevertheless, Jencks's analyses clearly indicate that IQ is the most important single predictor of an individual's ultimate position in American society. While there is considerable unpredictability for such indices as social status and income, IQ is more predictive than anything else.

The influence of IQ on the amount of education that a person obtains may be understood in terms of the unfolding of a set of interrelated social influences. We have seen that IQ is related to academic achievement. Individuals who do well in schools may develop positive views of their educational abilities that may foster academic aspirations. In addition, individuals who excel in their academic work may be assigned to educational tracks and to classes that are designed to prepare individuals for higher education. Educational counselors and administrators may encourage individuals who excel in their academic work to continue their education. Students assigned to classes with classmates who plan to continue their education my receive encouragement from their classmates to continue their education. This hypothetical scenario about interrelated influences that impact upon individuals who differ in IQ provides a basis for understanding the way in which IQ influences the amount of education that a person obtains. This scenario is not totally fictional. Rehberg & Rosenthal (1978) investigated the decision of high school students to continue their formal education. Their study was a longitudinal investigation of over 2000 high school students starting in the ninth grade and continuing until high school graduation. They related the decision to enroll in postsecondary education to measures of a pupil's background, IQ, and academic achievement, to the influence of parents, peers, and counselors, and to the curriculum that was elected. Table 9.1 presents a synthesis of their data indicating the way in which these variables influence the decision to obtain postgraduate education. The data in Table 9.1 include relationships for the same variables based on data obtained in the ninth grade, where the educational decision is based on intentions, and data from the same students who have graduated high school, where the dependent variable is the planned enrollment of students in college. These data indicate that individual differences in intelligence are a more important source of variance in the decision to continue education after high school graduation than they are at the beginning of high school. The influence of IQ and social class background change over the course of a person's high school career—the former influence tends to become larger, the latter influence tends to become smaller. The influence of IQ on the decision to continue education is, in terms of the path model that is developed, indirect. IQ influences the several variables that jointly determine the decision to continue one's education. IQ influences academic achievement. Indices of academic achievement influence the assignment of individuals to educational tracks and classes that are designed to prepare a person for higher education. Academic achievement influences the advice students receive from college counselors. And, class and curriculum placement influence friendship patterns and the kinds of influences that students receive from their peers. The influence of parental aspirations and expectations tends to decline over the course of a student's high school career. These changes are not dramatic, but they exert a cumulative influence that is documented in detail in Rehberg and Rosenthal's survey data. Rehberg and Rosenthal concluded that the educational system they studied is more responsive to "merit" (this assumes that high ability as assessed by IQ tests is an index of merit or at least educational

TABLE 9.1   Variables that Influence the Decision to Attend College[a]

	Ninth grade intention		Postsecondary enrollment	
	Male	Female	Male	Female
Social class	.46	.40	.36	.35
Ability	.39	.41	.43	.40
Parental educational stress	.40	.45	.29	.28
Further education taken for granted	.48	.47	.38	.31
Curriculum, grade 9	.42	.48	.29	.39
Peer college intentions, grade 9	.51	.44	.39	.35

[a] Based on Rehberg & Rosenthal (1978), Tables 3.6 and 7.1. (Copyright ©1978 by Longman Publishing Group)

merit) than to social class privilege. Of course, as indicated previously, the educational system is not completely based on merit since social class background continues to exert an independent influence on educational enrollment beyond secondary school.

Jencks (1979) also cited survey data that indicated that ability test scores become a more important influence on the decision to enroll in postgraduate education as students approach the end of their high school years. Apparently, the phenomena is characteristic of many educational systems in the U.S. He suggested that at the most general level the phenomenon is to be understood in one of two ways: (1) Schools treat individuals with different ability scores differently, generally providing more encouragement to academically talented students than to students with low test scores; and (2) individuals with high test scores are more adept at preparing themselves to continue their education during the high school years than students with low test scores. It is obvious that the way in which individual differences in IQ determine educational decisions and influence the amount of education that a person receives is attributable to the interactions of individuals with the educational system, and these influences must be understood as the result of a complex process that develops over time.

We have seen that there is relationship between intelligence and academic achievement. What determines this relationship? Behavior genetic procedures may be used to investigate the covariation between variables as well as individual differences in a variable. Cardon, DiLalla, Plomin, DeFries, & Fulker (1990) used the Colorado Adoption Project sample to study the relationship between reading skills and intelligence in a group of 7-year-old children who had completed 1 year of elementary school. They contrasted the relationship between IQ and reading skills of parents and children in adopted and control families. They found that the IQ and reading skill measures of adopted parents were not clearly related to the IQs and reading skills of their adopted children. For example, the correlations between the adopted mother's IQ and the IQ and reading skill performance of her adopted child were .07 and −.11, respectively. By contrast, the IQ of the biological mother in control families was related to the IQ of her natural children and to the reading skills of her natural children. The correlations were .21 and .17, respectively. Cardon et al. used these and other measures of the relationships between IQ and reading achievement for natural and adopted parents and their children to perform a behavior genetic analysis of the basis for the relationship between IQ and reading achievement. Their analysis indicated that reading achievement and IQ were equally heritable. Heritabilities were .36 and .38, respectively. The correlation between reading achievement and IQ was .43. They estimated that 90% of the covariance between reading achievement and IQ was attributable to shared genetic covariance. This implies that the genetic characteristics that determine individual differences in IQ are largely the same as those that determine individual differences in reading skills.

Brooks, Fulker, & DeFries (1990) reached a similar conclusion about the relationship between intelligence and reading skills on the basis of a twin study with a sample varying in age between 7 and 20. They obtained a correlation of .38 between their measure of IQ and the same measure of reading skill used in the Cardon *et al.* study. They found that the covariance between reading skill and IQ could be accounted for by a model that assumed that there was no between-family environmental influence on the relationship. The relationship was attributable to within-family sources of variance and genetic covariance. The genetic correlation between reading skill and IQ was .58.

Thompson, Detterman, & Plomin (1991) reported the results of a genetic covariance analysis of the relationship between cognitive abilities and scholastic achievement. They administered a battery of tests designed to obtain indices of spatial and verbal abilities and performance on achievement tests of reading, math, and language skills in the schools to a sample of 6- to 12-year-old twins. Behavior genetic analyses of their various measures indicated that measures of cognitive abilities had higher heritabilities than achievement tests. The estimated heritability of the spatial ability index was .70. The comparable heritability for the verbal ability index was .54. The estimated heritabilities for the three tests of achievement ranged from .17 to .27. The between-family environmental influences were higher on the achievement tests than on the ability indices. The achievement tests had between-family environmental influences ranging from .65 to .73. Spatial and verbal ability indices had estimated between-family environmental influences of .02 and .08, respectively. These data provide strong evidence for a conceptual distinction between achievement and ability. Heritabilities are higher for the latter; between-family environmental influences are higher for the former.

Thompson *et al.* also analyzed the genetic covariance between these two types of indices. Phenotypic correlations between verbal and spatial ability indices and measures of achievement ranged from .32 to .40. The correlations between these measures were higher for MZ twin pairs than for same-sex DZ twin pairs. The correlations between verbal and spatial ability indices and measures of achievement for MZ twins ranged from .31 to .40. The comparable correlations for the fraternal twins ranged from .18 to .23. The differences in the magnitude of the correlations imply that genetic factors influence the phenotypic correlations between ability and achievement. These data are compatible with a behavior genetic model that estimates that the genetic correlation for the phenotypic correlation of spatial and verbal ability and scholastic achievement is .80. These data are also compatible with a model that assigns a zero value for parameter estimates for the influence of between-family environmental variations on the phenotypic correlations between ability and achievement.

These three studies are the first to address the reasons for the relationship between academic achievement and IQ. It is premature to assume that the relationship between IQ and other academic achievements that are acquired in the schools will be genetically mediated. It is also the case that a model assuming that the genes that influence intelligence are the same as the genes that influence the development of academic achievements is plausible. Scores on a test of intelligence should not be construed as pure measures of ability. All tests of intelligence measure intellectual achievements that are determined by the ability to acquire knowledge. They are therefore tests of achievement. The distinction between ability and achievement is arbitrary and is a matter of degree. There are no pure tests of ability uncontaminated by the opportunity to acquire knowledge and intellectual skills. If individuals differ in a genetically determined aptitude to acquire knowledge and skills from common environmental exposures, it is reasonable to assume that that ability will be related to the acquisition of fluid ability as well as to benefit from the formal tuition of the schools. There may even be temperamental variables such as persistence, patience, curiosity, etc., that are heritable that influence the acquisition of the intellectual skills assessed by tests of intelligence and the acquisition of the content of the curriculum of the schools. The investigation of the genetic and environmental basis of the covariance between IQ and academic achievement leads to interesting questions about the kinds of environments that foster the development of genetic covariance. Are there educational settings that decrease the genetic covariance between IQ and academic achievements?

Modifiability

We have seen that IQ test scores are related to educational achievement. And, further, there is tentative evidence that the association between academic achievement and IQ may be mediated genetically. Does this imply that what children learn in schools is determined by genetic characteristics? And, leaving aside the issue of genetic covariance, does this imply that what children learn in schools is determined by the characteristics they bring to the schools? In this section I want to discuss the modifiability of the relationship between education and intelligence.

One aspect of this issue was discussed by Christopher Jencks (1972). Jencks analyzed differences in academic achievement associated with the public school that a student attended. He obtained aggregated indices of academic achievement for students in a school. Schools differ widely in the average level of academic achievement as assessed by tests of knowledge of the curriculum. It is easy to examine these data and conclude that some schools are better than others. That is, those schools whose pupils exhibited superior academic performance may be assumed to be more successful than those schools whose pupils exhibited inferior academic performance. The aggregated academic performance of pupils in a school is related to the socioeconomic characteristics of the pupils attending the school. For the most part, students in the U.S. are assigned by the geographical location of their residence to a particular school. Schools at the elementary school level do not influence the composition of their student body. But the composition of a student body can have an influence on the academic achievement of children in a school. This suggests that differences in the average academic achievement of pupils in a school may be attributable to differences in the social composition of the student body and not to intrinsic differences in the nature of the curriculum of the schools. Jencks found that aggregated indices of the social class background of a school usually correlated in excess of .9 with aggregated indices of the academic achievement of pupils in the school. Schools that were above the regression line relating aggregated academic achievement to aggregated social class background in a particular year might not be above the line in the following year. Schools that performed above their expected value in reading achievement might not perform above their expected value in mathematics achievement. Jencks concluded that variations among schools in the U.S. might account for as little as 2–3% of the variance in academic achievement after the composition of the social class background of the schools was taken into account. These analyses suggest that variations in what children learn in schools in the U.S. is not attributable to variations in the nature of the schools but is attributable to variations in the characteristics that children bring to the schools. One might say that the input determines the output.

Jencks's analysis deals with social class background and academic achievement. The relationship between social class background and academic achievement is mediated by individual differences in intelligence. Rehberg & Rosenthal (1978) summarized studies of the relationship of grades and IQ and social class background. Social class background has little or no predictive direct relationship to grades after one controls for such mediating influences as IQ and educational interest. IQ accounts for more variance in grades and indices of academic achievement than social class background. Virtually all of the relationship between IQ and grades and other indices of academic accomplishment in the schools is direct. That is, it is not diminished in path analyses that control for social class background. This suggests that the relationship between aggregated indices of academic performance characteristic of different schools and aggregated indices of the IQs of students in a school, including the aggregated indices of pupils obtained from IQ tests given prior to school entry, would be more substantial than the relationship between aggregated indices of social class background and educational accomplishments of pupils in different schools. ~~The IQ that children bring to the school determines variations in what children learn in the schools.~~

Jencks's views are controversial. Rutter, Maughan, Mortimore, Ouston, & Smith (1979) conducted a study in London, England, to demonstrate that there were wide disparities in the academic accomplishment of students with comparable social class backgrounds attending different schools. The difficulty with Rutter's analysis is that children in London are not assigned to secondary schools on the basis of their geographic residence and have a choice of schools. If the differences in accomplishment were apparent to researchers they might also have been apparent to parents in the community who might then elect to send academically talented children to those schools that have the best reputation. Unless there are good controls for the entry characteristics of children attending different schools in a system in which parents are given choice of the school to attend, it is difficult to know if variations in the academic achievement of pupils in different schools are to be attributable to variations in the quality of the schools or variations in the characteristics of different pupils in the schools.

Brookover, Beady, Flood, Schweitzer, & Wisenbaker (1979) argued that variations in academic achievement of pupils in different schools were related to the social climate of the school. They obtained a composite index of school climate that was based in part on measures of the attitudes of pupils and teachers about the possibility of academic success for pupils attending different schools in Michigan. They found that their school climate index was more predictive of the aggregated academic performance of pupils in the school than aggregated indices of the social class background of pupils in the schools. Their data are presented in Table 9.2 for two different orders of entry of variables in a hierarchical regression analysis. Although the school climate variable is more predictive of academic outcome than either race or social class background, it should be noted that a logical analysis of these data should be based on entering demographic variables in the equation prior to entering social climate variables. This assertion is based on an understanding of the

TABLE 9.2   Percentage of Variance in School Achievement Related to School Characteristics[a]

Variable	Percentage
Socioeconomic background	46
Plus percentage of whites	76
Plus school climate	83
Climate first	73
Plus socioeconomic background	75
Plus percentages of whites	83

[a]Based on Brookover, Beady, Flood, Schweitzer, & Wisenbaker (1979).

causal relationship that exists among these variables. Since pupils are assigned to school by geographic residence, school climate cannot influence the demographic characteristics of pupils in a school. The converse is not true. School climate and demographic characteristics are correlated. In this instance our understanding of the world permits us to infer something about the causal relationship between these variables. If the appropriate order of entry of variables is considered, it is apparent that the demographic background of pupils accounts for 76% of the variance in aggregated indices of academic accomplishment of different schools in the sample. Social climate adds 7% to the predictable variance. These data are interpreted by Brookover *et al.* as providing strong evidence for a model of school effects on academic achievement. Nevertheless, demographic characteristics of pupils account for more than 10 times as much variance as the variable that is assumed to capture a salient characteristic of schools that determines their influence on achievement.

The data obtained by Brookover and his associates may overestimate the importance of variability among schools. The influence of demographic characteristics on academic success is mediated by differences in intelligence test scores associated with race or class. Since intelligence is a better predictor than either race or class, it can be argued that the most relevant index of pupil characteristics was not included in this study. It is possible that aggregated indices of IQ would be more predictive of aggregated indices of academic performance than the demographic variables used in this study. In addition, school climate is not, strictly speaking, a measure of the characteristics of the school that is independent of characteristics of pupils in the school. One component in the index is students' belief in their academic success. Brookover *et al.* assume that this belief is caused by school characteristics. It may represent characteristics of pupils that are independent of demographic characteristics that predict academic achievement. These hypothetical characteristics may not be influenced by variations in the academic climate of a school that the person attends. Thus the interpretation of the influence of school effects provided by Brookover and his colleagues involves the unsupported assumption that beliefs about academic achievement held by pupils are influenced by characteristics of the school that pupils attend. Their interpretation would be more convincing if their measure of variations among schools did not include any information about the pupils who attend the school.

The analyses by Jencks and by Brookover *et al.* deal with variations among public schools. The relatively small variations in aggregated academic performance among different schools may be attributable to reduced variability in the educational practices of different schools. Coleman, Hoffer, & Kilgore (1982a, b) argued that students attending Catholic parochial schools at the secondary level had higher academic performance than pupils in public schools controlling for demographic backgrounds of pupils. Thus it is possible to argue that the relatively small impact of variations in schools may tell us more about the relative homogeneity of public schools than about the possible impact of variations in schools on the academic achievement of pupils in a school. The comparison of performance differences of pupils in Catholic and public schools is complicated by the fact that pupils are not randomly assigned to these two types of schools. Adjustments for initial differences in pupil characteristics are difficult since academically motivated and talented pupils might elect to attend Catholic schools if they believe that the public schools in their community are not adequate. A good analysis of these issues may be found in a series of articles dealing with the analysis of data from a large survey called the "High School and Beyond" study designed to assess the impact of Catholic secondary schools on pupils (Alexander & Pallas, 1985; Hoffer, Greeley, & Coleman, 1985; Jencks, 1985; Willms, 1985). This study provided information about the progress of students in Catholic and public high schools from sophomore year to senior year in a variety of academic subjects. The study assessed gains in academic work associated with public and Catholic school attendance. Since students in Catholic schools in this sample started with better academic performance in the sophomore year than students in the public schools, the magnitude of the estimated gains is dependent on the procedures that are used to adjust for initial differences in academic performance. Jencks (1985) presented an analysis of these data. He estimated that attendance at Catholic schools is associated with a gain in academic performance of .03 or .04 standard deviations per year compared to attendance in public schools. Since these are estimated gain scores, it can be assumed that initial ability differences are controlled. Jencks also estimated that attendance at Catholic schools from the first through twelfth grades may be associated with a gain of between .11 and .22 standard deviations relative to attendance in the public schools. Thus the .03- to .04-standard-deviation advantage per year may not be sustainable over the course of an extended exposure to Catholic education. While there is considerable uncertainty surrounding all of these estimates, it is clear that the impact of differences in educational accomplishments of pupils in Catholic versus public schools is relatively modest.

The research we have briefly reviewed on differences in academic achievement associated with different schools suggests that variations among schools are not major sources of variance in academic achievement. Schools do not make a large difference once one has accounted for the intellectual differences characteristic of children entering the schools. It is possible that the relatively modest effects of schools in this research are attributable to restrictions in variations among schools. One way to get some insight into this possibility is to compare the academic performance of children in different countries. Such comparisons may provide insight into possible differences in academic accomplishment associated with variations in schooling. A good example of such a study has been reported by Stevenson, Lee, Chen, Lummis, Stigler, Fan, & Ge (1990). They administered tests of mathematical knowledge to a representative sample of first and fifth grade children attending school in the Chicago metropolitan area and in Beijing, China. The children in Beijing were superior to the children in Chicago on most of the measures in the battery. At the fifth grade level, the Chinese children averaged 1.32 standard deviation units higher on the test battery than the children in Chicago. Although Chinese-American children scored higher on the battery of tests than other ethnic groups, their performance lagged behind that of Chinese students in Beijing. Although there is no control for entry characteristics in this study, these data do appear to clearly implicate differences in the curriculum in academic achievement. It is interesting to note that the parents and teachers of Chinese children had less formal education than the parents and teachers of American children. American children also were more confident of their mathematical ability than Chinese children and were more likely to believe that mathematics was an easy subject. Despite these differences, the American children were far behind the Chinese children. The differences are plausibly related to the amount of time devoted to mathematics in the elementary school and to the rigor of the curriculum. By performing cross-national comparisons it is possible to see that personal inputs do not constrain educational outputs. As we shall see in Chapter 10, differences in intelligence between Chinese-background individuals and individuals of other racial groups are small. Thus the large difference in academic performance obtained by Stevenson *et al.* (1990) cannot be attributed to intellectual differences. It is plausibly attributable to differences in the educational systems of China and the U.S. These data imply that individual differences in intelligence, though a major determinant of what is learned in school, do not preclude or constrain the development of a rigorous educational experience that will substantially modify educational outcomes. As we shall see, most educational reforms have had modest effects on academic achievement in the U.S. I suspect that this is not attributable to anything intrinsic about the limitations of educational reform given the entry characteristics of pupils. The modest effects attained may be attributable to the rather modest character of the reforms that have been studied. I suspect that American children are capable of attaining parity in mathematical literacy with Chinese children. In order to accomplish this goal it might be necessary to reform our educational system in a way that is more profound than the usual changes that are contemplated. We might, for example, need to lengthen the school day and the school year, increase the amount of homework given to children, increase the amount of time devoted to mathematics instruction, and increase the requirements for mathematical literacy among teachers in the upper elementary grades in order to have teachers with the knowledge required to teach a more advanced curriculum.

We have considered naturally occurring variations among schools as a source of variance in what is learned in the school. Another way of looking for variables that may modify the relationship between individual differences in intelligence and what is learned in the schools is to examine the influence of curriculum innovations on the relationship between intelligence and education. Cronbach & Snow (1977) presented a comprehensive review of studies of the relationship between individual differences in the characteristics of learners and variations in instructional methods. Their review of the literature was designed to provide evidence for the importance of what they called "aptitude × instructional interactions." Such interactions would be manifested by the discovery of a statistically significant interaction between student characteristics and instructional methods. This type of research attempts to determine if there are different instructional methods that are optimal for learners with different personal characteristics. The ultimate goal of this research from an applied point of view would be the assignment of individuals to instructional programs that are optimal for the learner. Cronbach and Snow's comprehensive review of the literature available to them led them to several generalizations about the importance of general intellectual ability in determining the outcome of education. They concluded their survey as follows:

> We once hoped that instructional methods might be found whose outcomes correlate very little with general ability. This does not appear to be a viable hope. Outcomes from extended education almost always correlate with pretested ability unless a ceiling is artificially imposed.
> The pervasive correlations of general ability with learning rate or outcomes limit the powers of ATI findings to reduce individual differences. [Cronbach & Snow, 1977, p. 500]

Note that this statement implies that the optimal basis for individualizing the curriculum based on individual differences among learners is knowledge of the learner's general intelligence rather than knowledge of the learner's specific ability scores. Learners of high general ability appear to outperform learners of low general ability under virtually all instructional contexts. It is also the case that there are many examples of aptitude × instructional interactions involving general intelligence. These interactions are virtually never disordinal. That is, they do not lead to a modification in the expectation of superior academic achievement for learners with high intelligence. What the interactions usually indicate is that there are instructional programs that can benefit low-ability learners, thereby decreasing the slope of the regression line relating general ability to achievement. There are also instructional programs that impede the progress of low-ability learners without decreasing the performance of high-ability individuals. The instructional programs that benefit low-ability learners may be described as those that provide students with structured information that relieves them of the burden of organizing materials for themselves. High-ability learners appear to benefit most from instructional programs that provide them with an opportunity to develop their own organizational structures (see Snow & Yalow, 1982).

There are many studies reviewed by Cronbach and Snow that provide evidence for these general statements (see also Snow and Yalow, 1982). Snow (1980) described a study by Sharpe that provides evidence of an interaction between measures of fluid and crystallized ability and instructional methods. Sharpe compared the performance of pupils in conventional classrooms with pupils assigned to IPI classrooms. IPI is a system of individually paced instruction relying on specific pretests of knowledge with frequent feedback to learners about their progress in accomplishing specifically described objectives. Also mastery tests are used to assess student progress. Sharpe found that pupils who scored low in crystallized ability benefited from IPI instruction; pupils who scored high in crystallized ability performed better in conventional classrooms than in IPI classrooms. The results for fluid ability were not significant, although he did find that pupils with high fluid ability performed better in conventional classrooms than in IPI classrooms.

The data obtained by Sharpe are similar to other examples of aptitude × instructional ability interactions that are reported in the literature. Note that the interactions obtained in this study involve interactions between measures of general intelligence and instructional methods. Variations in instructional outcomes associated with variations in general intelligence are present under both instructional programs investigated in this study—the innovative educational treatment did not eliminate the advantage associated with high intelligence. Or, to put the matter differently, the interactions were not disordinal leading to a condition in which high intelligence was not advantageous to the learner. The attempt to provide a more structured learning environment benefited learners with low ability. The structured learning environment produced a shallow slope relating an index of general intellectual ability to academic performance.

Bloom (1974, 1984) proposed that the relationship between general intelligence and what is learned in the schools could be reduced by the use of mastery learning procedures (see Block & Anderson, 1975). He noted that IQ tests scores are correlated with the time required to learn material presented to pupils. In the typical learning environment created in the public schools, times are allocated to the mastery of academic material that are not sufficient to permit slow learners with low IQ to master the material that is presented to them. In a typical elementary school classroom different students may be allocated times to learn that have a ratio of longest to shortest time of 3:1. The ratio of time required to master academic material in a typical classroom may be 5:1. Therefore, under ordinary instructional programs slow learners are not allocated a sufficient amount of time to master the curriculum of the schools. They are presented with new material before they have mastered the previous material, leading to the development of cumulative deficits. Bloom advocated the use of mastery learning procedures in order to solve this problem. Mastery learning permits pupils to have a sufficient amount of time to master material before being exposed to new material. Bloom argued that under mastery learning procedures pupils do not develop cumulative deficits. In addition, he asserted that slow learners exposed to mastery learning learn to learn more rapidly. After mastery learning experiences the ratio of time required to exhibit mastery for slow and rapid learners may be decreased to 1.5:1. These changes permit a larger percentage of students to master the curriculum of the public schools. And, the decrease in the time required to attain mastery leads to a decrease in the correlation between intelligence and the time required to master the curriculum. Note that Bloom does not claim that mastery learning procedures will eliminate the advantage that high-IQ pupils have over low-IQ pupils in attaining mastery of the curriculum of the schools. But the importance of IQ as a determinant of what is learned will be reduced.

Slavin (1987) reviewed research on mastery learning. He noted that studies reporting dramatic improvements as a result of the institution of mastery learning procedures were of very short duration. For studies of longer duration (4 or more weeks) there was no beneficial effect of mastery learning using standardized tests as criterion measures. For teacher-made testing, mastery learning was found to have small benefits of approximately .25 standard deviations compared to regular instructional procedures. In addition, he found that there was very little evidence of the claims made by Bloom that the time taken to master material decreased for slow learners, leading to a reduction in the ratio of times required to master material from slowest to fastest students. As a result, it was difficult to implement Bloom's educational procedures for long periods of time in the classroom. If students who learned rapidly were given new material as they mastered previous material and students who learned slowly were given a sufficient amount of time to master material before being introduced to new material, the range of materials being taught within a nonhomogeneously grouped classroom became very large and was difficult for teachers to manage. While mastery learning procedures may be useful for slow learners by providing a sufficient amount of time for them, thereby giving them success experiences and preventing the development of cumulative deficits, they clearly are not a panacea for eliminating individual differences. Indeed, the frequent use of mastery tests to assess pupil progress may actually impede the progress of rapid learners.

We briefly examined research in ordinary educational settings that evaluates attempts to reduce the influence of general intelligence on the outcomes of education. There are also studies dealing with populations that are assumed to be at special risk for school failure that are designed as interventions that will lead to more satisfactory educational outcomes for samples that are assumed to be at risk. Many of these projects are designed as educational interventions for black students attending schools in low-income urban areas (see Slavin, Karweit, & Madden, 1989, for a review of evaluation research on such programs). Few of these programs have been rigorously evaluated and their long-term effectiveness is, for the most part, yet to be documented. Chapter 6 of this book reviewed research reports from a consortium to evaluate longitudinal studies of Headstart programs for comparable populations. Recall that the review of that research indicated that such programs failed to produce sustainable increases in general intelligence and also failed to lead to long-term improvements in the educational achievement of pupils. A good example of an evaluation of a recently instituted intervention program is contained in an article published by Slavin, Madden, Karweit, Livermon, & Dolan (1990). They designed an intervention called "Success for All" that was instituted in the first three grades of an elementary school with a predominantly black pupil population in Baltimore. The intervention consisted in part of the use of certified reading teachers to provide one-to-one tutoring for children who developed problems in reading. In addition, there was a family support team that provided assistance to the parents of the pupils. At the end of the school year a battery of tests was used to assess pupil progress. The performance of pupils in this school was compared to the performance of pupils in a matched elementary school. California Achievement Tests of reading comprehension were .11, .23, and .63 standard deviations higher in the first, second, and third grades, respectively, in the experimental school after a 1-year exposure to the intervention. The mean performance on a battery of tests designed to assess specific reading skills as well as overall reading comprehension of the experimental school pupils exceeded the mean performance of the control group school pupils by .48, .22, and .81 standard deviations in the first, second and third grades, respectively.

The Slavin et al. (1990) study does not indicate whether the advantages associated with the introduction of professional tutors in the classroom are cumulative or sustainable. The effects do not appear to be large at the first and second grade levels for measures of reading comprehension, but they are moderately high at the third grade level. It is also interesting to note that the effects were larger on comprehensive batteries that included measures of specific reading skills than on a general measure of reading comprehension. It may be that such interventions are useful to provide relatively specific skills but are less helpful in improving higher-level understanding.

Palincsar & Brown (1984) reported the results of an educational intervention study designed to improve reading comprehension. They selected seventh grade pupils with adequate decoding skills who were approximately 2.5 years delayed in grade level performance on measures of reading comprehension. A subset of six of these pupils with IQs ranging from 67 to 99 (mean IQ = 83) were assigned to a reciprocal teaching intervention in which they were provided with instructions in the skills of summarizing, questioning, clarifying, and predicting the contents of reading passages for 30-minute sessions for a 20-day period. The students were instructed in groups of two and were required to lead the session in addition to being exposed to the expert modeling of these skills by teachers. Considerable evidence is provided in the report of this study that these students developed progress in the skills they were taught and practiced in the intervention. Their performance improved relative to control groups on probes of these skills when presented with new materials. Records of dialogue between teachers and learners demonstrated clear progress in the ability to summarize and predict the contents of reading programs. The skills acquired were present on the tests taken 2 months after the intervention. And, they exhibited evidence of an ability to generalize the skills they had acquired to the task of detecting incongruities in textual passages.

The Palincsar and Brown study may be considered as a demonstration of the possibility of intervention with children of moderately low IQ who are not able to comprehend text adequately. Although the Palincsar and Brown study provides clear evidence of a successful educational intervention, there are a number of respects in which the study demonstrates the limitations of the current "state of the art" in successful educational interventions. The results of the intervention were replicated in a second sample in which the pupils were reciprocally taught by teachers rather than by the researchers. While there may be doubts about the feasibility of large-scale interventions employing these techniques, let us assume that the gains reported by these teachers could be obtained for poor readers in any classroom. Even if this were true, there are a number of significant limitations and unresolved issues relevant to evaluating the intervention. First, the duration of the effects of the change is unknown. The posttest occurred only 2 months after the end of the intervention and the long-term effects of the intervention are not known. Second, the generalization probes, while demonstrating some ability to use the skills acquired with new texts in different contexts and to transfer these skills to related skills, are relatively limited. For example, no demonstration is made that the skills transfer to an ability to detect incongruities in mathematical word problems or to summarize lecture material. To assert this is not to denigrate the impressive utility of what was learned by the pupils but merely to indicate that the generalized skills that characterized the intellectual difference between high- and low-IQ pupils were not eliminated by the intervention used in this study. Third, although there was clear evidence of the development of new skills that were maintained and transferred to novel context in this study, the magnitude of the changes in more generalized skills may have been modest. On tests of ability to transfer the specific skills that were acquired of summarizing and predicting questions, subjects assigned to the control groups were approximately 1.9 and 1 standard deviations lower in performance on these skills, respectively, than students assumed to have normal comprehension skills. Subjects assigned to the reciprocal teaching groups had gained approximately 1.5 and 1 standard deviation units relative to the control groups on these transfer tests, respectively. Thus a substantial portion of the deficit exhibited in these skills was substantially eliminated. On the other hand, on a general test of reading comprehension, subjects assigned to the reciprocal teaching intervention exhibited an average gain of 15 months of progress. They began the study approximately 2.5 years behind in general reading comprehension and, assuming some gain in reading comprehension of normal students over the duration of the intervention, less than half of the deficit of these pupils on general reading comprehension that defined their selection for this intervention had been eliminated. The standard deviation of grade equivalents on the reading comprehension test was not provided, but a reasonable estimate of the standard deviation suggests that the gains for the six subjects assigned to the reciprocal teaching interventions for whom these data are provided was approximately .5 standard deviation. And, the enduring effects of the gains in this intervention are unknown.

The Palincsar and Brown study provides a good demonstration of the utility of a particular type of educational technique that can provide students with some useful skills. At the same time, when examined critically, it also demonstrated some of the limitations of our current effort to remediate the generalized learning deficits that are characteristic of individuals with moderate general intelligence who are at risk to demonstrate inadequate academic achievement.

There is a ubiquitous relationship between general intelligence and educational achievement. Our brief review of some representative intervention studies indicated that there is relatively little evidence that the relationship between intelligence and academic achievement is substantially modifiable using present instructional interventions. The discussion of the cross-cultural differences in mathematical achievement indicated that it is possible in principle to design educational interventions that will improve the overall performance of children in the public schools. There is relatively little evidence that such interventions will dramatically decrease the variability of indices of academic achievement. Nor are they likely to decrease the relationship between individual differences in intelligence and such indices.

Although IQ test scores predict academic achievement, they may be of little use in creating optimal instructional programs. They may be of some use in selecting students who are likely to benefit from accelerated and individualized experiences in the schools. IQ tests may be useful for generalized assignment to broadly different curricula. They are probably useless in designing a specific instructional program for a student. Anyone attempting to teach a person a specific skill needs to understand the specific knowledge and skills of the learner. Consider two opposite scenarios involving the relationship between IQ and performance at a particular academic task. Suppose a person with a high IQ performs poorly. A teacher could inform the learner that he or she has high IQ and is therefore capable of learning. This assertion provides little information to the learner and does not provide a diagnostic understanding of the deficiencies in the learner's performance. Suppose a learner with low IQ had adequately performed a task. Should the teacher inform the learner that he or she has violated the rules of psychological theory? The learner's ability to master academic material even though he or she is "not intelligent" and hence, by definition, "not able" to learn is an intellectual embarrassment. Knowledge of a person's IQ score in such a circumstance is useless. It is apparent that knowledge of an IQ test score is of little or no value to a teacher. IQ test scores may not even be an optimal basis for the assignment of individuals to broadly different curricula. Even though there is ample evidence that IQ does predict general academic performance, assignments of individuals to educational programs based on IQ may not be as valid as the assignment of individuals based on actual academic performance. Consider a hypothetical choice for the selection of a student for a class for "gifted" students. Assume that such a class will provide an enriched and accelerated academic program. Assume further that you are faced with a choice of selecting a student with relatively low IQ and excellent academic skills and performance or a student with relatively high IQ and a poor record of academic performance and relatively inadequate knowledge of the curriculum. In most circumstances it would probably be more rational to select the former than the latter student. There is little reason to use the predictive index in place of a measure of actual academic performance that serves as the validating criterion for the index. The criterion is probably superior to the measure that predicts the criterion.

This discussion suggests that IQ may not be particularly useful as an index to individualize instruction or to assign individuals to different instructional tracts. I believe that an end of the use of IQ tests in the schools would have little or no impact on education. The removal of the tests would not reduce the influence of the ubiquitous individual differences that influence academic achievement. Removing the tests would remove a tangible symbol of the pervasive importance of individual differences in academic achievement. The educational and social problems associated with those differences would remain after the tests are re-moved. In short, the tests do not create the problem, they merely are one way of informing us about the nature of the problem.

INTELLIGENCE AND OCCUPATIONS

Intelligence and the number of years of education that a person obtains are positively correlated. Occupational status and the number of years of education required for job entry into occupations of different status are positively correlated. This implies that intelligence test scores and oc-cupational status are positively correlated. Harrell & Harrell (1945) ob-tained IQ scores for white military recruits in World War II and related these scores to their civilian occupations. They found that the mean IQ for different occupations increased monotonically with the amount of formal education required for job entry. For example, they found that the highest mean IQs for their recruits were for individuals with civilian job classifications of accountant, lawyer, and engineer (IQ means of 128.1, 127.6, and 125.8, respective). The lowest mean IQs were for individuals with civilian occupations of farmhand, miner, and teamster (mean IQs of 94, 92, and 89, respectively). They also found that the range and standard deviation of the IQs of individuals were inversely related to the mean IQ of individuals in different occupations. For example, the range and stan-dard deviation of individuals with the civilian occupation of accountant were 94–157, S.D. = 11.7. The comparable numbers for individuals with the civilian occupation of teamster were 46–145 and 19.6. These data indicate that individuals with low IQs are not likely to be found in high-status occupations that require high levels of formal education as a condi-tion for entry into the occupation.

These analyses indicate that IQ and occupational status are related. Is intelligence related to success within an occupation? Ghiselli (1966, 1973) summarized studies relating general intelligence to job perfor-mance. He concluded that the correlations between general intelligence and job performance are frequently low and that they vary considerably and often in unpredictable ways from study to study. Hunter & Hunter (1984) used meta-analyses to reanalyze the studies examined by Ghiselli as well as other relevant data bases. They indicated that some of the variability in correlations relating intelligence to indices of job perfor-mance was attributable to statistical variability derived from the use of relatively small samples in several of the studies. The use of meta-analy-ses permits one to obtain estimates of the relationship between intel-ligence and indices of job performance that are not subject to large errors of estimate. Hunter and Hunter do not report specific statistical tests for the heterogeneity of effect size statistics in these various estimates. They asserted that there is little indication of statistically significant heterogeneity of correlations for different studies in their sample. Hunter and Hunter also indicated that where the necessary information was available, they corrected correlations for restrictions in range of talent in IQ and for unreliability of tests and criterion measures. For example, many of the studies relating IQ to job performance use supervisor ratings. They assumed that .80 was an upper-bound estimate of the reliability of supervisor's ratings. Table 9.3 presents the results of their reanalysis of Ghiselli's data relating indices of general intelligence to indices of job performance in different occupations. An examination of the reported correlations indicates that they range from .27 to .61. The correlations below .40 occur for jobs that are described by Hunter and Hunter as being low in complexity of intellectual demands. Hunter and Hunter estimated that the mean corrected correlation between IQ and measures of supervisor-rated job competence for various positions is .53. This estimate is based on 425 correlations obtained from over 30,000 subjects. Note that this is a corrected correlation with corrections for unreliability of measurement and restrictions in range of talent in the ability characteristics of applicants for positions. They also indicated that intelligence is related to indices of performance on the job that are used for promotion or certification of adequate job performance. They estimated that the correlation between these measures is .53. These correlations have relatively large standard deviations ($r = .15$), indicating that in any particular study, the corrected correlation between an ability index and a measure of job performance is likely to have a value that is deviant from the population value of .53. These data indicate that intelligence is a reasonably good predictor of performance in many different occupations.

It should be noted that the meta-analyses reported by Hunter and Hunter are based on correlations that are corrected values. These correc-

TABLE 9.3 Validity Correlations for Predicting Success in Different Occuaptions[a]

Job families	Mean validity			Beta weight		
	Cog[b]	Per	Mot	Cog	Mot	r
Manager	.53	.43	.26	.50	.08	.53
Clerk	.54	.46	.29	.50	.12	.55
Salesperson	.61	.40	.29	.58	.09	.62
Protective professions worker	.42	.37	.26	.37	.13	.43
Service worker	.48	.20	.27	.44	.12	.49
Trades and crafts worker	.46	.43	.34	.39	.20	.50
Elementary industrial worker	.37	.37	.40	.26	.31	.47
Vehicle operator	.28	.31	.44	.14	.39	.46
Sales clerk	.27	.22	.17	.24	.09	.28

[a]Based on Hunter & Hunter (1984).

[b]Cog, general cognitive ability; Per, general perceptual ability; Mot, general psychomotor ability; r, multiple correlation. Mean validities have been corrected for criterion unreliability and for range restriction.

tions are appropriate for theoretical purposes. The corrected data indicate that over a wide range of occupations, IQ accounts for approximately 25% of the variance of performance in a job as typically assessed by supervisors. These correlations may also be considered as indices of predictive validity. Here, the corrections may provide a distorted perspective on the value of IQ tests as a basis for personnel decisions and the selection of individuals for different jobs. Hunter and Hunter do not present uncorrected correlations in their paper. Corrections for restrictions in range may be inappropriate since the applied decision maker is confronted with the task of selecting individuals from a pool of applicants. The undoubtedly correct assertion that the correlation between IQ and performance in a job would be larger if the pool included individuals with IQs outside the range of the actual applicant pool is irrelevant to the decision maker unless he or she wishes to change the nature of the applicant pool to sample more widely from different IQ ranges. The corrections for attenuations are also problematic. The correction for unreliability of IQ scores is of little relevance to the applied decision maker since he or she never has a perfectly reliable index of intelligence available—only an actual score. So, too, the correction for unreliability of the criterion is also problematic. While supervisor ratings or any other measure of job performance are undoubtedly imperfect indices of a hypothetically pure measure of job performance, the inability to obtain an error-free measure might be interpreted as indicating that corrections for attenuation of criterion measures lead to selection of individuals who will outperform unselected individuals in ways that are not readily measured. In summary, these correction may overestimate the utility of the use of IQ tests for selection purposes. These comments should not be construed as arguing against the use of tests of general ability in selection situations. Hunter and Hunter presented a strong argument that such tests are as predictively valid as any readily available alternative. Perhaps what is important in these data is not the particular value of a corrected or an uncorrected validity coefficient relating IQ scores to job performance, but the apparent demonstration that IQ scores relate to many different kinds of job performance.

OTHER CORRELATES OF INTELLIGENCE

Individual differences in intelligence have been related to many different characteristics of individuals (see Brand, 1987, for a list of possible correlates of IQ scores). In many of these studies controls for social class are not used. It is difficult to know if IQ has an influence on some characteristic that is independent of various indices of social privilege. There is no literature assessing the influence of IQ on social behaviors that approaches the methodological sophistication and empirical adequacy of the studies we have reviewed relating IQ, education, and social class to occupational status and occupational mobility. There is, however, evidence that criminality and delinquency may be related to intelligence and that this relationship is not solely attributable to social class influences.

Intelligence and Criminality

There is a relationship between IQ and criminality and juvenile delinquency (Hirschi & Hindelang, 977). This relationship may be explained in different ways. Individuals who are officially classified as juvenile delinquents are more likely to be apprehended than individuals who commit crimes but are not apprehended. Intelligence may be related to the probability of being apprehended. It is possible that intelligence is unrelated to the probability of committing a crime but is inversely related to the probability of being apprehended for a crime that is committed. One argument against this interpretation of the relationship between intelligence and criminality is that it holds for self-reported incidences of criminal behavior as well as for officially recorded criminal behavior. Of course it could be argued that intelligence is related to the willingness to report that one has engaged in criminal behavior. A second explanation of the relationship between criminal behavior and intelligence assumes that it is attributable to social class influences. Criminality is related to social class background as is intelligence. This explanation implies that the relationship between intelligence and criminality would disappear if social class were controlled. Hirschi and Hindelang argued that this explanation is unlikely to be correct since the relationship between indices of criminality and intelligence holds among individuals with similar social class backgrounds.

Moffitt, Gabrielli, Mednick, & Schulsinger (1981; see also McGarvey, Gabrielli, Bentler, & Mednick, 1981) obtained records of juvenile criminal behavior from a cohort of Danish individuals born in Copenhagen. Their sample included 4552 males who were selected from their larger cohort who were tall. They had Danish military induction intelligence test scores for this sample as well as information about parental occupation. The correlation between IQ and the number of offenses committed by these subjects was $-.19$ and the partial correlation between IQ and criminality, holding constant socioeconomic status, was $-.17$. West & Farrington (1973) used a prospective design in which they obtained Raven test scores for children at age 8 and studied the incidence of juvenile delinquency for their subjects. They found that individuals who were recidivist juvenile delinquents were more likely to have low IQs than individuals who were either nondelinquent or had only a single incidence of delinquency. These relationships were present even after statistical controls for family income were used.

These results indicate that individual differences in intelligence are weakly related to juvenile delinquency and that this relationship is not solely or predominantly a function of social class background. They leave unresolved the basis for this relationship. It is possible that these relationships, like the relationship between intelligence and occupational status, are mediated by the influence of intelligence on education. That is, individuals with low intelligence are less likely than individuals with high intelligence to be rewarded for their performance in schools and may seek sources of prestige and rewards that are not related to educational performance. I am not aware of any studies that report the relationship between intelligence and criminality that statistically control for educational performance.

Intelligence and Fertility

IQ is related inversely to fertility. This relationship has been of considerable interest to individuals who are concerned with eugenic issues related to differences in reproduction. If individuals with low IQ reproduce at a higher level than individuals with high IQ, it is possible that these differential fertilities will lead to an intergenerational decrease in intelligence. In fact, R. B. Cattell (1936, 1937) predicted such a decrease. We now know that secular changes in intelligence have been associated with an increase rather than a decrease in intelligence and therefore Cattell's predictions were wrong. Nevertheless, they were instrumental in leading to investigations of the relationship between IQ and fertility.

Higgins, Reed, & Reed (1962) argued that the fertility patterns associated with IQ were not necessarily dysgenic (i.e., supportive of a pattern of reproduction in which individuals with genes that are likely to lead to low IQ reproduce at higher levels than individuals with genes likely to lead to high IQ, thereby creating an intergenerational decline in the gene pool with respect to the genetic potential for high IQ). They studied a large sample of individuals who had completed their fertility and they included individuals who had never married and had no children. They found that there was no relationship between IQ and fertility. These results were at odds with earlier studies reporting a negative relationship. The discrepancy in results was attributable to differences in methodology. Previous research had sampled schoolchildren and had related IQ to the number of siblings. These studies excluded individuals who had no offspring. Higgins *et al.* found that low-IQ individuals were less likely to marry than high-IQ individuals and were less likely to reproduce. If one considered the fertility of all members of the population there was little or no effect of IQ on fertility. These results were buttressed by additional data from other samples indicating that individuals with low IQ were more likely to have childless marriages (Bajema, 1971). These data convinced many individuals concerned with this problem that there was little or no relationship between IQ and fertility (Falek, 1971).

Vining (1982) challenged this conclusion. He noted that the samples investigated were not representative. They were white, native-born individuals, and they included cohorts born during a period of rising fertility. Vining argued that the relationship between fertility and IQ might vary for different groups in the U.S. and might vary for different cohorts. Van Court & Bean (1985) reported a comprehensive analysis of cohort effects on the relationship between IQ and fertility in the U.S. They used data collected from national opinion surveys that were assumed to sample representative samples of the U.S. population. These samples were administered a brief vocabulary test and this was used as an index of intelligence. The relationship between fertility and vocabulary scores for different cohorts for representative samples of the white population of the U.S. is presented in Table 9.4. These data indicate that the relationship has been consistently negative for most cohorts born in the twentieth century. This generalization is not valid for cohorts born between 1925 and 1935 whose peak fertility coincided with a period of high fertility.

Van Court and Bean did not have large numbers of nonwhites in their sample. There is data indicating that the relationship between IQ and fertility is different in black and white samples. Vining (1982) obtained high school IQ data from samples of black and white women who were between 24 and 34 in 1978. The samples were representative samples of the U.S. population, although the black sample was oversampled in order to increase the number of black respondents. He also obtained fertility information from these samples. Note that this is not a sample with completed fertility. Therefore, relationships between fertility and IQ in

TABLE 9.4 Correlations between Number of Offspring and Vocabulary Scores for Different Cohorts of the White Population of the U. S.[a]

Cohort	N	r
≤ 1894	91	−.04
1895–1899	120	−.17
1900–1904	195	−.23
1904–1909	273	−.17
1910–1914	307	−.08
1915–1919	363	−.13
1920–1924	424	−.12
1925–1929	364	.00
1930–1934	358	−.03
1935–1939	429	−.16
1940–1944	488	−.17
1945–1949	604	−.24
1950–1954	632	−.22
1955–1959	408	−.21
1960–1964	99	−.22

[a]Based on Van Court & Bean (1985).

TABLE 9.5 Fertility for Black and White Women Differing in IQ[a]

	<71	71–85	86–100	101–115	116–130	>130	All
White women	1.59	1.68	1.76	1.44	1.15	.92	1.46
N	17	122	522	907	438	60	2066
Black women	2.60	2.12	1.79	1.63	1.20	.00	1.94
N	50	165	159	88	10	1	473

[a]Based on Vining (1982).

these samples represent fertility experience up to age 34 and should not be assumed to reflect completed fertility. If high-IQ women have children when they are older than low-IQ women, the relationship between fertility and IQ in Vining's data will be overly negative. And, Vining found that the relationship between expected lifetime number of children (not actual number) and IQ was less negative than the relationship between actual number of children and IQ. Table 9.5 presents Vining's data on the relationship between early fertility for black and white women as a function of their IQ. Note that the relationship is different for black and white women. Fertility is higher in the black sample. The relationship between IQ and fertility appears to be nonlinear for the white sample. Fertility increases and peaks in the 86–100 IQ group and then declines as IQ increases. In the black sample fertility is a monotonically decreasing function of IQ, with the highest fertility occurring for women with IQs below 85. Since parental IQ is related to children's IQ, these data, if extrapolated, suggest that the difference in fertility patterns may contribute to intergenerational increases in the magnitude of the black–white difference in IQ test score. It should be noted that there is no evidence of such an increase (see Chapter 10). And, it is entirely possible that changes in opportunities available to black people in the U.S. may prove of greater significance in changing the relationship between black and white performance on IQ tests than differences in fertility rates for individuals with different IQs. In this connection it should be noted that Van Court and Bean's data suggest that the IQ–fertility relationship for most of the twentieth century has been dysgenic. Nevertheless, IQ has exhibited secular increases.

CONCLUSION

This chapter briefly reviewed data indicating that general intelligence is related to a variety of socially relevant indices. There appears to be little doubt that a person's score on a test of general intelligence is an important index of a person's behavior in a variety of contexts. It is difficult to think of any other single index that is as widely predictive or as predictive of socially important outcomes. And, it is clear that the predictability of IQ test scores is not solely or even predominantly attributable to the correlation between IQ and social class background. IQ tests index a characteristic of persons that is substantially independent of their social class background.

10

GROUP DIFFERENCES IN INTELLIGENCE

In what ways do race and gender influence performance on tests of intelligence?

BLACK–WHITE DIFFERENCES

Description

The study of racial differences in intelligence is as old as the study of individual differences in intelligence. Galton (1869) believed that there were racial differences in intelligence and that these differences were attributable to genetic differences between the races. There is a 1-standard-deviation difference in IQ between the black and white population of the U.S. (Loehlin, Lindzey, & Spuhler, 1975; Shuey, 1966). The black population of the U.S. scores 1 standard deviation lower than the white population on various tests of intelligence. Variations within race are clearly larger than variations between races. Excluding individuals who have very low IQ attributable to neurological damage, the within-race variability on intelligence tests is approximately 10 standard deviations. Thus the ratio of within-group variability to between-group variability in scores on tests of intelligence is large. Jensen (1980a) calculated the percentage of variance attributable to race and social class background on the Wechsler tests for a representative sample of 622 black and 622 white elementary school children in California. His analysis is presented in Table 10.1. Race, with socioeconomic status statistically controlled, accounts for 14% of the variance in IQ scores in this sample. Race and social class combined account for 22% of the variance. Variations within families among children reared together with the same racial and socioeconomic background accounts for 44% of the variance in these data, indicating that variations among individuals with identical socioeconomic backgrounds and racial backgrounds account for more vari-

280

TABLE 10.1 Percentage of Total Variance and Average IQ Difference in
WISC-R Full-Scale IQs Attributable to Each of Several Sources[a]

Source of variance	Variance (%)		Average IQ difference
Between races (independent of SES)	14	} 22	12
Between SES groups (independent of race)	8		6
Between families (within race and SES groups)	29	} 73	9
Within families	44		12
Measurement error	5		4
Total	100		17

[a]Based on Jensen (1980a).

ance in tests of intelligence than either race or socioeconomic status.
These data, which are roughly representative of what has been found in
other studies, indicate that variations in scores on tests of intelligence are
attributable primarily to characteristics of persons that are independent
of their racial and socioeconomic background. Although, in this chapter,
our emphasis shifts from a consideration of individual differences to a
consideration of differences among groups of individuals, it should be
recognized that an individual's performance on a test of intelligence is
never defined or predictable from his or her group identity. Research on
intelligence, properly considered, should invariably serve as an antidote
to stereotypes.

The 1-standard-deviation difference in IQ is magnified in importance
and visibility when IQ, or variables that are proxies for IQ, is used as a
basis of selection of individuals. The IQ distributions of black and white
populations overlap and approximately 16% of the black population, assuming normal curve statistics as a roughly accurate representation of the
underlying distributions, will have IQ scores that are above the white
mean. The ratio of white to black individuals at different points of the
distribution will vary widely. If IQ scores below 70 are used as a basis for
assigning individuals to special education classes, this IQ score for white
samples will be 2 standard deviations below the white mean, and it will
be 1 standard deviation below the black mean; and the ratio of white to
black individuals at or below the score of 70 will be approximately 1 to 7.
Therefore, if performance on IQ scores were the sole criterion for assignment to special education classes, the ratio of white to black individuals
assigned would be 1 to 7. Differences in ratios of individuals of different
races at different points of the IQ distribution become increasingly different at increasingly more extreme cutting points in the distribution. For

example, the ratio of white to black individuals with IQs above 115 is approximately 7 to 1, and the comparable ratio of individuals with IQs above 130 is almost 18 to 1. If individuals are selected for social roles such as admission to graduate schools or selective colleges that rely on high scores on IQ tests or variables that are highly correlated with IQ, the ratio of white to black individuals who meet selective admissions requirements will be above 1, and the size of the ratio will be determined by the extremity of the cutting score used. Gottfredson (1987) extended this analysis to a consideration of white to black employment ratios in different occupations and demonstrated that the differences in the ratio of white to black employment in different occupations were predictable from knowledge of the historical differences in the mean IQ of members of the occupation. The higher the average IQ of members of an occupation and the higher the "threshold" IQ for entry into the occupation, the higher the white to black ratio of employment in the occupation. These analyses clarify the social significance of a 1-standard-deviation difference in IQ between the black and white populations of the U.S. Although race is not highly predictive of IQ, IQ, or variables that are correlated with IQ, is correlated with entry into various social roles. And, for those social roles that have traditionally used IQ-related criteria restricting entry to individuals whose IQ scores are at the extremes of the distribution, there will be a large difference in per capita ratios of black and white individuals meeting the entry requirements. Thus the difference in IQ becomes socially visible and relevant to decisions about affirmative action.

Black–white differences in intelligence appear to have remained constant for several decades. Shuey (1966) calculated differences in individual IQ test performance for black and white schoolchildren tested before 1945 and between 1945 and 1965 and obtained a mean difference of 14 points for both periods. These means represent findings from over 300 studies. Loehlin et al. (1975) estimated black–white IQ differences for military recruits tested in World War I, World War II, and the Vietnam War. They estimated white–black mean differences in IQ of 1.16, 1.52, and 1.52 standard deviation units for these three wars, respectively. These data indicate that the differences have not declined. The results are complicated by different recruitment procedures and different tests. Nevertheless, these results provide little or no basis for assuming that the difference is diminishing. The secular changes in IQ that we considered in Chapter 6 have not diminished black–white differences in IQ. This implies that both the black and the white population of the U.S. have increased IQ at approximately the same rate over the last seven decades.

The black–white difference in IQ appears to be relatively constant over large segments of the life span. Although these differences are not present on the Bayley scales administered between 1 and 15 months of age (Bayley, 1969), the Bayley and other infant tests administered during the first year of life are not correlated with later IQ. Fagan & Singer (1983) found that black and white infants were not significantly different on tests of infant recognition memory that are predictively related to early childhood IQ. They demonstrated that a test of novelty preference administered to infants at 7 months of age was predictive of IQ at age $3\frac{1}{2}$ for both white and black children in their sample. The early childhood IQ test exhibited the usual black–white difference in performance. There were no black–white differences in performance on the novelty recognition task. The black infants scored slightly but not significantly better than the white infants on this measure. The black sample was small ($N = 16$) and the study requires replication. Taken at face value, these data suggest that there are no black–white differences on the earliest indices of information processing or novelty preference that are predictive of early childhood IQ. Therefore, the black–white difference in IQ most probably develops sometime after the first year of life.

Racial differences in IQ are clearly present prior to school entry. Broman et al. (1975) obtained a 1-standard-deviation difference on the Binet test for large samples of black and white children tested for the Collaborative Perinatal Project. Montie & Fagan (1988) obtained a 1-standard-deviation difference between white and black samples of 3 year olds on the Stanford–Binet. Jensen (1971) administered the Raven and the Peabody test to black and white students attending Berkeley elementary schools. He found that the black–white difference in performance on these tests varied on each of the tests over grades. The changes were not consistently related to age. There was no evidence of a systematic change in the magnitude of the black–white difference over the elementary school years. Gordon (1984) reviewed studies of the test–retest stability in IQ for black samples and found that there was, with the possible exception of Jensen's research on cumulative deficits discussed in Chapter 6, little or no evidence of a cumulative decline over the school-age years. The lack of evidence of a systematic increase or decrease in these differences suggests that the magnitude of black–white differences in performance on tests of intelligence does not change over the elementary school years. Data for high school age samples (see Shuey, 1966) and data for military recruits suggest comparable black–white IQ differences through the young adult period. Although we need more data about early childhood differences in IQ and data about performance on infant indices, the available data are compatible with the assertion that the black–white difference is present somewhere before the third year of life and remains more or less constant through the adult life span at approximately 1 standard deviation.

The black–white difference in performance on various tests of intelligence is not constant for different types of measures of intelligence. Loehlin et al. (1975) reviewed studies on profile differences between black and white samples and found that the results were somewhat inconsistent, although several studies indicate that the black samples tend to do somewhat better on tests of verbal ability than on tests of spatial and numerical reasoning (see Lesser, Fifer, & Clark, 1965; Stodolsky & Lesser, 1967). Jensen & Reynolds (1982) analyzed data for the national standardization sample of WISC-R. They studied black–white differences in performance on the Weschsler subtests with mean differences in full-scale scores partialled out. They found that the black sample exceeded the white sample on the Arithmetic and Digit Span subtests that load on the memory factor. The white samples were superior to the black samples on Comprehension, Block Design, Object Assembly, and Mazes. The latter three subtests are good markers for a spatial ability factor. These results suggest that the largest black–white differences in tests of ability will be obtained on spatial ability measures.

Jensen (1985a) proposed that the black–white difference on various tests of intelligence is predictable from knowledge of the g loading of the test. The more g loaded the test, the larger the black–white difference in favor of whites. Jensen called this the Spearman hypothesis since it is derived from a suggestion by Spearman. He distinguished between strong and weak forms of the hypothesis. The strong form of the hypothesis states that g constitutes the sole basis for differences in black–white performance on various tests of intelligence. The weak form of the hypothesis states that the differences are correlated with g, but that g is not the sole basis of the difference. The strong form of the hypothesis is contradicted by the data cited above reported by Jensen and Reynolds (1982). There are differences in subscale scores between black and white samples after removing the influence of full-scale IQ scores. The control for full-scale IQ may be interpreted as a control for g. Black–white differences in the residual variance on tests imply that some of the black–white difference in performance on IQ tests is attributable to factors other than g. Jensen was able to find 11 data sets that permitted him to test the Spearman hypothesis. For each of these data sets, black and white samples were administered a battery of tests. Jensen factor analyzed the tests separately for black and white samples and used these factor scores to derive a g loading for each test in each battery in the data set. He also obtained a measure of the black–white difference for each test in each data set expressed in terms of standard deviation units. He correlated the mean race difference scores with the g loadings of each test for each of the 11 samples. The correlation averaged over all of the data was .59. The tests with the highest g loadings had a white–black mean difference of 1.00 standard deviation for g loadings derived from a factor analysis of the scores of the black samples and .95 for g loadings derived from the white samples. (It should be noted that the factor structures of the tests and the g loadings of the tests derived from black and white samples were virtually identical.) The comparable differences for tests with the lowest g loadings in the studies were .59 and .55.

Jensen's results suggest that the magnitude of black–white differences on different tests of ability will be dependent on differences in the g loadings of the tests and differences in the tests loading on residual factors after g variance is removed. Of the two sources of individual differences, the former is more important than the latter. Jensen indicated that variations in g accounted for seven times more variance than variations in residual group factors in accounting for black–white differences in performance on the national standardization data for the WISC test analyzed by Jensen and Reynolds.

Naglieri & Jensen (1987) used the Spearman hypothesis to analyze claims that the Kaufman Assessment Battery for children (Kaufman & Kaufman, 1983a, b) yielded smaller black–white differences in intelligence than other standard intelligence tests. They tested a sample of black and white elementary school children who were matched for socioeconomic status on both the WISC and the Kaufman batteries. They found that the white sample had a WISC IQ that was .435 standard deviation units higher than the black sample. The comparable difference on the Kaufman total score was .317. They factor analyzed both tests together and obtained the g loadings of all of the subtests. The correlation between the g loadings of the tests and black–white differences on the tests was .78. Several of the g loadings of subtests included in the Kaufman battery were low. The factor analyses of these two tests clearly indicate that the non-g variance of the Kaufman tests is larger than the non-g variance of the WISC. The smaller black–white difference on the Kaufman test is entirely attributable to the use of tests that are less likely to be good measures of g. Blacks perform better than whites on tests of memory after the removal of g. It is possible to construct a test that will minimize the black–white difference in intelligence by using many subtests that are good markers for memory ability factors. The black–white difference in intelligence may be increased by the use of subtests that are good markers for spatial ability factors. These changes in the composition of subtest batteries on omnibus tests of intelligence may lead to changes in the magnitude of the black–white differences on the test without changing the underlying black–white difference in general intelligence. Naglieri and Jensen's analysis clearly demonstrates that the magnitude of the black–white difference in general intelligence is the same on the WISC and the Kaufman test even though the latter test leads to smaller differences than the former test.

I criticized the analyses reported by Jensen in favor of the Spearman hypothesis (Brody, 1987). I indicated that several of the studies used by Jensen were based on the WISC and that the Digit Span, Coding, and Tapping subtests of the WISC have relatively low loadings on the general factor and they do not appear to be good measures of abstract reasoning or general intelligence. Their inclusion in tests of intelligence does not constitute evidence that they are in point of fact good measures of intelligence. The inclusion of these tests in the battery may be taken as evidence of an error on the part of the test constructor. When tests whose g loadings are low are removed, the correlation between the g loadings of the remaining tests and the magnitude of the black–white differences on the tests is substantial on only one of the four studies based on the WISC. The correlations ranged from .12 to .16 for loadings based on the black samples and from .16 to .36 for loadings based on the white sample. Similar results were obtained for another of the studies containing tests whose g loadings were very much lower than other tests in the battery. I argued that Jensen's analyses in favor of the Spearman hypothesis were flawed because his results could be obtained by studying any battery of tests that contained good measures of g and other tests that were not measures of intelligence. Since blacks and whites do not differ on any and all cognitive tasks, any mixture of g-loaded tests and non-g-loaded tests would provide evidence for the Spearman hypothesis. I argued that differences in the g loadings of tests were too evanescent and fragile to constitute a dimension on which one could order several tests. Jensen (1987b) criticized my analysis. He indicated that his results were not an artifact of the inclusion of tests whose g loadings were sufficiently low to be considered outliers in the battery of tests. In order to demonstrate that his results held for different portions of the regression analysis, he divided his sample of tests into those that had g loadings above and below the median and found that the correlations between the g loadings of the tests and the black–white difference on tests with above-median g loadings were .33 and .34 for g loadings derived from the black and white samples, respectively. This analysis suggests that Jensen's results are not dependent on the use of tests that are not good measures of intelligence.

One difficulty with the empirical support in favor of Jensen's hypothesis is that the g loadings of the tests are empirically derived and without theoretical rationale. In Chapter 2 Gustafsson's research was reviewed. His analyses using confirmatory factor analyses provide a clear structural model for g. Recall that g is defined by tests of fluid ability such as the Raven. Gustafsson (1985) indicated that most of the tests that had high g loadings in the batteries investigated by Jensen were not tests of fluid ability that, on theoretical grounds, may be assumed to be isomorphic with g. I argued that tests that are presumed to be most g loaded on theoretical grounds do not invariably lead to the largest black–white differences in performance (Brody, 1987). I indicated that the Raven, a test that both Jensen and Gustafsson described as a test that is saturated with g variance, exhibits smaller black–white differences than tests that are not generally considered pure measures of g. For example, in one of the studies cited by Jensen, the black–white difference on the Raven was .91 standard deviation units and the comparable difference on the Peabody was 1.15. The Peabody is usually thought of as a nonculture-reduced measure of verbal ability. It is not a good measure of fluid ability. An optimal test of the Spearman hypothesis would require Jensen to investigate a battery of tests that contains a representative array of tests designed to sample the primary abilities. Gustafsson's analysis of such a battery indicated that the Raven is probably the best available measure of g. The fact that black–white differences are not invariably larger on the Raven than on other measures constitutes evidence against the strong version of Spearman's hypothesis. Given the evidence already obtained by Jensen it is unlikely that a rigorous test of the Spearman hypothesis using a representative battery of tests would provide evidence against the weak version of the hypothesis. The actual value of the correlation between black–white differences in tests and the magnitude of the g loading of tests of intelligence derived from a representative battery of tests remains to be determined.

The Meaning of Differences in Test Scores: Bias in Mental Tests

There is a black–white difference in scores on tests of intelligence. This is not in dispute. In order to evaluate the meaning of the difference in test scores it is necessary to examine the predictive and construct validity of intelligence tests administered to black and white samples. We want to know whether test scores obtained from black and white samples have the same meaning. Or, in somewhat more formal language, whether the nomological network of laws and relations that define the meaning of the test score and justify the inference from score to construct is the same for black and white samples. Or, to put the matter in another way, if I want to infer something about a person on the basis of his or her test score, is it necessary to consider the race of the person whose test score is being examined in order to increase the accuracy of the inference? The definitive discussion of this and related issues is found in Jensen's book, *Bias in Mental Testing* (Jensen, 1980a; see also Reynolds & Brown, 1984).

The most important applied issue with respect to the use of tests is their predictive validity. The relationship between a test score and an external criterion such as grades in school is defined by a regression line between test scores and the criterion that may be described in terms of three parameters—the slope of the regression line, the intercept of the line, and the standard error of estimate of the regression line. If a test is administered to two groups with different mean test scores, a test may be said to be an unbiased predictor if the groups do not differ significantly on any of the three parameters that define the regression line. An unbiased test in the sense defined above will predict the same criterion score for individuals with the same test score belonging to different groups with the same probability of error (I am ignoring issues related to the reliability of the test in this discussion. See Jensen, 1980a, Chapter 9, for a fuller discussion of this issue). Are IQ tests administered to black and white individuals unbiased with respect to their predictive validity?

Jensen reviewed studies relating performance on IQ tests to performance in elementary, secondary school, and colleges. Typically, but not invariably, the criterion was grades, although in some studies a test of academic achievement was used. Considering the diversity of settings, samples, and methods, the studies are remarkably consistent. The results of these investigations may be summarized using two generalizations. (1) The regression lines predicting academic performance for black and white students from tests of intelligence tend to be similar. (2) Where statistically significant differences between black and white regressions occur, they are almost invariably of the form of intercept bias. Where intercept bias exists, it involves an overprediction of performance for black individuals using the regression line derived from white samples. Linn (1973) analyzed bias in predicting college grades for black students from white regression lines on the SAT in 22 colleges. He found that the overprediction was .11, .29, and .45 standard deviation units of grade-point average for black students whose SAT scores were 1 standard deviation below the black mean, at the black mean, and 1 standard deviation above the black mean. The overprediction increased as test scores increased.

Studies of the relationship between intelligence tests and performance in various occupations also provide evidence of approximately equal predictive validity for white and black samples (Hunter, Schmidt, & Hunter, 1979). Where differences exist between regression statistics for black and white samples they are more likely to involve differences in intercepts, with the white intercept being higher than the black intercept. This implies that the use of a regression line derived from a white sample will result in overprediction of the performance of the black sample. Jensen analyzed regression statistics obtained by Ruch (1972) derived from studies comparing the predictive validity of paper-and-pencil tests for criteria of job performance administered to black and white samples. Considering the results of the studies collectively, Jensen's reanalysis indicated that there were significant intercept differences for various job-related criteria in 8 of the 20 studies. Of these, 11 regressions obtained from these 8 studies (some studies had more than one criterion measure) reported higher intercepts for white samples than for black samples and, for one regression, the intercept for the black sample was higher than the intercept for the white sample.

The most comprehensive investigation of the relationship between intelligence test scores and job performance for different racial groups is contained in the ETS–U.S. Civil Service Commission Study (Campbell, Crooks, Mahoney, & Rock, 1973). The study examined performance in three civil service jobs—medical technician, cartographic technician, and inventory management. For each job, a job analysis was prepared and supervisor ratings anchored by job descriptions were obtained. In addition, tests of job knowledge and measures based on work samples of actual performance were obtained. These criteria were predicted by tests selected for each occupation from the French battery of tests of different intellectual abilities. The samples were large, containing 731 white employees in the three job classifications and 168 black employees. There was relatively little difference in predictive validity from tests to criteria for black and white samples. For tests of job knowledge and for measures of work samples (but not for supervisor ratings) the differences that were obtained tended to be in the direction of white samples having higher intercepts than black samples, indicating that the performance of black individuals would be overpredicted from the white regression statistics. Differences between black and white samples on the French test batteries were present for individuals in each of the three job classifications. The differences ranged from .38 to .55 standard deviation units. The black–white differences in performance on tests for individuals holding the same job were also present on measures of job knowledge and work samples. The white samples had a mean that was .43 standard deviation units higher than the black samples on tests of job knowledge. Similarly, the white samples averaged .46 standard deviations higher on the work sample measures than the black samples. The white and black samples had smaller differences in supervisor's ratings. The white samples were .13 standard deviation units higher in ratings than the black samples. These results indicate that black–white differences in performance on aptitude tests may be mirrored by differences in measures of job knowledge and job performance.

This brief review of studies of the predictive validity of tests of intelligence for criteria such as job performance, academic achievement, and college grades indicates that the predictive validity of the tests is comparable for white and black samples.

These data have generated considerable controversy (see Elliot, 1987; Kaplan, 1985; Mercer, 1979, 1984). What do these data tell us about racial differences in intelligence as assessed by tests? Mercer (1984) argued that the findings demonstrating correlations between test scores and performance on achievement tests assessing knowledge of the standard curriculum of the schools is not surprising since the criterion and the tests were measures of the same thing and both reflected the degree of exposure of individuals in different racial groups to the majority culture that is reflected by the tests. She referred to data cited by Jensen (1980a) that indicated that tests of achievement may load as highly on g as tests of intelligence and that they are difficult to distinguish empirically by virtue of the high correlations between them.

Mercer's claim that the correlation between academic achievement and intelligence is attributable to the degree to which black and white individuals are exposed to a common cultural environment is easily refuted. Table 10.1, which is based on data collected by Mercer, indicates that most of the variance on tests of intelligence is attributable to differences within families for individuals of the same race reared in the same home. Whatever determines scores on tests of intelligence and *a fortiori* tests of achievement that are alleged to be measuring the same construct, cannot be solely, or predominantly, degree of exposure to white middle class culture. Mercer is correct in her assertion that it is often difficult to distinguish between tests of ability and tests of achievement. Indeed, on conceptual grounds it is certainly correct to say that all tests of intelligence or tests of ability are tests of achievement since they are measures of intellectual skills that are acquired. It may be correct to infer that individuals have a genotypic ability level that partially determines their phenotype. Indeed, there is good evidence for the existence of genotypes that influence intellectual phenotypes. There are, however, no tests of intelligence that are measures of a hypothetical genotype for intelligence. All existing tests are measures of phenotypes that may be construed as the learned intellectual achievements of an individual. To assert this, however, is not to assert that tests of achievement cannot be conceptually, or empirically, distinguished from tests of intelligence. It is possible to distinguish between these two types of measures in at least four ways. First, confirmatory factor analyses are able to clearly distinguish between fluid and crystallized ability measures and to define a general factor that is isomorphic with fluid ability. This suggests that appropriate factor analyses that include achievement tests with representative ability tests would lead to a hierarchical structure that differentiates between tests of academic achievement and tests of general intelligence that are best defined by tests of fluid ability. Second, tests of ability may be obtained chronologically prior to tests of achievement and used to predict achievements that an individual has not attained. Such chronologically prior predictions exist for tests of infant attention that predict later intelligence and for tests of intelligence that are administered prior to school entry. As we have seen, IQ test scores are predictive of what is learned in schools. It is therefore always possible to administer an IQ test prior to the presentation of some aspect of the curriculum and predict pupils' achievement scores on tests of that material. Third, IQ tests can include items that have quite different contents than tests of achievement. They can even include experimental tests of cognitive processes that are reviewed in Chapters 3 and 4 of this book that on the surface do not appear to reflect the content of achievement tests that are related to the curriculum of the schools. It should be noted, however, that scores on tests of abstract reasoning ability may be influenced by formal schooling as much as if not more than tests that are presumed to directly measure the content of the curriculum. Fourth, behavior—genetic analyses indicate that the heritability of tests of intelligence may be higher than the heritability of tests of achievement (see discussion of the Thompson, Detterman, & Plomin (1991) study in Chapter 9 of this volume).

Achievement and intelligence tests ought to become interrelated if intelligence relates to the acquisition of knowledge as it does. Over a long time period individual differences in intelligence will influence what is learned in the schools, and what is learned in the schools will influence a person's intellectual ability. Measures of achievement and measures of intelligence will become increasingly related. This relationship should not obscure their conceptual and empirical distinctiveness.

Is it possible to eliminate the black–white difference in intelligence test performance by changing the content of the tests? It is possible that items that are included on standard tests may assess information that is more likely to be available to white individuals than to black individuals. The classic example of such an item taken from the Weschsler tests is, "Who wrote Faust?" It is easy to take such an item and argue that it reflects nothing more than access to cultural information that is more readily accessible to individuals with exposure to white middle class culture than black culture. If items with such obvious cultural content are eliminated, would black–white differences in intelligence be eliminated? One of the best studies on this issue was performed by McGurk and reanalyzed by Jensen and McGurk (McGurk, 1953; Jensen & McGurk, 1987). McGurk obtained 226 items from group tests of intelligence and submitted them to a panel of 78 judges who were asked to rank them with respect to the degree to which they were culturally biased. He selected 184 of these items on which there was some evidence of agreement among the judges about the presence or absence of cultural bias and then administered a test of these items to a group of high school students to obtain indices of the difficulty of each item. Using these data he constructed a test consisting of 37 "biased" and 37 "unbiased" items that were matched in difficulty and administered this test to a large sample of black and white high school students. He then selected a sample of white and black students matched on school attended, enrollment in the same school since first grade, and socioeconomic status. McGurk found that the mean black–white differences on the two classes of items were larger on the items rated as noncultural than on the items that were rated as cultural. There was a significant race × item interaction. The results are reported in Table 10.2. These data imply that intuitions about the presence of bias in tests based on an examinations of item contents are not a reliable way of distinguishing among items that are likely to discriminate between members of different racial groups.

Davis and Eels (Eels, 1951) developed a test of intelligence that was designed to be nondiscriminatory. The test consisted of a series of cartoons representing individuals engaged in familiar activities. The test required individuals to answer questions about the activities of individuals depicted in the cartoons. The test did not achieve its purpose. Black–white differences in test scores on the Davis–Eels games were about the same order of magnitude as differences obtained in other tests (Ludlow, 1956).

TABLE 10.2   Black–White Difference in Items Rated as Culture Bound versus Items Rated as Nonculture Bound[a]

Test	White	Black	White − Black
Nonculture bound	15.61 (5.50)	12.61 (4.57)	3.00
Culture bound	10.46 (5.35)	8.99 (4.60)	1.47
Nonculture bound − culture bound	5.15	3.62	1.53

[a]Based on Jensen & McGurk (1987).

Williams (1972, 1974) developed the black intelligence test of cultural homogeneity (BITCH test) to assess knowledge of terms that were likely to be used in black cultural settings. He claimed that the test would be a valid index of the ability to survive in black cultural settings and would permit the computation of a survival quotient. Williams reports that it is a test on which black individuals score higher than white individuals. Scores on the BITCH test are not consistently related to scores on tests of intelligence. Mattarazzo & Weins (1977) reported a correlation of .16 for a white sample of applicants for a police job between BITCH test scores and Wechsler scores. The comparable correlation for the black applicants was −.33. Long & Anthony (1974) used the BITCH test with 30 black students who were assigned to special education classes. They found that all of the students who performed poorly on the WISC performed poorly on the BITCH test and the use of the BITCH test as a basis for assignment of students to special education classes would not have resulted in decisions that were at variance with those reached by use of the WISC. Mattarazzo and Weins found that the black police applicants whose mean IQ was 20 points above the black mean and who had an average of 2.5 years of college education were below the mean of the standardization sample for the BITCH test, who were 16- to 18-year-old high school students. It is clear that the scores on the BITCH test are not related to performance on any existing test of intelligence. The test does measure knowledge of terms and expressions that are more likely to be used in the black cultural community than in the white cultural community. It is not clear if the test may be used to predict anything about black individuals other than their knowledge of distinctive black cultural expressions. Implicit in the effort to develop this test is the assumption that standard tests of intelligence assess knowledge that is available to the white population of the U.S. and that standard tests do not provide useful information about black individuals other than the extent to which they have assimilated the white middle class culture of the U.S. This position discounts the evidence of the predictive validity of intelligence tests since the criterion is as biased as the test and is culturally saturated. Apparently, this view of cultural bias extends to knowledge of those areas of the curriculum that are least obviously relevant to a person's cultural outlook such as science and math. If one believes that it is important for black individuals to be knowledgeable about math and science as well as to study black cultural achievements and to be able to comprehend and analyze literary works of both black and white writers, then the abilities that are assessed by standard intelligence tests are predictively relevant to those cultural attainments. It would be useful to develop an intelligence test that was predictively related to the ability to acquire knowledge that did not exhibit black–white differences in performance. No such test exists. It should be understood that the attack on the validity of tests of intelligence is not only a critique of the tests but a critique of the value of the cultural achievements that are predicted by scores on the test. The view that the criteria predicted by IQ tests are not relevant for black students is explicitly stated by Mercer (1979), who developed a system of assessment that explicitly considers an individual's socioeconomic and racial background and provides additional points to an individual's score on tests to compensate him or her for the effects of impoverished or deviant cultural experiences. Mercer argued that it is unfair to judge the system of assessment that she developed with respect to traditional predictive validity criteria. Oakland (1979) reviewed studies using Mercer's System for Multicultural Pluralistic Assessment (SOMPA) and found that her procedures reduced the predictive validity of test scores for criteria of school achievement. Mercer simply regards this as an irrelevant issue.

Black–white differences in test score might be influenced by the way in which tests are administered. Jensen (1980a, Chapter 12) reviewed studies of the effects of the race of the examiner on racial differences in IQ test performance. He reviewed the results of 16 studies of this issue that he deemed methodologically adequate. For 10 of the 16 studies, there were no effects of the race of the examiner on the magnitude of black–white differences in IQ. The most comprehensive study was performed by Jensen (1974b), who had 8 black and 8 white examiners administer group tests including the Lorge–Thorndike test to 9000 schoolchildren in Berkeley, California. He found no race-of-examiner effect on the nonverbal portion of the test. He did find a 1-point diminution in the magnitude of the black–white difference in verbal IQ when children were tested by examiners of the same race. He also tested a number of children individually. He again found no effects on the nonverbal measure of the Lorge–Thorndike. On the verbal measure of the test, the magnitude of the black–white difference in IQ was increased by 3.2 points when scores were obtained by examiners of the same race as the children they tested. The available data suggest that the race of the examiner is not an important source of differences in test scores between black and white individuals.

It could be argued that race differences in examiners is not as important as class and professional position. Perhaps the race of the examiner is irrelevant if the black examiner occupies a position of authority and acts as a professional. It is possible that black individuals, particularly those from lower class backgrounds, may find the testing situation uncomfortable and this may lead them to perform at less than an optimal level. There are three arguments that may be advanced against this position. First, the Davis–Eels tests were designed to be administered in a relaxed and gamelike manner and we have seen that there was little indication that the magnitude of the black–white difference in performance on tests was diminished by these procedures. Second, the data supporting the Spearman hypothesis indicate that the magnitude of the black–white difference in test scores is in part a function of the g loading of the items on tests. It is hard to reconcile a generalized disposition to perform at a less-than-optimal level with a tendency to exhibit differential performance effects on different types of items. Third, a variant of the second argument may be derived by an examination of studies of digit span. Jensen & Figueroa (1975; see also Gordon, 1984) reported that backward digit span performance was more highly correlated with performance on the WISC than forward digit span performance. The ability to repeat digits in backward order may be interpreted as adding an element of transformational complexity to the simple forward digit span task. The black–white difference is more than twice as large on the backward digit span task as on the forward digit span task. Forward and backward digit span tasks are quite similar with respect to motivational and attentional demands. It is hard to imagine any nonintellective dimension that distinguishes them. The fact that black–white differences are larger on backward than forward digit span suggests that motivation and rapport with examiners is not a significant influence on the magnitude of black–white differences in scores on tests of intelligence.

Black–white differences in test scores might be influenced by the language of the test. There is a distinctive black dialect of English with some degree of grammatical distinctiveness that is spoken by a subset of the black population of the United States. It is possible that dialectical distinctiveness might influence test scores. Quay (1971, 1972, 1974) performed a series of studies in which he had the Stanford–Binet translated into black dialect. He found that variations in the language of the test had little or no influence on the performance of different groups of black children. The means obtained from the standard and dialectically translated versions of the test were comparable and item difficulties for different items were similar. These data suggest that the performance of black children on tests of intelligence is not depressed by their occasional use of a distinctive English dialect.

The difficulty of developing a test of intelligence that is both predictively valid and does not lead to black–white differences in test scores is largely attributable to the discriminating characteristics of items that are used on tests. Jensen (1980a, Chapter 11) reported the results of several studies of black–white differences on items used on tests of intelligence.

He correlated item difficulties on the WISC for samples of 6-, 7-, 9-, and 11-year-old black and white children. The correlation between indices of item difficulty in black and white samples for these four age groups ranged from .88 to .93. These data indicate that items that are difficult for members of one racial group are also difficult for members of the other racial group. The average correlation for these four age groups was .91. Jensen found that the cross-racial item difficulty correlations are higher if correlations were adjusted for differences in average level of performance between the races. In order to accomplish this, he correlated item difficulty scores for white samples with scores obtained from older black samples. The average correlation for three such comparisons of item difficulty between white samples and black samples that were either 1 or 2 years older was .98. These data indicate that adjustments for mental age differences for black and white samples tend to eliminate black–white differences in item difficulties.

Jensen also used analysis of variance procedures to identify possible black–white differences in response to different items on tests of intelligence. The group × item interaction in an analysis of variance can be used to detect items that may be biased in favor of one or another group. The ratio of group differences to the group × item interaction variance may be taken as an index of the relative importance of item biases in a test as a possible basis of group differences in performance on the test. Jensen indicated that for most standard tests of intelligence, the group × item interaction variance is relatively small and cannot account for a substantial portion of the difference in group scores.

The use of group × item interactions as a technique for assessing the possibility that items may not measure the same construct in different groups is not considered an ideal procedure by Jensen (1984). The results obtained may be affected by floor and ceiling effects as well as the possibility that an item may possess different degrees of diagnostic significance in different groups. The technique has been supplanted by newer methods of item response theory (Lord, 1980). These techniques require large samples of approximately 1000 in each of two groups whose item performances are being compared. The techniques involve comparisons of the probability of correct response to an item for individuals in different groups with the same ability. Since the samples are large, small differences in functions relating probability of passing an item to overall performance on the test will lead to statistically significant evidence of biases in items where bias is defined as a difference in the item response curve. Lord (1980) found statistically significant differences in item response characteristics for 38 out of 85 items on the Verbal SAT. Shepard, Camilli, & Williams (1984) found that 7 out of 34 items were biased against black samples in a mathematics test. Shepard (1987) indicated that the term *bias* in this context means only that the test is multidimensional and is a measure of different constructs in different groups. Six of the seven items on which white and black groups differed were word problems. If word problems are considered part of the domain of mathematical competence that is being assessed by the test, the item bias result may be interpreted as indicating that the differences between the groups cannot be expressed in terms of differences on a single dimension but may involve differences on more than one dimension that is being assessed by the item. The effects of eliminating the seven items which were biased against the black sample reduced the black–white difference on this test from .91 to .81 standard deviation units. Gordon (1987) indicated that the reduction of a .1-standard-deviation-unit difference in the black–white test score was exaggerated because Shepard *et al.* did not exclude three items that were biased against white subjects. If these items had been excluded the difference in test scores attributable to the removal of biased items would have been less than .1. Gordon also indicated that many of the studies of item bias use tests of achievement rather than tests of intelligence and he suggested that the former type of test may be more subject to the presence of bias than the latter. This brief review of the item bias literature leads to the following conclusions. Bias in items on standard tests exists if one searches for their presence using large samples and the most sophisticated psychometric techniques. The degree of bias is slight and adjustments for the presence of bias have negligible effects on the magnitude of black–white differences in performance on tests of achievement or tests of ability.

More generally, one can conclude from this review of research on bias in mental testing that the black–white difference in performance on tests of intelligence is not substantially attributable to differences in the construct validity of the tests for black and white samples. The factor analytic studies, item analysis research, and research on the predictive validity of tests suggests that the black–white difference in test scores is substantially attributable to differences in the construct that is assessed by the test.

Reasons for Differences in Test Scores

There are two general hypotheses about the basis for racial differences in intelligence—the genetic and the environmental. The genetic hypothesis was stated by Jensen as follows: ". . . something between one-half and three-fourths of the average IQ difference between American Negroes and whites is attributable to genetic factors, and the remainder to environmental factors and their interaction with the genetic differences" (Jensen, 1973, p. 363). Although Jensen's research since 1973 has been frequently directed to an understanding of racial differences in intelligence, he has not written extensively on the possible genetic basis of black–white differences in intelligence test scores. In 1987, he wrote,

As to the question of a genetic component in the black–white population difference in g, since 1969 I have always considered it a reasonable *hypothesis*, . . . I also consider it highly *plausible* that genetic factors are involved in the present black–white population difference. But plausibility falls far short of the status of a scientific fact. . . . There is as yet no empirical "proof" of this plausible genetic hypothesis of the kind that would be considered as definitive evidence in quantitative genetics. . . . the genetic hypothesis will remain untested in any acceptably rigorous manner for some indeterminate length of time, most likely beyond the lifespan of any present-day scientists. [Jensen, 1987c, p. 376, italics in original]

Jensen's statement about the current status of the genetic hypothesis of black–white differences in intelligence represents the views of the psychologist who is generally considered to be the most sophisticated defender of this position. His current statement of the status of the genetic hypothesis represents, on my reading of his work, a more cautious assessment of the status of the evidence for the hypothesis than that which he advanced in a book written in 1973. In that work he provided three kinds of arguments in favor of the genetic hypothesis. First, he argued that none of the known environmental variables on which the black and white populations of the U.S. differ are of sufficiently large magnitude to account for black–white differences in intelligence test scores. Second, the pattern of differences in test scores supported the hypothesis that differences on tests were predictable from a knowledge of the heritability of the test, suggesting that genetic differences were implicated. Third, test scores exhibited regressions toward racial means. Thus the IQ of the child of a black person with an IQ of 100 would be predicted to be somewhere between an IQ of 100 and the black mean IQ of 85. The predicted IQ of the child of a white person with an IQ of 100 would be expected to be 100. IQs in each case exhibit regressions toward their own means. Brody & Brody (1976) reviewed the evidence and logic of these various claims and indicated that the inference that there was a genetic basis of racial differences in intelligence was deficient on both logical and empirical grounds. In what follows I shall consider what I take to be the basis of Jensen's current thinking about the genetic hypothesis. Since Jensen has written relatively little about his current thinking other than to reaffirm his belief that the genetic hypothesis is plausible it is hard to reconstruct his contemporary thinking about this issue.

I do not know if Jensen still believes that regression arguments provide valid data in favor of the genetic hypothesis. The regression effect is based on the observation that black and white groups regress to their respective mean scores on tests of intelligence. Therefore, the expected value (where the term *expected* is used in the statistical sense of the value that is predicted that will minimize errors of prediction) of the IQ of a black person's sibling, parent, or child whose IQ is above the white mean is lower than the expected value of a white person's sibling, parent, or child with the same IQ. These regression phenomena are compatible with any hypothesis about the basis of black–white differences in performance on tests of intelligence. Regression effects must occur for mathematical reasons whenever a score from which one is predicting is extreme in its distribution. A black person whose IQ score is above the white mean has a score that is more deviant within the distribution of black scores than a white person with the same score in the distribution of white scores. Therefore, regression will be larger in this case for the black person. The phenomenon of differential regressions demonstrates nothing other than the observation that black persons can be considered members of a population that can be distinguished from another population (e.g., whites).

Since Jensen has not discussed regression effects recently I take it that the data that he finds persuasive derive from research of the nature of genetic and environmental influences on intelligence. There are a number of arguments associated with knowledge of the nature of genetic and environmental influences on intelligence that may be advanced in connection with the genetic hypothesis of race differences. Jensen argued that the evidence that intelligence is heritable within black and white groups is compatible with the hypothesis that the between-race difference is also attributable in part to genetic factors. There is little or no doubt that IQ is a heritable trait among white individuals. There is considerably less data on the heritability of IQ in black samples. In their comprehensive review of research on black–white differences in intelligence, Loehlin et al. (1975) were able to find only five studies that contained data relevant to an analysis of heritability of IQ in black samples. And, these studies do not provide ideal data for an analysis of heritability. Jensen (1973) reported data on sibling resemblance for black and white samples. Sibling resemblance does not provide an ideal data set for the computation of heritability indices. Scarr-Salapatek (1971) conducted a twin study in which she obtained comparisons between same-sex and opposite-sex twins for black and white samples. The lack of clear zygosity information detracts from the usefulness of these data. Vandenberg (1969, 1970) and Osborne & Gregor (1968) performed heritability analyses on a very small sample of black twins (32 MZ and 12 same-sex DZ) and reached somewhat different conclusions from each other about differences in heritability between black and white samples. It is obvious that the small DZ sample precludes any realistic analysis of heritability in the black sample. I am aware of only two studies that provide a reasonable basis for analyzing the heritability of intelligence in black samples. Nichols (1970, as reported in Loehlin et al., 1975) obtained correlations of .77 and .52 for a sample of 60 MZ and 84 DZ 4-year-old black twin pairs on the Stanford–Binet. Osborne (1978) administered a battery of tests to a black adolescent sample of 76 pairs of MZ twins and 47 pairs of DZ twins. He also tested a comparison sample of 171 white MZ twin pairs and 133 DZ twin pairs. He obtained several indices of intelligence from his test battery including a mean score and factor scores on verbal and spatial ability factors. On all of his measures of intelligence, the heritability of white and black samples was similar. For example, he obtained a mean score on his battery of 12 tests. The correlation for this measure for black MZ twins was .88 and the comparable correlation among black DZ twins was .51. The corresponding results for MZ and DZ correlations for the white sample were .85 and .62. These data indicate that the heritability of intelligence in the white and black samples was approximately equal. Osborne's data for the black sample are comparable to those reported in many other twin studies using white samples. Osborne's results suggest that intelligence is as heritable within the black population of the U.S. as it is within the white population. It is clear that we need considerably more data on the heritability of intelligence in black samples before we can confidently conclude that there are no differences in heritability between white and black samples. Adoption studies have not been reported for black samples relating the IQ of biological parents to the IQs of their adopted children. Despite the paucity of the available data, it is not unreasonable to conclude that IQ is equally heritable in the white and black populations of the U.S.

Let us assume that heritability for intelligence is equal in black and white populations. Let us assume further that heritability is high in both populations—perhaps even as high as .80, as suggested by Jensen. Do these assumptions imply that the racial difference in intelligence is due to genetic factors? It is easy to answer this question in one word—no. The reason on logical grounds is that the sources of between-group differences may be different from the sources of within-group differences (see Lewontin, 1975; see also MacKenzie, 1980, 1984). Lewontin presented examples from behavior genetic research in which within-group differences are heritable in two groups and between-group differences are entirely attributable to environmental causes. At best, evidence of within-group heritability suggests that it is possible to entertain a genetic hypothesis about between-group differences, but the hypothesis requires independent confirmation. Since black and white individuals are exposed to different environments it is always logically possible to attribute group differences in intelligence to environmental differences. Even if the heritability of intelligence were 1.00 in both groups, it is logically possible that differences between groups would be attributable to environmental sources of variance.

Heritability estimates within groups may provide some basis for an understanding of possible environmental hypotheses about the reasons for black–white differences in intelligence. As the heritability within groups increases, variations within groups on various environmental variables must have decreasing influence on the phenotype. If intelligence were totally heritable within a group, then any source of environmental variability within that group would be ruled out *ipso facto* as a possible basis for explanation of between-group differences in intelligence. Jensen used a variant of this argument to support his view that the racial difference is probably attributable to genetic differences. He argued that the amount of variance accounted for by known environmental variables within groups is too small to explain the between-group differences. This argument hinges on estimates of the magnitude of between-family environmental differences that are problematic. Jensen (1973) assumed that heritability for intelligence was .80 and that the remaining variance was equally divided between within-family and between-family environmental variance. These assumptions permitted him to calculate the magnitude of the between-family environmental differences that are required to produce a 1-standard-deviation difference in IQ as 4.6 standard deviation units. Known differences in between-family environmental variations between black and white populations are very much smaller in magnitude. For example, the mean difference in socioeconomic status is .53 standard deviation units. One can quarrel with the details of the quantitative analyses in this argument and still find the argument persuasive. Jensen's estimate for heritability is high and his estimate for between-family environmental influence is low—although as we have seen recent research is compatible with a relatively low estimate of between-family environmental influence on intelligence for older samples. Known environmental influences that are predictive of variations in intelligence within the white population cannot account for differences between black and white samples in intelligence. For example, the correlation between socioeconomic status and IQ is only .3, and socioeconomic status can only account for 10% of the variance in IQ. Some of this variance, on some accounts more than half, is attributable to genetic differences. If we assume that only 25% of the variation between socioeconomic groups is genetic, we are left with an estimate that environmental variations associated with being reared in different socioeconomic groups account for 7.5% of the variance in IQ. Assume that the black–white difference in socioeconomic status in the U.S. is .6 standard deviation units. It is obvious that a .6-standard-deviation-unit difference in a variable that may account for 7.5% of the variance in IQ cannot account for a 1-standard-deviation difference in test scores between the black and white populations of the U.S.

Mercer (1973) attempted to account for black–white differences in intelligence by appeal to environmental variables. She studied a sample of 339 black children who had a mean IQ of 90.5. She found five environmental characteristics that related to WISC IQ scores in this sample. These were living in a family with five or fewer members, having a mother with high educational aspirations, living in a family in which the head of the household was married, living in a family that was buying its own home or owned its own home, and living in a family that had a moderately high occupational status. For the subset of black children whose families had all of the characteristics described above, the mean IQ was 99.1. There were 17 black children in her sample whose families met each of the five criteria. Mercer concluded that for the subset of black children who were reared in an environment that was characteristic of the modal middle class white environment, the black–white IQ difference disappeared. She interpreted these results as providing support for an environmental interpretation of black–white differences in intelligence.

Jensen (1973) described this type of argument as an example of what he called the "sociologist's fallacy." The analysis implicitly refers to a hyperselected subset of the black sample. In effect, it assumes that the subset of the black sample that has all of the characteristics of a modal white sample shares with that sample their characteristic modal IQ. It leaves unresolved why only 17 of the 339 children in the black sample share the modal characteristics of the white sample. Implicitly, the analysis assumes that all of the variables that are correlated with IQ have a one-way causal influence. It ignores the possibility that IQ may influence socioeconomic status, decisions about family size, and lifestyles. The difficulty is that many of the variables that influence IQ are also influenced by IQ and the covariance of IQ and various environmental variables that are related to IQ is causally ambiguous. All of the joint variance cannot be reasonably allocated to a unicausal explanation that assumes that socioeconomic variables influence IQ and IQ does not influence socioeconomic variables (see Loehlin et al., 1975, p. 166).

It is probably correct to say that measurable aspects of the environment considered in their appropriate causal role cannot account for the black–white difference in IQ test scores. It is possible that an accumulation of environmental influences that have a small but detectable influence on IQ might collectively account for the difference. Lynn (1990c) suggested that nutritional variables might contribute to black–white differences in intelligence. He analyzed data collected by Broman et al. (1987) as part of the Collaborative Perinatal Project. They administered the WISC to a sample of over 17,000 white children and 18,900 black children and measured the head circumference of each of the subjects in their sample. Table 10.3 presents Lynn's calculations of the mean head circumference and height for black and white children in this study. The black sample had a mean head circumference that was approximately .5 standard deviations lower than that of the white sample. There were no differences in the height of these two groups and therefore it was not necessary to correct head circumference for height differences.

The appropriate interpretation of data on racial differences in head circumference is not clear. Lynn (1990c) noted that head circumference has increased 1 standard deviation in western countries in the last 50 years. He argued that this increase is attributable to changes in nutrition. Therefore, he interpreted the racial differences in head circumference as being attributable to nutritional influences. Rushton (1990) argued that

TABLE 10.3   Mean Head Circumference for Black and White 7 Year
Olds from the Collaborative Perinatal Project[a]

	Black		White	
	Mean	S.D.	Mean	S.D.
Head circumference (cm)	50.91	1.57	51.72	1.53
Height (cm)	122.90	6.48	122.53	5.63

[a]Based on Lynn (1990c).

racial differences in head circumference have a genetic origin, are related
to brain size, and are to be interpreted as evidence for a genetic hypothesis
about differences in intelligence. It is not self-evident that the racial difference in head circumference obtained in these studies reflects genetic
differences. It should be noted that Rushton does not provide data on the
heritability of head circumference. Until we have a clearer understanding
of the genetic and environmental influences on the development of head
circumference, it is difficult to provide an interpretation of these data. In
a sense it is as difficult to determine the reasons for a racial difference in
head circumference as it is to determine the reasons for a racial difference
in IQ.

Another variable that may contribute to racial differences in intelligence is lead exposure. Research reviewed in Chapter 6 indicates that
exposure to lead may adversely influence the development of intelligence.
It is reasonable to assume that the black population, with many individuals living in inner cities in deteriorated housing conditions, is more
likely to be exposed to high concentrations of lead than the white population of the U.S. Although lead exposure may have a small influence on
the development of IQ and may not play a role in the development of
intelligence in more than an undefined subset of the black population,
lead as a variable may be paradigmatic of a series of variables that may
collectively account for the black–white difference in IQ. That is, there
may be a large set of variables that share the characteristic of having an
unequal frequency of occurrence in the black and white populations of
the U.S., each of which might have a small influence on IQ. Note that this
suggestion is merely an argument about the plausibility of an environmental hypothesis about the causes of the racial difference in IQ. Since
we do not have evidence indicating that the racial IQ gap may be accounted for by the measurement of a large number of variables (with
appropriate controls for the influence of genetic differences on the variables), the argument remains at the level of an untested hypothesis that
may be plausible.

Flynn (1980, 1984, 1987) presented a variant of this argument. He noted
that evidence of secular changes in IQ indicates that environmental
events exist that could account for a 1-standard-deviation difference in IQ,

although he admitted that we are not able to specify the environmental events that produced this change. Since the environmental influences are undefined we do not know whether they provide an account of black–white differences in IQ.

There is an additional environmental explanation of the black–white IQ gap. There may be environmental influences on IQ that cannot be measured on a common scale for black and white populations of the U.S. That is, there may be experiences that black individuals are likely to encounter that white individuals never encounter. It is not hard to imagine many such influences. Black and white Americans are reared in quasisegregated environments frequently having relatively little social contact with each other. There are different cultural exposures in music and the arts and language. Experiences of discrimination and racism are encountered at one time or another or even constantly by black Americans and not by white Americans. We have little or no scientific data that quantifies the effects of living in a quasiseparate environment on the development of IQ in black individuals. Nevertheless, the possibility exists that the cumulative effects of experiences that occur frequently to black individuals and virtually never to white individuals may account for some or all of the black–white IQ gap.

Jensen is probably correct in asserting that known environmental influences that are measurable (and cannot themselves be attributed to genetic influences) do not account for the black–white IQ gap. But this observation does not render a genetic hypothesis more plausible than an environmental hypothesis about the gap (see MacKenzie, 1984). Genetic hypotheses are not necessarily favored by the failure of environmental hypotheses to be confirmed. That is, the genetic hypothesis is in the same logical position as the environmental hypothesis. The assertion that known environmental influences do not account for the IQ gap leaves the possibility that unknown environmental or genetic influences are responsible for the gap. The genetic hypothesis, has exactly the same status as an unmeasured source of variance as that of an unmeasured set of environmental variables.

The arguments for and against the genetic hypothesis for racial differences in intelligence test scores that we have examined may be described as indirect arguments. Direct tests of hypotheses about genetic and environmental differences could be obtained, in principle, by the use of a cross-fostering experimental design in which individuals with white and black genotypes are assigned to opposite race environments. While there are no complete cross-fostering studies of this type available, there are studies that provide information about black children who are reared in white environments. Flynn (1980) argued that studies that directly test genetic and environmental hypotheses, however imperfectly, provide evidence that is more relevant to an evaluation of these hypotheses than the indirect arguments presented by Jensen.

There are four studies that assess the IQs of black children who have been reared in predominantly white environmental settings. Scarr & Weinberg (1976) obtained IQ scores for a sample of black children who were transracially adopted by upper middle class white parents in Minnesota whose mean IQ was 119.5. The mean IQ of 154 natural children of these parents was 116.7. The transracially adopted children of these parents were tested at a mean age of 74 months (S.D. = 30). All of the children were 4 yr. or older at the time of testing. The mean IQ of 29 adopted children whose biological parents were both black was 96.8. The mean IQ of 68 adopted children who had one black biological parent was 109.

These data provide several sources of information relevant to an evaluation of hypotheses about racial differences in intelligence. The mean IQ of all of the transracially adopted children in this study was 106—a value above the white mean. Scarr and Weinberg reported that the educational levels of the biological parents of the adopted children were comparable to those of the black population. If we assume on the basis of this information that the biological parents of the children had IQs that are representative of the black population, then these data suggest that a representative sample of black children reared in upper middle class white homes would have IQs that are above the white mean. Although the Scarr and Weinberg study is plausibly interpretable as providing evidence for the malleability of IQs for black children, these data should not be construed as providing definitive evidence in favor of an environmental hypothesis about racial differences in intelligence test scores. The children at the time of testing were relatively young and the full effects of genetic influences on IQ are not apparent until the postadolescent period. In addition, the influence of the family environment on IQ appears to decline after early childhood. Scarr and Weinberg prepared an abstract of a paper to be delivered at a meeting of the Behavior Genetic Society reporting the results of a 10-year follow-up study of the transracially adopted children. The abstract indicated that the IQs of the adopted children declined during that period. The paper was not delivered. Neither the abstract, nor the paper reporting the results of the study, have been published. The abstract did not report any of the details of the follow-up study. The magnitude of the decline in IQ was not reported in the abstract. In the absence of these details, it is impossible to evaluate reports of a possible decline of the IQs of the transracially adopted children in the Scarr and Weinberg study. At very least, their data indicate that the developmental history of IQ scores of black children reared in white environments is different from the developmental history of the scores of black children reared in black environments. Recall that black children reared in black environments exhibit IQ scores that are approximately 1 standard deviation below the white mean by age 3. If the transracially adopted children in the Scarr and Weinberg study had IQs that regressed toward the black mean at older ages, their documented IQs at age 6 were more characteristic of white adoptees.

Scarr and Weinberg found, in common with other studies of adoption reviewed in Chapter 5, that adopted children had IQs that were lower than the IQs of the natural children of the adoptive parents. These data provide evidence for a genetic influence on IQ. The difference in IQ of the children with two black parents as opposed to one black parent might also be interpreted as providing support for a genetic interpretation of racial differences in IQ, except that Scarr and Weinberg indicated that the social history of these two groups of children were different. Children with two black parents were adopted at a later age, had more preadoption placements, and had shorter exposures to the adopted home than children with one black parent. When these variables were statistically controlled, the influence of the racial background of the transracially adopted child on IQ was substantially reduced.

Moore (1985, 1986) obtained Wechsler test scores for a sample of 23 black children who were adopted by black middle class families and a sample of 23 black children who were adopted by white middle class families. The educational levels of the black and white adoptive mothers were equal. The educational level of the black fathers was slightly lower than the educational level of the white fathers. The children were tested between ages 7 and 10. The children adopted by black families had a mean IQ of 103.6 and the children adopted by white families had a mean IQ of 117.1. There were no differences in the IQs of children with one or two black parents. Moore's results provide support for Scarr and Weinberg's environmental interpretation of the differences between black and biracial children's IQs. Her study, however, is not definitive for two reasons. First, the children were young. Second, no information was provided about the biological parents of these children. Moore indicated that the characteristics of the biological mothers of the adopted children whose families chose to participate in the study were comparable to the characteristics of the biological mothers of the children whose adopted family did not choose to participate in the study. Thus, information about the biological mothers is available but Moore did not report these data. If the biological parents of the children adopted by white parents were comparable to the biological parents of the children adopted by black parents, then the Moore study would provide strong evidence in favor of an environmental interpretation of black–white differences in IQ.

Moore also studied the behavior of children in the examination and in another session in which mothers were asked to help their children solve a block design problem from the Wechsler test. She found that transracially adopted children responded differently to the demands of the IQ test than children adopted by black families. The transracially adopted children appeared more confident of their abilities as problem solvers and were more likely to expand on the reasons for their answers than the children adopted by black families. The white mothers of the adopted children were more likely to joke, grin, and laugh as a way of releasing tension when their children worked on the block design than the black mothers. The black mothers were more likely to be critical of their children's performance than were the white mothers. These differences in behavior and social interaction were related to differences in performance on the IQ tests. Moore argued that differences in the intellectual socialization experiences characteristic of black and white rearing could result in differences in the intellectual performance of children. Moore's presentation did not indicate whether these differences in observed behavior accounted for all of the IQ differences obtained in the study. It is not clear whether she has isolated the critical environmental variables that might account for racial differences in IQ test scores.

Tizard (1974) compared white and black (West Indian) children reared in residential nurseries in England. There were 149 children tested who ranged in age from 2 years to 4 years and 11 months. The children were tested with the Reynall test and the Minnesota nonverbal test, and a subset of the older children were given a WISC. The results were quite consistent across the measures. The mean IQ of children with either one or two black parents was slightly higher than the mean IQ of children whose biological parents were both white. Tizard indicated that there were no conspicuous differences in the backgrounds of the biological parents of the children. Her results suggest that black children reared in the same environment as white children will develop comparable IQs. It should be noted that the children were quite young at the time of testing and the black children were West Indian blacks. These data support an environmental interpretation of black–white differences in IQ. The development of IQ appears to be constant for black and white children reared in comparable environments.

Arguably, Eyferth (1959, 1961; Eyferth, Brandt, & Hawel, 1960) reported the most important direct study of the reasons for black–white differences in intelligence test performance. Eyferth studied a sample of 181 children whose biological fathers were black soldiers serving in the Army of Occupation in Germany at the end of World War II. The children were reared by their biological mothers, who were white German women. The children were compared to a sample of white children whose biological fathers had been white soldiers in the same army in Germany. The mothers of the two samples were carefully matched on a number of variables including place of residence, socioeconomic background, and composition of the family that reared the child. Approximately 75% of the fathers of the children were American soldiers; the remaining fathers were French troops who were either black or white. The children were tested with a German version of the WISC at ages between 5 and 13. Two-thirds of the children were tested when they were between 10 and 13 years of

age. The mean IQ of the white children was 97.2 and the mean IQ of the
black children was 96.5. These data suggest that children with one black
parent who are reared in similar circumstances to children with two
white parents will have comparable performance on IQ tests. The conditions of rearing in Germany, apart from the distinctive subcultural experiences of American blacks and under conditions that are similar for black
and white children, provide a clear test of the hypothesis that black–
white differences in IQ are attributable to environmental events. The
Eyferth study provides strong evidence in favor of an environmental interpretation of black–white differences in IQ. There are three possible
objections to this interpretation of the results. First, information about
the characteristics of the biological fathers was not available. It is possible
that they were not a representative sample of black and white soldiers or
of the black and white populations of the U.S. Flynn (1980) presented a
thorough analysis of this issue. He indicated that sexual relationships
between soldiers of the occupation and German women after World War II
were widespread and were not confined to any particular segment of the
Army of Occupation. In addition, he argued that Army test score records
indicated that black soldiers did in fact have lower IQs than white soldiers. Eyferth's results would have provided more definitive information
if data about the biological fathers of these children had been reported.
Nevertheless, there is no reason to believe that the white and black biological fathers were not representative of their groups and therefore it is
reasonable to assume that they differed in IQ. Second, it is possible to
argue that children resulting from interracial matings will have higher
IQs than children who had two black parents because of the effects of
heterosis. This is a well-known genetic phenomenon in which outbred
groups exhibit increases in a trait. Eysenck (1984) argued that Eyferth's
results might be attributable to heterosis. This is not a highly plausible
hypothesis. Heterosis has been found for a number of traits in animal and
plant studies. Its existence in human populations is extremely problematic for such traits as height (see Loehlin et al., 1975). And there is
little or no evidence for such a phenomenon for intelligence, although
there is some problematic evidence for the opposite effects of inbreeding
depression on IQ. Each of the other transracial adoption studies that we
have considered permits comparisons between children with two black
parents and children with one black parent. Only the Scarr and Weinberg
study provided evidence that could be interpreted as supporting the existence of heterosis, and there were persuasive reasons to assume that the
differences obtained in that study were attributable to differences in the
preadoption experiences of children. The Tizard and Moore studies both
obtained data that are incompatible with the existence of heterosis.
Therefore, heterosis does not provide a convincing explanation of the
results of the Eyferth study. Third, the children tested in the Eyferth
study, though older than those tested in other transracial adoption stud-

ies, are still not at the age at which IQ test scores are most heritable. While the Eyferth study is not definitive, it is probably the most convincing study we have available and its results support an environmental interpretation. If a substantial portion of the IQ difference between black and white populations in the U.S. were attributable to genetic differences, the black children in the Eyferth study should have had IQs that were several points lower than the white children. The fact that they did not constitutes evidence against a genetic hypothesis.

If we consider the transracial adoption studies collectively, they provide evidence in favor of an environmental interpretation of black–white differences in IQ test score. With the possible exception of the unpublished follow-up data in the Scarr and Weinberg study which cannot be evaluated, the data indicate that black children reared in white environments have IQ test scores that are characteristic of white children reared in white environments.

There is an additional source of direct evidence on the reasons for black–white differences in intelligence. The black population of the U.S. consists of individuals who differ with respect to their degree of black and white ancestry. A genetic hypothesis predicts that there should be a positive correlation between the degree of white ancestry of a black person and his or her IQ. Although this hypothesis appears to be straightforward it is not easy to test. There is no simple and direct way of measuring the degree of black ancestry of a black person. Variations in skin color, the most visible manifestation of racial admixture, may in part be attributable to variations in skin color among African ancestors of American blacks (see Harrison & Owen, 1964). Also, white ancestry might at one time or another provide social advantages for black individuals. It is generally recognized that studies of the influence of racial admixture on IQ should be pursued using latent biological markers such as blood groups as a basis of estimating ancestry. This is difficult to do since blood markers that might once have been indicative of African ancestry may no longer covary in the same way that they did among African ancestors. Loehlin *et al.* (1975, pp. 124–125) indicated that blood gene markers characteristic of European ancestry in two samples of black individuals were uncorrelated. Thus genes indicative of European ancestry may no longer covary in the same way in contemporary black populations. Although the assessment of degree of white ancestry among black samples is not a simple matter, the data that are available suggest that IQ is not related to degree of white ancestry in black samples. Scarr, Pakstis, Katz, & Barker (1977; see also Jensen, 1981; Scarr, 1981) calculated the probability that an individual's blood group was characteristic of a white or black sample and the probability that an individual's blood group markers were characteristic of white ancestral samples. They obtained a correlation between these two probability measures and performance on four tests of ability in a sample of black schoolchildren. The correlations between their two measures of white ancestry and a composite general ability measure were −.05 and −.03. These data provide no evidence that white ancestry among black individuals correlates with intelligence.

Witty & Jenkins (1936) studied a sample of black children who had IQs of 140 or higher. They assumed that a genetic hypothesis would predict that black individuals with very high IQs are more likely to have white ancestry than black individuals with less atypical IQs. They relied on geneological data to estimate the degree of white ancestry of their sample of 28 children and reported that the degree of racial admixture present in this group was comparable to that which was present in a larger group of 63 black children with IQs above 125 and that the degree of racial admixture was comparable to that reported in a large sample of American blacks studied by Herskovitz (1930). MacKenzie (1984) argued that the geneological data might not be accurate and that the Herskovitz sample might not be a relevant control group for a study using a local rather than a national sample. While the Witty and Jenkins study is far from ideal, at very least it fails to provide data in support of a genetic hypothesis about racial differences in IQ. This study considered in conjunction with the Scarr *et al.* study indicates that there is no relationship between degree of white ancestry and intelligence in black samples.

Conclusion

After a century of research and speculation about black–white differences in intelligence it is, I think, fair to say that we know relatively little about the reasons for the difference. We do know that the differences in intelligence test performance are not attributable in any obvious way to bias in the tests and that the differences in test scores reflect differences not in particular bits of cultural knowledge but in more general and abstract abilities. And, we know that the differences are related to criteria such as the acquisition of knowledge that are valued by many if not all individuals in both the black and the white communities of the United States. The reasons for the differences are probably to be found in the distinctive cultural experiences encountered by black individuals in the United States. While it may be difficult to definitively rule out a genetic hypothesis on the basis of the available evidence, I think that it is also fair to say that there is no convincing direct or indirect evidence in favor of a genetic hypothesis of racial differences in IQ.

It is sometimes wrongly assumed that the ideological and social consequences of a genetic explanation for black–white differences in scores on tests of intelligence are somehow devastating and that environmental explanations lead to much more satisfactory social outcomes. It should be noted that many of the consequences of a genetic or environmental explanation may not be those that are envisioned in popular discussions. Since genetic influences are not immutable and the influence of the genotype on the phenotype is variable, it is quite possible that a genetic basis for racial differences in intelligence might be more remediable than an environmental difference. Some of the alleged environmental influences on intelligence that are assumed to account for racial differences in intelligence test performance are not easily remediated. If, for example, prenatal influences are important, we can in principle, although not easily in practice, provide better prenatal care for black women. If black children have been damaged by inadequate prenatal care we may not find it easy to remediate the intellectual consequences of this damage for children who have been prenatally deprived. If, as Moore suggests, black middle class parents provide intellectual socialization experiences that are less than optimal to develop good performance on IQ tests, will it be easy to develop new socialization methods for black parents?

Research on black–white differences in intelligence fails to provide answers to three critical questions. (1) What are the reasons for the difference? (2) Can we eliminate it? (3) If we cannot eliminate the difference, can we design an environment in which the effects of individual differences in intelligence are mitigated such that they are not determinative to the extent they are now of racial differences in performance in the schools and in other socially relevant contexts? If we could make progress on the third question the answers to the first two questions would appear to be less pressing. It is possible that the answer to the first question might enable us to eliminate the difference or to design ways to mitigate the difference. If so, the study of the reasons for black–white differences would be socially useful.

THE INTELLIGENCE OF JAPANESE
AND CHINESE GROUPS

There are many studies comparing black and white samples on tests of intelligence. There are relatively few studies comparing Japanese and Chinese samples to white samples on tests of intelligence. P. E. Vernon (1982) summarized studies of the performance of the descendants of Asian immigrants living in North America on tests of intelligence. He also included data on the performance of Chinese samples in Hong Kong. Lynn (1987) also summarized the available literature.

There was little adequate data on the intelligence test performance of Japanese- and Chinese-background children in America or Canada until the 1970s. A number of studies were published as early as the 1920s. The samples were small and not particularly representative. These studies usually found that these groups exhibited deficits relative to whites in measures of verbal intelligence and performed as well as white groups on measures of nonverbal intelligence. The deficits in measures of verbal intelligence may be reasonably attributable to the possibility that many of the subjects in these early studies were reared in homes in which English was not spoken. Data on the intelligence test performance of representative samples of Japanese and Chinese groups were not available until after World War II.

The two most comprehensive investigations of the performance of Chinese and Japanese groups in America were reported by Flaugher & Rock (1972) and by Coleman and his colleagues as part of the Coleman report on the performance of American schoolchildren (Coleman, Campbell, Hobson, McPartland, Moody, Weinfield, & York, 1966). Flaugher & Rock (1972) administered group tests of intelligence to a sample of 18,000 high school juniors in Los Angeles. They found that Asian-American students (primarily Japanese-Americans in this sample) scored above white students on tests of reasoning and tests of spatial and number abilities. Asian-American students scored lower on tests of verbal ability than white students. The most comprehensive data available are contained in the Coleman report of the performance of 650,000 American schoolchildren. Children classified as having an Asian background had the highest performance of any group investigated. The Asian students exceeded the white mean at each grade investigated on tests of nonverbal ability. Their scores were approximately .25 standard deviations higher on these measures than that of other groups. Asian groups were above the mean on verbal intelligence in the first three grades and then exhibited declines in performance relative to other groups. Their verbal test scores were approximately .10 standard deviations below that of white groups.

Studies of Asian-background children in America going back to the earliest fragmentary reports of tests administered after World War I exhibit a consistent pattern of results—stronger performance on nonverbal than on verbal tests and relatively little evidence for deficits in general intelligence even for children who have deficits in the use of the English language. It should be noted that these results contradict Mercer's analysis of black–white differences in intelligence in that they indicate that tests of intelligence do not measure the degree of acquaintance of individuals with white middle class culture.

The results of the intelligence test performance of Asian Americans are buttressed by studies of the performance of Japanese individuals on tests of intelligence originally standardized on American samples. Lynn (1987) summarized the results of three large-scale studies of the performance of Japanese on standardized tests of intelligence (see also Lynn & Hampson, 1986a). The studies include a Japanese standardization of the McCarthy scales for children ages 2–8, and two standardizations of the Wechsler tests, for children aged 4–6 (for the WISC) and for samples between 6 and 16 (for the Japanese version of the WAIS). Lynn compared the performance of Japanese groups to that of American white groups on these tests. He adjusted the scores to take account of secular trends in intelligence and

TABLE 10.4   Mean IQ of Japanese Children Relative to American White Mean of 100 and Standard Deviation of 15[a]

Age	Spearman's g	Verbal	Visuospatial	Test
2.5	94.4	92.8	97.0	McCarthy
3	94.1	92.5	96.5	McCarthy
3.5	96.6	94.7	99.5	McCarthy
4	95.9	93.1	99.6	McCarthy
4.5	97.1	93.8	101.6	McCarthy
5	97.2	92.6	103.7	McCarthy
5.5	98.7	93.8	105.7	McCarthy
6.5	101.2	97.1	107.2	McCarthy
7.5	98.5	93.9	104.5	McCarthy
8	97.7	92.7	104.7	McCarthy
6	100.6	96.2	103.8	WPPSI
6	101.2	97.8	106.2	WISC-R
7	100.0	95.6	106.0	WISC-R
8	102.1	97.9	106.5	WISC-R
9	102.3	99.0	105.8	WISC-R
10	104.1	101.0	106.5	WISC-R
11	104.0	100.7	106.2	WISC-R
12	104.4	100.9	106.1	WISC-R
13	103.4	100.3	104.8	WISC-R
14	104.0	100.8	105.4	WISC-R
15	104.2	101.3	105.4	WISC-R
16	103.3	100.8	103.0	WISC-R

[a]Based on Lynn (1987).

obtained scores for general intelligence as well as scores for verbal and spatial ability. Table 10.4 presents his analyses. Table 10.4 indicates that the performance of Japanese groups is slightly lower than that of American whites on the McCarthy tests given to young children. The Japanese samples exceed the American white samples on the Wechsler tests. After age 8, the differences are approximately .25 standard deviations. A second feature of these data is that at all ages the Japanese samples score higher on spatial measures than on verbal measures. Ignoring age trends, Japanese samples score approximately .33 standard deviations higher on measures of spatial ability than on measures of verbal ability.

Lynn also reported data for performance of Chinese groups on tests of intelligence in Hong Kong, Singapore, and Taiwan. Chinese 13 year olds in Hong Kong obtained an IQ of 113.3 on the Raven Progressive Matrices. This value was an estimated score adjusting for secular changes in IQ. A comparable study in Singapore reported an IQ of 103.3 for Chinese 13 year olds. And, Chinese 16 year olds in Taiwan administered Cattell Culture-Fair tests obtained adjusted means of 101 and 103 for indigenous Taiwanese and Chinese immigrant groups, respectively. These data indicate that Chinese-background children in Asia have nonverbal intelligence test performance that is equal to or slightly superior to the performance of American and British samples. Lynn (1987) indicated that there are three aspects of these data that require interpretation. (1) Chinese- and Japanese-background children score lower on tests of intelligence administered prior to age 6 than American and British children. (2) After age 6, Chinese- and Japanese-background individuals have marginally higher general intelligence than British and American white individuals. (3) Chinese- and Japanese-background individuals have higher spatial than verbal abilities.

Lynn's summary of the differences between Chinese and Japanese individuals and white Americans has been challenged (see Sue and Okazaki, 1990; 1991). The differences are based on scores that are adjusted for secular trends. In addition, the comparisons are of retrospective data sets that were not based on samples constructed on the same basis. There may also have been differences in the way in which tests were administered in different countries at different times. It is obviously difficult to arrive at conclusions about cross-cultural differences in performance on tests when these differences are not based on data sets that are explicitly collected for the purpose of cross-cultural comparisons.

Stevenson, Stigler, Lee, Kitamura, & Hsu (1985) obtained ability scores from representative samples of first and fifth grade pupils from Minneapolis, Minnesota, Taipei, Taiwan, and Sendai, Japan on a battery of verbal and nonverbal tests. Although there were significant differences in test scores on some tests in the battery, the overall differences in scores were small and inconsistent. The data obtained in this study, which was specifically designed as a test of cross-cultural differences in performance, do not support Lynn's analysis of racial differences in test performance.

Lynn (1991) indicated that the Stevenson *et al.* study was not conclusive. He cited data indicating that individuals in Minnesota had above average IQs. It should be noted that the comparison cities chosen by Stevenson *et al.* were designed to be comparable to Minneapolis. All of this points to the difficulty of making cross-cultural comparisons. Unless there are comprehensive comparisons of samples designed to be representative of the populations of different countries who are tested in the same manner on the same tests, it is difficult to reach conclusions about the performance of individuals in different groups. Thus, it is possible to argue that Lynn's conclusions about the nature of racial differences in IQ may not be justified.

Lynn (1987) asserted that these findings were not easily interpretable by environmental hypotheses and he advanced a biological theory to explain these results. Lynn assumed that the relatively low performance of preschool Japanese groups is attributable to a genetic influence on the rate of maturation among individuals he designates as mongoloids. It should be noted that the empirical basis for the assumption that pre- school-age IQ is lower in Japanese samples is weak. It is based on research using the McCarthy scales. Recall that Naglieri & Jensen (1987) demonstrated that the g loading of the McCarthy scales for children was lower than the g loading of the WISC. The magnitude of age-related differences in the performance of American white and Japanese individuals on intelligence tests may be attributable to the use of different tests at different ages that assess somewhat different constructs. Also, the relative improvement in Japanese samples may be attributable to the effects of differences in schooling. Japanese elementary education may be more rigorous than American elementary education. Cross-national comparisons of academic achievement consistently find that the performance of American elementary schoolchildren is lower than the performance of children in Asian countries. The differences are particularly acute in mathematics achievement (see discussion of the Stevenson *et al.* (1990) study in Chapter 9). Elementary education in Asian countries in mathematics is more intensive than elementary mathematics education in America. This differential emphasis on formal and abstract elements in the curriculum might influence the development of fluid intelligence and account for some of the differences in intelligence noted by Lynn.

Lynn proposed that differences between individuals with Asian backgrounds and Caucasians in intelligence are explained by genetic differences in brain functioning. He proposed that the former group experienced a shift in neurological structure during the Ice Age. The left hemisphere of the brain of individuals with Asian backgrounds evolved structures capable of processing visuospatial information. Therefore, the brains of individuals with Asian backgrounds have a higher proportion of cortical tissue devoted to processing spatial information than the brains of Caucasians. Consequently, the brains of individuals with Asian backgrounds are more likely to have a smaller proportion of cortical tissue available for processing verbal information.

Lynn cited three kinds of evidence in favor of this theory. Frydman & Lynn (1989) reported the results of a transracial adoption study in which 19 Korean children were adopted by middle class Belgian parents. These children had a WISC verbal IQ of 110.6 and a performance IQ of 123.5 at age 10. Fryden and Lynn interpret these data as support for a genetically programmed tendency for individuals of Asian backgrounds to have higher spatial than verbal abilities. Although this interpretation of these data is plausible, alternative interpretations are possible. Although the differences between verbal and nonverbal IQs are statistically significant, it should be noted that the sample is small and that the study requires replication before it can be confidently asserted that transracially adopted Asian-background children have higher performance than verbal IQs. It should also be noted that these children were adopted at a mean age of 19 months with differences in the age of adoption varying from 3 to 72 months. Therefore, most of these children had less exposure to French than children reared from birth in French-speaking areas of Belgium. Their lower performance on tests of verbal ability may reflect nothing more than a lower level of exposure to the French language. In order to rule out this alternative hypothesis it would be necessary to study children of Asian backgrounds who were adopted at birth by Caucasians. An analogous interpretation of many of the studies demonstrating differences in verbal and nonverbal intelligence for Asian-Americans is plausible. That is, relatively poorer performance on tests of verbal intelligence may be attributable to decreased exposure to English for children who are not native speakers of the language or who are reared by parents who are not native speakers of the language. It should be noted that this interpretation will not account for observations of a comparable pattern of results for Japanese children reared in Japan.

Lynn (1987) presented data indicating that verbal and spatial abilities are negatively correlated when g is held constant. P. A. Vernon (1990) argued that this relationship was a statistical artifact since $g = V + P$ where V and P represent performance and verbal IQ, respectively. Therefore, holding g constant will lead to an inverse relationship between V and P. Lynn (1990b) disagreed with Vernon's analysis. He noted that g, or a composite IQ, is a function of all the tests that constitute the test battery. Partial correlations among verbal tests, with g held constant, are positive. Similarly, partial correlations among spatial tests are positive with g held constant. By contrast, partial correlations between verbal and spatial tests are negative with g held constant. It seems to me that Vernon's analysis is more nearly correct. It is possible to factor analyze omnibus tests of intelligence such as the Wechsler tests and obtain spatial and verbal ability factors defined by such markers as Vocabulary and Block Design. The existence of such factors is not in dispute. With g held constant it is mathematically necessary that they are inversely related simply because their identity as separate factors is attributable to the high positive correlations among the subtests that define each of the factors. Therefore, the inverse relationship between spatial and verbal ability factors is analytically equivalent to the assertion that spatial and verbal ability factors exist (the term *exist* is used here solely in the statistical sense of being definable by an observed pattern of correlations). The existence of an inverse pattern of correlations cannot be used to provide evidence for a neurological model of the biological basis of spatial and verbal abilities since the inverse relationship is an analytical consequence of the existence of separate spatial and verbal ability factors.

Lynn (1987) cited data from cognitive experimental studies indicating that there are differences in the lateralized functioning of Caucasian and Asian groups. Hatta & Dimond (1980) presented irregular geometric visual stimuli to the right or left hemisphere of Japanese and English college students using a tachistoscope. Subjects were required to recognize the stimuli presented to them. The percentage of correct recognitions for the Japanese and English students for stimuli presented to the right and left visual field is presented in Table 10.5. Japanese students had more accu-

TABLE 10.5 Mean Percentage of Correct Recognition
of Random Forms in the Left and Right Visual Fields
of Japanese and English Subjects[a]

Subjects	Left visual field	Right visual field
Japanese		
Mean	38.49	44.10
Standard deviation	12.46	10.42
English		
Mean	45.69	31.31
Standard deviation	10.78	10.93

[a]Based on Hatta & Dimond (1980).

rate recognition of complex visual stimuli presented to the right visual field (left hemisphere) than English students. Although English students were slightly better than Japanese students in recognizing visual stimuli presented to the left visual field (right hemisphere), the differences were not statistically significant. The significant interaction of visual field × social background of subjects is interpreted by Hatta and Dimond as supporting a model of differential lateralization of brain function among English and Japanese individuals. Japanese individuals, in contradistinction to English individuals, are assumed to be capable of bilateral processing of stimuli and superior processing of visual stimuli in the left hemisphere.

Tsunoda (1978) obtained data supporting a hypothesis of differential lateralization of function among Japanese and Caucasian individuals. He reported a right-ear (left-hemisphere) advantage for the recognition of auditory stimuli such as a bird singing or the chirping of a cricket in Japanese subjects and a left-ear (right-hemisphere) advantage for recognition of the same stimuli among Western subjects. These data are interpreted by Lynn (1987) as supporting the assumption that the right hemisphere is freed for the processing of spatial information among Japanese.

Although both the Hatta and Dimond and the Tsunoda studies provide evidence for differential lateralization of functioning between Japanese and Western subjects, neither study provides strong support for a general theory of genetically determined differences in brain functioning between Caucasian and Asian individuals. Evidence indicating differential lateralization effects is not presented for other Asian groups. Both Tsunoda and Hatta and Dimond assume that the differential lateralization that they obtained is attributable to the characteristics of Japanese orthography, which requires mastery of Kanji, a form of written language which is nonphonetic and ideographic. Thus language function among Japanese requires the involvement of skills that are normally dependent upon right-hemisphere specialization. If this analysis is correct, differential lateralization of function would not be obtained for individuals of Japanese background who have never been exposed to Kanji. Evidence indicating that there are left-hemisphere advantages for processing spatial information among individuals with Asian backgrounds would have to be far more extensive before it could reasonably be concluded that there is a racially based difference in lateralization of function. In addition, it would be necessary to obtain evidence for the heritability of lateralization of functioning before it would be reasonable to entertain a hypothesis of a genetic difference in brain functioning. And, it would be necessary to demonstrate that indices of lateralization are related to patterns of psychometrically assessed abilities.

It is possible to summarize the evidence in favor of Lynn's genetic theory about the basis of differences between Caucasian and Asian individuals by indicating that there is little or no persuasive evidence in favor of the theory. The inverse relationship between verbal and spatial reasoning is probably a statistical artifact of the existence of separate spatial and verbal ability factors; the single transracial adoption study cited requires replication and is capable of alternative interpretations; and the data on differential lateralization of brain function do not include studies of several Asian groups and do not include studies of individuals of Asian backgrounds not exposed to ideographic representations of language that might plausibly be assumed to influence the way in which the hemispheres process different kinds of information. To assert this is not to assert that there is decisive evidence against the theory. Rather it is to assert that the evidence offered in favor of the theory is thin and not compelling.

GENDER DIFFERENCES IN INTELLIGENCE

Meta-analyses have become the preferred way of summarizing literature on sex differences in cognitive functioning. There are three meta-analyses available that summarize studies of sex differences in verbal ability, spatial ability, and mathematical ability.

Hyde & Linn (1988) analyzed 165 studies including over a million subjects in their analysis of gender differences in verbal ability. They obtained an effect size of .14 for the mean difference between females and males, indicating female superiority in verbal ability of approximately one-seventh of a standard deviation. When they calculated a weighted mean in which the mean difference for each study was weighted by sample size, the effect size became −.04, indicating no difference in verbal ability. The difference between the weighted mean and the unweighted mean was substantially attributable to the results of a single study with a sample size of 977,361 subjects. Ramist & Arbeiter (1986) reported that males performed better than females on the SAT verbal test for college admission. When the results of this study were removed from the analysis, the effect size became .11, indicating that females did slightly better on tests of verbal ability than males.

Hyde and Lynn examined gender differences in studies as a function of several different characteristics of the studies. There was relatively little difference in outcome as a function of the age of the sample. Among the study characteristics that related to outcome were the year of publication of the study. Studies that were published in 1973 or earlier, and that were included in Maccoby and Jacklin's classic review of studies of gender differences, had an effect size of .23 (Maccoby & Jacklin, 1974). Studies published after 1973 had an effect size of .10, indicating that gender differences in verbal ability have declined.

Hyde and Linn attribute the anomalous SAT results to the possibility that the content of the questions in the SAT may be biased. SAT questions may be more likely to reflect the subjects with which males are more familiar than females. It is also possible that there are unrepresentative samples of males and females taking the SAT. They indicated that females taking the SAT in 1985 had lower socioeconomic status than males taking the test. Irrespective of the reasons for the anomalous results of the SAT study, the Hyde and Linn analysis of gender-related differences in mean verbal ability supports the conclusion that such differences are extremely small. A tenth of a standard deviation difference, perhaps the best current estimate of the magnitude of gender differences in verbal ability, has little or no practical or theoretical significance. These findings pose some difficulties for theories of brain lateralization that have been advanced to explain gender differences in ability that are based in part on the assumption that females have higher verbal ability than males (see Levy, 1976).

Linn & Petersen (1985) reported the results of a meta-analysis of tests of spatial ability published after Maccoby and Jacklin's review of this literature in 1974 and prior to 1982. Their analysis is based on 172 measures of effect size differences between males and females on various measures of spatial ability. They distinguished among three different spatial abilities—spatial perception, the ability to determine spatial relationships with respect to the orientation of the body as indexed by performance on the rod and frame test in which an individual is required to determine the verticality of a rod placed in a tilted frame; mental rotation, the speed and accuracy of ability to rotate two- and three-dimensional figures as indexed by tasks of the type studied by Shepard & Metzler (1971); and spatial visualization, the ability to perform complex multistep manipulations of spatially presented information as indexed by performance on the embedded figures test in which subjects are required to identify forms embedded in a complex design that serves to obscure the location and representation of the embedded figure. Using this analysis scheme, Linn and Petersen obtained mean effect size differences of male means minus female means of .44 for spatial perception, .73 for measures of rotation, and .13 for measures of visualization. Linn and Petersen find relatively little evidence of age differences in these effect size indices. And, for studies of rotation, the spatial ability with the largest gender difference, there is no evidence that the magnitude of gender differences is related to the age of the subjects in the study. These results pose difficulty for theories of gender difference that implicate biological changes associated with puberty as being critical for the emergence of gender differences in spatial ability (see Waber, 1976, 1979).

Hyde, Fennema, & Lamon (1990) reported the results of a meta-analysis of studies of gender differences in mathematics performance. Their analysis included 259 comparisons based on the testing of close to 4 million subjects. The weighted mean effect size for the male mean minus the female mean was .20, indicating that males scored approximately one-fifth of a standard deviation better than females on tests of mathematics. The magnitude of the difference was related to the year of publication of the study. The effect size index was .31 for studies published in 1973 or earlier and .14 for studies published after 1973. In addition, the magnitude of gender differences varied with the selectivity of the sample. For unselected representative samples the effect size was −.05, indicating slight female superiority in mathematics performance. For studies of samples with above-average mathematical performance the effect sizes varied between .33 and .54. These data suggest that there is little or no difference in mathematical performance between male and female subjects in the population, but males are more likely to outperform females in samples selected for above-average mathematical performance. The three meta-analyses of gender differences in ability described above all find evidence of a secular trend of decreasing gender differences in performance. Feingold (1988) reported an analysis of gender differences in the standardization data for the Differential Aptitude Test and the Preliminary Scholastic Aptitude Test (PSAT) for tests administered at different times. These analyses are particularly informative about secular trends since they are based on representative samples of high school students given the same tests. Table 10.6 presents his analysis of gender differences in several components of the Differential Aptitude Test as a function of the year in which the test was administered. The results are unusually consistent. On all measures gender differences have declined from tests administered in 1947 to tests administered in 1980. The magnitude of gender differences in these tests declined approximately .27 standard deviations from 1947 to 1980, and these declines occurred for tests in which females outperformed males in 1947 and for tests in which males outperformed females in 1947. These results indicating a secular trend of declining gender differences in abilities are also supported by results on the PSAT. Effect sizes for gender differences in verbal ability scores declined from −.12 in 1960 to −.02 in 1983. Effect sizes for mathematical ability

TABLE 10.6   Secular Trends in Gender Differences
in Differential Aptitude Test Performance[a]

Test	Year	Male mean − female mean (standard deviation units)
Spelling	1947	−.54
	1962	−.53
	1972	−.47
	1980	−.45
Language	1947	−.49
	1962	−.41
	1972	−.40
	1980	−.40
Clerical	1947	−.62
	1962	−.53
	1972	−.44
	1980	−.34
Mechanical reasoning	1947	1.33
	1962	1.00
	1972	.83
	1980	.76
Spatial relations	1947	.37
	1962	.26
	1972	.19
	1980	.15
Verbal reasoning	1947	.14
	1962	.06
	1972	.01
	1980	−.02
Abstract reasoning	1947	.23
	1962	.09
	1972	.02
	1980	−.04
Numerical reasoning	1947	.21
	1962	.10
	1972	−.01
	1980	−.10

[a]Based on Feingold (1988).

declined from .34 to .12 over this period. The demonstration of the declining significance of gender differences in abilities is probably not plausibly
explainable by reference to biological explanations. These results would
appear to implicate secular changes in our culture. These might plausibly
include a decline in sex stereotyping of activities, interests, and curricular
choices among high school students.

Gender differences in ability measures are more likely to be present in
samples that are above average in abilities. This is clearly true for mathematical ability and appears to also be true for ability measures where
there is little or no difference in gender or where females perform better
than males. Recall that Hyde and Linn reported that males had higher

mean scores on the SAT verbal test than females. The SAT is taken by a select group of high school students. It is possible to explain an advantage for males over females at the high end of the distribution of scores on an ability where there is a small mean difference in scores in favor of males. Small differences in central tendency of a distribution are magnified at the extremes of the distribution. This explanation will not account for higher performance of males for above-average ability groups where females have a higher mean than males. There is a second, and perhaps more significant, reason for the relatively superior performance of males in mathematics among high-ability groups. There are variance differences between males and females. Males generally have higher variance on ability scores. Therefore, more males than females are likely to be found in the tails of the distribution. Lubinski & Humpreys (1990) analyzed Project Talent data (Flanagan, Dailey, Shaycroft, Gorham, Orr, & Goldberg, 1962) on gender differences in abilities. Their sample consisted of close to 100,000 tenth grade students designed to be a representative sample of American students in 1960. Using these data they formed a composite measure of mathematics ability in their sample. The mean for males was approximately .18 of a standard deviation higher than the mean for females on this measure, a value that is congruent with other reported differences for this historical period. Males also had a standard deviation that was approximately 8% higher than females on this measure. Gender differences in variance were present on indices in which females had higher mean scores than males. For example, on a composite index of intelligence, females had a mean that was .02 standard deviations higher than males. Males had a standard deviation of IQ scores that was approximately 3% higher than females. Lubinski and Humphreys selected a sample of individuals who had scores in the highest 1% of math scores in the male and female subsamples. Among this group of individuals who were highly selected for a measure of mathematical aptitude that was highly correlated with their index of general intelligence, male subjects had composite indices of intelligence that were approximately one-fifth of a standard deviation higher than female subjects. This mean difference reversed the small female advantage in IQ among the unselected subjects. Differences in variability can account for the finding that males are likely to be disproportionately represented in high-ability groups above a high cutting score. These analyses explain the results of the Johns Hopkins talent search studies in which a self-selected sample of mathematically precocious seventh grade children take the SAT test for mathematical ability designed for twelfth grade college applicants. Using a cutting score of 500, the male-to-female ratio is 2:1; using a cutting score of 700, the male-to-female ratio is 13:1 (Benbow, 1988; Benbow & Stanley, 1981). These results are not substantially attributable to biases in self-selected samples. Comparable results were obtained by Lubinski and Humphreys in their analysis of Project Talent data. Benbow also indicated that these differences in ratios have not exhibited secular changes. The phenomena of large numbers of males at extremely high scores may therefore coexist with a declining mean difference in ability levels. Benbow obtained data on the distribution of math ability scores in male and female samples in her studies. Figure 10.1 presents these data. An examination of Fig. 10.1 indicates that males and females are equally well represented at the lower end of the distribution, but there is an excess number of males at the high end of the distribution. Comparable results were reported by Feingold (1988) for an analysis of scores on the SAT verbal test. Secular changes in verbal ability have diminished the excess number of male subjects at the low end of the distribution but have left unchanged an excess number of males at the high end of the distribution.

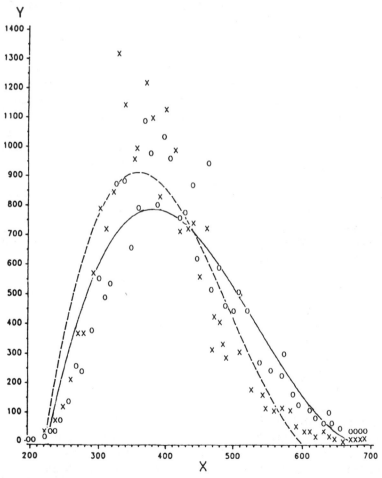

FIGURE 10.1   Distribution on SAT Q scores for mathematically precocious male (O) and female (X) students. (Based on Benbow, 1988.)

We have examined sex differences in three different special abilities. Since standardized IQ tests are usually constructed to remove gender differences in means, relatively little recent research has focused on gender differences in general ability. It should be noted that math, verbal, and spatial abilities are highly correlated. For example, Lubinski and Humphreys reported correlations between their mathematical ability composite and scores on an IQ composite, a verbal ability composite, and a spatial ability composite ranging from .62 to .83 in their male and female samples designed to be representative of tenth grade high school students in 1960. The highest correlations are obtained in both male and female subjects between mathematical composite scores and general IQ, followed by correlations of .75 between mathematical composite scores and verbal ability scores. The lowest correlations are obtained between mathematical ability scores and spatial ability scores. This finding poses difficulty for theories of mathematical ability that link it to spatial ability and assume that differences in spatial ability explain gender differences in mathematical ability.

The contemporary research on gender differences in intelligence leads to several generalizations. They are as follows.

1. Gender differences in general intellectual ability are small and virtually nonexistent.
2. Secular changes have diminished gender differences in special ability scores.
3. Mean differences in verbal ability and mathematical ability in the general population have virtually disappeared.
4. Males appear to be more variable in a number of ability measures and this difference in variability, particularly at the high end of the distribution of ability, may contribute to an excess number of males above relatively high cutting scores.
5. There are gender differences on tests of spatial ability. The magnitude of the difference appears to vary with the type of test and may be as high as .75 standard deviation units in favor of males over females for tests of mental rotation.

Generalizations (1) and (3) do not require explanation. There is little to explain about the absence of effects. Perhaps the two most challenging generalizations that require explanation are generalization (4) and (5). Little is known about gender differences in variability and most of the literature on gender differences has been devoted to the explanation of differences in means rather than variability. It may be that variability differences have important social consequences. For example, if selective institutions use high cutting scores on the SAT as one means of selecting their students, they will find more males meeting this criterion than females. It is clear that we need to know more about the reasons for differences in variability, and research on gender differences might profitably concern itself with this issue.

Generalization (5) has been the subject of a considerable body of speculation and theoretical analysis. Studies of performance on rotation tasks provide information about the processes that distinguish male and female performance on these tasks. Linn & Petersen (1985) indicated that gender differences are less likely to be found on measures of the intercept of the function relating decision time to the angle of rotation. Gender differences are more likely to be present on measures of slope. Lohman (1986) analyzed gender differences in speed–accuracy tradeoffs in a mental rotation task. He found that differences in the slope of decision times as a function of angle of rotation were attributable to differences in speed–accuracy tradeoffs. Females reached asymptotic performance in their speed–accuracy tradeoff curves more rapidly than males on the longest rotation tasks. Males and females did not differ significantly in speed of rotation when the accuracy of rotation was controlled. It took females longer to solve the more difficult problems. Slope differences in spatial rotation measures may be determined by the time taken to solve the more difficult problems. Therefore, some of the gender differences may be attributable to gender differences in caution and decision criteria used to attain a given level of accuracy. It is also the case that these data suggest that there are gender differences in the difficulty level of rotation problems.

What accounts for the gender differences in spatial ability? The analysis of performance on rotation tasks presented in Chapter 4 based on the Minnesota study of twins reared apart by McGue and Bouchard indicated that the parameters of percentage correct, slope, and intercept are heritable. McGue and Bouchard also found that none of their measures of parental characteristics and childhood environmental factors correlated with performance on spatial ability indices in their adult sample of twins. There is little ambiguous evidence that relates specific socialization experiences to performance on either general or specific intellectual abilities. Correlations between specific socialization experiences and specific abilities are not easily interpreted since the activities that children engage in may in part be determined by genetically influenced characteristics of children that determine their activities and the response of parents to children. In addition, evidence that opposite-sex DZ twins are as alike as same-sex DZ twins in general ability suggests that gender-specific socialization practices do not influence general intelligence. I am not aware of data on specific abilities dealing with this issue. If opposite-sex DZ twins were as similar on measures of spatial ability as same-sex DZ twins, this would suggest that differences in gender-specific socialization experiences do not influence the development of specialized intellectual abilities. This discussion supports two rather tentative conclusions. First, there is little convincing data that supports a socialization explanation of gender differences in spatial ability. This assertion does not imply that such an interpretation is not plausible or could not be developed. It implies only that strong evidence in favor of such an interpretation does not exist. What of the possibility of a genetic explanation of the difference? The fact that spatial ability is a heritable trait indicates that genetic factors might be implicated in gender differences. This is a very weak conclusion. It does not indicate that biological factors are implicated.

There are two related biological explanations for sex differences in abilities that have been proposed. One is a structural theory based on the assumption that there is a difference in cerebral lateralization among males and females. The second theory attempts to relate sex differences in abilities to hormonal differences.

Levy (1969, 1976) proposed that males are more lateralized than females. She assumed that females had more bilateral representation for verbal abilities than males. She assumed that spatial ability was mediated by the right hemisphere and that the representation of verbal processing in the right hemisphere of females decreased the ability for spatial processing in females in the right hemisphere, leading to a male advantage. Levy's hypothesis is based on a series of assumptions: Males are more lateralized than females and lateralization with specialization of function for spatial processing in the right hemisphere is associated with superior performance on tests of spatial ability. Hahn (1987; see also Bryden, 1982; McGlone, 1980) reviewed research on sex differences in cerebral lateralization derived from five different areas of investigation—dichotic listening, tachistoscopic presentations, EEGs, haptic identifications, and somatosensory discrimination. His review deals with studies from infancy through age 15. He concluded that there was little consistent evidence indicating sex differences in lateralization. The studies he reviewed either reported no sex differences or, where sex differences were obtained using a particular paradigm, they were not replicated by other investigators. It should be noted that many of the studies reviewed had relatively small samples and may have had relatively low power to reject null hypotheses derived from the assumption of equality in cerebral lateralization for males and females. Hahn suggested that performance on the tasks used to assess laterality might be influenced by several methodological variables that might influence the degree of lateralization of performance on the tasks as well as results related to sex differences in cerebral lateralization.

Voyer & Bryden (1990) reported the results of a study of sex differences in the lateralization of rotation that provides information about sex differences in cerebral lateralization and the relationship between lateralization and spatial ability. They obtained measures of spatial ability using a paper and pencil test of rotation developed by Vandenberg & Kuse (1978). They also presented visual rotation problems to the right and left visual hemifield using a tachistoscope. They found a gender × visual field interaction for performance on the tachistoscopic visual rotation task.

Males exhibited superior performance on rotation problems presented to the left hemifield (right hemisphere) and females exhibited superior performance for rotation problems presented to the right hemifield. They obtained a measure of the lateralization of performance on the rotation problem by subtracting the reaction times for right visual field presentations from the reaction times for left visual field presentations. A negative value for this index would indicate a right hemisphere advantage for processing rotation problems. They found that this lateralization index was positively correlated for both male and female subjects with performance on their paper and pencil test of rotation performance (correlations for males and females were .37 and .52, respectively). These data suggest that superior processing of rotation problems in the left hemisphere is associated with superior spatial ability! Indeed, there was an ability × lateralization interaction for the tachistoscopic presentation of stimuli, indicating that subjects who were high in spatial ability tended to have a right-visual-field (left-hemisphere) advantage for solving rotation problems. Other groups had a left-visual-field advantage. Thus the pattern of cerebral lateralization that was exhibited by females in this study was characteristic of superior spatial ability. Voyer and Bryden suggested that there is a right-hemisphere advantage for processing novel stimuli and a left-hemisphere advantage for processing familiar stimuli. They assumed that subjects who had superior spatial ability would be more likely than low-spatial-ability subjects to be familiar with rotation problems and would therefore exhibit a left-hemisphere advantage for this task. Whether or not this ad hoc hypothesis is correct, the results obtained by Voyer and Bryden are illustrative of the complexities inherent in attempts to use cerebral lateralization as an explanation for gender differences in spatial ability. Even where cerebral lateralization differences are obtained that are congruent with theoretical expectations derived from Levy's model, the relationship with spatial ability indices may not be congruent with theoretical assumptions relating lateralization to differences in spatial abilities.

Kimura & Hampson (In press) summarized evidence suggesting that male and female differences in cognitive abilities are related to hormonal differences. There is evidence relating variation in hormonal characteristics to cognitive performance. Resnick, Berenbaum, Gottesman, & Bouchard (1986) administered a battery of cognitive ability tests to females who had congenital adrenal hyperplasia. These females are prenatally exposed to adrenal androgens. They compared these females to sibling or cousin controls on a variety of cognitive abilities. The experimental and control groups had relatively equal general intelligence as indexed by performance on the Raven test. The control group had Raven test performance that was .08 standard deviations higher than that of the females with congenital adrenal hyperplasia. The experimental subjects had spatial ability scores that averaged .665 standard deviations higher than the scores of the control subjects. These results indicate that females who are exposed prenatally or perinatally to androgens will exhibit superior spatial ability. The results are based on small samples (N = 13 in the experimental group, N = 8 in the control group) but they do support the assumption that sex differences in spatial ability may be related to hormonal differences between males and females.

Shute, Pellegrino, Hubert, & Reynolds (1983) measured androgens in the blood in normal male and female students. They found that females with high levels of androgens had higher spatial ability scores than females with low levels of androgens. For males, the results were in the opposite direction. These results, when combined, provide evidence for a curvilinear relationship between androgen levels and performance on tests of spatial ability. Very high levels of androgen characteristic of males with high androgen levels are associated with relatively poor performance on tests of spatial ability. Low levels of androgen characteristic of females with low androgen levels are also associated with poor spatial ability. Intermediate levels of androgen characteristic of males with low androgen levels or females with high androgen levels are associated with superior performance on tests of spatial ability.

Hampson (1990) administered a battery of tests to women when they were assumed to be menstruating or in the midluteal phase of the menstrual cycle. She assumed that the high levels of progesterone and estrogen characteristic of the midluteal phase of the menstrual cycle would lead to better performance on tests in which females tended to perform better than males and to poorer performance on tests in which females performed more poorly than males. She found that women who took the spatial ability tests when they were menstruating performed better than women who took the test during the midluteal phase of their cycle. This effect was not present on other ability tests that favored females. For these tests, women taking the test initially during the midluteal phase performed better than women taking the test when they were menstruating. Thus the differences in performance on spatial ability tests were not attributable to a generalized superiority on all tests of ability. Hampson also included within-subject comparisons on tests of abilities. Each subject took the battery of tests twice during each phase of her menstrual cycle (there were counterbalanced orders of test taking). There were no statistically significant differences in performance on tests of spatial abilities based on the within-subject comparisons. Hampson attributed the lack of significant within-subject differences on tests of spatial ability to carryover practice effects from the first to the second administration of the test. The failure to obtain within-subject differences on measures of spatial ability makes it difficult to interpret Hampson's results.

Kimura & Hampson (In press) reported the results of a study of postmenopausal women who were receiving estrogen therapy. They contrasted the performance of these women on tests of spatial ability during low- and high-estrogen phases of their therapy. They found no significant differences in spatial abilities as a function of the administration of endogenous estrogens in this study.

It should be clear from this brief review that there may be relationships between hormones and performance on various tests of cognitive abilities. The relationships are complex and are not consistent. Studies in this area rarely provide clear and unambiguous findings in support of clearly articulated theoretical assertions. The precise nature of the biological differences that may contribute to gender differences in performance on spatial ability tests is not known.

This brief survey of research on gender differences in intelligence leads to the following conclusion. There are two kinds of gender differences in intelligence. Males are more variable than females, leading to an excess number of males above high cutting scores. Males score higher than females on tests of spatial ability. There are no explanations for these differences that have received consistent empirical support.

11

BEYOND IQ: SOCIAL INTELLIGENCE AND PERSONALITY

SOCIAL INTELLIGENCE

Intelligence is often defined in terms of ability to solve personal problems. Sternberg (1985) defined intelligence as "purposive adaptation to, and selection and shaping of, real-world environments relevant to one's life" (Sternberg, 1985, p. 45). It is commonly believed that academic intelligence as assessed by IQ tests is imperfectly related to ability to function intelligently in everyday life. We all know academically intelligent individuals whose personal lives are a shambles. Indeed, we all know academically intelligent individuals who do not function well in academic settings because of emotional problems. In this chapter we shall consider several attempts to go beyond IQ to a consideration of the diverse relationships between intelligence and other personal characteristics that may influence a person's ability to function "intelligently" in a variety of social settings. These issues may be pursued from two somewhat contradictory perspectives. Some may believe that intelligence as conventionally assessed by IQ tests is unimportant and has little or nothing to contribute to our understanding of a person's social success. Others believe that IQ may be an important influence on academic performance but academic success has little or nothing to do with success in other areas.

Sternberg (1985) presented profiles of three graduate students in Yale's Department of Psychology to explicate his triarchic theory of intelligence. Alice is described as an admissions officer's dream—a student with high grades, high test scores, and good recommendations. She is described as having high analytical and critical intelligence. She was IQ test smart but she was unable to develop her own ideas. Sternberg described her as being deficient in both practical and synthetic intelligence despite her high IQ.

Barbara is described as the admissions officer's nightmare—a student with good grades and "abysmal" aptitude test scores. She was exceptionally creative and able to view things in a novel way.

Celia was somewhere between Alice and Barbara. She did not have Alice's analytic abilities nor was she as creative as Barbara. She had "street smarts." She was able to figure out the demands of the situations she encountered and adjust her behavior to meet those demands.

Sternberg described each of these graduate students as being intelligent in a different way and these differences are taken as the basis for the explication of a theory of intelligence that goes beyond IQ and emphasizes different aspects of intellectual functioning. From my perspective, this analysis omits much of what is important about IQ. What is important about intelligence is that it is an individual-difference characteristic that predicts whether or not a person will be successful enough academically to be admitted to Yale's Department of Psychology as a graduate student, or, to consider the opposite extreme, whether or not a person will have difficulty mastering the academic curriculum of the elementary school. To focus on differences among students with the academic intelligence to be admitted to Yale's graduate school exemplifies an elitist conception of intelligence. Once one has attained a certain level of intelligence, how much intelligence you have, or the various forms in which it is expressed, may not matter. If you have money to buy food, it does not matter whether bread is available or not—you can eat cake.

There are a number of attempts to measure characteristics of persons that are independent of academic intelligence as assessed by IQ tests that are assumed to predict the ability to function intelligently in a variety of social settings. Epstein & Meier (1989) developed an inventory designed to measure competence in constructive thinking. They assumed that academic intelligence is a measure of the rational components of the mind and that it is unrelated to an experiential component of the mind that is assumed to operate preconsciously and to influence an individual's emotional life (see Epstein, 1988, for an explication of the theory). The Constructive Thinking Inventory measures dimensions of thought that are designed to measure the effectiveness of an individual's ability to control his or her emotional life and to cope with problems of living. Table 11.1 presents examples of items from the inventory.

Epstein and Meier administered the inventory to a sample of 174 undergraduates. They also obtained self-report information abut the subject's "success in living." They included items that measured success in a work setting (these included reports about the number of hours worked during the past year and an index of employer satisfaction with the worker based on such indices as invitations to return, salary increases, and estimated favorableness of a letter of recommendation that the employer would write for the employee—as judged by the student filling out the forms), success in social situations, success in love relationships, an index of self-discipline referring to overeating and the use of alcohol or other mind-altering drugs, and a medical checklist of common student ailments.

Epstein and Meier found that scores on the Constructive Thinking

TABLE 11.1 Examples of Items from Constructive Thinking Inventory[a,b]

Emotional Coping
   I worry a great deal about what other people think of me. $(-)$
   I don't let little things bother me.
   I tend to take things personally.
Behavioral Coping
   I am the kind of person who takes action rather than just thinks or complains about a situation.
   I avoid challenges because it hurts too much when I fail. $(-)$
   When faced with upcoming unpleasant events, I usually carefully think through how I will deal with them.
Categorical Thinking
   There are basically two kinds of people in this world, good and bad.
   I think there are many wrong ways, but only one right way, to do almost anything.
   I tend to classify people as either for me or against me.
Superstitious Thinking
   I have found that talking about successes that I am looking forward to can keep them from happening.
   I do not believe in any superstitions. $(-)$
   When something good happens to me, I believe it is likely to be balanced by something bad.
Naive Optimism
   If I do well on an important test, I feel like a total success and that I will go very far in life.
   I believe that people can accomplish anything they want to if they have enough willpower.
   If I were accepted at an important job interview, I would feel very good and think that I would always be able to get a good job.
Negative Thinking
   When I am faced with a new situation, I tend to think the worst possible outcome will happen.
   I tend to dwell more on pleasant than unpleasant incidents from the past. $(-)$
   I get so distressed when I notice that I am doing poorly in something that it makes me do worse.

[a]Based on Epstein & Meier (1989).
[b]Items are scored on a 1–5 scale for the degree to which they are true or false. Items followed by a $(-)$ are scored in reverse direction.

Inventory were unrelated to intelligence. They found that IQ scores loaded .10 on a general factor defined by the separate components of the Constructive Thinking Inventory. Table 11.2 presents correlations between IQ scores and Constructive Thinking scores and the several indices of "success in living." These data indicate that the Constructive Thinking Inventory is a better predictor of success in living than IQ. IQ scores are more predictive of academic achievement than Constructive Thinking Inventory scores. On each of the other outcome variables, constructive thinking scores are more predictive than IQ.

These data raise several interpretive issues. First, it should be noted that students in a university are selected for intelligence. They are not

TABLE 11.2 Correlations between Constructive Thinking, IQ, and Criteria of Success in Learning[a]

	Work	Love	Social relationships	Academic achievement	Psychological symptoms	Physical symptoms	Self-discipline problems	Alcohol and drug problems
CTI scale	.19	.26	.36	.14	-.39	-.22	-.25	-.22
IQ scale	.11	-.04	-.13	.43	.17	-.04	-.14	-.02

[a]Based on Epstein & Meier (1989).

selected for skill in constructive thinking. Therefore, correlations between IQ and some of these outcome variables will be subject to reductions attributable to restrictions in range of talent.

Second, the correlations between constructive thinking scores and the outcome variables are relatively low. Excluding academic achievement, they range in magnitude from .19 to .39. These data indicate that scores on the Constructive Thinking Inventory have lower relationships to these indices of success in living than IQ has to academic achievement. The obtained relationships between constructive thinking indices and indices of successful living may over- or underestimate the "true" relationships among these variables. Constructive thinking and indices of success in living derive principally from self-report measures. Generalized dispositions to describe oneself in negative terms may influence both variables. Obtained correlations between IQ and success in school are more nearly determined by independently obtained behavioral indices. Note that IQ is a behaviorally derived index. That is, it is based on an individual's ability to answer various questions and to solve various problems. IQ tests do not ask individuals to rate their vocabulary—a measure of a person's vocabulary is derived from the ability of an individual to correctly define words. By contrast, the items in the behavioral coping index measure self-described beliefs and reactions. A person who says that he or she takes action rather than complains about a situation is presenting a characterization of a behavioral tendency. This type of item is analogous to asking a person if he or she has a large vocabulary.

The indices of success in living are also determined principally by self-reports about behavior rather than by actual objective indices of behavior. By contrast, the dependent variable of academic success is determined by independent ratings of a person's performance by teachers or by performance on standardized tests that consist of measures of behavior, i.e., the ability of an individual to correctly answer a question. Thus the validity of IQ measures as determinants of academic achievement rests on relationships between independently assessed indices of behavior. The validity of the constructive thinking score is based on correlations among items that are based for the most part on self-reports of behavioral tendencies obtained at the same time from the same individuals. The issue of temporal continuity underscores another important difference between validity correlations for IQ and the validity correlations reported by Epstein and Meier. Research reviewed in Chapter 9 indicates that it is possible to administer an IQ test to children in kindergarten and predict performance on reading tests administered to the children several years after the IQ test is administered. Note that the IQ score is obtained when the majority of the children taking the test do not know how to read. Thus IQ is predictive of future behavior. It is also the case that these correlations may underestimate the true relationship between constructive thinking and success in living. Better measures based on objective

indices might indicate that constructive thinking is more substantially related to successful living than is indicated by the correlations reported by Epstein and Meier.

Third, the Constructive Thinking Inventory is related to measures of personality. Epstein and Meier reported that Constructive Thinking Inventory scores correlate .54 with a measure of neuroticism or tendency to negative thinking derived from an adjective checklist. Epstein and Meier also indicated that the correlations between the neuroticism index and the measures of success in living were lower than those between scores on constructive thinking and success in living. While the measure of constructive thinking appears to be partially independent of neuroticism as assessed by an adjective checklist, the relationship between other indices of neuroticism based on standard self-report measures and the kinds of dependent variables used by Epstein and Meier remains to be determined. There is a large literature relating neuroticism as assessed by self-report indices or ratings to other measures. It is beyond the scope of this volume to present an explication of contemporary trait theories of personality (see Brody, 1988, for a review of trait theories). There is evidence that personality may be described in terms of a limited number of general traits including such traits as neuroticism, extraversion, and impulsivity. It is not clear if the Constructive Thinking Inventory measures characteristics of persons that are substantially independent of standard trait measures. It is possible that Epstein and Meier have simply put old wine in new bottles. That is, they may have rediscovered that personality traits relate to social behavior.

I have raised a number of questions about the research of Epstein and Meier. My analysis of their research has, in some respects, indicated that the evidence reported for the predictive validity of the index of constructive thinking compares unfavorably with the evidence for the validity of IQ tests in what may be a somewhat more limited sphere of social competence. It should be noted that such a comparison is, in a sense, unreasonable. IQ tests have been available for over 80 years and evidence of their predictive validity at least for performance in academic contexts is extensive. The potential utility of the Constructive Thinking Inventory remains to be extensively investigated.

Wagner & Sternberg (1986; Wagner, 1987; Sternberg, Wagner, & Okagaki, (in press) developed a theory of tacit knowledge which they defined as knowledge about managing oneself, managing others, and managing a career. They assumed that success in many different work settings was dependent upon tacit knowledge. Such knowledge is rarely explicitly taught despite its potential importance for success. They developed measures of tacit knowledge by interviewing successful professionals in a field and then constructing work-related situations that present alternative courses of action to individuals. Correct responses to the sit-

uations were developed by obtaining the consensus judgments of experienced and successful professionals. Table 11.3 presents examples of two items used in this research, one for academic psychologists and one for business managers.

Wagner and Sternberg provided two kinds of evidence for the validity of their indices of tacit knowledge. First, they demonstrated that groups who differed with respect to exposure to professional settings differed in their tacit knowledge. For example, undergraduates, graduate students in psychology, and academic psychologists differed with respect to their scores on a tacit knowledge test. Similarly, business managers received higher scores on a tacit knowledge measure than business school students. They also related performance on measures of tacit knowledge to within-group differences in measures of professional success. Table 11.4 presents a summary of some of the validity correlations for tacit knowledge measures obtained in several different studies. Note that the correlations are moderately high. Tacit knowledge appears to be related to diverse indices of professional accomplishment. The correlations, which are uncorrected, approach .5, suggesting that tacit knowledge scores account for 25% or more of the variance in professional accomplishment.

Wagner and Sternberg reported that tacit knowledge scores are uncorrelated with general intelligence—at least within the samples they studied that tend to be somewhat restricted in range of talent for general intelligence. While the magnitude of the reported correlations obtained is impressive, the conceptual interpretation of these findings is somewhat vexed. Tacit knowledge is related to experience. For example, Wagner and Sternberg reported that the tacit knowledge scores of psychology faculty were 1.26 standard deviation units higher than the scores of undergraduates. Tacit knowledge scores for business managers correlated .30 with years of experience as a manager. These relationships point to an important conceptual difference between validity coefficients for general intelligence and validity coefficients for tacit knowledge scores. Since intelligence is relatively stable and does not substantially increase as a result of professional experience in a particular occupation, intelligence may properly be described as a prior ability of a person. Intelligence is an individual-difference characteristic that a person brings to the job and thus a person's scores on an intelligence test may be used to predict future performance. Some primordial aspects of intelligence are present in a person's genotype, and individual differences in intelligence are primordially manifested in the first year of a person's life. There is no evidence that individual differences in tacit knowledge are heritable or are in some primordial or latent sense manifested in the first year of life (although it is not utterly absurd to imagine that the ability to acquire knowledge is related to temperamental characteristics of a person that are partially influenced by genotypes and are primordially manifested in the first year

TABLE 11.3   Items Used to Assess Tacit Knowledge[a]

Academic Psychology Item

It is your second year as an assistant professor in a prestigious psychology department. This past year you published two unrelated empirical articles in established journals. You don't believe, however, that there is a research area that can be identified as your own. You believe yourself to be about as productive as others. The feedback about your first year of teaching has been generally good. You have yet to serve on a university committee. There is one graduate student who has chosen to work with you. You have no external source of funding, nor have you applied for funding.

Your goals are to become one of the top people in your field and to get tenure in your department. The following is a list of things you are considering doing in the next 2 months. You obviously cannot do them all. Rate the importance of each by its priority as a means of reaching your goals.

_____ a. Improve the quality of your teaching
_____ b. write a grant proposal
_____ c. begin long-term research that may lead to a major theoretical article
_____ d. concentrate on recruiting more students
_____ e. serve on a committee studying university-community relations
_____ f. begin several related short-term research projects, each of which may lead to an empirical article

.
.
.

_____ o. volunteer to be a chairperson of the undergraduate curriculum committee

Business Manager Item

It is your second year as a midlevel manager in a company in the communications industry. You head a department of about 30 people. The evaluation of your first year on the job has been generally favorable. Performance ratings for your department are at least as good as they were before you took over, and perhaps even a little better. You have two assistants. One is quite capable. The other just seems to go through the motions but to be of little real help.

You believe that although you are well liked, there is little that would distinguish you in the eyes of your superiors from the nine other managers at a comparable level in the company.

Your goal is rapid promotion to the top of the company. The following is a list of things you are considering doing in the next 2 months. You obviously cannot do them all. Rate the importance of each by its priority as a means of reaching your goal.

_____ a. find a way to get rid of the "dead wood," e.g., the less helpful assistant and three or four others
_____ b. participate in a series of panel discussions to be shown on the local public television station
_____ c. find ways to make sure your superiors are aware of your important accomplishments
_____ d. make an effort to better match the work to be done with the strengths and weaknesses of individual employees

.
.
.

_____ n. write an article on productivity for the company newsletter

[a]Based on Wagner & Sternberg (1986).

TABLE 11.4 Examples of Validity Correlations for Tacit Knowledge[a]

Group	Measure	r[b]
Academic psychologists	Citations	.23
Academic psychologists	Citations	.44
Academic psychologists	Publications	.32
Academic psychologists	Publications	.28
Business manager	Salary	.21
Bank manager	Percentage salary increase	.48
Bank manager	Performance rating	.37
Life insurance people	Yearly quality awards	.35

[a]Based on Wagner & Sternberg (1986), Wagner (1987); Sternberg, Wagner & Okagaki (in press).

[b]All correations based on tacit knowledge are scored in the positive direction, indicating that superior tacit knowledge is associated with higher performance on the measure.

of life). More critically, tacit knowledge measures are not obtained prior to entry into an occupation in this research program. Therefore, it is not at all clear if they are or are not predictively relevant to future performance.

The concurrent nature of the validity correlations for tacit knowledge indices fails to provide a basis for distinguishing between two different interpretations of the relationships between tacit knowledge and occupational success. (1) The individuals who rapidly acquire tacit knowledge use this knowledge to perform the tasks required for professional success in an optimal manner. On this analysis, tacit knowledge is causally related to professional achievement. (2) Individuals who are professionally successful are placed in roles that permit them to acquire tacit knowledge. Tacit knowledge is a by-product of professional success and is not causally related to professional success. One way to distinguish between these two interpretations of the relationship between tacit knowledge and occupational success is to attempt to inculcate tacit knowledge and demonstrate that obtained increases in tacit knowledge are associated with better occupational performance. Sternberg et al. (in press) briefly reported that such efforts had been successful with schoolchildren. If it can be established that increases in tacit knowledge increase occupational success, then it would be reasonable to assume that tacit knowledge is causally related to occupational success. It is my guess that such efforts will be only marginally successful. Here is a speculative justification for this guess. It would be relatively easy to provide individuals with tacit knowledge. For example, the tacit knowledge information contained in the test for academic psychologists could be assembled in a relatively short book including examples of various situations and the responses of experts. If individuals assimilated this information would it improve their performance as academic psychologists? I think it might be useful but I doubt if it would have a major impact on their eventual success. It is my impression after serving as mentor to a number of academic psychologists that their eventual success in terms of such measures as citation indices has little or nothing to do with their tacit knowledge of appropriate strategies to be followed. Individuals differ in talent for research. Many beginning academic psychologists understand that their eventual success in the profession is contingent on developing programmatic research. Many are unable to do so in part because they do not have the talents required to be a successful researcher. Tacit knowledge in academic psychology as measured by Wagner and Sternberg is inversely related to time spent teaching. Many academic psychologists like teaching and administration and find these activities rewarding. Their efforts in these activities may not be seen as counterproductive. Thus their failure to spend more time in research, irrespective of the reward structure of many academic institutions, may be in part a matter of choice rather than a poor decision determined by a deficiency in tacit knowledge. Similarly, skill in interpersonal relations and the ability to manage other individuals may not be solely or even substantially determined by tacit knowledge. Such abilities may derive in part from personality characteristics that are not easily altered. What may be implicit in the Wagner and Sternberg analysis is a belief that knowledge determines action. Knowing what to do may not be a sufficient basis for doing the right thing. There is a rational and cognitive model of motivation and personality that is implicit in the research on tacit knowledge. People will behave in an optimal manner if they know what they should do. By contrast, it is possible to argue that we often know what we should do, but for a variety of reasons, not always rational, we may find it difficult to do what we know we should do. A full discussion of this issue is clearly beyond the scope of this book (see Brody, 1983a, for a discussion of the cognitive theory of motivation, and Brody, 1988, for a discussion of change and stability in personality—both issues that bear on the question of the role of belief in transforming human action).

The discussion of research on tacit knowledge has detoured. To return to the research, it is clear that a promising beginning has been made on the development of measures that are related to competence in a variety of settings. It remains to be determined whether these measures are causally related to success or are merely a by-product of success.

Do people differ in social skills? Is there anything analogous to g in the domain of social intelligence? We shall review several attempts to measure individual differences in social intelligence. Rosenthal, Hall, DiMatteo, Roberts, & Archer (1979) developed a test of the ability to understand social behaviors called the Profile of Nonverbal Sensitivity (PONS). The test consists in the film presentation of 220 scenes in which a person depicts an affective state. The scenes vary with respect to the nature of emotion that is depicted and also with respect to the amount of information conveyed to the viewer. The film may depict various parts of the body (e.g., the face only) and may or may not include auditory information. Viewers are asked to answer multiple choice questions about each of the film depictions.

Rosenthal *et al.* reported the results of an extensive set of investigations using the PONS test. They demonstrated that the test is reliable (test–retest $r = .69$) and that it appears to measure a general ability to accurately judge emotional expressions. It is possible to derive a number of subscores from the inventory by considering the type of emotional expression depicted (e.g., positive versus negative) or the kind of representation presented (e.g, including or excluding the face). Different subscores derived from the PONS are positively correlated. Rosenthal *et al.* obtained median correlations among several subscores in six different samples and then obtained the median of these medians. The median correlation was .39. This result indicates that ability to accurately judge the emotional meaning of the scenes depicted in the PONS is a skill that predicts performance in several variants of this task. They also found that PONS scale scores are only weakly related to general intelligence. They obtained correlations between the PONS and various indices of academic intelligence (IQ, SAT, etc). The median r was .14. These results indicate that the abilities measures by the PONS test are relatively independent of general intelligence. Is the PONS test related to other social skills? Rosenthal *et al.* related PONS scores to self-reports about interpersonal success. Table 11.5 presents a summary of these studies. An examination of the data in Table 11.5 indicates that the correlations are quite low. Therefore, skill at interpreting emotional states is not highly correlated with self-reported interpersonal success. Scores on the PONS test are also only weakly related to ratings by others of interpersonal or nonverbal sensitivity. Rosenthal *et al.* obtained a weighted mean correlation of .16 between PONS scores and ratings obtained from supervisors, teachers, and peers in a variety of studies that included 587 subjects. These results indicate that the PONS is only weakly related to rated interpersonal skill. Rosenthal *et al.* present little or no evidence that scores on the PONS are correlated substantially with any measure of interpersonal skill. Thus the ability measured by the PONS does not appear to be substantially related to any important external criterion.

Sternberg and Smith (as cited in Sternberg, 1985) investigated the ability to judge the meaning of social situations using two different judgment tasks. They presented pictures of a man and woman interacting and asked their subjects to judge whether they were individuals who were strangers or a couple who had a close relationship. In their second task, subjects were presented with pictures of a pair of individuals interacting and asked to judge which was the other's work supervisor. They found that each of their tasks was reliable. The correlation between the two measures was .09, suggesting that ability to make accurate judgments in one social

TABLE 11.5 Correlations between PONS and Self-Reported Interpersonal Success[a]

Subjects	N	Quality of same-sex relationship	Quality of opposite-sex relationship	Number of friends	Speed in making friends	Understanding in relationship	median
Adults	326	.20	-.02	.10	.08	.06	.08
College students	378	.06	.05	.04	.08	-.02	.05
High school students	369	.08	.02	.04	.08	-.06	.06
Median		.08	.02	.04	.08	.06	

[a]Based on Rosenthal, Hall, Dimatteo, Rogers, & Archer (1979).

context is unrelated to the ability to make accurate judgments in a second context. Performance on these tasks was not predicted by scores on the PONS or by scores on the Cattell Culture-Fair Test of Intelligence. These results suggest that the skills measured by the PONS are relatively specific to the format of items used in that test. They do not appear to be substantially related, or related at all, to the ability to make judgments about the social relationships of individuals from pictures of their interactions.

Ford & Tisak (1983; see also Brown & Anthony, 1990; Keating, 1978) studied relationships between social and academic intelligence and the relationship between these intelligences and an interview measure of social competence. They administered a battery of social intelligence tests and academic intelligence tests to a sample of 218 high school students. The social intelligence measures used included a personality test (the Hogan Empathy Scale) (Hogan, 1969), measures of rated social competence obtained from self, peers, and teachers, and a behavioral measure of competence based on performance in an interview situation. They found that the several measures of social intelligence were positively correlated (average $r = .36$). The correlation is spuriously low. Several social intelligence indices had low reliabilities. These data indicate that different indices of social intelligence form a positive manifold. Social intelligence was weakly related to academic intelligence. The average r was .26. The result may be spuriously high since it included teacher ratings that might be assumed to reflect academic ability. When teacher ratings were removed from the subset of social intelligence measures, the average correlation between indices of academic intelligence and social intelligence decreased to .20. The correlations among the several indices of social intelligence involve agreements between various ratings and self-reports. Only one behavioral index was used—performance in an interview situation. The five nonbehavioral indices of social intelligence correlated between .23 and .47 with performance in the interview situation. The correlation between four indices of academic intelligence and performance in the interview correlated between .20 and .31. The social intelligence measures were marginally better predictors of performance in the interview situation than the indices of academic intelligence.

This brief review of measures of social intelligence indicates that limited progress has been made in understanding this construct. Three fundamental questions about the domain of social intelligence are, in my judgment, unresolved. First, is there a positive manifold for different behavioral measures of social intelligence? There is relatively little evidence that different behavioral measures of social intelligence are empirically related. It is not hard to think of an indefinitely large set of social skills that would form a universe of potential tests analogous to the domain of general cognitive competence. Certainly the skills measured by the PONS test as well as those measured by Sternberg and Smith would belong to the domain of social intelligence. In addition to skill at decoding nonverbal messages, social intelligence might include a variety of performance skills related to mastery of appropriate behaviors in different social settings. These might include anything from the general ability to make friends to knowing how to comfort a bereaved person. Because it is relatively difficult to obtain measures of skilled performance in realistic social contexts, little or no adequate research has been reported indicating whether or not correlations among a battery of tests of diverse social skills would exhibit a positive manifold. Correlations among ratings of social intelligence do provide evidence for a positive manifold. By contrast, the Sternberg and Smith study suggests that social skills that appear to be conceptually similar may not exhibit positive relationships. It may be that social intelligence is domain specific and highly differentiated (see Cantor & Kihlstrom, 1987). Or, it may be that the relationships among diverse social abilities have not been adequately explored and that something analogous to a generalized social intelligence does exist.

Second, to what extent do measures of social intelligence relate to real-world competence? The research fails to provide a clear answer to this question. Most of the obtained correlations with external criteria are low. Whether this is due to inadequacies of measurement or to intrinsically weak relationships is not clear.

Third, in what way is social intelligence related to personality traits? Most of the attempts to relate measures of social intelligence to personality have not used measures of the best-defined personality traits. There are data suggesting that personality may be defined in terms of a limited number of traits such as neuroticism, extraversion, and impulsivity (Brody, 1988). There is limited information available about the relationships between measures of social intelligence and basic personality traits. Rosenthal *et al.* reported inconsistent relationships between the PONS and scores on extraversion. Epstein reported that the Constructive Thinking measure of social competence was inversely related to neuroticism. He did not, however, use standardized measures of neuroticism. It may be that many of the measures of social skills and general social competence that are being developed by researchers in social intelligence are related to well-defined measures of personality.

PERSONALITY AND INTELLIGENCE

Personality and intelligence are related in diverse ways. We shall consider evidence for four types of relationships.

1. Personality characteristics may modify the relationship between intelligence and academic performance.
2. Personality characteristics may influence the development of intellectual skills.

3. Personality characteristics may influence performance on a test of intelligence.

4. There may be conceptual analogies between personality and intelligence. In particular both may be construed as traits.

Evidence for each of these four types of relationships is discussed as follows:

1. There are studies relating personality and intelligence to academic success. Kipnis (1971) reported a series of studies relating scores on a self-report measure of impulsivity to academic success. He found that impulsivity was related to academic success and seemed to moderate the influence of individual differences in intelligence on school success. Table 11.6 presents data from one of Kipnis's studies indicating a relationship between intelligence as indexed by SAT scores, impulsivity, and college grade-point average. The data in Table 11.6 indicate that individuals who score high on impulsivity and who have high SAT scores tend to have lower grade-point averages than individuals who have high SAT scores and score low on impulsivity. Kipnis also reported that individuals who are impulsive are more likely to flunk out of college than individuals who are not impulsive. Smith (1967) also reported that impulsivity related to academic success in college. He found a correlation of .47 between peer ratings of impulse control before college entry and grade-point average.

Evidence for a relationship between personality characteristics and school success is also present for temperamental variables. Matheny, Dolan, & Wilson (1976) asked school authorities to nominate children in their twin study who were experiencing academic difficulty. A control group was formed from the same cohort of twins. At a median age of 10, the children who were nominated were described as having reading test scores that were 1.9 grade equivalents lower than those of the children in the control group. It was found that at age 6 twins in the index group had Wechsler intelligence test scores that were 8 points lower than scores of twins in the control group. These results suggest that the differences in academic performance between the index and the control children are not likely to be attributable to differences in their intelligence. The standard

TABLE 11.6 Mean GPA for Individuals
Differing in SAT Scores and Impulsivity[a]

SAT	Impulsivity	
	High	Low
High	2.23	2.63
Low	1.70	1.81

[a]Based on Kipnis (1971).

deviation of grade-equivalent scores at an average age of 10 is not given in the report. It is unlikely to be very much larger than 1. Differences in reading score and the general school difficulty exhibited by the index twins relative to the control group twins cannot be accounted for by the relatively small difference they exhibited on intelligence test scores. Matheny et al. reported that the index twins were significantly different from the control twins on measures of temperament derived from the preschool period. The index twins were reported to be overly active (87 versus 26% for the control group), distractable (89% for the index versus 22% for the control group children), and were more likely to be described as experiencing feeding and sleeping problems as infants. The variables that differentiated between the index twin cases and the control cases were heritable; the concordances for monozygotic twin pairs for these variables were higher than the concordances for dyzygotic twins. These results suggest that their are temperamental variables that are genetically influenced that moderate the relationship between intelligence and academic achievement.

2. Personality characteristics may influence the development of intelligence. Huesmann, Eron, & Yarmel (1987) studied the relationship between intelligence and aggression using a longitudinal design. They obtained measures of aggression and intellectual competence at age 8 and again 22 years later when their subjects were age 30. At age 8 they obtained IQ scores and a measure of aggression based on peer nominations. At age 30 they used the Wide Ranging Achievement Test as a measure of intellectual competence and they obtained an aggression index from the Minnesota Multiphasic Personality Inventory. They reported that the correlation between age 8 IQ and their measure of intellectual competence at age 30 was .49. Using a multiple regression technique, they found that age 8 peer-nominated aggression correlated $-.21$ with age 30 intellectual competence. The multiple correlation using both of these age 8 indices to predict age 30 scores was .61. Age 8 aggression scores add significantly to the ability to predict age 30 intellectual competence. The correlation between age 8 and age 30 aggression scores was .30. The addition of IQ at age 8 to the prediction equation did not add significantly to the ability to predict aggression at age 30. Huesmann et al. indicated that intelligence is inversely related to aggression at age 8 but has little or no influence on changes in aggression after age 8. By contrast, aggressive tendencies that exhibit some continuity between age 8 and age 30 appear to interfere with opportunities for learning and may continue to depress intellectual functioning. The Huesmann et al. study presents evidence suggesting that personality characteristics may act over a long period of time to depress intellectual functioning.

3. Personality characteristics may influence performance on tests of intelligence. Some of the complexities in the relationship between personality characteristics and performance on group tests of intelligence are

illustrated in data obtained by Revelle, Humphreys, Simon, & Gilliland
(1980). They used practice items from the SAT as a measure of intellectual
performance. They administered this test to individuals differing in an
impulsive component of extraversion at different times of the day. They
assumed that time of day and differences in extraversion (impulsivity)
would influence physiological arousal and that differences in arousal
would influence intellectual performance. They assumed that introverts
(low-impulsive subjects) do not differ from extraverts (high-impulsive
subjects) in their chronic level of arousal but rather with respect to the
time of day in which they are most aroused. Nonimpulsive subjects (introverts) are likely to be highly aroused in the morning but not in the
evening. Impulsive subjects (extraverts) are assumed to be low in arousal
in the morning but high in arousal in the evening. Revelle *et al.* (1980)
reported the results of a series of studies of the influence of time of day,
impulsivity as measured by personality inventories, and caffeine, which
they assumed to be a nonspecific energizer that adds to the overall level of
arousal present in a particular subject on intellectual performance. Figure
11.1 presents the results of these studies and indicates that impulsive
subjects given caffeine in the morning exhibited a clear improvement in
task performance. Subjects low in impulsivity who were assumed to be
high in arousal in the morning showed a clear decrement in performance
when given caffeine in the morning. The opposite pattern of results was
obtained in the evening—that is, caffeine increased the performance of
those subjects low in impulsivity and led to performance decrements
among those high in impulsivity and who were assumed to be at high
levels of arousal in the evening. They interpreted this rather complex, but
replicated, pattern of interactions by appeal to the assumption that caf-

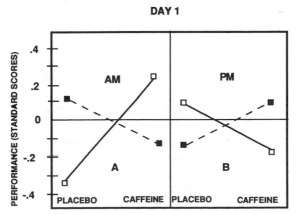

FIGURE 11.1 Performance in standard score units for high-impulsive (———) and low-
impulsive (- - - - -) subjects as a function of time of day and caffeine. (Based on Revelle,
Humphreys, Simon, & Gilliland, 1980.)

feine added to the arousal level of their subjects and that low-impulsive subjects who were highly aroused in the morning become overaroused when given caffeine and thus their performance deteriorated. The high-impulsive subjects given caffeine in the morning were underaroused, and the addition of caffeine brought them to an arousal level that was optimal for task performance.

4. There are conceptual relationships between the domains of personality and intelligence. Cantor & Kihlstrom (1987) explored these relationships from a perspective that construes intelligence and personality as context- and situationally determined individual-difference characteristics. Personality and intelligence may also be analyzed from a trait theoretical perspective (see Brody, 1988, for a fuller explication of some conceptual analogies between personality traits and general intelligence). This perspective may be justified by reference to the analogies in the following paragraphs between personality traits and general intelligence.

General intelligence and personality traits are longitudinally consistent characteristics of persons. Evidence for the longitudinal consistency of intelligence is reviewed in Chapter 8. Conley (1984) reviewed the evidence for the longitudinal consistency of personality traits and found that test–retest correlations for personality characteristics are only marginally lower than comparable correlations for general intelligence. In addition, there is evidence for the longitudinal persistence of latent personality traits inferred from diverse methods of measurement (see Brody, 1988, Chapter 2).

Personality characteristics and general intelligence exhibit cross-situational consistencies. Evidence for the existence of the cross-situational consistency of general intelligence is found in the ubiquitous finding of positive manifolds among diverse intellectual measures. Also, evidence indicating relationships between general intelligence and performance in educational settings as well as performance in laboratory measures of information-processing skills indicates that general intelligence is a disposition that influences individual differences in diverse settings. The existence of comparable cross-situational consistencies for personality traits is more problematic. In part, the lack of evidence of cross-situational consistencies in personality derives from the difficulties of obtaining behavioral measures of personality characteristics in diverse situations. I have argued that evidence of cross-situational consistencies for personality traits exists. Careful measurement of individual differences in behavior in diverse settings as well as longitudinal studies of consistencies in trait-related behaviors do provide evidence for the importance of generalized personality dispositions that influence behavior in many different settings (see Brody, 1988, Chapter 2).

Evidence reviewed in Chapter 6 of this book indicates that it is relatively difficult to modify general intelligence with existing technologies. A comparable argument may be made for personality characteristics. For example, there is relatively little evidence that enduring changes in neurotic dispositions may be obtained as a result of therapeutic interventions (see Brody, 1983b, 1985, 1990; Prioleau, Murdock, & Brody, 1983).

Evidence reviewed in Chapter 5 indicates that general intelligence is a heritable characteristic. Evidence for the heritability of personality characteristics exists (see Brody, 1988, Chapter 3; Plomin, Chipuer, & Loehlin, 1990). There are differences in the details of the way in which genetic and environmental characteristics influence intelligence and personality. Indeed, there are differences in the behavior genetic models that also are appropriate for different personality traits. There are similarities—both personality and intelligence are heritable characteristics and recent research indicates that within-family environmental differences are an important source of variance for both intelligence and personality.

Evidence in favor of a heritable component of individual differences is compatible with the search of the biological basis of individual differences. Tentative evidence for this approach for intelligence is reviewed in Chapter 7 of this book. A review of research on the biological basis of personality may be found in Zuckerman (1991).

Intelligence and personality dispositions influence socially relevant behaviors. Chapter 9 of this book presents evidence of this influence for intelligence. Comparable evidence indicating that personality characteristics are predictive of a variety of socially relevant outcomes may be found in my book on personality (Brody, 1988).

Trait conceptions are related to biological dispositions. Biological dispositions cannot account for individual differences. A reductive model of individual differences divorced from social contexts cannot account for the influence of the environment on the development and expression of phenotypes. In order to understand the way in which biological dispositions are actualized, it is necessary to understand the characteristics of the social world that provide the arena for the actualization of dispositions. One can understand individual lives in terms of three distinct influences—biological dispositions, chance encounters, and social reality. George Eliot's novel, *Middlemarch*, provides an apt example of the way in which these influences combine to influence the life of a fictional character. Dorothea Brooke is a young woman who is intelligent, passionate, idealistic, and possessed of a "hereditary strain of Puritan energy." She impetuously enters into an inappropriate marriage with an older clergyman who pretends to be engaged in great works of scholarship. If we try to understand Dorothea Brooke's life we must allow for personal dispositions (character), chance encounters, and an understanding of the social world in which she lived. It would be impossible to predict from a knowledge of Dorothea's personal dispositions that she would encounter Dr. Causabon. Understanding her character one could understand why she would choose to marry him and why her marriage would be a source of great unhappiness to her. In order to understand Dorothea's life it is necessary to understand the structure of the society in which she lived and the limited opportunities for meaningful social action provided to women of her social background in nineteenth-century England. We can hardly begin to contemplate Dorothea's frustrations or, for that matter, the genius of her creator, by appeal to scores on limited number of personal dispositions or traits. At the same time we cannot begin to understand either the life of the fictional character of her creator without understanding the personal dispositions that each brought to the worlds, both fictional and real, in which they lived.

12

EPILOGUE: THE FUTURE
OF INTELLIGENCE

RESEARCH

The first systematic theory of intelligence presented by Spearman in 1904 is alive and well. At the center of Spearman's paper of 1904 is a belief that links exist between abstract reasoning ability, basic information-processing abilities, and academic performance. Contemporary knowledge is congruent with this belief. Contemporary psychometric analyses provide clear support for a theory that assigns fluid ability, or g, to a singular position at the apex of a hierarchy of abilities. Fluid ability is linked to information-processing skills that emerge in the first year of life. And fluid ability is linked to the acquisition of academic skills. There is at least tentative evidence from genetic covariance analyses that the linkages between fundamental information-processing capacities, fluid ability, and the acquisition of academic knowledge are partially mediated by genetic characteristics. Changes in intelligence over the life span are also linked to a model of genetic unfolding. This interrelated complex of influences and ramifications of individual differences are probably linked to biological processes and may ultimately be partially understood by reference to the structure and function of the human nervous system. While there are enormous gaps in our understanding, the study of the behavior genetics of intelligence supports a model of biologically based individual-difference characteristics whose ramifications extend from performance on basic information tasks to educationally mediated social mobility. I think that in the next decades progress will be made in elucidating the biological basis of intelligence.

There are a number of respects in which a Spearmanian conception of intelligence is incomplete. Fluid ability is "invested" in a number of specific abilities and specialized procedural knowledge structures that influence a person's ability to act intelligently in a variety of social contexts. Investment is a metaphorical term, not a theory. We know little or nothing about the processes by means of which generalized dispositions

349

emerge into specialized knowledge. In part, this gap is attributable to an ideological divide in contemporary research on intelligence. One group of psychologists pursuing a Spearmanian vision of the field study intelligence as a decontextualized biologically based general disposition. A second group of psychologists attempts to go beyond IQ and emphasizes multiple skills and abilities that are expressed in different ways in different social contexts. At some point we shall have to find ways of integrating these different visions of the field. Put another way, the study of intelligence will need to become genuinely biosocial rather than merely social or merely biological.

A Spearmanian conception of intelligence is incomplete for a second reason. The study of individual differences in intelligence ignores individual differences in the meaning of the construct of intelligence for different individuals. Individuals with the same level of general intelligence may use different procedures to solve the same problem, and the same individual at different times may solve the same problem in different ways. Thus tasks may differ in the intellectual processes that they elicit. The heritability of intelligence for different groups of individuals may be different and the generality of the construct of general intelligence itself may vary for different groups or over the life span. Thus individuals may not only vary in intelligence but also in the meaning of the construct of intelligence. Such a conception of intelligence need not end in a morass of idiographic nongeneralizable meanings in which each person is intelligent in his or her own unique way. There may be general laws that predict variations in the construct of intelligence for different groups. For example, the heritability of intelligence and the extent to which a g factor accounts for variations in the intellectual performance of a person may be related to the level of intelligence of a person, or to the age of a person, or to the social background of a person. Such emerging laws qualify the meaning of the construct of intelligence and add the study of variations in the construct to the study of variations in the level of the construct.

THE FUTURE OF TESTS

The study of intelligence is controversial because of its association with tests of intelligence. Would the world be different if the tests did not exist? I think not—or at least not substantially different. Consider some of the possible uses of IQ tests and the effects of the elimination of the tests. Binet designed tests to identify children who required special educational services. IQ tests are still used for this purpose. Judgments about the need for special educational placements of children are made by considering additional information about a child including his or her functioning in the classroom. The tests may, on occasion, wrongly indicate that a particular child should be placed in special education and, equally, the tests may correctly indicate that a particular child should not be placed in a special education class. On balance, I suspect that the tests are more nearly right than wrong and that placement in special education can be made with greater accuracy with the tests than without them. Special education placement for children at the borderline may or may not be beneficial for the children. In theory, the smaller classes and extra attention provided to children in such classes may assist them and may even prepare them to benefit from the regular educational program if they are "mainstreamed." The it is also the case that such placement may result in a neglect of the child's educational needs and may serve to "warehouse" children by placing them in a setting in which little is expected of them and little is obtained. Recall the results of the evaluation of Headstart programs reported by Consortium for Longitudinal studies (see Chapter 6). They reported that participation in Headstart programs reduced the frequency of placement in special education classes. They also reported that participation in Headstart programs did not influence the acquisition of academic skills. This suggests that special education placement, like tracking programs in general, may have marginal influences on what children learn in school. The other alleged psychological consequences of attendance in special education may be equally inconsistent. For example, special education placement may lower a student's self-esteem and serve to stigmatize the student. A program that mainstreams students with marginal academic abilities may also serve to lower a student's self-esteem by providing a reference group of students who are academically more talented than the marginal student. These speculations lead me to two tentative conclusions. First, the elimination of IQ tests for placement in special education would probably have only a marginal influence on placements. The same students would, for the most part, be assigned to these classes. Second, the marginal changes in placements in special education would not have a dramatic effect on what pupils learn in school.

IQ tests are not only used for selection of pupils for programs that are assumed to benefit poor learners; they are also used to select individuals who are assumed to be academically gifted. Consider the use of the SAT tests of academic aptitude for admission to selective colleges in the U.S. The tests are not described as tests of intelligence and, I suspect for political purposes, the tests are scored on a different scale (originally designed to have a mean of 500 and a standard deviation of 100 rather than a mean of 100 and a standard deviation of 15). The SAT tests are correlated with IQ tests and may be considered as group tests of intelligence. It would be quite easy to replace the SAT tests of academic aptitude with tests of achievement. Indeed, admission to English universities is based substantially on performance on tests of achievement based on the secondary school curriculum. American universities rely on grades in secondary school, interviews, letters of recommendation, as well as performance on tests of academic achievement and academic aptitude.

Since tests of aptitude and achievement are substantially correlated and since both are correlated with grades in secondary school there is a substantial amount of redundant information in any student's admission folder. The elimination of academic aptitude tests would not deprive selective colleges of a substantial amount of information about a potential candidate for admission. There is even a conceptual argument to be made for greater reliance on tests of achievement than on tests of ability. The former are the criterion variable used to validate the latter. It is more reasonable to use the criterion rather than the measure that predicts the criterion. Where discrepancies exist between these two indices it is more reasonable to rely on the measure of achievement rather than on the measure of aptitude. Students who have high ability and who have not acquired knowledge and students who have low ability but who have acquired knowledge are both more likely to persist in their characteristics than to change. Given a choice, institutions might well prefer a good student to a mediocre student irrespective of the differences in their academic aptitudes.

It is difficult to use measures of academic achievement for admission in the United States because of the disparity of educational opportunities available to students in different schools. It is unreasonable to compare the knowledge of French of a student who attended a high school that provides 5 years of instruction in the subject with a student who has studied French in a high school that provides only 3 years of instruction in the subject. Selection of students by increased reliance on tests of academic achievement from subsets of applicant pools that provide students with relatively equal educational opportunities appears to be both fair and reasonable. The use of achievement tests to select students with unequal educational opportunities is not fair. The use of academic aptitude tests may be justified to evaluate students who attend secondary schools that do not provide an advanced curriculum. Such schools may offer few advanced placement classes, have limited foreign language courses, and have few advanced math and science courses. Such schools have few academically rigorous courses of any kind and frequently have few students who will attend selective colleges and universities. Academically talented students who attend such schools may have good grades and poor academic achievement as assessed by standardized tests of achievement. In such a case, measures of academic aptitude may be useful to a college. Note that this recommendation for the use of aptitude tests is contrary to many popular discussions of the use of such tests. That is, it is usually argued that aptitude tests should be used to assess those who are "privileged" and should not be used to assess the disadvantaged. In support of this latter position it should be noted that variations in educational opportunity may have larger effects on fluid ability measures than on crystallized ability. Therefore, better secondary school education may influence performance on measures of aptitude as much as or more than performance on measures of achievement. My preference for a larger role for aptitude tests in the selection of students whose academic background is weak stems in part from the belief that credentials of students for selective colleges who attend high schools with inadequate curricula are difficult to assess. I have taught students with excellent secondary school grades from schools that had few students going to selective colleges who had great difficulty in my classes. In many instances these students had low SAT scores.

The use of standardized tests for selection is complicated by differences in the test scores of black and white applicant pools. If admission to selective colleges and professional schools is based on test scores, the proportion of black and white applicants who will be admitted will be different. Therefore, the use of tests may be viewed as a way of excluding black individuals. Many colleges and universities are committed to increasing the racial diversity of their student bodies and increasing the representation of minorities on their campuses. The discussion of research on black–white differences in intelligence in Chapter 10 of this book can contribute in a small way to an understanding of this issue. We do know that tests exhibit little or no predictive bias for black and white students for measures of academic success. Therefore, test scores are equally informative about the expected academic performance of black and white students. The use of achievement tests rather than aptitude tests would, if anything, be more detrimental to equal admissions opportunities for black and white students. Achievement tests are highly correlated with aptitude tests. In addition, students who have inadequate secondary education are unlikely to obtain good scores on tests of achievement irrespective of their academic abilities. Thus the use of any standardized test, indeed the use of any objective criterion, is likely to decrease the enrollment opportunities of black students. These assertions present the limits of scientific knowledge on this issue. Whether equal admissions standards should be applied to candidates from different racial groups or whether affirmative action standards should be used to increase minority representation is not a scientific question. One's position on this question is determined by a sense of history and values. I find an intellectual position that advocates race-neutral treatment of individuals attractive. It is intellectually coherent—race ought not to serve as a barrier to individuals and equally it ought not to serve as an entitlement. At the same time, I believe that such a conceptually coherent position ignores the history of racial exclusion, prejudice, and separatism that has marked race relations in America. And, it is difficult to advocate racially neutral positions in the face of the history of racism in America. Accordingly, for what it is worth, I favor affirmative action polices. I state my position on this issue not because I believe that my own values and experiences carry any special importance or should be persuasive in any way. Rather, I state this preference to indicate that there is no necessary connection between scientific questions related to the validity of tests of intelligence and public policy questions. What I believe is scientifically correct is that tests inform us that race in America is weakly linked to differences in academic aptitude. Attacking the tests will do little to mask the underlying reality revealed by the tests. Eliminating the tests will not eliminate differences in academic performance. If IQ tests had not been invented or if they were banned from public use the differences in academic aptitude would not be eliminated. We would have a slightly less precise and quantitative representation of these differences and we would still be faced with the social problems that derive from the need to educate children with different degrees of academic aptitude in schools. I believe that we need to find ways to increase the academic rigor of our educational system—American children are not well educated in comparison to children in other countries. We need to find better ways of educating students with marginal intellectual abilities and we also need to find ways of fostering the education of students with unusually high intellectual ability. Intelligence tests might be useful adjuncts to this process. They provide ways of indexing intellectual competencies and monitoring educational outcomes for students with different abilities. Since the tests provide limited information about the specific knowledge and reasoning processes of individuals, their role in educational reform is limited. I suspect that their elimination would have little or no impact on our ability to reform and improve the education of American children.

I believe that we have come as far as we can with the assessment of intelligence by psychometric procedures. It is certainly possible to marginally improve current practices of assessing intelligence. IQ tests could be given on more than one occasion in order to aggregate measures to obtain a more reliable individual index. Existing widely used standard measures could be improved. The Wechsler tests include subtests with relatively low g loadings and are not optimal measures of intelligence. Tests could be created that reflect what we know about the hierarchical structure of intellect. Such tests would measure g as well as second-order specialized ability factors as well as scores on more specialized factors. While such a hierarchical and differentiated view of the intellectual abilities of an individual would bring current assessment practices into agreement with current theoretical understanding, it is not at all clear that this gain in assessment would be useful. To a considerable extent, relationships between psychometric intelligence and performance are mediated by g. And, current tests do provide an adequate index of g. While better indices of g could be obtained, they are likely to be substantially correlated with IQ and are thus unlikely to present independent information about a person that is more than marginally useful.

Is it possible to use new technologies to assess individual differences? It is not hard to imagine the development of assessment batteries using computers. In principle, there are many potential advantages in the use of computerized assessment procedures. Tests could be individuated. Branching programs could be used that would skip problems and questions and that would permit one to determine the limits of an individual's ability rapidly and efficiently. In addition, the use of computers would permit one to obtain measures of a number of different basic information-processing abilities. Such assessment could even be linked to psychophysiological measures, providing additional insight into the ways in which individuals solve various kinds of intellectual tasks. It is not hard to imagine the development of an interactive computerized assessment procedure. I believe that the development of this type of assessment tool would be useful for researchers. I do not know if it would have many practical applications. It is difficult to relate individual abilities to the design of methods of instruction that draw on the particular abilities of the learner. We have not made a great deal of progress since Cronbach and Snow comprehensively considered the problems of aptitude × instructional interactions 15 years ago. Assessments of the particular knowledge structures of a learner may be of great value to a teacher. Assessment of abilities may be too removed from the actual instructional setting to provide an ideal way of individualizing instructional programs. Whether we will be able to design instructional methods that are optimal for learners who differ with respect to their structure of intellectual abilities and whether a computerized assessment procedure providing information about information-processing abilities will provide a basis for individualizing instruction remains to be determined.

Fifteen years age I co-authored a book on intelligence. Since then the field has made major advances. New understanding has been attained about the hierarchical structure of abilities. New developments in behavior genetics and the emergence of developmental behavior genetics provide insights into the ways in which genetic and environmental events combine to influence general intelligence over the life span. Our understanding of the development of intelligence has been enhanced by research on infant intelligence and intelligence among the aged. Perhaps of greatest significance is the attempt to study intelligence with the techniques of the contemporary experimental psychologist. This effort marks a return to the use of techniques advocated by such pioneers as Spearman and has invigorated the field and added greatly to the sophistication of process-oriented studies of individual differences in intelligence. And, finally, a renewed interest in the social context in which intellectual skills influence performance enlarges our understanding of the scope of research on intelligence. The field that exists today is more intellectually demanding, diverse, and interesting than the field I wrote about in 1976. I do not believe that our intellectual progress has had a major impact on the development of tests of intelligence. Perhaps new developments in the field will be less closely tied to the use of tests. Of greater concern to me is that our intellectual progress has not had any great impact on our ability to modify intelligence or to modify the relationship between general intelligence and what is learned in the schools. Thus the social problems that have been inextricably linked with the study of intelligence remain equally urgent and equally unremediated. In this respect we have made little progress. Intelligence is not the most important thing about a person. It may tell us little or nothing about a person's character or effectiveness in a particular social role. It is not, however, an irrelevant characteristic of a person. If we value education, we should be interested in a characteristic of persons that predicts their educational performance. Scores on tests of intelligence are not important—the same may not be said for the characteristic that is imperfectly assessed by the tests.

LITERATURE CITED

Abdel-Rahim, A. R., Nagoshi, C. T., & Vandenberg, S. G. (1990). Twin resemblances in cognitive abilities in an Egyptian sample. *Behavior Genetics*, **20**, 33–43.

Agrawal, N., Sinha, S. N., & Jensen, A. R. (1984). Effects of inbreeding on Raven Matrices. *Behavior Genetics*, **14**, 579–585.

Alderton, D. L., Goldman, S. R., & Pellegrino, J. W. (1985). Individual differences in process outcomes for analogy and classification solution. *Intelligence*, **9**, 69–85.

Alexander, K. L., & Pallas, A. M. (1985). School sector and cognitive performance. *Sociology of Education*, **58**, 115–128.

Allport, D. A. (1980). Pattern and action. In G. L. Claxton (Ed.), *Cognitive psychology: New directions*. London: Routledge and Kegan Paul.

Anastasi, A. (1981). Coaching, test sophistication and developed abilities. *American Psychologist, Special Issue*, **36**, 1086–1093.

Anderson, J. E. (1939). The limitation of infant and preschool tests in the measurement of Intelligence. *Journal of Psychology*, **8**, 351–379.

Anderson, J. E. (1946). The prediction of terminal intelligence from infant and preschool tests. *Yearbook of the National Society for the Study of Education*, **39**, Part I.

Anderson, M. (1986). Inspection time and IQ in young children. *Personality and Individual Differences*, **7**, 677–686.

Bajema, C. (1971). The genetic implication of population control. *Bio-Science*, **21**, 71–75.

Baker, L. A., Vernon, P. A., & Ho, H. Z. (In press). The genetic correlation between intelligence and speed of information processing. *Behavior Genetics*.

Baltes, P. B., & Schaie, K. W. (1976). On the plasticity of intelligence in adulthood and old age: Where Horn and Donaldson fail. *American Psychologist*, **31**, 720–725.

Baltes, P. B., & Willis, S. L. (1979). The critical importance of appropriate methodology in the study of aging: The sample case of psychometric intelligence. In F. Hoffmeister and C. Müller (Eds.), *Brain function in old age*. Heidelberg: Springer.

Baltes, P. B., Kliegl, R., & Dittmann-Kohli, F. (1988). On the locus of training gains in research on the plasticity of fluid intelligence in old age. *Journal of Educational Psychology*, **80**, 392–400.

Barrett, P., Eysenck, H. J., & Lucking, S. (1986). Reaction time and intelligence: A replicated study. *Intelligence*, **10**, 9–40.

Bashi, J. (1977). Effects of inbreeding on cognitive performance. *Nature*, **266**, 440–442.

Bayley, N. (1969). *The Bayley Scales of infant development*. New York: Psychological Corporation.

Belmont, L., & Marolla, F. A. (1973). Birth order, family size, and intelligence. *Science*, **182**, 1096–1101.

Benbow, C. P. (1986). Physiological correlates of extreme intellectual precocity. *Neuropsychologia*, **24**, 719–725.

Benbow, C. P. (1988). Sex differences in mathematical reasoning ability in intellectually talented preadolescents: Their nature, effects, and possible causes. *Be-*

havioral and Brain Sciences, **11,** 169–232.

Benbow, C. P., & Stanley, J. C. (1981). Mathematical ability: Is sex a factor? *Science,* **212,** 118–119.

Benson, V. E. (1942). The intelligence and later success of sixth grade pupils. *School and Society,* **55,** 163–167.

Benton, A. (1980). The neuropsychology of facial recognition. *Psychologist,* **35,** 176–186.

Berbaum, M. L., Marcus, G. B., & Zajonc, R. B. (1982). A closer look at Gailbraith's "closer look." *Developmental Psychology,* **18,** 174–180.

Berbaum, M. L., & Moreland, R. L. (1980). Intellectual development within the family: A new application of the confluence model. *Developmental Psychology,* **16,** 506–516.

Binet, A. (1890). La perception des longeurs et des nombres chez quelques petits enfants. *Revue Philosophique,* **29,** 186–200.

Binet, A. (1905). Analyse de C. E. Spearman, the proof and measurement of association between two things and general intelligence objectively determined and measured. *L'Annee Psychologique,* **11,** 623–624.

Binet, A. (1908). Le developpement de l'intelligence chez les enfants. *L'Annee Psychologique,* **14,** 1–94.

Binet, A. (1911). Nouvelles recherches sur la mesure du niveau intellectual chez les enfants d'ecole. *L'Annee Psychologique,* **17,** 145–201.

Binet, A., & Henri, V. (1896). La psychologie individuelle. *L'Annee Psychologique,* **2,** 411–465.

Binet, A., & Simon, T. (1905a). Sur la necessite d'etablir un diagnostic scientifique des etats inferieurs de l'intelligence. *L'Annee Psychologique,* **11,** 163–190.

Binet, A., & Simon, T. (1905b). Methodes nouvelles pour le diagnostic du niveau intellectual des anormaux. *L'Annee Psychologique,* **11,** 191–244.

Binet, A., & Simon, T. (1905c). Application des methodes nouvelles au diagnostic du niveau intellectuel chez des enfants normaux et anormaux d'hospice et d'ecole primaire. *L'Annee Psychologique,* **11,** 245–336.

Binet, A., & Simon, T. (1916). *The development of intelligence in children.* Reprinted, 1983. Salem, NH: Clyer.

Birch, H. G., & Gussow, J. D. (1970). *Disadvantaged children: Health, nutrition, and school failure.* New York: Grune & Stratton.

Blagg, N. (1991). *Can we teach intelligence? A comprehensive evaluation of Feuerstein's instrumental enrichment program.* Hillsdale, NJ: Erlbaum.

Blau, P. M., & Duncan, O. D. (1967). *The American occupational structure.* New York: Wiley.

Blinkhorn, S. F., & Hendrickson, D. E. (1982). Average evoked responses and psychometric intelligence. *Nature,* **195,** 596–597.

Block, J. H., & Anderson, L. W. (1975). *Mastery learning in classroom instruction.* New York: Macmillan.

Bloom, B. S. (1964). *Stability and change in human* characteristics. New York: Wiley.

Bloom, B. S. (1974). Time and learning. *American Psychologist,* **29,** 682–688.

Bloom, B. S. (1984). The 2 sigma problem: The search for methods of instruction as effective as one-to-one tutoring. *Educational Research,* **13,** 4–16.

Bock, G., Stebbins, L. B., & Proper, E. C. (1977). *Education as experimentation: A planned variation model* (Vol. IV-B. *Effects of follow through models*). Cambridge, MA: Abt Associations.

Bornstein, M. H. (1989). Stability in early mental development: From attention and information processing in infancy to language and cognition in childhood. In M. H. Bornstein & N. A. Krasnegor (Eds.), *Stability and continuity in mental development.* Hillsdale, NJ: Erlbaum.

Bornstein, M. H. (1985a). Habituation of attention as a measure of visual information processing in human infants: Summary, systematization, and synthesis. In G. Gottlieb and N. A. Kransnegor (Eds.), *Measurement of audition and vision in the first year of postnatal life: A methodological overview.* Norwood, NJ: Ablex.

Bornstein, M. H. (1985b). How infant and mother jointly contribute to developing cognitive competence in the child. *Proceedings of the National Academy of Sciences, 82,* 7470–7473.

Bornstein, M. H. (1984). *Infant attention and caregiver stimulation: Two contributions to early cognitive development.* Paper presented at the International Conference on Infant Studies, New York City, NY.

Bornstein, M. H., & Sigman, M. D. (1986). Continuity in mental development from infancy. *Child Development, 57,* 251–274.

Bouchard, T. J., Jr. (1982). Review of identical twins reared apart: A reanalysis. *Contemporary Psychology, 27,* 190–191.

Bouchard, T. J., Jr (1983). Do environmental similarities explain the similarity in intelligence of identical twins reared apart? *Intelligence, 7,* 175–184.

Bouchard, T. J., Jr., Lykken, D. T., McGue, M., Segal, N. L., & Tellegen, A. (1990). Sources of human psychological differences: The Minnesota Study of Twins Reared Apart. *Science, 250,* 223–228.

Bouchard, T. J., Jr., & McGue, M. (1981). Familial studies of intelligence: A review. *Science, 212,* 1055–1059.

Bouchard, T. J., Jr., & Segal, N. L. (1985). Environment and IQ. In B. B. Wolman (Ed.), *Handbook of intelligence: Theories, measurements, and applications.* New York: Wiley.

Brackbill, Y., & Nichols, P. L. (1982). A test of the confluence model of intellectual development. *Developmental Psychology, 18,* 192–198.

Bradley, R., & Caldwell, B. (1976). Early home environment and changes in mental test performance from 6 to 36 months. *Developmental Psychology, 12,* 93–97.

Bradley, R., & Caldwell, B. (1980). Home environment, cognitive competence and IQ among males and females. *Child Development, 51,* 1140–1148.

Brand, C. R. (1987). The importance of general intelligence. In S. Modgil and C. Modgil (Eds.), *Arthur Jensen: Consensus and controversy.* New York: Falmer.

Brand, C. R., & Deary, I. J. (1982). Intelligence and "inspection time." In H. J. Eysenck (Ed.), *A model for intelligence.* New York: Springer.

Brebner, J., & Nettlebeck, T. (1986). Inspection time. *Personality and Individual Differences, 7,* 603–749.

Brewer, N., & Smith, G. A. (1984). How normal and retarded individuals monitor and regulate speed and accuracy of responding in serial choice tasks. *Journal of Experimental Psychology: General, 113,* 71–93.

Brody, E. B., & Brody, N. (1976). *Intelligence: Nature, determinants and consequences.* New York: Academic Press.

Brody, N. (1983a). *Human motivation: Commentary on goal-directed action.* New York: Academic Press.

Brody, N. (1983b). Where are the emperor's clothes? *Behavioral and Brain Sciences, 6,* 303–308.

Brody, N. (1985). Is psychotherapy better than a placebo? *Behavioral and Brain Sciences, 7,* 758–762.

Brody, N. (1987). Jensen, Gottfredson, and the black–white difference in intelligence test scores. *Behavioral and Brain Sciences, 10,* 507–508.

Brody, N. (1988). *Personality: In search of individuality.* San Diego: Academic Press.

Brody, N. (1990). Behavior therapy versus placebo: Comment on Bowers and Clum's meta-analysis. *Psychological Bulletin, 107,* 106–109.

Broman, S. H., Nichols, P. L., & Kennedy, W. A. (1975). *Preschool IQ prenatal and early developmental correlates.* Hillsdale, NJ: Erlbaum.

Broman, S. H., Nichols, P. L., Shaughnessy, P., & Kennedy, W. (1987). *Retardation in young children.* Hillsdale, NJ: Erlbaum.

Brookover, W., Beady, C., Flood, P., Schweitzer, J., & Wisenbaker, J. (1979). *School social systems and student achievement: Schools can make a difference.* New York: Praeger.

Brooks, A., Fulker, D. W., & DeFries, J. C. (1990). Reading performance and general cognitive ability: A multivariate genetic analysis of twin data. *Personality and Individual Differences,* **11,** 141–146.

Brown, L. T., & Anthony, R. G. (1990). Continuing the search for social intelligence. *Personality and Individual Differences,* **11,** 463–470.

Bryden, M. P. (1982). *Laterality: Functional asymmetry in the intact brain.* New York: Academic Press.

Burks, B. S. (1928). The relative influence of nature and nurture upon mental development: A comparative study of foster parent–foster child resemblance and true parent–true child resemblance. *Yearbook of the National Society for the Study of Education,* **27,** 219–316.

Burt, C. (1909–1910). Experimental tests of general intelligence. *British Journal of Psychology,* **3,** 94–177.

Busse, T. V., Ree, M., Gutride, M., Alexander, T., & Powell, L. S. (1972). Environmentally enriched classrooms and the cognitive perceptual development of Negro preschool children. *Journal of Educational Psychology,* **63,** 15–21.

Butler, S. R., Marsh, H. W., Sheppard, M. J., & Sheppard, J. L. (1985). Seven-year longitudinal study of the early prediction of reading achievement. *Journal of Educational Psychology,* **77,** 349–361.

Cahan, S., & Cohen, N. (1989). Age versus schooling effects on intelligence development. *Child Development,* **60,** 1239–1249.

Caldwell, B., & Bradley, R. (1978). *Home observation for measurement of the environment.* Little Rock: University of Arkansas.

Campbell, F. A., & Ramey, C. T. (1990). The relationship between cognitive development, mental test performance, and academic achievement in high-risk students with and without early educational experience. *Intelligence,* **14,** 293–308.

Campbell, J. T., Crooks, L. A., Mahoney, M. H., & Rock, D. A. (1973). *An investigation of sources of bias in the prediction of job performance—A six-year study* (ETS Report PR-73-37). Princeton, NJ: Educational Testing Service.

Cantor, N., & Kihlstrom, J. F. (1987). *Personality and social intelligence.* Englewood Cliffs, NJ: Prentice-Hall.

Capron, C., & Duyme, (1989). Assessment of effects of socioeconomic status on IQ in a full cross-fostering design. *Nature* **340,** 552–553.

Cardon, L. R., DiLalla, L. F., Plomin, R., DeFries, J. C., & Fulker, D. W. (1990). Genetic correlations between reading performance and IQ in the Colorado Adoption Project. *Intelligence,* **14,** 245–257.

Carlson, J. S., & Jensen, C. M. (1982). Reaction time, movement time, and intelligence: A replication and extension. *Intelligence,* **6,** 265–274.

Carlson, J. S., & Widaman, K. F. (1987). Elementary cognitive correlates of g: Progress and prospects. In P. A. Vernon (Ed.), *Speed of information-processing and intelligence.* Norwood, NJ: Ablex.

Caron, A. J., Caron, R. F., & Glass, P. (1983). Responsiveness to relational information as a measure of cognitive functioning in nonsuspect infants. In T. Fields and A. Sostek (Eds.) *Infants born at risk: Physiological, perceptual, and cognitive processes.* New York: Grune and Stratton.

Carpenter, P. A., Just, M. A., & Schell, P. (1990). What one intelligence test measures: A theoretical account of the processing in the Raven Progressive Matrices Test. *Psychological Review,* **97,** 404–431.

Carroll, J. B. (1988). Yes, there's g, and what else. Unpublished manuscript based on a colloquium presented at the University of Delaware, Nov. 17, 1988.

Caruso, O. R., Taylor, J. J., & Detterman, D. K. (1982). Intelligence research and intelligent policy. In D. K. Detterman & R. J. Sternberg (Eds.), *How and how much can intelligence be increased?* Norwood, NJ: Ablex.

Cattell, J. M. (1890). Mental tests and measurements. *Mind,* **15,** 373–381.

Cattell, J. M., & Farand, L. (1890). Physical and mental measurements of the students of Columbia University. *Psychological Review,* **3,** 618–648.

Cattell, R. B. (1936). Is our national intelligence declining? *Eugenics Review,* **28,** 181–203.

Cattell, R. B. (1937). *The fight for our national intelligence.* London: King & Sons.

Cattell, R. B. (1941). Some theoretical issues in adult intelligence testing. *Psychological Bulletin,* **38,** 592.

Cattell, R. B. (1963). Theory of fluid and crystallized intelligence: A critical experiment. *Journal of Educational Psychology,* **54,** 1–22.

Cattell, R. B. (1971). *Abilities: Their structure, growth and action.* Boston: Houghton-Miflin.

Cattell, R. B. (1987). *Intelligence: Its structure, growth and action.* Amsterdam: North-Holland.

Ceci, S. J. (1990). *On intelligence . . . more or less. A bio-ecological treatise on intellectual development.* Englewood Cliffs, NJ: Prentice Hall.

Ceci, S. J., & Liker, J. (1986). A day at the races: A study of IQ, expertise, and cognitive complexity. *Journal of Developmental Psychology: General,* **115,** 255–266.

Ceci, S. J., & Liker, J. (1988). Stalking the IQ–experience relationship: When the critics go fishing. *Journal of Experimental Psychology: General,* **117,** 96–100.

Chipuer, H. M., Rovine, M. J., Plomin, R. (1990). LISREL modeling: Genetic and environmental influences on IQ revisited. *Intelligence,* **14,** 11–29.

Clarke, A. M., & Clarke, A. D. B. (1976). *Early experience: Myth and evidence.* New York: Free Press.

Cohen, J. (1952). A factor-analytically based relationale for the Wechsler–Bellevue. *Journal of Consulting Psychology,* **16,** 272–277.

Cohen, J. (1959). A factor analytically based rationale of the Wechsler Adult Intelligence Scale. *Journal of Consulting Psychology,* **21,** 451–457.

Cohn, S. J., Cohn, C. M. G., & Jensen, A. R. (1988). Myopia and intelligence: A pleiotropic relationship? *Human Genetics,* **80,** 53–58.

Cole, S. (1979). Age and scientific performance. *American Journal of Sociology,* **84,** 958–977.

Coleman, J. S., Campbell, E. O., Hobson, C. J., McPartland, J., Moody, A. M., Weinfield, F. D., & York, R. L. (1966). *Equality of educational opportunity.* Washington, DC: U.S. Government Printing Office.

Coleman, J. S., Hoffer, T., & Kilgore, S. (1982a). Cognitive outcomes in public and private schools. *Sociology of Education,* **55,** 65–76.

Coleman, J. S., Hoffer, T., & Kilgore, S. (1982b). *High school achievement.* New York: Basic.

Conley, J. J. (1984). The hierarchy of consistency: A review and model of longitudinal findings on adult differences in intelligence, personality and self opinion. *Personality and Individual Differences,* **5,** 11–26.

Consortium for Longitudinal Studies (Ed.) (1983). *As the twig is bent . . . Lasting effects of preschool programs.* Hillsdale, NJ: Erlbaum.

Cooper, L. A., & Shepard, R. N. (1973). Chronometric studies of the rotation of mental images. In W. G. Chase (Ed.), *Visual information processing.* New York: Academic Press.

Crombie, I. K., Todman, J., McNeill, G., Florey, C. D., Menzies, I., & Kennedy, R. A. (1990). Effect of vitamin and mineral supplementation on verbal and non-verbal reasoning of school children. *Lancet,* **335,** 744–747.

Cronbach, L. J. (1968). Intelligence? Creativity? A parsimonious reinterpretation of the Wallach–Kogan data. *American Educational Research Journal,* **5,** 491–511.

Cronbach, L. J., & Snow, R. E. (1977). *Aptitudes and instructional methods.* New York: Irvington.

Damasio, A. R. (1985). Prosopognosia. *Trends in Neuroscience,* **8,** 132–135.

Daniels, D., & Plomin, R. (1985). Differential experience of siblings in the same family. *Developmental Psychology,* **21,** 747–760.

Deary, I. J. (1980). *How general is the mental speed factor in "general" intelligence:*

An attempt to extend inspection time to the auditory modality. B. S. honors thesis, University of Edinburgh, Scotland.

Deary, I. J. (1986). Inspection time: Discovery or rediscovery? *Personality and Individual Differences, 7,* 625–632.

Deary, I. J. (1988). Basic processes in human intelligence. In H. J. Jerison and I. Jerison (Eds.), *Intelligence and evolutionary biology.* Berlin: Springer.

Deary, I. J. (1989). Auditory inspection time: Review, recent research and reassessment. In D. Vickers and P. L. Smith (Eds.), *Human information processing: Measures, mechanisms, and models.* Elsevier Amsterdam: North-Holland.

Deary, I. J., & Caryl, P. G. (1990). Inspection time and cognitive ability. In K. J. Gilhooly, M. T. G. Keane, R. H. Logie, & G. Erdos (Eds.), *Lines of thinking.* London: Wiley.

Deary, I. J., & Caryl, P. G. (In press). Intelligence, EEG and evolved potentials. In P. A. Vernon (Ed.), *Biological approaches to the study of human intelligence.* Norwood, NJ: Ablex.

Deary, I. J., Caryl, P. G., Egan, V., & Wight, D. (1989). Visual and auditory inspection time: Their interrelationship and correlations with IQ in high ability subjects. *Personality and Individual Differences, 10,* 525–533.

Deary, I. J., Head, B., & Egan, V. (1989). Auditory inspection time, intelligence and pitch discrimination. *Intelligence, 13,* 135–147.

DeFries, J. C., Johnson, R. C., Kuse, A. R., McClearn, G. E., Polovina, J., Vandenberg, S. G., & Wilson, J. R. (1979). Familial resemblance for specific cognitive abilities. *Behavior Genetics, 9,* 23–43.

DeFries, J. C., Plomin, R., & LaBuda, M. C. (1987). Genetic stability of cognitive development from childhood to adulthood. *Developmental Psychology, 23,* 4–12.

Detterman, D. K. (1987). What does reaction time tell us about intelligence? In P. A. Vernon (Ed.), *Speed of information-processing and intelligence.* Norwood, NJ: Ablex.

Detterman, D. K., & Daniel, M. H. (1989).

Correlations of mental tests with each other and with cognitive variables are highest for low IQ groups. *Intelligence, 13,* 349–359.

Detterman, D. K., & Spry, K. M. (1988). Is it smart to play the horses? Comment on "A Day at the Races: A Study of IQ, Expertise, and Cognitive Complexity" (Ceci & Liker, 1986). *Journal of Experimental Psychology: General, 117,* 91–95.

Detterman, D. K., & Sternberg, R. J. (1982). *How and how much can intelligence be increased.* Norwood, NJ: Ablex.

Detterman, D. K., Thompson, L. A., & Plomin, R. (1990). Differences in heritability across groups differing in ability. *Behavior Genetics, 20,* 369–384.

Dixon, R. A., Kramer, D. A., & Baltes, P. B. (1985). Intelligence: A life-span developmental perspective. In B. B. Wolman (Ed.), *Handbook of intelligence: Theories, measurements and applications.* New York: Wiley.

Dodd, S. L. (1928). The theory of factors. *Psychological Review, 35,* 211–234.

Dodd, S. L. (1929). Sampling theory of intelligence. *British Journal of Psychology, 19,* 306–327.

Drillien, C. M. (1964). *The growth and development of the prematurely born infant.* Baltimore: Williams and Wilkens.

Duncan, O. D., Featherman, D. L., & Duncan B. (1972). *Socioeconomic background and achievement.* New York: Seminar Press.

Dunham, J. L. Guilford, J. P., & Hoepfner, R. (1966). Abilities related to classes and the learning of concepts. *Reports from the Psychological Laboratory, 39.*

Eels, K. (1951). *Intelligence and cultural differences.* Chicago: University of Chicago Press.

Elliot, R. (1987). *Litigating intelligence.* Dover, MA: Auburn House.

Epstein, S. (1988). Cognitive-experimental self-theory: Implication for developmental psychology. *Minnesota Symposium on Child Psychology.* Hillsdale, NJ: Erlbaum.

Epstein, S., & Meier, P. (1989). Constructive thinking: A broad coping variable with specific components. *Journal of Person-*

ality and Social Psychology, **57**, 332–350.

Eyferth, K. (1959). Eine untersuchung der Neger-Mischlingskinder in Westdeutschland. *Vita Humana*, **2**, 102–114.

Eyferth, K. (1961). Leistungen verschiedener Gruppen von Besatzungskindern in Hamburg—Weschler Intelligenztest für kinder (HAWIK). *Archiv für die gesamte Psychologie*, **113**, 222–241.

Eyferth, K., Brandt, U., & Hawel, W. (1960). *Farbige kinder in Deutschland*. Munich: Juventa Verlag.

Eysenck, H. J. (1939). Primary mental abilities. *British Journal of Educational Psychology*, **9**, 260–265.

Eysenck, H. J. (1967). Intelligence assessment: A theoretical and experimental approach. *British Journal of Educational Psychology*, **37**, 81–98.

Eysenck, H. J. (1984). The effect of race on human abilities and mental test scores. In C. R. Reynolds, and R. T. Brown (Eds.), *Perspectives on bias in mental testing*. New York: Plenum.

Eysenck, H. J. (1988). Editorial: The concept of "Intelligence": Useful or useless? *Intelligence*, **12**, 1–16.

Eysenck, H. J., & Barrett, P. (1985). Psychophysiology and the measurement of intelligence. In C. R. Reynolds & V. L. Willson (Eds.), *Methodological and statistical advances in the study of individual differences*. New York: Plenum.

Fagan, J. F. (1984). The relationship of novelty preferences during infancy to later intelligence and later recognition memory. *Intelligence*, **8**, 339–346.

Fagan, J. F., & McGrath, S. K. (1981). Infant recognition memory and later intelligence. *Intelligence*, **5**, 121–130.

Fagan, J. F., & Singer, L. T. (1983). Infant recognition memory as a measure of intelligence. In L. P. Lipsett (Ed.), *Advances in infancy research*. (Vol. 2). Norwood, NJ: Ablex.

Falek, A. (1971). Differential fertility and intelligence: Resolution of two paradoxes and formulation of a third. *Journal of Human Evolution*, **1**, 11–15.

Fancher, R. E. (1985). Spearman's original computation of g. A model for Burt?

British Journal of Psychology, **76**, 341–352.

Farber, S. L. (1981). *Identical twins reared apart: A reanalysis*. New York: Basic Books.

Feingold, A. (1988). Cognitive gender differences are disappearing. *American Psychologist*, **43**, 95–103.

Feshbach, S., Adelman, H., & Fuller, W. (1977). Prediction of reading and related academic problems. *Journal of Educational Psychology*, **69**, 299–308.

Feuerstein, R. (1979). *The dynamic assessment of retarded performers: The learning potential assessment device. Theory, instruments, and techniques*. Baltimore: University Park Press.

Feuerstein, R., Rand, Y., Hoffman, M. B., & Miller, R. (1980). *Instrumental enrichment: An intervention program for cognitive modifiability*. Baltimore: University Park Press.

Firkowska, A., Ostrowska, A., Sokolowska, M., Stein, Z. A., Susser, M., & Wald, I. (1978). Cognitive development and social policy: The contribution of parental occupation and education to mental performance in 11 year olds in Warsaw. *Science*, **200**, 1357–1362.

Fischbein, S. (1980). IQ and social class. *Intelligence*, **4**, 51–63.

Flanagan, J. L., & Cooley, W. W. (1966). *Project talent: One year follow-up studies*. Pittsburgh: University of Pittsburgh.

Flanagan, J. C., Dailey, J. T., Shaycroft, M. F., Gorham, W. A., Orr, O. B., & Goldberg, I. (1962). *Design for the study of American youth*. Boston: Houghton-Mifflin.

Flaugher, R. I., & Rock, D. A. (1972). *Patterns of ability factors among four ethnic groups*. Princeton, NJ: Educational Testing Service.

Flynn, J. R. (1980). *Race, IQ and Jensen*. London: Routledge & Kegan Paul.

Flynn, J. R. (1984). The mean IQ of Americans: Massive gains 1932–78. *Psychological Bulletin*, **95**, 29–51.

Flynn, J. R. (1987). Massive IQ gains in 14 nations: What IQ tests really measure. *Psychological Bulletin*, **101**, 171–191.

Fodor, J. A. (1983). *The modularity of mind. An essay on faculty psychology*. Cambridge: MIT Press.

Ford, M. E., & Tisak, M. S. (1983). A further search for social intelligence. *Journal of Educational Psychology, 75,* 196–206.

Frearson, W. M., Barrett, P., & Eysenck, H. J. (1988). Intelligence, reaction time and the effects of smoking. *Personality and Individual Differences, 9,* 497–519.

Frearson, W. M., & Eysenck, H. J. (1986). Intelligence, reaction time (RT) and a new "odd-man-out" RT paradigm. *Personality and Individual Differences, 7,* 807–817.

Freeman, F. N., Holzinger, K. J., & Mitchell, B. C. (1928). The influence of environment on the intelligence, school achievement, and conduct of foster children. *27th Yearbook of the National Society for the Study of Education, 27,* Part I.

Frydman, M., & Lynn, R. (1989). The intelligence of Korean children adopted in Belgium. *Personality and Individual Differences, 10,* 1323–1325.

Fulton, M., Thomson, G., Hunter, R., Raab, G., Laxen, D., & Hepburn, W. (1987). Influence of blood lead on the ability and attainment of children in Edinburgh. *Lancet, 1,* 1221–1226.

Gailbraith, R. C. (1982a). Just one look was all it took: Reply to Berman, Markus and Zajonc. *Developmental Psychology, 18,* 181–191.

Gailbraith, R. C. (1982b). Sibling spacing and intellectual development: A closer look at the confluence models. *Developmental Psychology, 18,* 151–173.

Gailbraith, R. C. (1983). Individual differences in intelligence: A reappraisal of the confluence model. *Intelligence, 7,* 183–194.

Galton, F. (1869). *Hereditary genius: An inquiry into its laws and consequences.* London: MacMillan.

Galton, F. (1879). Psychometric experiments. *Brain, 2,* 149–162.

Galton, F. (1883). *Inquiries into human faculty, and its development.* London: MacMillan.

Galton, F. (1885). On the anthropometric laboratory at the late International Health Exhibition. *Journal of the Anthropological Institute, 14,* 205–219.

Garber, H. L. (1988). *The Milwaukee Project: Preventing mental retardation in children at risk,* Washington, DC: American Association on Mental Retardation.

Gardner, H. (1983). *Frames of mind: The theory of multiple intelligences.* New York: Basic.

Ghiselli, E. E. (1966). *The validity of occupational aptitude tests.* New York: Wiley.

Ghiselli, E. E. (1973). The validity of aptitude tests in personnel selection. *Personnel Psychology, 26,* 461–477.

Gibson, J. J. (1979). *The ecological approach to visual perception.* Boston: Houghton-Mifflin.

Gladwin, T. (1970). *East is a big bird.* Cambridge, MA: Belknap Press.

Glutting, J. J., & McDermott, P. A. (1990). Principles and problems in learning potential. In C. R. Reynolds and R. W. Kamphaus (Eds.), *Handbook of psychological and educational assessment of children: Intelligence and achievement.* New York: Guilford Press.

Glutting, J. J., & McDermott, P. A. (In press). Childhood learning potential as an alternative to traditional ability measures. *Psychological Assessment: A Journal of Consulting and Clinical Psychology,* in press.

Goldberg, R. A., Schwartz, S., & Stewart, M. (1977). Individual differences in cognitive processes. *Journal of Educational Psychology, 69,* 9–14.

Gordon, R. A. (1984). Digits backward and the Mercer–Kamin law: An empirical response to Mercer's treatment of internal validity in IQ tests. In C. R. Reynolds & J. R. Brown (Eds.), *Perspectives on bias in mental testing.* New York: Plenum.

Gordon, R. A. (1987). Gordon replies to Shepard. In S. Modgil & C. Modgil (Eds.), *Arthur Jensen: Consensus and controversy.* New York: Falmer.

Gottfredson, L. S. (1987). The practical significance of black–white differences in intelligence. *Behavioral and Brain Sciences, 10,* 510–512.

Gottfried, A. W. (1984). Home environment and early cognitive development: Integration, meta-analysis, and conclusions. In A. W. Gottfried (Ed.), *Home environ-*

ment and early cognitive development: Longitudinal research. Orlando: Academic Press.

Gottfried, A. W., & Gottfried, A. E. (1984). Home environment and cognitive development in young children of middle-socioeconomic-status families. In A. W. Gottfried (Ed.), *Home environment and early cognitive development.* Orlando: Academic Press.

Guilford, J. P. (1964). Zero intercorrelations among tests of intellectual abilities. *Psychological Bulletin, 61,* 401–404.

Guilford, J. P. (1967). *The nature of human intelligence.* New York: McGraw-Hill.

Guilford, J. P. (1974). Rotation problems in factor analysis. *Psychological Bulletin, 81,* 498–501.

Guilford, J. P. (1977). *Way beyond the IQ: Guide to improving intelligence and creativity.* Buffalo, NY: Creative Education Foundation.

Guilford, J. P. (1981). Higher-order structure-of-intellect abilities. *Multivariate Behavioral Research, 16,* 411–435.

Guilford, J. P. (1985). The structure-of-intellect model. In B. B. Wolman (Ed.), *Handbook of intelligence: Theories, measurements and applications.* New York: Wiley.

Guilford, J. P., & Hoepfner, R. (1971). *The analysis of intelligence.* New York: McGraw-Hill.

Gustafsson, J. E. (1984). A unifying model for the structure of intellectual abilities. *Intelligence, 8,* 179–203.

Gustafsson, J. E. (1985). Measuring and interpreting g. *Behavioral Brain Sciences, 8,* 231–232.

Gustafsson, J. E. (1988). Hierarchical models of individual differences. In R. J. Sternberg (Ed.), *Advances in the psychology of human intelligence* (Vol. 4). Hillsdale, NJ: Erlbaum.

Guttman, L. (1954). A new approach to factor analysis: The radex. In P. F. Lazarsfeld (Ed.), *Mathematical thinking in the social sciences.* Glencove, IL: Free Press.

Guttman, L. (1965). The structure of the interrelations among intelligence tests. *Proceedings of the 1964 Invitational Conference on Testing Problems.*

Princeton, NJ: Educational Testing Service.

Guttman, L. (1970). Integration of test design and analysis. *Proceedings of the 1969 Invitational Conference on Testing Problems.* Princeton, NJ: Educational Testing Service.

Hahn, W. K. (1987). Cerebral lateralization of function: From infancy through childhood. *Psychological Bulletin, 101,* 376–392.

Haier, R. J. (In press). Cerebral glucose metabolism and intelligence. In P. A. Vernon (Ed.), *Biological approaches to human intelligence.* Norwood, NJ: Ablex.

Haier, R. J., Robinson, D. L., Braden, W., & Krengel, M. (1984). Psychometric intelligence and visual evoked potentials: A replication. *Personality and Individual Differences, 5,* 487–489.

Haier, R. J., Robinson, D. L., Braden, W., & Williams, D. (1983). Electrical potentials of the cortex and psychometric intelligence. *Personality and Individual Differences, 4,* 591–599.

Haier, R. J., Siegel, B., Jr., Neuchterlein, K. H., Hazlett, M. E., Wu, T. C., Paek, J., Browning, H. L., & Buchsbaum, M. S. (1988). Cortical glucose metabolic rate correlates of reasoning and attention studied with positron emission tomography. *Intelligence, 12,* 199–217.

Hampson, E. (1990). Variations in sex-related cognitive abilities across the menstrual cycle. *Brain and Cognition, 14,* 26–43.

Harnqvist, K. (1968a). Relative changes in intelligence from 3–18. I. Background and methodology. *Scandinavian Journal of Psychology, 9,* 50–64.

Harnqvist, K. (1968b). Relative changes in intelligence from 13–18. II. Results. *Scandanavian Journal of Psychology, 9,* 65–82.

Harrell, T. W., & Harrell, M. S. (1945). Army General Classification Test scores for civilian occupations. *Educational and Psychological Measurement, 5,* 229–239.

Harrison, G. A., & Owen, J. J. (1964). Studies on the inheritance of human skin color. *Annals of Human Genetics, 28,* 27–37.

Hatta, T., & Dimond, S. J. (1980). Comparison of lateral differences for digit and random form recognition in Japanese and Westerners. *Journal of Experimental Psychology: Human Perception and Performance, 6,* 368–374.

Haywood, H. C., & Arbitman-Smith, R. (1981). Modification of cognitive functions in slow-learning adolescents. In P. Mittler, (Ed.), *Frontiers of knowledge in mental retardation* (Vol. 1. *Social, educational, and behavioral aspects*). Baltimore: University Park Press.

Hearnshaw, L. S. (1979). *Cyril Burt: Psychologist.* London: Hodden and Houghton.

Hebb, D. O. (1942). The effects of early and late brain injury upon test scores and the nature of normal adult intelligence. *Proceedings of the American Philosophical Society, 85,* 275–292.

Heber, R., & Garber, H. (1972). An experiment in prevention of cultural-familial retardation. In D. A. A. Primrose (Ed.), *Proceedings of the Second Congress of the International Association for the Scientific Study of Mental Deficiency.* Warsaw: Polish Medical Publishers.

Heber, R., & Garber, H. (1975). Progress Report II: An experiment in the prevention of cultural-familial retardation. In D. A. A. Primrose (Ed.), *Proceedings of the Third Congress for the Scientific Study of Mental Deficiency* (Vol. 1). Warsaw: Polish Medical Publishers.

Henderson, N. D. (1982). Human behavior genetics. *Annual Review of Psychology, 33,* 403–440.

Hendrickson, D. E. (1982). The biological basis of intelligence. Part II: Measurement: In H. J. Eysenck (Ed.), *A model for intelligence.* New York: Springer-Verlag.

Hendrickson, D. E., & Hendrickson, A. E. (1980). The biological basis of individual differences in intelligence. *Personality and Individual Differences, 1,* 3–33.

Herrman, L., & Hogben, L. (1933). The intellectual resemblance of twins. *Proceedings of the Royal Society of Edinburgh, 53,* 105–129.

Herskovitz, M. J. (1930). *The anthropometry of the American Negro.* New York: Columbia University Press.

Hertzog, C. (1989). Influences of cognitive slowing on age differences in intelligence. *Developmental Psychology, 25,* 636–651.

Hick, W. E. (1952). On the rate of gain of information. *Quarterly Journal of Experimental Psychology, 4,* 11–26.

Higgins, J. V., Reed, E. W., & Reed, S. C. (1962). Intelligence and family size: A paradox resolved. *Eugenies Quarterly, 9,* 84–90.

Hirschi, T., & Hindelang, M. J. (1977). Intelligence and delinquency: A revisionist review. *American Sociological Review, 42,* 571–587.

Ho, H. Z., Baker, L., & Decker, S. N. (1988). Covariation between intelligence and speed of cognitive processing: Genetic and environmental influences. *Behavior Genetics, 18,* 247–261.

Hoffer, T., Greeley, A. M., & Coleman, J. S. (1985). Achievement growth in public and Catholic schools. *Sociology of Education, 58,* 74–97.

Hogan, R. (1969). Development of an empathy scale. *Journal of Consulting and Clinical Psychology, 33,* 307–316.

Horn, J. L. (1985). Remodeling old models of intelligence. In B. B. Wolman (Ed.), *Handbook of intelligence: Theories, measurements and applications.* New York: Wiley.

Horn, J. L., & Cattell, R. B. (1966). Refinement and test of the theory of fluid and crystallized intelligence. *Journal of Educational Psychology, 57,* 253–270.

Horn, J. L., & Donaldson, G. (1976). On the myth of intellectual decline in adulthood. *American Psychologist, 3,* 701–719.

Horn, J. L., Donaldson, G., & Engstrom, R. (1981). Apprehension, memory and fluid intelligence decline in adulthood. *Research on Aging, 3,* 33–84.

Horn, J. L., & Knapp, J. R. (1973). On the subjective character of the empirical base of Guilford's structure-of-intellect model. *Psychological Bulletin, 80,* 33–43.

Horn, J. L., & Knapp, J. R. (1974). Thirty wrongs do not make a right: Reply to Guilford. *Psychological Bulletin, 81,* 502–504.

Horn, J. L., & Stankov, L. (1982). Auditory and visual factors of intelligence. *Intelligence, 6*, 165–185.

Horn, J. M., Loehlin, J. C., & Willerman, L. (1979). Intellectual resemblance among adoptive and biological relatives: The Texas Adoption Project. *Behavior Genetics, 9*, 177–207.

Horn, W. F., & Packard, T. (1985). Early identification of learning problems: a meta-analysis. *Journal of Educational Psychology, 77*, 597–607.

Howe, M. J. A. (1988a). Intelligence as an explanation. *British Journal of Psychology, 79*, 349–360.

Howe, M. J. A. (1988b). The hazard of using correlational evidence as a means of identifying the causes of individual ability differences: A rejoinder to Sternberg and a reply to Miles. *British Journal of Psychology, 79*, 539–545.

Huesmann, L. R., Eron, L. D., & Yarmel, P. W. (1987). Intellectual functioning and aggression. *Journal of Personality and Social Psychology, 52*, 218–231.

Humphreys, L. G. (1967). Critique of Cattell: Theory of fluid and crystallized intelligence: A critical experiment. *Journal of Educational Psychology, 58*, 120–136.

Humphreys, L. G. (1976). A factor model for research on intelligence and problem solving. In L. Resnick (Ed.), *Proceedings: The nature of intelligence*. New York: Wiley.

Humphreys, L. G. (1985). General intelligence: An integration of actor, test, and simplex theory. In B. B. Wolman (Ed.), *Handbook of intelligence: Theories, measurement, and applications*. New York: Wiley.

Humphreys, L. G. (1989). Intelligence: Three kinds of instability and their consequences for policy. In R. L. Linn (Ed.), *Intelligence*. Urbana: University of Illinois Press.

Humphreys, L. G. (1990). Erroneous interpretation of difference scores: Application to a recent example. *Intelligence, 14*, 231–233.

Humphreys, L. G., & Parsons, C. K. (1979). A simplex process model for describing differences between cross-lagged correlations. *Psychological Bulletin, 86*, 325–334.

Hunt, E. (1978). Mechanics of verbal ability. *Psychological Review, 85*, 109–130.

Hunt, E. (1987). The next word on verbal ability. In P. A. Vernon (Ed.), *Speed of information-processing and intelligence*. Norwood, NJ: Ablex.

Hunt, E., Davidson, J., & Lansman, M. (1981). Individual differences in long-term memory access. *Memory and Cognition, 9*, 599–608.

Hunt, E., Frost, N., & Lunneborg, C. (1973). Individual differences in cognition: A new approach to intelligence. In G. Bower (Ed.), *Advances in learning and motivation* (Vol. 7). New York: Academic Press.

Hunt, E., Lunneborg, C., & Lewis, J. (1975). What does it mean to be high verbal? *Cognitive Psychology, 7*, 194–227.

Hunt, J., M. (1961). *Intelligence and experience*. New York: Ronald Press.

Hunter, J. E., & Hunter, R. F. (1984). Validity and utility of alternative predictors of a job performance. *Psychological Bulletin, 96*, 72–98.

Hunter, J. E., Schmidt, F. L., & Hunter, R. (1979). Differential validity of employment tests by race: A comprehensive review and analysis. *Psychological Bulletin, 86*, 721–735.

Hyde, J. S., Fennema, E., & Lamon, S. J. (1990). Gender differences in mathematics performance: A meta-analysis. *Psychological Bulletin, 107*, 139–155.

Hyde, J. S., & Linn, M. C. (1988). Gender differences in verbal ability: A meta-analysis. *Psychological Bulletin, 104*, 153–169.

Irwin, R. J. (1984). Inspection time and its relation to intelligence. *Intelligence, 8*, 47–65.

Jacobsen, L. L., Berger, S. M., Bergman, R. L., Milham, J., & Greeson, L. E. (1971). Effects of age, sex, systematic conceptual learning sets and programmed social interaction on the intellectual and conceptual development of pre-school children from poverty backgrounds. *Child Development, 42*, 1399–1415.

Jencks, C. (1972). *Inequality: A reassessment of the effect of family and schooling in America. New York: Basic Books.

Jencks, C. (1979). Who gets ahead? The determinants of economic success in America. New York: Basic Books.

Jencks, C. (1985). How much do high school students learn? Sociology of Education, 58, 128–135.

Jensen, A. R. (1971). Do schools cheat minority children? Educational Research, 14, 3–28.

Jensen, A. R. (1973). Educability and group differences. London: Methuen.

Jensen, A. R. (1974a). Cumulative deficit: A testable hypothesis. Developmental Psychology, 10, 996–1019.

Jensen, A. R. (1974b). The effect of race of examiner on the mental test scores of white and black pupils. Journal of Educational Measurement, 11, 1–14.

Jensen, A. R. (1977). Cumulative deficit in IQ of blacks in the deep south. Developmental Psychology, 13, 184–191.

Jensen, A. R. (1978). Genetic and behavioral effects of non-random mating. In R. T. Noble & N. Weyl (Eds.), Human variation: The biopsychology of age, race, and sex. New York: Academic Press.

Jensen, A. R. (1980a). Bias in mental testing. New York: Free Press.

Jensen, A. R. (1980b). Use of sibling data in educational and psychological research. American Educational Research Journal, 17, 153–170.

Jensen, A. R. (1981). Obstacles, problems, and pitfalls in differential psychology. In S. Scarr (Ed.), Race, social class, and individual differences in I.Q. Hillsdale, NJ: Erlbaum.

Jensen, A. R. (1982a). Reaction time and psychometric g. In H. J. Eysenck (Ed.), A model for intelligence. Berlin: Springer-Verlag.

Jensen, A. R. (1982b). The chronometry of intelligence. In R. J. Sternberg (Ed.), Advances in research in intelligence (Vol. 1). Hillsdale, NJ: Erlbaum.

Jensen, A. R. (1984). Test bias: Concepts and criticisms. In C. R. Reynolds & R. T. Brown (Eds.), Perspectives on bias in mental testing. New York: Plenum.

Jensen, A. R. (1985a). The nature of the black–white difference on various psychometric tests: Spearman's hypothesis. Behavioral and Brain Sciences, 8, 193–263.

Jensen, A. R. (1985b). Methodological and statistical techniques for the chronometric study of mental abilities. In C. R. Reynolds & V. L. Willson (Eds.), Methodological and statistical advances in the study of individual differences. New York: Plenum.

Jensen, A. R. (1987a). Individual differences in the Hick paradigm. In P. A. Vernon (Ed.), Speed of information-processing and intelligence. Norwood, NJ: Ablex.

Jensen, A. R. (1987b). Further evidence for Spearman's hypothesis concerning black–white differences in psychometric tests. Behavioral and Brain Sciences, 10, 512–519.

Jensen, A. R. (1987c). Differential psychology: Towards consensus. In S. Modgil & C. Modgil (Eds.), Arthur Jensen: Consensus and controversy. New York: Falmer.

Jensen, A. R. (1989). Review: Raising IQ without increasing g? A review of The Milwaukee Project: Preventing Mental Retardation in Children at Risk. Developmental Review, 9, 1989.

Jensen, A. R., & Figueroa, R. A. (1975). Forward and backward digit-span interaction with race and IQ: Predictions from Jensen's theory. Journal of Educational Psychology, 67, 882–893.

Jensen, A. R., & McGurk, F. C. J. (1987). Black–white bias in "cultural" and "noncultural" test items. Personality and Individual Differences, 8, 295–301.

Jensen, A. R., & Reynolds, C. R. (1982). Race, social class and ability patterns on the WISC-R. Personality and Individual Differences, 3, 423–438.

Jensen, A. R., Schafer, E. W. P., & Crinella, F. M. (1981). Reaction time, evoked brain potentials, and psychometric g in the severely retarded. Intelligence, 5, 179–197.

Jensen, A. R., & Sinha, S. N. (In press). Physical correlates of human intelligence. In P. A. Vernon (Ed.), Biological approaches to human intelligence. Norwood, NJ: Ablex.

Jensen, A. R., & Vernon, P. A. (1986). Jensen's reaction-time studies: A reply to Longstreth. *Intelligence*, **10**, 153–179.

Jones, D. C., & Carr-Saunders, A. M. (1927). The relation between intelligence and social status among orphan children. *British Journal of Psychology*, **17**, 343–364.

Jones, H. E., & Bayley, N. (1941). The Berkeley growth study. *Child Development*, **12**, 167–173.

Joynson, R. B. (1989). *The Burt affair*. London: Routledge, Chapman, Hall.

Juel-Nielsen, K. (1965). Individual and environment: A psychiatric-psychological investigation of MZ twins reared apart. *Acta Psychiatrica Scandinavica* (Suppl. 183). Copenhagen: Munksgaard.

Kail, R., & Pellegrino, J. W. (1985). *Human intelligence: Perspectives and prospects*. New York: Freeman.

Kamin, L. J. (1974). *The science and politics of IQ*. Potomac, MD: Erlbaum.

Kamin, L. J. (1980). Inbreeding depression and IQ. *Psychological Bulletin*, **87**, 469–478.

Kaplan, R. M. (1985). The controversy related to the use of psychological tests. In B. B. Wolman (Ed.), *Handbook of intelligence: Theories, measurements and applications*. New York: Wiley.

Karlsson, J. L. (1976). Genetic factors in myopia. *Acta Geneticae Medicae et Gamellologiae*, **25**, 292–294.

Kaufman, A. S. (1975). Factor analysis of the WISC-R at 11 age levels between 6-½ and 16-½ years. *Journal of Consulting and Clinical Psychology*, **43**, 135–147.

Kaufman, A. S., & Kaufman, N. L. (1983a). *K-ABC administration and scoring manual*. Circle Pines, MN: American Guidance Service.

Kaufman, A. S., & Kaufman, N. L. (1983b). *K-ABC interpretive manual*. Circle Pines, MN: American Guidance Service.

Keating, D. P. (1978). A search for social intelligence. *Journal of Educational Psychology*, **70**, 218–223.

Keating, D. P., & Bobbitt, B. L. (1978). Individual and developmental differences in cognitive-processing components of mental ability. *Child Development*, **49**, 155–167.

Keating, D. P., List, J. A., & Merriman, W. E. (1985). Cognitive processing and cognitive ability: A multivariate validity investigation. *Intelligence*, **9**, 149–170.

Kelderman, H., Mellenbergh, G. J., & Elshout, J. J. (1981). Guiford's facet theory of intelligence: An empirical comparison of models. *Multivariate Behavioral Research*, **16**, 37–61.

Kimura, D., & Hampson, E. (In press). Neural and hormonal mechanisms mediating sex differences in cognition. In P. A. Vernon, (Ed.), *Biological approaches to human intelligence*. Norwood, NJ: Ablex.

Kipnis, D. (1971). *Character structure and impulsiveness*. New York: Academic Press.

Kranzler, J. H., & Jensen, A. R. (1989). Inspection time and intelligence: A meta-analysis. *Intelligence*, **13**, 329–347.

LaBuda, M. C., DeFries, J. C., & Fulker, D. W. (1987). Genetic and environmental covariance structures among WISC-R subtests: A twin study. *Intelligence*, **11**, 233–244.

Landsdown, R., & Yule, W. (Eds.). (1986). *The lead debate: The environment, toxicology, and child health*. London: Croom Helm.

Lansman, M., Donaldson, G., Hunt, E., & Yantis, S. (1982). Ability factors and cognitive processes. *Intelligence*, **6**, 347–386.

Larson, G. E. (1990). Novelty as "representational complexity": A cognitive interpretation of Sternberg and Gastel (1989). *Intelligence*, **14**, 235–238.

Larson, G. E., & Alderton, D. L. (1990). Reaction time variability and intelligence: "Worst performance" analysis of individual differences. *Intelligence*, **14**, 309–325.

Larson, G. E., Merritt, C. R., & Williams, S. E. (1988). Information processing and intelligence: Some replication of task complexity. *Intelligence*, **12**, 131–147.

Larson, G. E., & Saccuzzo, D. P. (1986). Jensen's reaction-time experiments: Another look. *Intelligence*, **10**, 231–238.

Larson, G. E., & Saccuzzo, D. P. (1989). Cognitive correlates of general intelligence: Toward a process theory of g. *Intelligence, 13,* 5–31.

Lavin, D. E. (1965). *The prediction of academic performance: A theoretical analysis and review of research.* New York: Russell Sage Foundation.

Lawrence, E. M. (1931). An investigation into the relation between intelligence and inheritance. *British Journal of Psychology* (Monograph Supplement), **16,** 1–80.

Leahy, A. (1935). Nature-nurture and intelligence. *Genetic Psychology Monographs, 17,* 236–308.

Lesser, G. S., Fifer, F., & Clark, H. (1965). Mental abilities of children from different social-class and cultural groups. *Monographs of the Society for Research in Child Development, 30* (4).

Levy, J. (1969). Possible basis for the evolution of lateral specialization of the human brain. *Nature, 224,* 614–615.

Levy, J. (1976). Cerebral lateralization and spatial ability. *Behavior Genetics, 6,* 171–188.

Lewis, M., & Brooks-Gunn, J. (1981). Visual attention at three months as a predictor of cognitive functioning at two years of age. *Intelligence, 5,* 131–140.

Lewontin, R. C. (1975). Genetic aspects of intelligence. *Annual Review of Genetics, 9,* 387–405.

Linn, M. C., & Petersen, A. C. (1985). Emergence and characterization of sex differences in spatial ability: A meta-analysis. *Child Development, 56,* 1479–1498.

Linn, R. L. (1973). Fair test use in selection. *Review of Education Research, 43,* 139–161.

Livingstone, M., & Hubel, D. H. (1988). Segregation of form, movement, and depth: Anatomy, physiology, and perception. *Science, 240,* 740–749.

Locurto, C. (1990). The malleability of IQ as judged from adoption studies. *Intelligence, 14,* 275–292.

Loehlin, J. C. (1989). Partitioning environmental and genetic contributions to behavioral development. *American Psychologist, 44,* 1285–1292.

Loehlin, J. C., & DeFries, J. C. (1987). Geno-type–environment correlation and IQ. *Behavior Genetics, 17,* 263–277.

Loehlin, J. C., Horn, J. M., & Willerman, L. (1989). Modeling IQ change: Evidence from the Texas Adoption Project. *Child Development, 60,* 993–1004.

Loehlin, J. C., Lindzey, G., & Spuhler, J. M. (1975). *Race differences in intelligence.* San Francisco: Freeman.

Loehlin, J. C., Willerman, L., & Horn, J. M. (1988). Human behavior genetics. *Annual Review of Psychology, 39,* 101–133.

Loevinger, J. (1951). Intelligence. In H. Nelson (Ed.), *Theoretical foundations of psychology.* New York: Van Nostrand.

Lohman, D. F. (1986). The effect of speed–accuracy tradeoff on sex differences in mental rotation. *Perception and Psychophysics, 39,* 427–436.

Long, P. A., & Anthony, J. J. (1974). The measurement of retardation by a culture-specific test. *Psychology in the Schools, 11,* 310–312.

Longstreth, L. E. (1984). Jensen's reaction-time investigations of intelligence: A critique. *Intelligence, 8,* 139–160.

Longstreth, L. E. (1986). The real and the unreal: A reply to Jensen and Vernon. *Intelligence, 10,* 181–191.

Longstreth, L. E., Davis, B., Carter, L., Flint, D., Owen, J., Rickert, M., & Taylor, E. (1981). Separation of home intellectual environment and maternal IQ as determinants of child's IQ. *Developmental Psychology, 17,* 532–541.

Lord, F. M. (1980). *Applications of item response theory to practical testing problems.* Hillsdale, NJ: Erlbaum.

Lorge, I. (1945). Schooling makes a difference. *Teachers College Record, 46,* 483–492.

Lubin, M., & Fernandez, J. M. (1986). The relationship between psychometric intelligence and inspection time. *Personality and Individual Differences, 7,* 653–657.

Lubinski, D., & Humphreys, L. G. (1990). A broadly based analysis of mathematical giftedness. *Intelligence, 14,* 327–355.

Ludlow, H. G. (1956). Some recent research on the Davis–Eels game. *School and Society, 84,* 146–148.

Lynn, R. (1987). The intelligence of the mongoloids: A psychometric, evolutionary and neurological theory. *Personality and Individual Differences, 8,* 813–844.

Lynn, R. (1990a). The role of nutrition in secular increases in intelligence. *Personality and Individual Differences,* **11,** 273–285.

Lynn, R. (1990b). Negative correlations between verbal and visuo-spatial abilities: Statistical artifact or empirical relationship? *Personality and Individual Differences,* **11,** 755–756.

Lynn, R. (1990c). New evidence on brain size and intelligence: A comment on Rushton and Cain and Vanderwolf. *Personality and Individual Differences,* **11,** 795–797.

Lynn, R. (1991). Educational achievements of Asian-Americans. *American Psychologist,* **46,** 875–876.

Lynn, R. (In press). Nutrition and intelligence. In P. A. Vernon (Ed.), *Biological approaches to human intelligence.* Norwood, NJ: Ablex.

Lynn, R., & Hampson, S. (1986a). Intellectual abilities of Japanese children: An assessment of 2-½–8-½-year-olds derived from the McCarthy scales of children's abilities. *Intelligence,* **10,** 41–58.

Lynn, R., & Hampson, S. (1986b). The rise of national intelligence: Evidence from Britain, Japan, and the U.S.A. *Personality and Individual Differences,* **7,** 23–32.

Maccoby, E. E., & Jacklin, C. N. (1974). *The psychology of sex differences.* Stanford, CA: Stanford University Press.

MacKenzie, B. (1980). Hypothesized genetic racial differences in IQ: A criticism of three proposed lines of evidence. *Behavior Genetics,* **10,** 225–234.

MacKenzie, B. (1984). Explaining race differences in IQ: The logic, the methodology, and the evidence. *American Psychologist,* **39,** 1214–1233.

MacKenzie, B., & Bingham, E. (1985). IQ, inspection time, and response strategies in a university population. *Australian Journal of Psychology,* **37,** 257–268.

MacKenzie, B., & Cumming, S. (1986). How fragile is the relationship between inspection time and intelligence? The effects of apparent-motion cues and previous experience. *Personality and Individual Differences,* **7,** 721–729.

Marcus, G. B., & Zajonc, R. B. (1977). Family configuration and intellectual development. *Behavioral Science,* **22,** 137–142.

Marjoribanks, K., & Walberg, H. J. (1975). Birth order, family size, social class, and intelligence. *Social Biology,* **22,** 261–268.

Marshalek, B., Lohman, D. F., & Snow, R. E. (1983). The complexity continuum in the radex and hierarchical models of intelligence. *Intelligence,* **7,** 107–127.

Matheny, A. P., Jr., Dolan, A. B., & Wilson, R. S. (1976). Twins with academic learning problems. *American Journal of Orthopsychiatry,* **46,** 464–469.

Mattarazzo, J. D. (1972). *Wechsler's measurement and appraisal of adult intelligence* (5th ed.). Baltimore: Williams & Wilkins.

Mattarazzo, J. D., & Weins, A. N. (1977). Black intelligence test of cultural homogeneity and Wechler Adult Intelligence Scale scores of black and white police applicants. *Journal of Applied Psychology,* **62,** 57–63.

Matthews, G., & Dorn, L. (1989). IQ and choice reaction time: An information processing analysis. *Intelligence,* **13,** 299–317.

McGarvey, B., Gabrielli, W. F., Jr., Bentler, P. M., & Mednick, S. A. (1981). Rearing social class, education, and criminality: A multiple indicator model. *Journal of Abnormal Psychology,* **90,** 354–364.

McGlone, J. (1980). Sex differences in brain asymmetry: A critical survey. *Behavioral and Brain Sciences,* **3,** 215–264.

McGue, M., & Bouchard, T. J., Jr. (1989). Genetic and environmental determinant of information processing and special mental abilities: A twin analysis. In R. J. Sternberg (Ed.), *Advances in the psychology of human intelligence* (Vol. 5). Hillsdale, NJ: Erlbaum.

McGurk, F. C. J. (1953). On white and Negro test performance and socioeconomic factors. *Journal of Abnormal and Social Psychology,* **48,** 448–450.

McMichael, A. J., Baghurst, P. A., Wigg, N. R., Vimpani, G. V., Robertson, E. F., & Roberts, R. J. (1988). Port Pirie cohort study: Environmental exposure to lead and children's abilities at the age of four years. *New England Journal of Medicine,* **319,** 468–475.

Mehrota, S. N., & Maxwell, J. (1950). The intelligence of twins: A comparative study of eleven-year-old twins. *Population Studies*, **3**, 295–302.

Mercer, J. R. (1973). *Labeling the retarded.* Berkeley, CA: University of California Press.

Mercer, J. R. (1979). *System of multicultural pluralistic assessment (SOMPA): Technical manual.* New York: Psychological Corporation.

Mercer, J. R. (1984). What is a racially and culturally nondiscriminatory test? A sociological and pluralistic perspective. In C. R. Reynolds and R. T. Brown (Eds.), *Perspectives on bias in mental testing.* New York: Plenum.

Messick, S. (1980). *The effectiveness of coaching for the SAT: Review and reanalysis of research from the fifties to FTC.* Princeton, NJ: Educational Testing Service.

Messick, S., Jungeblut, A. (1981). Time and method in coaching for the SAT. *Psychological Bulletin*, **89**, 191–216.

Miller, D. J., Ryan, E. B., Aberger, E., McGuire, M. D., Short, E. J., & Kenny, D. A. (1979). Relationships between assessment of habituation and cognitive performance in the early years of life. *International Journal of Behavioral Development*, **2**, 159–170.

Moffitt, T. E., Gabrielli, W. F., Mednick, S. A., & Schulsinger, F. (1981). Socioeconomic status, IQ and delinquency. *Journal of Abnormal Psychology*, **90**, 152–156.

Montie, J. E., & Fagan, J. F., III. (1988). Racial differences in IQ: Item analysis of the Stanford–Binet at 3 years. *Intelligence*, **12**, 315–332.

Moore, E. G. J. (1985). Ethnicity as a variable in child development. In M. B. Spencer, G. K. Brookins, & W. R. Allen (Eds.), *Beginnings: The social and affective development of black children.* Hillsdale, NJ: Erlbaum.

Moore, E. G. J. (1986). Family socialization and the IQ test performance of traditionally and transracially adopted black children. *Developmental Psychology*, **22**, 317–326.

Naglieri, J. A., & Jensen, A. R. (1987). Comparison of black–white differences on the WISC-R and K-ABC: Spearman's hypothesis. *Intelligence*, **11**, 21–43.

Nagoshi, C. T., & Johnson, R. C. (1985). Ethnic group-by-generation interaction in the Hawaii Family Study of Cognition. *Intelligence*, **9**, 259–264.

Nathan, M., & Guttman, R. (1984). Similarities in test scores and profiles of kibbutz twins and singletons. *Acta Geneticae Medicae at Gemellogiae*, **33**, 213–218.

Needleman, H. C., Gunnoe, C., Leviton, A., Reed, R., Peresie, H., Maher, C., & Barrett, P. (1979). Deficits in psychologic and classroom performance of children with elevated dentine lead levels. *New England Journal of Medicine*, **300**, 689–695.

Neel, J. V., Schull, W. J., Yamamoto, M., Uchida, S., Yanase, T., & Fujiki, N. (1970). The effects of parental consanguinity and inbreeding in Hirado, Japan: II. Physical development, tapping rate, blood pressure, intelligence quotient, and school performance. *American Journal of Human Genetics*, **22**, 263–286.

Nettlebeck, T. (1973). Individual differences in noise and associated perceptual indices of performance. *Perception*, **2**, 11–21.

Nettlebeck, T. (1987). Inspection time and intelligence. In P. A. Vernon (Ed.), *Speed of information processing and intelligence.* Norwood, NJ: Ablex.

Nettlebeck, T., Edwards, C., & Vreugdenhil, A. (1986). Inspection time and IQ: Evidence for a mental speed–ability association. *Personality and Individual Differences*, **7**, 633–641.

Nettlebeck, T., & Kirby, N. H. (1983). Measures of timed performance and intelligence. *Intelligence*, **7**, 39–52.

Nettlebeck, T., & Lally, M. (1976). Inspection time and measured intelligence. *British Journal of Psychology*, **67**, 17–22.

Newman, H. H., Freeman, F. N., & Holzinger, K. H. (1937). *Twins: A study of heredity and environment.* Chicago: University of Chicago Press.

Nichols, P. I. (1970). The effects of heredity and environment on intelligence test performance in 4 and 7 year white and Negro sibling pairs. Doctoral dissertation, University of Minnesota. Ann Arbor, MI: University Microfilms, No. 71-18, 874.

Oakland, T. (1979). Research on the ABIC and ELP: A revisit to an old topic. *School Psychology Digest*, **8**, 209–230.

O'Connor, M. J., Cohen, S., & Parmalee, A. H. (1984). Infant auditory discrimination in preterm and full-term infants as a predictor of 5-year intelligence. *Developmental Psychology*, **20**, 159–170.

Osborne, R. T. (1978). Race and sex differences in heritability of mental test performance: A study of negroid and caucosoid twins. In R. T. Osborne, C. E. Noble, & N. Weyl (Eds.), *Human variation: The biopsychology of age, race, and sex*. New York: Academic Press.

Osborne, R. T., & Gregor, A. J. (1968). Racial differences in heritability estimates for tests of spatial ability. *Perceptual and Motor Skills*, **27**, 735–739.

Paine, R. S. (1957). The variability in manifestations of untreated patients with phenylketonuria (phenylpyruvia aciduria). *Pediatrics*, **20**, 290–301.

Palincsar, A. A., & Brown, A. L. (1984). Reciprocal teaching of comprehension-fostering and comprehension-monitoring activities. *Cognition and Instruction*, **1**, 117–175.

Parks, R. W., Lowenstein, D. A., & Dondrell, K. L. (1988). Cerebral metabolic effects of a verbal fluency test. A PET scan study. *Journal of Clinical and Experimental Neuropsychology*, **10**, 565–575.

Partanen, J., Bruun, K., & Markkanen, T. (1966). *A study of intelligence, personality, and use of alcohol of adult twins*. Stockholm: Almqvist & Wiksell.

Pasamanick, B., & Knobloch, H. (1966). Retrospective studies of the epidemiology of reproductive casualty, old and new. *Merrill-Palmer Quarterly*, **12**, 7–26.

Paterson, D. G. (1930). *Physique and intellect*. New York: Century.

Peak, H., & Boring, E. G. (1926). The factor of speed in intelligence. *Journal of Experimental Psychology*, **9**, 71–94.

Pearson, K. (1901a). On the systematic fitting of curves to observations and measurements. *Biometrika*, **1**, 265–303.

Pearson, K. (1901b). The lines of closest fit to a system of points. *Philosophical Magazine*, **2**, 559–572.

Pedersen, N. L., McLearn, G. E., Plomin, P., & Friberg, L. (1985). Separated fraternal twins: Resemblance for cognitive abilities. *Behavior Genetics*, **15**, 407–419.

Perrett, D. L., Mistlin, A. J., & Chitty, A. J. (1987). Visual neurones responsive to faces. *Trends in Neuroscience*, **10**, 358–364.

Peterson, J. (1926). *Early conceptions and tests of intelligence*. Westford, CT: Greenwood Press.

Phillips, K., & Fulker, D. W. (1989). Quantitative genetic analysis of longitudinal trends in adoption designs with application to IQ in the Colorado Adoption Project. *Behavior Genetics*, **19**, 621–658.

Pinneau, S. R. (1961). *Changes in intelligence quotient: Infancy to maturity*. New York: Houghton-Mifflin.

Plomin, R. (1986). *Development, genetics, and psychology*. Hillsdale, NJ: Erlbaum.

Plomin, R. (1987). Genetics of intelligence. In S. Modgil & L. Modgil (Eds.), *Arthur Jensen: Consensus and controversy*. New York: Falmer.

Plomin, R. (1988). The nature and nurture of cognitive abilities. In R. J. Sternberg (Ed.), *Advances in the psychology of human intelligence*. Vol. 4. Hillsdale, NJ: Erlbaum.

Plomin, R., & Daniels, D. (1987). Why are children in the same family so different from each other? *Behavioral and Brain Sciences*, **10**, 1–16.

Plomin, R., & DeFries, J. C. (1985). *Origins of individual differences in infancy: The Colorado Adoption Study*. Orlando, FL: Academic Press.

Plomin, R., & Loehlin, J. C. (1989). Direct and indirect IQ heritability estimates. *Behavior Genetics*, **19**, 331–342.

Plomin, R., Chipuer, H. M., & Loehlin, J. C. (1990). Behavioral genetics and personality. In L. A. Pervin (Ed), *Handbook of personality: Theory and research*. New York: Guilford Press.

Plomin, R., DeFries, J. C., & Fulker, D. W. (1988). *Nature and nurture during infancy and early childhood*. New York: Cambridge University Press.

Posner, M. I., Boies, S. J., Eichelman, W. H., & Taylor, R. L. (1969). Retention of visual and name order of single letters. *Jour-

nal of Experimental Psychology, 79, 1–16.

Prioleau, L., Murdock, M., & Brody, N. (1983). An analysis of psychotherapy versus placebo studies. *Behavioral and Brain Sciences, 6,* 275–310.

Quay, L. C. (1971). Language, dialect, reinforcement, and the intelligence test performance of Negro children. *Child Development, 42,* 5–15.

Quay, L. C. (1972). Negro dialect and Binet performance in severely disadvantaged black four-year-olds. *Child Development, 43,* 245–250.

Quay, L. C. (1974). Language dialect, age, and intelligence-test performance in disadvantaged black children. *Child Development, 45,* 463–468.

Raaheim, K. (1974). *Problem solving and intelligence.* Oslo, Norway: Universitets Forlaget.

Ramey, C. T., & Haskins, R. (1981). The modification of intelligence through early experience. *Intelligence, 5,* 5–19.

Ramey, C. T., Holmberg, M. C., Sparling, J. H., & Collier, A. M. (1977). An introduction to the Carolina Abecedarian Project. In B. M. Caldwell and D. J. Stedman (Eds.), *Infant education: A guide for helping handicapped children in the first three years.* New York: Walker.

Ramey, C. T., Lee, M. W., & Burchinal, M. R. (1990). Developmental plasticity and predictability: Consequences of ecological change. In M. H. Bornstein and N. A. Krasnegor (Eds.), *Stability and continuity in social development.* Hillsdale, NJ: Erlbaum.

Ramist, L., & Arbeiter, S. (1986). *Profiles, college bound seniors, 1985.* New York: College Entrance Examination Board.

Raz, N., Millman, D., & Sarpel, G. (1990). Cerebral correlates of cognitive aging: Gray–white matter differentiation in the medial temporal lobes, and fluid versus crystallized abilities. *Psychobiology, 18,* 475–481.

Raz, N., Moberg, P. J., & Millman, D. (1990). Effects of age and age-related differences in auditory information processing on fluid and crystallized intelligence. *Personality and Individual Differences, 11,* 1147–1152.

Raz, N., & Willerman, L. (1985). Aptitude-related differences in auditory information processing: Effects of selective attention and tone duration. *Personality and Individual Differences, 6,* 299–304.

Raz, N., Willerman, L., Igmundson, P., & Hanlon, M. (1983). Aptitude-related differences in auditory recognition masking. *Intelligence, 7,* 71–90.

Raz, N., Willerman, L., & Yama, M. (1987). On sense and senses: Intelligence and auditory information processing. *Personality and Individual Differences, 8,* 201–210.

Reed, T. E., & Jensen, A. R. (1991). Arm nerve conduction velocity (NCV), brain NCV, reaction time, and intelligence. *Intelligence, 15,* 33–47.

Rehberg, R. A., & Rosenthal, E. R. (1978). *Class and merit in the American high school: An assessment of the revisionist and meritocratic arguments.* New York: Longman.

Resnick, S. M., Berenbaum, S. A., Gottesman, I. I., & Bouchard, T. J., Jr. (1986). Early hormonal influences on cognitive functioning in congenital adrenal hyperplasia. *Developmental Psychology, 22,* 191–198.

Revelle, W., Humphreys, M. S., Simon, L., & Gilliland, K. (1980). The interactive effect of personality, time of day, and caffeine: A test of the arousal model. *Journal of Experimental Psychology: General, 109,* 1–31.

Reynolds, C. R., & Brown, R. T. (Eds.) (1984). *Perspectives on bias in mental testing.* New York: Plenum.

Roberts, R. D., Beh, H. C., & Stankov, L. (1988). Hick's law, competing-task performance, and intelligence. *Intelligence, 12,* 111–130.

Robinson, D. L., Haier, R. J., Braden, W., & Krengel, M. (1984). Psychometric intelligence and visual evoked potentials: A review. *Personality and Individual Differences, 5,* 487–489.

Rose, D. H., Slater, A., & Perry, H. (1986). Prediction of childhood intelligence from habituation in early infancy. *Intelligence, 10,* 251–263.

Rose, R. R., & Kaprio, J. (1987). Shared experience and similarity of personality:

Positive data from Finnish and American twins. *Behavioral and Brain Sciences*, **10**, 35–36.

Rose, S. A., & Wallace, I. F. (1985). Visual recognition memory: A predictor of later cognitive functioning in preterms. *Child Development*, **56**, 843–852.

Rosenthal, R., Hall, J. H., DiMatteo, M. R., Rogers, P. L., & Archer, D. (1979). *Sensitivity to nonverbal communication: The PONS test*. Baltimore: Johns Hopkins University Press.

Rosner, M., & Belkin, M. (1987). Intelligence, education and myopia in males. *Archives of Ophthalmology*, **105**, 1508–1511.

Royce, J. M., Darlington, R. B., & Murray, H. W. (1983). Pooled analyses: Findings across studies. In Consortium for Longitudinal Studies (Ed.), *As the twig is bent . . lasting effects of preschool programs*. Hillsdale, NJ: Erlbaum.

Ruch, W. W. (1972). A reanalysis of published differential validity studies. Paper presented at meeting of American Psychological Association, Honolulu, Hawaii, September 1972.

Rush, D., Stein, Z., & Susser, M. (1980). *Diet in pregnancy: A randomized controlled trial of nutritional supplements*. New York: Liss.

Rush, D., Stein, Z., Susser, M., & Brody, N. (1980). Outcome at one year of age: Effects of somatic and psychological measures. In D. Rush, Z. Stein, and M. Susser (Eds.), *Diet in pregnancy: A randomized controlled trial of nutritional supplements*. New York: Liss.

Rushton, J. P. (1990). Race, brain size and intelligence: A rejoinder to Cain and Vanderwolf. *Personality and Individual Differences*, **11**, 785–794.

Rutter, M., Maughan, B., Mortimore, P., Ouston, J., & Smith, A. (1979). *Fifteen thousand hours: Secondary schools and their effects on children*. London: Open Books.

Salthouse, T. A. (1982). *Adult cognition: An experimental psychology of human aging*. New York: Springer-Verlag.

Salthouse, T. A. (1985). *A theory of cognitive aging*. Amsterdam: Elsevier North-Holland.

Salthouse, T. A. (1988). The role of processing resources in cognitive aging. In M. L. Howe & C. J. Brainerd (Eds.), *Cognitive development in adulthood: Progress in cognitive development research*. New York: Springer-Verlag.

Sausanne, G. (1979). On the relationship between psychometric and anthropometric traits. *American Journal of Physical Anthropology*, **51**, 421–423.

Scarr, S. (1981). *Race, social class and individual differences, new studies of old problems*. Hillsdale, NJ: Erlbaum.

Scarr, S., & McCartney, K. (1983). How people make their own environments. *Child Development*, **54**, 424–435.

Scarr, S., Pakstis, A. J., Katz, S. H., & Barker, W. B. (1977). Absence of a relationship between degree of white ancestry and intellectual skills in a black population. *Human Genetics*, **39**, 69–86.

Scarr, S., & Weinberg, R. A. (1976). I.Q. test performance of black children adopted by white families. *American Psychologist*, **31**, 726–739.

Scarr, S., & Weinberg, R. A. (1983). The Minnesota Adoption Studies: Genetic differences and malleability. *Child Development*, **54**, 260–267.

Scarr-Salapatek, S. (1971). Race, social class, and I.Q. *Science*, **174**, 1285–1295.

Schafer, E. P. W. (1982). Neural adaptability: A biological determinant of behavioral intelligence. *International Journal of Neuroscience*, **17**, 183–191.

Schaie, K. W. (1980). Age changes in intelligence. In R. L. Sprott (Ed.), *Age, learning, ability, and intelligence*. New York: Van Nostrand Reinhold.

Schaie, K. W. (1988). Internal validity threats in studies of adult cognitive development. In M. L. Howe & C. J. Brainerd (Eds.), *Cognitive development in adulthood*. New York: Springer-Verlag.

Schaie, K. W. (1990). The optimization of cognition functioning in old age: Predictions based on cohort-sequential and longitudinal data. In P. M. Baltes & M. M. Baltes (Eds.), *Successful aging: Perspectives from the behavioral sciences*. Cambridge: Cambridge University Press.

Schaie, K. W., & Hertzog, C. (1983). Fourteen-year cohort-sequential analyses of adult intellectual development. *Developmental Psychology*, **19**, 531–543.

Schaie, K. W., & Strother, C. R. (1968). A cross-sequential study of age changes in cognitive behaviors. *Psychological Bulletin*, **70**, 671–680.

Schaie, K. W., & Willis, S. L. (1986). Can decline in adult intellectual functioning be reversed? *Developmental Psychology*, **22**, 223–232.

Schaie, K. W., Willis, S. L., Jay, G., & Chipuer, H. (1989). Structural invariance of cognitive abilities across the adult life span: A cross-sectional study. *Developmental Psychology*, **25**, 652–662.

Schiff, M., Duyme, M., Dumaret, A., & Tomkiewicz, S. (1982). How much could we boost scholastic achievement and IQ scores? A direct answer from a French adoption study. *Cognition*, **12**, 165–196.

Schiff, M., & Lewontin, R. (1986). *Education and class: The irrelevance of IQ genetic studies.* Oxford: Clarendon Press.

Schoenthaler, S. J., Amos, S. P., Eysenck, H. J., Peritz, E., & Yudkin, J. (1991). Controlled trial of vitamin-mineral supplementation: Effects of intelligence and performance. *Personality and Individual Differences*, **12**, 351–362.

Schull, W. J., & Neel, J. V. (1965). *The effects of inbreeding on Japanese children.* New York: Harper & Row.

Scribner, S., & Cole, M. (1981). *The psychology of literacy.* Cambridge, MA: Harvard University Press.

Segal, N. L. (1985). Monozygotic and dyzygotic twins: A comparative analysis of mental ability profiles. *Child Development*, **56**, 1051–1058.

Shagass, C., Roemer, R. A., Straumanis, J. J., & Josiassen, R. C. (1981). Intelligence as a factor in evoked potential studies in psychopathology. Comparison of low and high IQ subjects. *Biological Psychiatry*, **11**, 1007–1029.

Sharp, S. E. (1898–1899). Individual psychology: A study in psychological method. *American Journal of Psychology*, **15**, 201–293.

Shepard, L. A. (1987). The case for bias in tests of achievement and scholastic aptitude. In S. Modgil & C. Modgil (Eds.), *Arthur Jensen: Consensus and controversy.* New York: Fulmer.

Shepard, L., Camilli, G., & Williams, D. M. (1984). Accounting for statistical artifacts in item bias research. *Journal of Educational Statistics*, **9**, 93–128.

Shepard, R., & Metzler, J. (1971). Mental rotation of three dimensional objects. *Science*, **171**, 701–703.

Shields, J. (1962). *Monozygotic twins brought up apart and brought up together.* London: Oxford University Press.

Shuey, A. M. (1966). *The testing of negro intelligence.* (2nd ed.). New York: Social Science Press.

Shute, V. J., Pellegrino, J. W., Hubert, L., & Reynolds, R. W. (1983). The relationship between androgen levels and human spatial abilities. *Bulletin of the Psychonomic Society*, **21**, 465–468.

Shuter-Dyson, R., & Gabriel, C. (1983). *The psychology of musical ability* (2nd ed.). London: Methuen.

Sigman, M. D. (1983). Individual differences in infant attention: Relations to birth status and intelligence at five years. In T. Field & A. Sostek (Eds.), *Infants born at risk: Physiological, perceptual, and cognitive processes.* New York: Grune & Stratton.

Sigman, M. D., Cohen, S. E., Beckwith, L., & Parmalee, A. H. (1986). Infant attention in relation to intellectual abilities in childhood. *Developmental Psychology*, **22**, 788–792.

Sigman, M., Neumann, C., Jansen, A. A. J., & Bwibo, N. (1989). *Cognitive abilities of Kenyan children in relation to nutrition, family characteristics, and education.* Child Development, **60**, 1463–1474.

Skodak, M., & Skeels, M. H. (1949). A final follow-up study of one hundred adopted children. *Journal of Genetic Psychology*, **75**, 85–125.

Slavin, R. E. (1987). Mastery learning reconsidered. *Review of Educational Research*, **57**, 175–213.

Slavin, R. E., Karweit, N. L., & Madden, N. A. (1989). *Effective programs for students at risk.* Boston: Allyn and Bacon.

Slavin, R. E., Madden, N. A., Karweit, N. L.,

Livermon, B. J., & Dolan, L. (1990). Success for all: First-year outcomes of a comprehensive plan for reforming urban education. *American Educational Research Journal, 27,* 250–278.

Smith, G. M. (1967). Usefulness of peer ratings of personality in educational research. *Educational and Psychological Measurement, 27,* 967–984.

Smith, M. (1985). Recent work on low level lead exposure and its impact on behavior, intelligence, and learning: A review. *Journal of the American Academy of Child Psychiatry, 24,* 24–32.

Snow, R. E. (1990). Aptitude processes. In R. E. Snow, P. A. Federico, & W. E. Montague (Eds.), *Aptitude, learning, and instruction:* (Vol. 1. *Cognitive processes analysis of aptitude*). Hillsdale, NJ: Erlbaum.

Snow, R. E., & Yalow, E. (1982). Education and intelligence. In R. Sternberg (Ed.), *Handbook of human intelligence.* Cambridge: Cambridge University Press.

Snygg, D. (1938). The relation between the intelligence of mothers and of their children living in foster homes. *Journal of Genetic Psychology, 52,* 401-406.

Sokolov, Y. N. (1958/1963). *Perception and the conditioned reflex.* (Translated by S. W. Waydenfeld.) New York: Macmillan.

Sokolov, Y. N. (1969). The modeling properties of the nervous system. In M. Cole & F. Maltzman (Ed.), *A handbook of contemporary Soviet psychology.* New York: Basic Books.

Sommer, R., & Sommer, B. A. (1983). Mystery in Milwaukee: Early interventions, IQ, and psychology textbooks. *American Psychologist, 38,* 982–985.

Spearman, C. (1904a). The proof and measurement of association between two things. *American Journal of Psychology, 15,* 72–101.

Spearman, C. (1904b). "General Intelligence" objectively determined and measured. *American Journal of Psychology, 15,* 201–293.

Spearman C. (1923). *The nature of "intelligence" and the principles of cognition.* London: MacMillan.

Spearman, C. (1927). *The abilities of man.* London: MacMillan.

Spearman, C. (1930). C. Spearman. In C. Murchison (Ed.), *A history of psychology in autobiography* (Vol. 1). Worcester, MA: Clark University Press.

Spearman, C., & Holzinger, K. J. (1924). The sampling error in the theory of two factors. *British Journal of Psychology, 15,* 17–19.

Spearman, C., & Krueger, F. (1906). Die Korrelation zwischen Verschiedenen geistigen Leistungsfähigkeiten. *Zeitschrift fur Psychologie und Physiologie der Sinnesorgane, 44,* 50–114.

Spitz, H. H. (1986). *The rising of intelligence.* Hillsdale, NJ: Erlbaum.

Stankov, L. (1983). The role of competition in human abilities revealed through auditory tests. *Multivariate Behavioral Research Monographs,* **(83)**1.

Stankov, L. (1986). Kvashchev's experiment: Can we boost intelligence? *Intelligence,* **10,** 209–230.

Stankov, L. (1987). Competing task and attentional resources: Exploring the limits of primary–secondary paradigm. *Australian Journal of Psychology,* **39,** 123–137.

Stankov, L. (1988). Single tests, competing tasks and their relationship to broad factors of intelligence. *Personality and Individual Differences,* **9,** 25–33.

Stankov, L., & Horn, J. L. (1980). Human abilities revealed through auditory tests. *Journal of Educational Psychology,* **72,** 21–44.

Stein, Z. A., & Kassab, H. (1970). Nutrition. In J. Wortis (Ed.), *Mental retardation* (Vol. 2). New York: Grune & Stratton.

Stein, Z. A., Susser, M., Saenger, G., & Marolla, F. (1975). *Famine and human development. The Dutch hunger winter of 1944/45.* New York: Oxford University Press.

Stern, W. (1912). *Die psychologischen Methoden der Intelligenzprufung.* Leipzig: Barth.

Sternberg, R. J. (1977). *Intelligence, information processing and analogical reasoning: The componential analysis of human abilities.* Hillsdale, NJ: Erlbaum.

Sternberg, R. J. (1980). Sketch of a componential subtheory of human intelligence. *Behavioral and Brain Sciences*, **3**, 573–614.

Sternberg, R. J. (1981). Intelligence and non-entrenchment. *Journal of Educational Psychology*, **73**, 1–16.

Sternberg, R. J. (1982). Natural, unnatural, and supernatural concepts. *Cognitive Psychology*, **14**, 451–488.

Sternberg, R. J. (1985). *Beyond IQ: A triarchic theory of intelligence.* New York: Cambridge University Press.

Sternberg, R. J. (1986). *The triarchic mind: A new theory of human intelligence.* New York: Viking.

Sternberg, R. J. (1990). Critiques of the smart: A reply to Humphreys and Larson. *Intelligence*, **14**, 239–244.

Sternberg, R. J., & Gardner, M. K. (1983). Unities in inductive reasoning. *Journal of Experimental Psychology: General*, **112**, 80–116.

Sternberg, R. J., & Gastel, J. (1989a). Coping with novelty in human intelligence: An empirical investigation. *Intelligence*, **13**, 187–197.

Sternberg, R. J., & Gastel, J. (1989b). If dancers ate their shoes: Inductive reasoning with factual and counterfactual premises. *Memory and Cognition*, **17**, 1–10.

Sternberg, R. J., & Powell, J. S. (1983). Comprehending verbal comprehension. *American Psychologist*, **38**, 878–893.

Sternberg, R. J., Wagner, R. K., & Okagaki, L. (In press). Practical intelligence: The nature and role of tacit knowledge in work and at school.

Sternberg, R. J., & Weil, E. M. (1980). An aptitude–strategy interaction in linear syllogistic reasoning. *Journal of Educational Psychology*, **72**, 226–234.

Sternberg, S. (1970). Memory-scanning: Mental processing revealed by reaction time experiments. In J. S. Antrobus (Ed.), *Cognition and affect.* Boston: Little Brown.

Stevenson, H. W., Lee, S-Y., Chen, C., Lummis, M., Stigler, J., Fan, L., & Ge, F. (1990). Mathematics achievement of children in China and the United States. *Child Development*, **61**, 1053–1066.

Stevenson, H. W., Stigler, J. W., Lee, S., Lucker, G., Kitamura, S., & Hsu, C. (1985).

Cognitive performance and academic achievement of Japanese, Chinese, and American children. *Child Development*, **56**, 718–734.

Stevenson, J., Graham, P., Fredman, G., & McLoughlin, V. (1987). A twin study of genetic influences on reading and spelling ability and disability. *Journal of Child Psychology and Psychiatry*, **28**, 229–247.

Stodolsky, S. S., and Lesser, G. (1967). Learning patterns in the disadvantaged. *Harvard Educational Review*, 37, 546–593.

Stough, C. K. K., Nettlebeck, T., & Cooper, C. J. (1990). Evoked brain potentials, string length and intelligence. *Personality and Individual Differences*, **11**, 401–406.

Streissguth, A. P., Barr, H. M., Sampson, P. D., Darby, B. L., & Martin, O. C. (1990). IQ at age 4 in relation to maternal alcohol use and smoking during pregnancy. *Developmental Psychology*, **25**, 3–11.

Sue, S., Okazaki, S. (1990). Asian-American educational achievements: A phenomenon in search of an explanation. *American Psychologist*, **45**, 913–920.

Sue, S., & Okazaki, S. (1991). Explanations for Asian–American achievements: A reply. *American Psychologist*, **46**, 878–880.

Sundet, J. M., Tambs, K., Magnus, P., & Berg, K. (1988). On the question of secular trends in the heritability of intelligence test scores: A study of Norwegian twins. *Intelligence*, **12**, 47–59.

Tambs, K., Sundet, J. M., Magnus, P. (1984). Heritability analysis of the WAIS subtests: A study of twins. *Intelligence*, **8**, 283–293.

Taylor, H. F. (1980). *The IQ game: A methodological inquiry into the heredity–environment controversy.* New Brunswick, NJ: Rutgers University Press.

Teasdale, T. W., Fuchs, J., & Goldschmidt, E. (1988). Degree of myopia in relation to intelligence and educational level. *Lancet*, **1**, 1351–1354.

Teasdale, T. W., & Owen, O. R. (1984). Heredity and familial environment in intelligence and educational level—a sibling study. *Nature*, **309**, 620–622.

Teasdale, T. W., & Owen, O. R. (1989). Continuing secular increases in intelligence and a stable prevalence of high intelligence levels. *Intelligence, 13,* 255–262.

Teasdale, T. W., Sorenson, T. I. A., & Owen, O. R. (1989). A secular decline in the association of height with intelligence and educational level. *British Medical Journal, 298,* 1291–1293.

Tenopyr, M. L., Guilford, J. P., & Hoepfner, R. A. (1966). A factor analysis of symbolic memory abilities. *Reports from the Psychological Laboratory* (No. 38). University of Southern California, Los Angeles.

Terman, L. M., & Childs, H. G. (1912). A tentative revision and extension of the Binet–Simon measuring scale of Intelligence. *Journal of Educational Psychology, 3,* 61–74.

Tetewsky, S. J., & Sternberg, R. J. (1986). Conceptual and lexical determinants of nonentrenched thinking. *Journal of Memory and Language, 25,* 202–225.

Thompson, L. A., Detterman, D. K., & Plomin, R. (1991). Associations between cognitive abilities and scholastic achievement: Genetic overlap but environmental differences. *Psychological Science, 2,* 158–165.

Thomson, G. H. (1916). A hierarchy without a general factor. *British Journal of Psychology, 8,* 271–281.

Thomson, G. H. (1939). *The factorial analysis of human ability.* London: Houghton–Mifflin.

Thorndike, R. L. (1987). Stability of factor loadings. *Personality and Individual Differences, 8,* 585–586.

Thurstone, L. L. (1931). Multiple factor analysis. *Psychological Review,* 38, 406–427.

Thurstone, L. L. (1938). *Primary mental abilities.* Chicago: University of Chicago Press.

Thurstone, L. L., & Thurstone, T. G. (1941). *Factorial studies of intelligence.* Chicago: University of Chicago Press.

Tizard, B. (1974). IQ and Race. *Nature, 247,* 316.

Treisman, A. M. (1982). Perceptual grouping and attention in visual search for features and for objects. *Journal of Experimental Psychology: Human Perception and Performance, 8,* 194–214.

Treisman, A. M., & Gormican, S. (1988). Feature analysis in early vision: Evidence from search asymmetries. *Psychological Review, 95,* 15–48.

Treisman, A. M., & Souther, J. (1985). Search asymmetry: A diagnostic for preattentive processing of separable features. *Journal of Experimental Psychology: General, 114,* 285–310.

Tsunoda, T. (1978). Logos and pathos: Differences in mechanism of vowel sound and natural sound perception in Japanese and Westerners and in regard to mental structure. *Journal of Dental Health, 28,* 35–43.

Tuddenham, R. D. (1948). Soldier intelligence in World War I and II. *American Psychologist, 3,* 54–56.

Van Court, M., & Bean, F. D. (1985). Intelligence and fertility in the United States: 1912–1982. *Intelligence, 9,* 23–32.

Vandenberg, S. G. (1969). A twin study of spatial ability. *Multivariate Behavioral Research, 4,* 273–294.

Vandenberg, S. G. (1970). A comparison of heritability estimates of U.S. Negro and white high school students. *Acta Geneticae Medicae et Gemellologiae, 19,* 280–284.

Vandenberg, S. G., & Kuse, A. R. (1978). Mental rotations, a group test of three-dimensional spatial visualization. *Perceptual and Motor Skills, 47,* 599–604.

Vandenberg, S. G., & Vogler, G. P. (1985). Genetic determinants of intelligence. In B. B. Wolman (Ed.), *Handbook of intelligence: Theories, measurements and applications.* New York: Wiley.

Vandenberg, S. G., & Wilson, K. (1979). Failure of the twin situation to influence twin differences in cognition. *Behavior Genetics, 9,* 55–60.

Van Valen, L. (1974). Brain size and intelligence in man. *American Journal of Physical Anthropology, 40,* 417–424.

Vernon, P. A. (1983). Speed of information processing and general intelligence. *Intelligence, 7,* 53–70.

Vernon, P. A. (1989). The heritability of measures of speed of information processing. *Personality and Individual Differences,* **10,** 573–576.

Vernon, P. A. (1990). The effect of holding g constant on the correlation between verbal and nonverbal abilities: A comment on Lynn's "The intelligence of the Mongoloids . . ." (1987). *Personality and Individual Differences,* **11,** 751–754.

Vernon, P. A. (In press). The use of biological measures to estimate behavioral intelligence. In P. A. Vernon (Ed.), *Biological approaches to human intelligence.* Norwood, NJ: Ablex.

Vernon, P. A., & Jensen, A. R. (1984). Individual and group differences in intelligence and speed of information processing. *Personality and Individual Differences,* **5,** 911–23.

Vernon, P. A., & Mori, M. (1989). Intelligence, reaction times and nerve conductance velocity. *Behavior Genetics* (Abstracts), **19,** 779.

Vernon, P. A., Nador, S., & Kantor, L. (1985). Reaction times and speed-of-processing: Their relationship to timed and untimed measures of intelligence. *Intelligence,* **9,** 357–374.

Vernon, P. E. (1961). *The structure of human abilities* (2nd ed.). London: Methuen.

Vernon, P. E. (1982). *The abilities and achievements of Orientals in North America.* New York: Academic Press.

Vickers, D. (1970). Evidence for the accumulator model of psychophysical discrimination. *Ergonomics,* **13,** 37–58.

Vickers, D., Nettelbeck, T., & Willson, R. J. (1972). Perceptual indices of performance: The measurement of "inspection time" and "noise" in the visual system. *Perception,* **1,** 263–295.

Vining, D. R. (1982). On the possibility of the re-emergence of a dysgenic trend with respect to intelligence in American fertility differentials. *Intelligence,* **6,** 241–264.

Vogel, W., & Broverman, D. M. (1964). Relationship between EEG and test intelligence. A critical review. *Psychological Bulletin,* **62,** 132–144.

Voyer, D., & Bryden, M. P. (1990). Gender, level of spatial ability, and lateralization of mental rotation. *Brain and Cognition,* **13,** 18–29.

Waber, D. P. (1976). Sex differences in cognition: A function of maturation rate. *Science,* **192,** 572–574.

Waber, D. P. (1979). Cognitive abilities and sex related variations in the maturation of cerebral cortical functions. In M. A. Wittig & A. C. Peterson (Eds.), *Sex related differences in cognitive functioning.* New York: Academic Press.

Wagner, R. K. (1987). Tacit knowledge in everyday social behavior. *Journal of Personality and Social Psychology,* **52,** 1236–1247.

Wagner, R. K., & Sternberg, R. J. (1986). Tacit knowledge and intelligence in everyday life. In R. J. Sternberg & W. K. Wagner (Eds.), *Practical intelligence.* Cambridge: Cambridge University Press.

Welford, A. T. (Ed.) (1980). *Reaction Times.* New York: Academic Press.

West, D. J., & Farrington, D. P. (1973). *Who becomes delinquent?* London: Heinemann.

White, K. R. (1982). The relation between socioeconomic status and academic achievement. *Psychological Bulletin,* **81,** 461–481.

Widaman, K. F., & Carlson, J. S. (1989). Procedural effects on performance in the Hick paradigm: Bias in reaction time and movement time parameters. *Intelligence,* **13,** 63–85.

Willerman, L. (1979). Effects of families on intellectual development. *American Psychologist,* **34,** 923–929.

Willerman, L., & Bailey, J. M. (1987). A note on Thomson's sampling theory for correlations among mental tests. *Personality and Individual Differences,* **8,** 943–944.

Willerman, L., Schultz, R., Rutledge, J. N., & Bigler, E. (1989). *Magnetic resonance imaged brain structures and intelligence.* Paper presented to the 19th annual meeting of the Behavior Genetics Association, Charlottesville, VA.

Williams, R. L. (1972). *The BITCH Test (Black Intelligence Test of Cultural Homogeneity).* St. Louis, MO: Washington University.

Williams, R. L. (1974). Scientific racism and

IQ: The silent mugging of the black community. *Psychology Today*, **7**, 32–41.

Willis, S. L., & Baltes, P. B. (1980). Intelligence in adulthood and aging: Contemporary issues. In L. W. Poon (Ed.), *Aging in the 1980s: Psychological issues*. Washington, DC: American Psychological Association.

Willis, S. L., & Schaie, K. W. (1986). Practical intelligence in later adulthood. In R. J. Sternberg & R. K. Wagner (Eds.), *Practical intelligence: Nature and origins of competence in the everyday world*. Cambridge: Cambridge University Press.

Willms, J. D. (1985). Catholic school effects on academic achievement: New evidence from the High School and Beyond follow-up study. *Sociology of Education*, **58**, 98–114.

Wilson, R. S. (1983). The Louisville Twin Study: Developmental synchronies in behavior. *Child Development*, **54**, 298–316.

Wilson, R. S. (1986). Continuity and change in cognitive ability profile. *Behavior Genetics*, **16**, 45–60.

Winick, M., Meyer, K., & Harris, R. (1975). Malnutrition and environmental enrichment by adoption. *Science*, **190**, 1173–1175.

Wissler, C. (1901). The correlates of mental and physical tests. *Psychological Review*, (Monograph No. 3).

Witty, P. A., & Jenkins, M. D. (1936). Intrarace testing and Negro intelligence. *Journal of Psychology*, **1**, 179–192.

Wolf, R. M. (1965). The measurement of environments. In C. W. Harris (Ed.), *Proceedings of the 1964 Invited Conference on Testing Problems*. Princeton, NJ: Educational Testing Service.

Wolf, T. H. (1973). *Alfred Binet*. Chicago: University of Chicago Press.

Yamane, S., Kaij, S., & Kawano, K. (1988). What facial features activate face neurons in the inferotemporal cortex? *Experimental Brain Research*, **73**, 209–214.

Yarrow, L. J., Klein, R. P., Lomonoco, S., & Morgan, G. A. (1975). Cognitive and motivational development in early childhood. In B. X. Friedlander, G. M., Sterritt, and G. E. Kirk (Eds.), *Exceptional infant* (Vol. 3). New York: Brunner/Mazel.

Yudkin, J. (1988). Letter to the editor. *Lancet*, **1**, 407.

Zajonc, R. B. (1976). Family configuration and intelligence. *Science*, **192**, 227–236.

Zajonc, R. B. (1983). Validating the confluence model. *Psychological Bulletin*, **93**, 457–480.

Zajonc, R. B., & Bargh, J. (1980). The confluence model: Parameter estimation for six divergent data sets on family factors and intelligence. *Intelligence*, **4**, 349–361.

Zajonc, R. B., & Markus, G. B. (1975). Birth order and intellectual development. *Psychological Review*, **82**, 74–88.

Zajonc, R. B., Markus, H., & Markus, G. B. (1979). The birth order puzzle. *Journal of Personality and Social Psychology*, **37**, 1325–1341.

Zhang, Y., Caryl, P. G., & Deary, I. J. (1989a). Evoked potential correlates of inspection time and intelligence. *Personality and Individual Differences*, **10**, 379–384.

Zhang, Y., Caryl, P. G., & Deary, I. J. (1989b). Evoked potentials, inspection time and intelligence. *Personality and Individual Differences*, **10**, 1079–1094.

Zigler, E., Abelson, W. D., & Seitz, V. (1973). Motivational factors in the performance of economically disadvantaged children on the Peabody Picture Vocabulary Test. *Child Development*, **44**, 295–303.

Zigler, E., & Valentine, J. (1979). *Project Head Start: A legacy of the war on poverty*. New York: Free Press.

Zuckerman, M. (1991). *Psychobiology of personality*. New York: Cambridge University Press.

AUTHOR INDEX

SUBJECT INDEX

Achievement–intelligence distinction, 20, 289–291
  fluid versus crystallized ability, 20
  black–white differences, 289–291
Additive genetic influence, 127
Adoption effect, 148–150
Adoptive parent–adopted child relationship, 138–142, 144–145
Age decline, 234–251
  everyday tasks, 247
  gray matter characteristic, 246
  interindividual constancy versus interindividual variability, 248–250
  intervention, 247–249
  multi versus unidimensionality, 249–250
  multi versus unidirectionality, 249–250
  pitch discrimination, 245–246
  resource theory, 241–244
  speed influence, 241–243
  see also Life span development
Age grading, 7
Aggregation, see Hotchpotch principle
Aptitude × instruction interaction, 265–266
  see also Mastery learning
Asian–white difference, 310–317
  biological basis, 313–317
  laterality, 315–317
  spatial versus verbal ability, 311–313
Assortative mating, 130
Attenuation correction, 3

Behavior–genetic parameters, 150–158
  cohort effect, 151–152
  direct versus indirect estimate, 150–151
  IQ variation, 153
  LISREL estimate, 154–156
  social class influence, 153
Behavior genetics, see Behavior genetic parameters, Heritability, Partition of phenotypic variance

Between-family influence, 127, 168–173
Bias in tests, 287–296
  criterion bias, 289–291
  examiner effect, 293–294
  intercept bias, 288
  item characteristic, 294–295
  item response theory, 295–296
  item selection, 291–292
  linguistic distinctiveness, 294
  predictive validity for occupational performance, 288–289
  predictive validity for school performance, 287–288
  see also Black Intelligence Test of Cultural Homogeneity, Black–white difference
Binet's test, 6–8
Biological correlates, 215–227
  See also Brain size, Electroencephalogram, Evoked potential, Head circumference, Myopia, Nerve conductance velocity, Positron emission tomography
Biological environment, 206–214
  see also Perinatal influence, Prenatal influence, Lead exposure, Nutrition
Biological parent–adopted child relationship, 137–145, 147
  parental IQ, 138–141, 144–145
  parental IQ surrogate, 144–145
Biologically unrelated siblings reared together, 139, 145–146
Biological sibling relationship, 137, 147
  reared apart, 147
  reared together, 137
Birth order, see Confluence theory
Black Intelligence Test of Cultural Homogeneity, 292
Black–white difference, 280–310
  African ancestry, 308–309
  age influence, 282–283

ISBN 0-12-134251-4